BREAKING THE FRAMES

WORLD COMICS AND GRAPHIC NONFICTION SERIES

Frederick Luis Aldama and Christopher Gonzalez, Editors

The World Comics and Graphic Nonfiction Series includes monographs and edited volumes that focus on the analysis and interpretation of comic books and graphic nonfiction from around the world. The books published in the series use analytical approaches from literature, art history, cultural studies, communication studies, media studies, and film studies, among other fields, to help define the comic book studies field at a time of great vitality and growth.

MARC SINGER

BREAKING THE FRAMES

POPULISM AND PRESTIGE IN COMICS STUDIES

UNIVERSITY OF TEXAS PRESS AUSTIN

Cover art credits, from top to bottom, left to right: *Jerry Siegel, Joe Shuster, Ed Dobrotka, and John Sikela, "Superman, Matinee Idol,"* Superman *issue 19 (DC Comics, 1942), p. 6; Kyle Baker,* Nat Turner *(Abrams, 2008), p. 18; Alan Moore and Kevin O'Neill,* The League of Extraordinary Gentlemen Century: 2009 *(Top Shelf Productions/Knockabout Comics, 2012), n.p.; Alan Moore and Kevin O'Neill,* The League of Extraordinary Gentlemen, *vol. 1, issue 1 (America's Best Comics, 1999), front cover; David B.,* Epileptic, *translated by Kim Thompson (Pantheon, 2005), p. 14; Mark Waid and Alex Ross,* Kingdom Come *issue 1 (DC Comics, 1996), p. 9; Alan Moore and Kevin O'Neill,* The League of Extraordinary Gentlemen Century: 2009 *(Top Shelf Productions/Knockabout Comics, 2012), n.p.; Marjane Satrapi,* Persepolis, *vol. 1 (Pantheon, 2003), p. 117, translated by Blake Ferris; Robert Crumb, rejected cover for the* New Yorker *(2009); and Chris Ware, "God,"* McSweeney's Quarterly Concern *issue 13 (2004), dust jacket.*

Requests for permission to reproduce material from this work should be sent to:
Permissions
University of Texas Press
P.O. Box 7819
Austin, TX 78713-7819
utpress.utexas.edu/rp-form

♾ The paper used in this book meets the minimum requirements of ANSI/NISO Z39.48-1992 (R1997) (Permanence of Paper).

LIBRARY OF CONGRESS CATALOGING-IN-PUBLICATION DATA

Names: Singer, Marc, author.
Title: Breaking the frames : populism and prestige in comics studies / Marc Singer.
Other titles: World comics and graphic nonfiction series.
Description: First edition. | Austin : University of Texas Press, 2018. | Series: World comics and graphic nonfiction series | Includes bibliographical references and index.
Identifiers: LCCN 2017054496
ISBN 978-1-4773-1709-9 (cloth : alk. paper)
ISBN 978-1-4773-1710-5 (pbk. : alk. paper)
ISBN 978-1-4773-1711-2 (library e-book)
ISBN 978-1-4773-1712-9 (non-library e-book)
Subjects: LCSH: Comic books, strips, etc.—History and criticism. | Popular culture and literature.
Classification: LCC PN6714 .S56 2018 | DDC 741.5/9—dc23
LC record available at https://lccn.loc.gov/2017054496

doi:10.7560/317099

CONTENTS

ACKNOWLEDGMENTS

This book could not have been started, much less finished, without the scholarly community created by my friends and colleagues in the field of comics studies. While I have some grave reservations about current and future directions in that field, I am also indebted to the thoughtful work and generous advice of my fellow scholars. I particularly need to single out the expert guidance of Bart Beaty: whether he was navigating me through the world of French small-press comics, theorizing the construction of value in the comics world, furnishing sources that could be found nowhere else on this side of the Atlantic, or providing judicious comments on the manuscript, his assistance and friendship have been invaluable. He deserves much of the credit and absolutely no accountability for what follows in these pages. The same holds true for Joseph Witek, whose feedback was as important to this manuscript as his scholarship has been to comics studies, and for Charles Hatfield and Ian Gordon, who kindly supplied articles and images, not to mention good fellowship and general counsel over the years.

I would also like to thank Jim Burr and Sarah McGavick for bringing this project to Texas and guiding it to completion, Christopher González for his work with the World Comics and Graphic Nonfiction Series, and Frederick Luis Aldama for his enthusiastic support every step of the way. They have made the University of Texas Press a home for comics studies, and I am grateful for the opportunity to work with them. That gratitude extends to the efforts of Robert Kimzey, Nancy Bryan, and everyone at the press who worked so hard to publish and promote this book.

This project began during a sabbatical leave from Howard University. My most heartfelt thanks to my colleagues in the Department of English and especially our chair, Dana Williams, for their steadfast support of my research. I am deeply appreciative of my good fortune in finding a department that encourages teaching and scholarship in comics studies.

Portions of chapter 1 previously appeared in *Studies in Comics*, vol. 4, no. 2 (2013), and an earlier version of chapter 4 appeared in *The Comics of Chris Ware: Drawing Is a Way of Thinking* (2010), edited by David M. Ball and Martha Kuhlman. Reviews of the *Critical Inquiry* special issue *Comics & Media* for *European Comic Art* (Autumn 2015) and of *Building Stories* for the *Cincinnati Review* (Summer 2013) provided early opportunities to work out some of the ideas that shaped this project. I am grateful to all my editors, especially Julia Round, Chris Murray, David Ball, and Martha Kuhlman, for their assistance in developing these arguments and for allowing me to expand on them here.

Finally, thanks as always to Christy and Eric for everything they do to support my work and everything they do that has nothing to do with work. They always know when to give me time to write and, more importantly, when it's time to pull me away.

BREAKING THE FRAMES

INTRODUCTION

POW! ZAP!

COMICS AREN'T JUST FOR CULTURAL STUDIES PROFESSORS ANYMORE

The temptation is to give in to hyperbole: *A strange dispute rocked the world of comics in the spring of 2015!* In fact, the quarrel was as typical and as ephemeral as the texts that provoked it. Harvard University history professor Jill Lepore wrote "Looking at Female Superheroes with Ten-Year-Old Boys," a column for the *New Yorker* in which, with the help of her youngest son and one of his friends, she reviewed the Marvel Studios film *Avengers: Age of Ultron* and the first issue of the Marvel Comics series *A-Force*. The intersection of the magazine's rarefied sensibilities and Marvel's bombastic entertainment was unusual but not nearly as strange as it would have been even a few years earlier. Since the turn of the twenty-first century, comics have made inroads into nearly every corner of American culture, from Hollywood blockbusters and network television series to gallery exhibitions and literary magazines. If anything, the *New Yorker* was ahead of the curve; since Françoise Mouly joined the staff as art editor in 1993, it has been remarkably receptive to comics, commissioning covers by acclaimed artists such as Robert Crumb and Chris Ware and running essays on historical pioneers such as Bernard Krigstein and Jack Cole.[1] Given the magazine's long-standing interest in comics and the superhero genre's increasing centrality to American culture, the *New Yorker*'s decision to review a contemporary superhero comic feels less like a surprise than an acknowledgment of the inevitable.

The results of this interaction were no less inevitable. After dismissing the movie in a few sentences, Lepore trains her attention on *A-Force*, a comic book that assembles all of Marvel's female superheroes onto one team for no purpose that Lepore can gather, other than the fact that they are all women. (The comic was one of dozens of spin-off titles released as part of Marvel's *Secret Wars* crossover event; other series were populated entirely by cowboys, zombies, and similar high-concept shtick.) She mostly relies on her son and his friend to interpret the book for her, highlighting the baroque narrative continuity and endlessly self-replicating characters that serve to make *A-Force* absolutely incomprehensible to anyone not steeped in Marvel's current publishing line. She also skewers Marvel's superficial engagement with feminism, noting that many of the company's female superheroes are derivative versions or gender-swapped copies of popular male characters. Operating more through snark and insinuation than argument, Lepore implies that Marvel's female casting and *A-Force*'s female cast amount to little more than marketing hooks.

In the process, however, she also objects to the "pervy characters and costumes" and complains that the female superheroes "all look like porn stars." Lepore maintains that this lascivious subtext is written into their DNA, noting that William Moulton Marston, the creator of Wonder Woman, was an advocate for the benefits of pornography and a contributor to a men's magazine, writing copy for artist George Petty's voluptuous pin-up girls. (The anecdote also provides a convenient opportunity to promote Lepore's recent book *The Secret History of Wonder Woman.*) She doesn't acknowledge that Marston's feminism, kinky and idiosyncratic but also outspoken and sincere, makes his female heroes more ideologically committed than Marvel's, or that his family's sex-positive position on pornography is, for some contemporary feminists, far more progressive than her own. For Lepore, any idealized female figure is a sexual object, the cast of *A-Force* no less than the Petty Girls: "Their power is their allure [. . .]. Even their bodies are not their own." Filtering her review through the sensibilities of two preteen boys, Lepore suggests that female superheroes have always been pin-up girls or porn stars, and can be nothing else.

This argument prompted some heated reactions from comics fans, and from one comics creator. In "Dr. Lepore's Lament," a response posted on her website, G. Willow Wilson, who created *A-Force* with cowriter Marguerite Bennett and artist Jorge Molina, castigates Lepore for her glib comparisons and censorious tone. Beyond addressing Lepore's criticisms, however, Wilson also promotes a model of reading that would rule out virtually any criticism at all. She repeatedly complains about Lepore's decontextualized reading of *A-Force,* listing the following contexts that are necessary to its interpretation: its status as the first issue in a limited series; its status as part of the *Secret Wars* crossover; its place in the larger Marvel universe; its emergence from and response to fan criticisms of gender representation in superhero comics; its departure from older conventions of representing female superheroes, such as revealing costumes or contorted poses; and its refusal to engage in past practices such as objectifying or brutalizing female characters. Some of these points are laudable (though they set a very low standard), while others are familiar evasions that comics creators and fans have used to dismiss criticism of any serialized publication, but they all suggest that only die-hard superhero fans will be able to make sense of *A-Force*. Wilson not only concedes that her readers must be deeply invested in comics fandom, she practically boasts about it, marshaling claims that *A-Force* is not written for outsiders as defenses against any criticism from them.

This appeal to the comics community to rally against criticism from the outside is augmented by a generous helping of anti-intellectualism. Wilson first rejects "whatever self-congratulatory bar of high culture Dr. Lepore requires us to leap over in order to be considered 'real' artists" even though Lepore issues no such challenge in her review. Wilson then attempts to draw up the battle lines between insider and outsider with another reference to Lepore's elitism:

> It is a shame that, in this recent wave of mainstream media attention toward comics, *actually reading comic books* does not appear to be a prerequisite. And it shows. Where is the call to action in Dr. Lepore's article? What is the aspirational message we are meant to take away? Who does she imagine she is helping? [. . .]
>
> Dr. Lepore provides no answers, and in all likelihood, she never intended to. Her article is a very crisp demonstration of the difference between criticism from within the community—criticism from people who love comics and want to see them succeed—and criticism from the self-appointed gatekeepers of art and culture, who categorically do not give a shit.

This resentment of cultural elites certainly extends to Lepore's academic credentials; the latent animosity bursts out into the open in the closing lines, where Wilson declares, "I imagine Dr. Lepore and I want the same thing: better, more nuanced portrayals of women in pop culture. What I don't understand is why someone in her position would, from her perch a thousand feet up in the ivory tower, take pot shots at those of us who are in the trenches, doing exactly that." The idea that Lepore's commitment to feminism might require criticizing even well-intentioned comic books is simply out of the question. For Wilson, criticism only counts when it's aspirational; it was a useful tool for calling forth comics that don't objectify women, but it's not supposed to be trained on those comics in turn. It's certainly not supposed to find them wanting. Wilson prefers criticism from people who love comics and want to see them succeed, promoting future creation, community, and above all consumption.

My aim is not to belabor this or that point in an online dustup over a comic book, nor to choose sides between Wilson and Lepore. Instead I want to highlight the telling divergences between their critical approaches, but also the surprising convergences—for the only thing that was at all strange about this exchange, which followed well-worn formulas for critical discussions of popular culture, was that both parties held one principal but unspoken assumption. Lepore's review is indicative of the approach taken by many academics who are unfamiliar with comics: she doesn't engage with the actual comic in any detail, doesn't place it in the contexts of its publication or its genre, and doesn't seem to think it merits any more sustained critical argument. Wilson's response is equally indicative of the approach taken not only by fans and creators but by many academics who identify as fans and who are intimately familiar with the world of comics: defensive, anti-intellectual, and adamant that good criticism should be aspirational, Wilson also exempts comics from sustained critical argument if that argument should prove too unsympathetic. What one rules out in her offhand dismissal, the other rejects in favor of populist resentment. Neither approach is adequate to interpreting even the most mundane comics, particularly in an academic context. This book attempts to chart another course, showing how comics studies can benefit from more careful engagement with comics texts and their many material, historical, and cultural contexts.

Extending this debate to the academic study of comics requires an important caveat. It's one thing to criticize Harvard scholar Jill Lepore for her breezy indifference, even when she's writing for a popular magazine, but G. Willow Wilson is not an academic. This doesn't indemnify her from criticism either, but it complicates any attempt to cast her comments as representative of the populist tendency in comics studies. However, many academics who work in comics studies share the same assumptions and make the same arguments, including the celebration of unreflective reading and the suspicion of academic scholarship. Sometimes they even take the opportunity to prescribe these values for the field as a whole.

ACADEMIC ANTIELITISM AS COMICS CRITIQUE

In his introduction to *Critical Approaches to Comics: Theories and Methods*, a casebook edited by Matthew J. Smith and Randy Duncan, Henry Jenkins casts these arguments in more academically palatable terms. The title, "Should We Discipline the Reading of Comics?," implies an uncertainty formed by Jenkins's experiences watching the trials and tribulations of disciplinary formation in film and media studies (4–6). But no such ambivalence can be found in his opening paragraph, which constructs an idyllic myth of childhood reading to argue that comics are by nature and habit undisciplined:

> Even as a child, I knew that reading comics demonstrated a thorough lack of discipline [. . .] there was not yet a canon (fan or academic) to tell us what we were supposed to read. We read for no purpose other than pleasure—there was no method to tell us how we were supposed to read. Indeed, many adults were there to remind us what a monumental waste of time all of this was—there was nothing like Publish or Perish pushing us to read more comics. (1)

Jenkins acknowledges that this description is a nostalgic myth, and his introduction assumes that the formation of a discipline of comics studies is inevitable. He outlines a number of reasonable expectations for a such a discipline: that it should take comics seriously as objects of study, that it should interpret them in the contexts of their own traditions and vocabularies, that comics scholars should be familiar with these contexts, and that we shouldn't have to explain or defend our discipline every time we engage in it. Nevertheless, his introduction continues to privilege fan modes of reading (leisurely, random, secretive) over academic ones (professional, orderly, public). Presuming to speak for the collection's editors and contributors—and perhaps all comics scholars?—Jenkins declares, "We want a homeland where comics geeks of all disciplines can come together—perhaps a return to the treehouse where we used to talk about the latest comics with our buddies, or perhaps something which is one part local comics shop and one part university bookstore" (2). This tone persists to the end of the piece, where his use of the first-person plural becomes somewhat more supplicatory but the presumption that comics scholars should be first and foremost comics fans remains just as strong: "Let's hold onto what made talking about comics fun in the first place even as we seek admission into the ivy-covered halls. [. . .] And let's get together on Wednesdays when the new comics come into the shops" (10).

At this point I should probably mention that I was one of the contributors to *Critical Approaches to Comics*, and Henry Jenkins does not speak for me. I hope he doesn't speak for the majority of comics scholars, although as I was working on this project I sometimes had my doubts. I have no interest in returning to some prelapsarian or prepubescent treehouse, and I'm not looking to establish a geek homeland. I'm looking for a professional academic discipline, one that is open to scholars from other disciplines, and comics fans too, but also those who have never read a comic before. I hope comics studies will welcome any methodology or theoretical framework, provided that scholars are willing to put in the work of familiarizing themselves with the field and its subjects.[2] I also hope those scholars will maintain the highest professional standards of their chosen methodologies, whether they work in literary criticism, art history, sociology, linguistics, or any other field. The practices of academic scholarship are not simply professional markers or passwords; they help to ensure that our research is informed by the most relevant theories, supported by the best available evidence, engaged in dialogues with other scholars, and able to withstand intellectual scrutiny. As this volume will make clear, these standards are not always sustained, but without them comics studies will not be an academic discipline at all. We'll just be a bigger treehouse.

Jenkins takes a different view in his introduction, evincing a deep and not altogether unwarranted suspicion of academic discourse. He wants to avoid the pitfalls that have characterized other disciplines in media studies: isolating themselves from fans and creators, establishing exclusive canons or hierarchies of taste, regarding media forms in isolation, getting dragged into endless and unresolvable arguments over definitions, and anything else that results in overly restrictive disciplinary frameworks. However, his aversion to elitism and exclusivity sometimes bleeds over into a general animosity toward academic discourse, as when he frets about "Young Turks spouting credentializing theory" (4)—a cliché that seems more germane to the "theory wars" of the 1980s and 1990s than to most comics conferences I have attended. Comments such as these suggest that snobbery can cut both ways, and in fact Jenkins is quick to lecture fans as well as academics for their exclusionary practices—"These very different branches of research need to stop rolling their eyes and snickering behind each other's backs. They need to learn to talk to and with each other" (5)—even if he frames them in a curiously personified and personalized manner.

The rest of his introduction tends to hold academics solely responsible for this isolation, however, even though his scant examples cut in the other direction. Jenkins contrasts two anthologies, *A Comics Studies Reader* (edited by Jeet Heer and Kent Worcester and published by the University Press of Mississippi) and *The Best American Comics Criticism* (edited by Ben Schwartz and published by Fantagraphics), as representatives of the academic and fan/practitioner approaches to comics studies. He notes that Schwartz's collection includes no academics while Heer and Worcester's reader "includes mostly academic contributors," concluding that each discourse has excluded the other (5). Yet that "mostly" should signal that these two books are not equally exclusionary—in fact, about one quarter of Heer and Worcester's contributors are journalists, fans, or practicing comics artists, what Jenkins terms "the Seldes and Spiegelman clans" of the fan-scholars (5), including none other than Gilbert Seldes and Art Spiegelman. Stranger still, the book's coeditor, Jeet Heer, is himself listed by Jenkins as one of the "fan intelligentsia" (5) whose point of view is supposedly represented in Schwartz's book but not Heer's. To complicate the picture still further, Heer and Worcester had previously collaborated on another anthology, *Arguing Comics: Literary Masters on a Popular Medium* (also published by the University Press of Mississippi), which surveys writings on comics by journalists, essayists, and public intellectuals dating back to the 1890s, consolidating and canonizing the public traditions of comics scholarship and presenting them to an academic audience. Jenkins cites this volume in his notes (13n5), but it doesn't otherwise trouble his picture of an academic discipline that shuts out other discourses about comics. His prescriptions are instead bolstered by sourceless condemnations of hypothetical scholars, as Jenkins shadowboxes against a series of imaginary rivals.

A markedly different appraisal of the challenges and shortcomings of North American comics scholarship had been offered some years earlier by Joseph Witek. In "American Comics Criticism and the Problem of Dual Address," Witek also notes the tensions and animosities that sometimes arise between academics and other comics scholars. He attributes these frictions to suspicion or outright hostility on the part of artists and critics from the fan tradition, citing representative objections to academic jargon (or, in some cases, the very prospect of the academic study of comics) from critic Robert C. Harvey, educator Leonard Rifas, and comics artist Art Spiegelman. Tellingly, none of these figures have been marginalized in the academic discourse about comics: Harvey has been published by the University Press of Mississippi, Rifas is a scholar and teacher (as well as a fellow contributor to *Critical Approaches to Comics*), and Spiegelman is widely read as both an artist and a critic. Far from depicting an academic discipline saturated with snobbery toward these voices, Witek describes one that has tried too hard to be all things to all readers: the field has limited its ability to generate new knowledge because it has addressed itself to an impossibly variegated audience and done so "from a defensive crouch" (219). The crouch, at least, is easy to understand, as even the use of the mildest and most accessible critical terminology is enough to provoke a stinging rebuke from critics like Harvey, who resent the intrusion of academic discourse into a space they regard as their own (Witek 222). However, comics scholars who renounce the markers of academic discourse—chief among them a specialized vocabulary and the citation of other scholars working in the same field—have surrendered the ability to conduct their research as part of a larger critical conversation with a shared sense of its own history (Witek 223). We have impeded our own work, Witek says, and it has done nothing to appease the Harveys of the world.

Witek is willing to risk charges of exclusivity if it means expanding the limits of our knowledge and our craft as scholars (224); Jenkins takes the opposite approach in his introduction to *Critical Approaches to Comics*, stressing that academics must learn to speak to many different audiences in a kind of multiple address (6). The merits and drawbacks of Jenkins's method are on full display in his brief reading of Kim Deitch's *The Search for Smilin' Ed*, which he offers as a potential model for comics scholarship. Jenkins makes the case that comics must be read transmedially by scholars who look to explore connections across media rather than attempt to craft medium-specific arguments that regard each form in isolation. Deitch's graphic novel is well chosen for these purposes, and Jenkins details its many representations of and connections to other popular media, such as film and television. Yet having asserted that a comics studies narrowly focused on comics and only comics would falter when confronted with Deitch's work (10), he fails to show where his transmedial approach would thrive. For all the time Jenkins spends describing how we should read *The*

Search for Smilin' Ed, he never quite gets around to reading it, let alone explaining what new insight or understanding such a reading would yield. The contours of his approach are laid out with clarity, but their applications and purposes remain unclear. This unilluminating reading might seem to confirm Witek's warning that "in the attempt to address so many audiences at once, we have disabled ourselves from talking to each other" (223), yet Jenkins specifically addresses an audience of other comics scholars and does so in the interest of promoting a distinct critical methodology. For all that he prescribes a "radically undisciplined" approach to comics studies (6), his proposed methods and values fit neatly within a coherent and well-defined academic discipline: comparative in its approach to media, inclusive in both its subjects and its participants, deeply suspicious of canons and hierarchies, and quick to accuse other academics of elitism, Jenkins's piece represents a highly orthodox application of the disciplinary assumptions of cultural studies.

As it has developed since the 1960s, the field of cultural studies has opened the academy to the examination of popular culture—a necessary and long-overdue project without which comics studies, and this book, would not be possible. As theorized and practiced by scholars such as John Fiske, however, the discipline's assumptions have hardened into a mode of cultural populism that celebrates any and all manifestations of popular culture while dismissing their critics as elitists. Jim McGuigan, in his book *Cultural Populism*, suggests that the political and intellectual assumptions of cultural populism are distinct from the study of popular culture, a practice that he welcomes; indeed, to the extent that these assumptions encourage an appreciative, open-minded attitude toward popular tastes, McGuigan is happy to identify himself as a cultural populist (3–4). McGuigan specifically criticizes the "*uncritical* populist drift in the study of popular culture" (5, his emphasis), a drift that has led certain strands of cultural studies to limit their focus to a narrow and self-affirming set of theoretical positions while they neglect economic and historical contexts that can't be explained through textual interpretation alone. McGuigan calls instead for a "critical populism" (5) that can study popular texts while still accounting for the material conditions of their production. Respectful and essentially sympathetic in his critiques, McGuigan nevertheless raises serious concerns about the populist tendency in cultural studies. He observes that the "uncritical endorsement of popular taste and pleasure [. . .] is curiously consistent with economic liberalism's concept of 'consumer sovereignty'" (6), an idea that scholars today are more likely to subsume under the political logic of neoliberalism. Thomas Frank has similarly noted that cultural populism is perfectly complementary with the neoliberal ideology that he terms market populism, which characterizes free markets as expressions of the popular will and mediums of democratic consent (xiv). Although most cultural studies scholars identify strongly with progressive or leftist politics, Frank notes that cultural populism shares market populism's disdain for intellectual elites—whom it imagines as anyone who presumes to criticize the tastes of the people or their articulations in the cultural marketplace (287, 289–292).

In *American Idyll: Academic Antielitism as Cultural Critique*, Catherine Liu traces this ethos to a much longer populist tradition that resents intellectuals and experts, sometimes with good reason and sometimes with disastrous consequences. For Liu, the emergence of cultural studies marked the entry of that anti-intellectual tradition into the academy itself, an arrival that corresponded with a larger shift in the system of higher education. Liu observes that in the postwar period, the model of a liberal education centered on the humanities and stressing the values of "reason, difficulty, intellectual history, and tradition" enjoyed substantial institutional support from the university and the state (170). As the postwar economic expansion ended and public investment in education eroded, that institutional support withered. While universities were shifting over to private funding and contingent employment, the liberal education they once promoted was replaced by a mode of critique (by no means limited to cultural studies, but certainly inclusive of it) that stresses transgression, emancipation, antielitism, and solidarity with popular opinion (170). There is much to be said for these values—again, it's hard to imagine a comics studies without them. But in dismissing the values of reason, evidence, expertise, the whole sphere of the intellectual, the populist strain of cultural studies also runs the risk of losing some of the most powerful tools of cultural critique. A "radically undisciplined" discipline may find itself left only with an unquestioning affirmation of the popular and an equally vapid condemnation of a nebulously defined elite.

This mode of cultural populism is now so ascendant within academia that it has even spread to scholars who are not themselves populists. Jenkins is suspicious of writers who only study comics that accord with the values of middlebrow literature (2), and he expresses grave reservations over artists and critics who look to form aesthetic canons that would exclude most comics from consideration (4). Yet even the scholars who are most engaged in those projects, scholars who have sought to build a comics studies that conforms to traditional notions of literary prestige, transform into the most effusive fans when the time comes to discuss the comics they deem worthy of inclusion. Some of the most carefully researched and skillfully argued pieces will rule out any oppositional stance toward their subjects in order to celebrate comics, both individually and collectively, in terms that are remarkably similar to Jenkins's own. For all that they seek to champion the comics form, however, many of the authors of these pieces remain woefully (and sometimes willfully) ill informed about the art, industry, and criticism of comics, as they often have not bothered to familiarize themselves with their subjects. This troubling trend holds true for new comics readers and lifelong fans, fire-breathing populists and ideological crusaders of every stripe. These scholars don't always work within Jenkins's preferred disciplinary framework, but they are still undisciplined.

The problem that faces comics studies isn't cultural studies per se, nor even the orthodoxies of cultural populism, but rather a certain style of scholarship that assumes comics, because they are a popular form, don't warrant the rigors of sustained critical attention. This style of writing can encompass work on every kind of comic, from the most popular entertainment to the most prestigious works of art (categories that prove increasingly hard to distinguish in the comics world anyway, and with diminishing returns). The resulting criticism exhibits any number of problems, including

- constructing elitist hierarchies of taste
- constructing antielitist (but equally patronizing) condemnations of critical judgment
- abandoning the standards and practices of academic scholarship
- ignoring or misreading other comics scholarship
- relying on a single theory or theorist to do all the interpretive work
- applying that theory inflexibly to reach preordained conclusions
- ignoring the roles of comics artists, ownership practices, or production and creative labor in general
- not reading the comics selected for discussion
- not regarding comics as worthy of academic study

This last complication occurs in scholarly books claiming to study comics with a regularity that is both surprising and depressing. But no matter the subject or discipline, the comics populists and their more highbrow counterparts share one common method and flaw: they avoid challenging and critically informed readings in favor of superficial or celebratory ones.

In the interest of grounding this argument in more examples, of not boxing at shadows, I will survey several works of comics scholarship, ranging in focus from the popular to the literary, that draw from this common set of problems—especially in their failure to treat the comics as subjects of critical analysis, or their disciplines as methods of critical analysis, or both.

COMICS AND . . .

These shortcomings are perhaps most apparent in the "comics and . . . " books that have exploded in popular-culture publishing over the last decade. These books interpret popular comic book characters, usually superheroes, through the lens of some academic discipline such as psychology or philosophy—or, more frequently, they introduce readers to these disciplines through the examples of comic book characters. They often belong to larger series that apply the same disciplinary frameworks to popular franchises in other media, with publishers ranging from academic presses to boutique houses that operate outside the paradigms of scholarly discourse. The Smart Pop series from BenBella Books advertises the participation of comics and science fiction writers, not scholars, though some scholars do take part; at the other end of the spectrum, the Blackwell Philosophy and Pop Culture series is published by John Wiley & Sons, who also publish the *Journal of Popular Culture* and hundreds of other academic journals. University presses such as Oxford have also begun to enter the field of popular-culture publishing, which offers the possibility of attracting a broader readership not limited to the academy. Regardless of who publishes them, these series often sit uneasily between the standards of popular and academic writing. Typically timed to coincide with the release of blockbuster films, the books rarely apply any systematic critical approach to the characters' circulation between different media forms and industries. Instead, they are far more likely to invest the characters with a kind of Platonic agency that isn't bound to any text at all. Robin S. Rosenberg has written several examinations of the psychology of superheroes, but while she cites comics as evidence, she doesn't attribute them to any authors; to do so would mean acknowledging that Superman or Batman have been scripted by hundreds of writers across eighty years of publication, complicating her assumption that they have singular, consistent selves to psychoanalyze. Analyses such as Rosenberg's focus on the characters as they are broadly represented across multiple media, not the specific texts that generate them. The actual comics are irrelevant—as are the films and television shows and animation, all just so many interchangeable vehicles for the characters under analysis.

If the psychological approach often displays an indifference to its source material, the philosophical approach is founded on a more or less explicit contempt. William Irwin, editor of the Blackwell series, admits in "Philosophy and/as/of Popular Culture" that his interest is not in studying popular culture but in promoting philosophy: "to paraphrase a British philosopher, 'we need a spoonful of sugar to help the medicine go down.' We need to start with popular culture and use it to bring people to philosophy" (47). Regarding his subjects as Trojan horses for delivering philosophical concepts, Irwin scoffs at the study of popular culture for its own sake and believes cultural studies scholars "take themselves and their subject matter too seriously" (56). He maintains that philosophers should only use popular culture to illustrate philosophical points, never as a source of meaning or an object of interpretation in its own right. (Irwin's antipathy to interpretation extends to literary criticism and critical theory in general; he is an adherent and defender of E. D. Hirsch's theories of authorial intention.) However, even Irwin must concede that his volumes are works of philosophy only "in some loose sense of the word" (47), and he may oversell their potential; in a generally sympathetic overview for the *Chronicle of Higher Education*, Stephen T. Asma suggests that audiences typically come for the sugar and leave the medicine behind. Irwin views the study of popular culture as a means to an end, and that end is fairly clear: the Blackwell series has produced fifty-two volumes in ten years and shows no signs of abating, while Asma reports that Open Court's book *The Simpsons and Philosophy*, also edited by Irwin, sold more than a quarter of a million copies. These volumes provide a steady stream of revenue for their publishers, but they add little to the disciplines of philosophy or cultural studies.

To select one example more or less at random, *Watchmen and Philosophy: A Rorschach Test*, edited by Mark D. White, includes fifteen essays that explain the characters from Alan Moore and Dave Gibbons's *Watchmen* through the ideas of Immanuel Kant, John Stuart Mill, Friedrich Nietzsche, and Henri Bergson, among others. The approach is not inapposite, as the ethical dilemmas posed by Moore and Gibbons lend themselves to discussions of utilitarianism and deontology or fatalism and free will. Most of the essays, however, do little work beyond explaining the philosophical contexts of dilemmas that Moore and Gibbons have already laid out with remarkable clarity. Certainly the contributors have little to say about *Watchmen* as a text, citing no other scholarship on the series and scarcely mentioning the book's creators: the index lists just fifteen pages that cite writer Alan Moore and eight that mention artist Dave Gibbons (mostly the same ones). Only one contributor discusses the art in *Watchmen,* and that discussion barely takes up three pages. Most of the essays offer few insights into the comic beyond basic explanations of its plot and characters, much as they offer few insights into the philosophers beyond basic explanations of their ideas. (Citations of contemporary scholarship in philosophy—that is, citations that regard philosophy as anything other than another kind of primary source to be juxtaposed against *Watchmen*—are almost as rare as citations of scholarship on comics.) *Watchmen and Philosophy* follows an all-too-common script in comics studies, in which the arguments never advance beyond the straightforward application of some branch of philosophy or critical theory to a comic book. The comic demonstrates the widely understood tenets of the theory; the theory explicates the broadly shared readings of the comic. The essays are not doing any new work on either front.

In *How to Read Superhero Comics and Why,* Geoff Klock notes the problems of selecting a single mode of analysis and applying it to comics in an unreflective fashion. His example is archetypal criticism of the Carl Jung/Joseph Campbell variety, and he observes that tracing mythic archetypes in comics usually "amounts to little more than extensive footnoting" (8). At its best, this type of criticism simply directs the reader to consult the scholars whose ideas it summarizes rather than contributing any new analysis of its own. Arguably, Klock's book itself follows this model: though he presents detailed and thoughtful close readings of individual comics, his larger argument amounts to little more than a rote application of Harold Bloom's psychopoetics with a little Slavoj Žižek on the side. Every comic, every scene, every image is reduced to an allegory for the writer's anxiety of influence and shorn of any other meaning or context. In fact, Klock goes out of his way to rule out any historical or cultural contexts for his readings, distinguishing his work from cultural studies (10–11) and scoffing at any attempts to describe the comics he studies as postmodern (3). His readings are circumscribed entirely within Bloom's poetics, which insist that "the meaning of a poem can only be a poem, but *another poem—a poem not itself*" (Bloom 70, his emphasis). For Klock, who never questions Bloom's methods or his assumptions, the meaning of a superhero comic can only be another superhero comic. As an assessment of contemporary superhero publishing, this is largely correct, for reasons I will discuss in chapter 2, and yet those reasons are in large part historical and economic ones, not simply matters of psychology. By depriving himself of any contexts outside the superhero genre (and a narrowly psychologistic approach to the genre at that), Klock has limited his readings to a re-creation of Bloom's poetics within the world of superhero comics—a transplantation to unlikely soil, but nothing more.

This poetics of influence also leads Klock to prioritize the contributions of writers ahead of artists, who barely factor into his analysis unless they also write their own scripts. But at least Klock recognizes that writers and artists (along with inkers, colorists, letterers, editors, and other production staff) participate in the creation of comics; many of the academics who write about superheroes pay the creators no such mind. Lillian S. Robinson's *Wonder Women* provides selective and scattered readings of six decades of female superheroes, but other than William Moulton Marston, whose eccentric beliefs and unorthodox living arrangements have fascinated so many scholars, Robinson scarcely mentions the writers or artists who created them. (The slender index to *Wonder Women* is filled with fictional characters but lists no more than a handful of creators.) Like Rosenberg and too many other scholars, Robinson erases the creative labor of comics, treating the superheroes as products of an anonymous and undifferentiated mass culture. While this strategy may enable Rosenberg's psychological assumptions, it undercuts Robinson's intermittent attempts at historicizing the superwomen because it removes them from the processes of their own production.

Like many academics who dabble in comics studies, even those who identify themselves as lapsed fans or childhood readers, Robinson demonstrates a lack of familiarity with the most basic conventions of reading and writing about comics. She repeatedly refers to "origins stories" and "text bands" rather than using the well-established names for origin stories, narrative captions, and similar conventions. She discusses "the comic book genre" (x) in the singular, by which she means superhero comics, and she describes comics as "the quintessence of American popular culture" (1), echoing decades-old canards that presented comics as an original and characteristically American art form. These nationalistic claims have long since been displaced by accounts that trace the origins of comics to Europe in the early nineteenth century (Dierick and Lefèvre) if not the early modern era (Kunzle), but that work has made no impact on Robinson's book, which cites only a few works of comics scholarship and fewer still that are written from an academic perspective. For all that she is occasionally willing to voice her criticisms of a particular comic or character, Robinson identifies with her subjects primarily as a fan who is "trying to rescue" Wonder Woman and other female superheroes "from an ultimately hollow status as an unexamined pop icon" (xii). Unfortunately, she hasn't opted to examine their genre, their medium, their art form, or most of the scholarly discourse about them.

Sometimes it's not even clear whether Robinson has read the comics she selects for discussion. While surveying the Emma Peel–inspired Wonder Woman comics that were published from 1968 to 1972, Robinson refers to one character, the villainous Dr. Cyber, by two different names ("Cyber" and the "Beauty Hater") that correspond to the different copy used on the covers—giving no confidence that she has read anything beyond the covers. Even taken on its own terms, her research is incomplete: Robinson claims that "the covers from this period show [Wonder Woman] battling more female foes than ever" (81), but she lists just six covers out of a twenty-five-issue span (issues 177 to 201). A perusal of the Grand Comics Database reveals that the previous twenty-five issues included seven covers featuring Wonder Woman in battle with various female antagonists, as did the next twenty-five ("Wonder Woman").[3] Robinson's approach combines the worst qualities of the hardcore fan and the slumming academic: she devotes more attention to the fictional characters than to their creators, but she doesn't bother to read them in any depth.

Perhaps the most egregious oversight comes in her abbreviated discussion of *Promethea*, by Alan Moore, J. H. Williams III, and Mick Gray. Technically, it's not a discussion of *Promethea* at all but rather a rejoinder to Klock's reading of *Promethea*, yet even on that account it falls short. Robinson opens by referring to Promethea as "a transsexual hero who first appeared in 1995" (125). The errors are already piling up: Promethea first appeared in 1999, as a consultation of Klock's book or the comics themselves would confirm, and she isn't a single character but rather a divine being who merges with a succession of mortal hosts. One of her previous hosts, the fictitious comic book writer Bill Woolcott, was a gay man who transformed into a female superhero, but every other host (including Sophie Bangs, the comic's protagonist) is female. However, Bill Woolcott isn't the source of Robinson's confusion. Klock begins his discussion of *Promethea* with an analysis of another, far more minor supporting character, Roger of the Five Swell Guys. Roger is the sole female member of New York City's premier hero team, but this wasn't always the case. Roger was once a man, before a past adventure, never shown in *Promethea* and already over before the series began, transformed him into a woman. Ironically, despite (or perhaps because of?) this transformation, Roger remains the team's most physically imposing member, the muscle of the Five Swell Guys. Klock, always on the lookout for commentaries on other comics, suggests that Roger parodies a pattern of representation in which female superheroes are simply written as male characters with exaggerated, stereotypically feminine bodies (111). He then reads the Sophie Bangs Promethea as a counterpoint, an authentically feminine character whose more realistic body type departs from superhero comics' huge-breasted, wasp-waisted norm (112)—a norm that is arguably embodied by Roger, who bears the statuesque physique of most female superheroes and who tends to lose her clothes when she gets into a fight.

Robinson, however, conflates these two characters—a mistake she compounds by combining two different quotes from two consecutive pages of Klock's book—and responds to Klock as if Roger and Promethea are one and the same:

> Aside from the egregious use of terms like *feminine* and *male mentality* as if they mean something—and the same thing to writer and reader—this statement misses the irony in claiming that a character he describes as "literally" a man in a woman's body is the most real woman of all. And, although it would certainly be nice to see a variety of body types valorized among female superheroes, to identify one with wide hips who is nonetheless incapable of child-bearing as the "real" woman only increases the unconscious irony. (125–126)

Robinson raises some important objections to Klock's claims, specifically his assumption that there is a singular feminine identity or male mentality and his failure to consider the possibility that superheroes with more conventionally sexualized bodies can still present feminine and feminist perspectives. But these arguments are undermined when Robinson doesn't realize that Klock is referring to two completely different characters. (Nor is she in any position to chide him for his essentialism while she implies trans women aren't "real" women and defines womanhood through the ability to bear children.) To be fair, Klock's decision to open his discussion of *Promethea* with an analysis of Roger would be genuinely confusing to someone who hasn't read the comic—but if she hasn't read the comic, why is Robinson discussing it at all? For all its pretensions to feminism, *Promethea* furnishes ample material for a feminist critique, but Robinson is in no position to offer one. Unfortunately, her lack of preparation doesn't deter her from weighing in, or from opening her response to Klock with a hearty "Wrong again!" (125). It's hard to imagine any scholar taking such a cavalier approach within other, more established critical discourses. But in comics studies, it gets you a book contract.

TERMS OF EXCLUSION

Despite their centrality to the "comics and . . . " books, superheroes are no longer the sole or even the primary subjects of many academic studies of comics. Much of the recent activity in comics scholarship comes from my own home discipline, the field of literary studies, and focuses on the traditions of underground and alternative comics. This wasn't always the case; in 2009, Paul Lopes could conduct a brief survey of comics scholarship in the introduction to his book *Demanding Respect: The Evolution of the American Comic Book* and come up with a list consisting largely of histories and audience studies (xxii–xxiii). Since then, however, comics studies has seen an influx of literary scholars, the majority of whom tend to write about graphic memoirs, histories, journalism, or realistic fiction. These scholars avoid some of the more egregious oversights of the populists—they are conversant with a much wider range of critical theory, and most are adept close readers of the comics texts—but their investment in established notions of literary value contributes a new set of challenges. As Jenkins cautions, many literature scholars have sought to establish (or at least have done nothing to expand) a restrictive canon consisting of just a few critically acclaimed comics; frequently, they have sought to rename the comics form itself.

Some of the most prominent literary scholars have demonstrated a peculiar and persistent anxiety over the history and connotations of the word "comics," which has resulted in endless nominations of replacements for the term. Such anxieties have their antecedents among comics fans; writing for amateur press associations and fanzines, Richard Kyle first coined the term "graphic novel" to denote ambitious, artistically mature stories in comics form back in 1964 (Hatfield, *Alternative Comics* 165n10). The term was later used by comics artist Will Eisner when he sought to promote his 1978 book *A Contract with God* to bookstores and general audiences; by the mid-1980s, the label had become common in both the comics industry and the book trade (*Alternative Comics* 29–30). Comics artists and critics have long used the term with some uneasiness, however, viewing it as an attempt to bestow a borrowed dignity on comics or simply as a misnomer: many of the "graphic novels" stocked on bookshelves are collections of serialized comics lacking any novelistic telos or scope, and even *A Contract with God* is a collection of short stories (*Alternative Comics* 29). The term "novel" also implies a fictionality that runs counter to the testimonial impulse that fuels the autobiographies and other nonfiction accounts that have won so much critical attention in recent decades. There are ample reasons for scholars to be wary of the graphic novel label in spite of its commercial success.

Such skepticism, however, doesn't quite account for the zeal with which some scholars have attempted to coin new names for the comics form. Hillary Chute and Marianne DeKoven edited a special issue of *Modern Fiction Studies* on "graphic narrative" (767), William Kuskin uses "graphia" (9) in his special issue of *English Language Notes*, and education professors such as Courtney Lee Weida have favored "graphica" (99). Many of the artists who emerged from the undergrounds prefer to take their comix with an *X* to separate them from the commercial mainstream; in 1988, Art Spiegelman proposed the term "commix" since the form mixes words and pictures ("Commix" 61). He later streamlined it to "co-mix," a term that *Critical Inquiry* editor W. J. T. Mitchell received with enthusiasm, at least for one paragraph ("Comics" 260). But no term is perfect: Spiegelman's coinages are both too idiosyncratic and too similar to existing names, not redefinitions so much as mercurial whims of an artist who has also proposed "*Nincompictopoop*" and "*Ikonologosplatt*" for the same purposes ("Picturing" n.p.). "Graphic narrative" is useful in shedding the fictive connotations of "graphic novel," but it would seem to exclude nonnarrative works of the type collected by Andrei Molotiu in *Abstract Comics: The Anthology*; on the other hand, "graphia" or "graphica" might potentially include any graphic mark or expression, limiting their usefulness as descriptors. There is, of course, one term that already describes the entire field of production in comics, however broadly we wish to define it. That term is "comics," and the lengths some literary scholars go to in order to avoid it says much about the assumptions that guide them.[4]

"Comics" isn't a perfect descriptor either. A relic of the days when the most popular and prominent comics were humorous newspaper strips, it may seem particularly ill suited for the earnest memoirs, hard-hitting reportage, and deadly serious superhero narratives that most interest academics today. But etymological precision doesn't seem to be the reason that literature scholars eschew the term; after all, we still discuss "the novel" even though the form is no longer all that new, and we still use the term "tragedy" even if most performances are (I hope) no longer followed by the ritual sacrifice of a goat. We accept that these terms acquired new meanings over time because those meanings preceded us; the novel and the tragedy had already carved out cultural spaces for their present forms before they became objects of study in the academy. Comics also preceded our critical attention, but their claims to cultural capital and prestige (at least in Anglophone criticism) are new and unsettled enough that some scholars still attempt to rename them. This impulse might arise from a lack of familiarity with the form, fear of its historical connotations, pressure to conform to lingering cultural hierarchies, or the type of entrepreneurial claim-staking that the modern university rewards. Whatever their motivations, these efforts regard comics as a kind of unexplored territory ripe for academic discovery—an assumption that requires scholars to ignore the considerable body of scholarship already written about comics.

Even the most thoroughly researched articles sometimes display shocking blind spots. Hye Su Park, writing a bibliographic essay that purports to "serve as a broad survey" (149) of criticism on Art Spiegelman's *Maus*, claims that "*Maus* criticism is sorely lacking in substantial examinations on issues surrounding gender, race, religion, and critical pedagogy" (148). In fact, such examinations have ranked among the chief concerns of the ample body of criticism that didn't make it into Park's survey. Her claim about the neglect of race and religion is particularly striking in its oversight, as Spiegelman's use of animal metaphors to represent different racial, ethnic, and religious groups is one of the oldest and most contentious topics in *Maus* criticism. Those metaphors have been roundly condemned by critics such as Robert C. Harvey in *The Art of the Comic Book* (243–245) and defended by scholars such as Joseph Witek in *Comic Books as History* (102–114). Witek's chapter on *Maus* was the first scholarly work on Spiegelman published in English, and it has since become a touchstone for Spiegelman criticism; referenced in many of the articles Park cites, it nevertheless appears nowhere in her "broad survey." Park not only ignores the foundational work on her subject, she then declares the remainder of that work sorely lacking in the very discussions she has overlooked.

This problem is hardly limited to a single article, as seen in Chute and DeKoven's pronouncement "There does not yet exist an established critical apparatus for graphic narrative" (770). Charles Hatfield has noted that literary-critical writing on comics frequently fails to engage with other work in comics studies, and often doesn't address other comics beyond its own narrow canon of graphic memoirs ("Studies" 411). As a result, the few titles that have been admitted into that canon are wrenched out of their historical, material, and aesthetic contexts, and Hatfield laments that "A kind of willed forgetting seems to shape the academic and literary criticism of comics" (419). That forgetting could furnish a whole new set of examples for Witek's warning about scholarship that doesn't speak to other scholarship, although in this case the problem originates not in a desire to address fan audiences but in an inclination to ignore the history of comics and comics studies. Hatfield describes how the literary critics' flattening and compartmentalization of comics history has enabled journalists who promote an elitist and exceptionalist view in which mature, complex, critically acclaimed comics like *Maus* or Alison Bechdel's *Are You My Mother?* are not regarded as comics at all (419–421). After shrinking the canon, jettisoning the context, and neglecting other scholarship, the only remaining step is to remove the surviving masterpieces from the world of comics entirely.

GUILTY PLEASURES

In 2012, the University of Chicago hosted "Comics: Philosophy and Practice," a conference that gathered seventeen acclaimed North American underground and alternative comics artists. Two years later that symposium would form the backbone of *Comics & Media,* a special issue of *Critical Inquiry* edited by Hillary Chute and Patrick Jagoda, who wisely caution readers against "the twinned discourses that so often plague discussions of emergent forms: cheerleading on one hand and the performance of marginality on the other" (3). The editors also note that Tom Gunning and Scott Bukatman, film theorists who didn't participate in the conference but who contributed original articles for the issue, step back from those discourses with ease. The problem with such measured but highly selective praise is the resulting implication that the other participants might not. Intentional or otherwise, this implication is borne out in the conference transcripts and the other parts of the journal. University of Chicago professor Deborah Nelson introduced the panel "Comics and Autobiography" by observing that autobiography has become one of the most popular, innovative, and ubiquitous genres in American culture, "however much the *New York Times* and other cultural guardians chastise us for our appetites" (Gloeckner et al. 86). This self-conscious positioning in opposition to the cultural gatekeepers would seem to be contradicted by Nelson's presence on a University of Chicago conference panel focused primarily on autobiographical comics. Nor is this gambit restricted to autobiography: no matter how many institutions open their doors to comics, from the National Endowment for the Arts to the Whitney Biennial to the *New York Times* itself, the conference guests and moderators continue to position comics as a marginal art form.

This positioning is by no means limited to a single conference or journal, but is endemic to comics artists and scholars alike. *Demanding Respect*, Paul Lopes's social history of the American comic book, is primarily concerned with chronicling the medium's lack of prestige and demonstrating how it has triumphed over the disdain of critics and legislators. Christopher Pizzino, who sees comics' poor cultural stature not as an obstacle overcome but as a persistent barrier to their legitimation, traces this theme in the comics themselves in *Arresting Development: Comics at the Boundaries of Literature*, making the performance of marginality central to the medium's artistic successes. While this status anxiety is arguably outdated—of the four major works Pizzino examines, only Alison Bechdel's *Fun Home* was published entirely in this century—comics creators have been reluctant to abandon it. Indeed, some of the most acclaimed artists regularly incorporate that anxiety into their work even as they continue to rake in the awards. In his comic "Ruin: Your Life, Draw: Cartoons!" Chris Ware's hyperbolically morose narration laments that cartoonists must consign themselves to lives of poverty, public scorn, and "utter social disregard," an odd complaint coming from an artist whose accolades include multiple book prizes, fellowships, and museum exhibitions, not to mention the conference invitations. (Ware spoke at the Chicago conference and incorporated "Ruin: Your Life" into the version of his conference poster that appears in *Critical Inquiry*.) Ware, of course, knows that his career has not followed the dismal trajectory outlined in the comic, yet the aggressively self-effacing posture is part of his routine, serving much the same purpose as the quote he includes from *Peanuts* cartoonist Charles Schulz: "Cartooning will destroy you. It will break your heart." Ware is fond of this quote, having previously cited it in a 2001 interview (Phipps); so too did Ware's friend and fellow conference guest Ivan Brunetti, in a 2006 strip titled "Cartooning Will Destroy You." As Bart Beaty has noted, these invocations attempt to claim Schulz as a tortured, melancholic artist in the tradition of the Romantic genius, and the field of cartooning as fertile ground for such genius (*Comics* 94–95). If the wildly popular creator of Snoopy can be cast as a tortured soul who suffered for his art, then comics as a whole are simultaneously marginalized and validated as a serious art form disconnected from the tastes and institutions of mass culture. By this logic, the marginalization is the validation.

With the comics artists performing their own marginality, the academics are free to supply the cheerleading. Far from ignoring comics creators, the scholars who participated in the Chicago conference were just as deferential to the artists as their more populist counterparts are to fictional characters. Moderators serenaded their guests and presented them with homemade dolls, far exceeding the routine unctions that kick off most conference keynotes. Chute and Jagoda display a similar deference in *Comics & Media*, most patently in their treatment of Robert Crumb's rejected cover for the *New Yorker* depicting a transgender couple applying for a marriage license before a befuddled clerk (plate 1). *Comics & Media* features this image twice, once accompanying the transcript of a panel with Crumb and Françoise Mouly (Mouly 196) and again on the cover, in a clear statement of solidarity with Crumb. As the transcript makes clear, however, *New Yorker* editor David Remnick did not reject the piece lightly. The cover was slated to run in June 2009, after California's short-lived recognition and abrupt repeal of same-sex marriage propelled the issue to national attention. In that context, Mouly reports, Remnick felt Crumb was portraying gay couples in an outdated and arguably homophobic manner. Mouly seems to share this interpretation, telling the Chicago conference that "a lot of the fight for gay marriage is one for normalization—today's gay advocates are not presenting themselves as freaks" (Mouly 193). This position invites more interrogation, notably for its confusion of homosexuality with transgender identity and for Mouly's indirect reference to the transgender couple as "freaks." However, all these confusions originate with Crumb's cartoon. Remnick has a point about Crumb's treatment of his subjects: his framing places the couple in full figure, making them the objects of the joke and turning the clerk's window into a mirror that reflects or models an anxious normative gaze. Even worse, the helpful sign that points the way to a "gender inspection" appears to mock the happy couple rather than the society that doesn't know what to do with them. Unfortunately, any such critical considerations were left out of the panel discussion, which ranged from Crumb's indignation to Mouly's feeble apologies. The panel and the journal present the cover as further evidence that Crumb and the other assembled comics artists are edgy, oppositional, marginalized figures even as they continue to dominate the covers of the *New Yorker*. The rejected cover received an equally enthusiastic reception from the conference audience, which applauded when it was displayed—or at least that's how the editors choose to represent the crowd's no doubt varied reactions.

The editors would very much like readers of *Critical Inquiry* to know what fun the conference was; so, too, would the conference moderators, who routinely expressed their amazement that they were discussing comics in an academic setting. (The artists, many of whom speak regularly at conferences and universities, didn't seem nearly as surprised.) No guest saw more validation visited upon his every utterance than Crumb: the moderators deferred to his constant interruptions of his fellow guests, and the editors make sure to note the audience's laughter at his quips. Some outbursts, however, went unrecorded. In a postmortem interview with Chute for the *University of Chicago Magazine*, Elizabeth Station—although quite a sympathetic interviewer in the conference mold ("Pulling this off makes you a rock star. How do you feel about that?")—asks, "How about that moment when Crumb referred to a young women [*sic*] who asked him a question as a 'cute thing'?" Chute writes it off as part of the cartoonist's irrepressible counter-cultural ethos: "Sometimes there were tense moments [. . .]. But that's what happens when you bring actual artists into this environment. You can't just clean everyone up and sanitize them in the way you might when everyone there is a practicing professor or scholar" (Station). While Chute maintains that the tension was productive, this particular clash of cultures didn't find its way into *Critical Inquiry*. Chute and Jagoda have carefully sanitized Crumb by leaving out his patronizing and sexist remark; had Station not asked about the incident, there would be no record anywhere that it ever happened. Reverence for the guests has supplanted fidelity to the event and stifled a genuine exchange of ideas and perspectives.

For all that the editors and moderators seek to celebrate the artists (or protect them from themselves), their investment in the continued marginalization of comics sometimes takes on a curiously patronizing tone. In his conversations at the conference with Art Spiegelman and Joe Sacco, *Critical Inquiry* general editor W. J. T. Mitchell is especially prone to fetishize the medium of comics as a "guilty pleasure" (Mitchell and Spiegelman 21–22) and a "second childhood" that refuses to grow up (Sacco and Mitchell 53). Both artists push back on this formulation, with Sacco in particular rejecting Mitchell's claims ("To me it is not an extension of my childhood so much. I think the drawing grew up with me in some ways") and urging him not to confuse the subversive tradition of the undergrounds with being childish (53). Having spent most of his career creating comics for adults, Sacco understandably insists on preserving that space. Mitchell, ever the deferential host, quickly repeats these sentiments, lamenting that comics have been dismissed as childish only to reassert the charge in the same breath, claiming for comics "the ability to penetrate official so-called grown-up views of the world—that's another way in which I think of it as a second childhood" (54). While Mitchell seeks to praise comics with these intimations of their illicit charms, his insistence on defining them as childish suggests a lingering inability to distinguish between the historical audiences for North American comics and the possibilities of the comics form. The persistence of these preconceived notions shapes not only his contributions but the conference and the journal issue as a whole.

Although some of the participating artists, notably Spiegelman, are well-versed in the material history of comics as a mass medium and its impact on the form (for example, through advances in printing technology), the editors are more interested in separating the emergent literary canon of comics artists from that history. In his afterword for the journal, where the artists can no longer challenge him, Mitchell joins the endless quest for a new name for comics, seeking one that will highlight their supposed roles as genre and medium while "defying any singular identity confined to their specific history in mass print media" ("Comics" 260). Though he says he wants to preserve that history in an indecisive and ungainly "comics/co-mix" homonym, his comments both at the conference and in the afterword imply that the history of North American comics is limited to a singular identity as a juvenile mass medium: if "comics" are the guilty pleasure of perpetual childhood, then the artists celebrated at the Chicago conference must work in some other form with a different name. The conference enforces this partitioning, focusing solely on artists from the undergrounds and their inheritors in the alternative comics movement. When the history of comics as a mass medium leaks into the conversation, it does so only by way of comments from artists such as Spiegelman, or the post facto contributions of scholars such as Gunning and Bukatman. From the perspective of the conference organizers and editors, any comics originating from that tradition are simply interesting historical documents, personal milestones in the formation of the legitimate artists or, occasionally, sources they might raid for inspiration—as Chute herself (in collaboration with Alison Bechdel) contributes a quartet of comic strips inspired by the web cartoonist Kate Beaton (Chute and Bechdel 52) but doesn't examine Beaton's work or invite her to participate in the conference or the journal. Comics in popular genres might be fodder for an artist's development or templates for their own derivative gags, but not works of art worthy of study or discussion in their own right.

Even as the special issue excludes most genres of comics from consideration, it also flattens the critical language that scholars might use to discuss them, with some contributors repurposing the very concept of genre itself. Gunning and Katalin Orbán both use the term to describe publication formats such as the comic strip or graphic novel, a sense not far removed from the Romantic use of "genre" to describe entire literary forms such as poetry, novels, or drama (Gunning 46). Yet to refer to "the graphic novel genre," as Orbán does (Orbán 169), occludes the broad range of generic production within a format that includes fantasy, humor, memoir, journalism, realistic fiction, experimental narrative, and more. Mitchell confuses the matter even further, describing comics as a medium that can be applied to any genre before suggesting that the distinction between genre and medium is trivial if not meaningless ("Comics" 256, 259). Part of the problem may be that neither term is adequate to describe the entire field of comics. If "genre" is defined by particular narrative conventions or social uses, then "medium" is tied too closely to material form itself: properly speaking, the comic book constitutes one medium, the newspaper comic strip another, webcomics still another, and so on. Treating the graphic novel as a publication format (and as just one among many possible formats) rather than a single all-encompassing genre would acknowledge this generic and transmedial diversity while foregrounding the material production that so many comics scholars overlook.

If our scholarship requires another term that isn't bound by the material limits of medium or the narrative constraints of genre, we might consider discussing comics as form. Most of the *Critical Inquiry* contributors are reluctant to do so, given formalism's association with outmoded discourses of medium specificity. In their most dogmatic applications, especially as practiced by modernist art critic Clement Greenberg, appeals to medium specificity attempted to dictate the most essential and pure forms of expression in any medium, a notion thoroughly rebutted by Noël Carroll (3–36), among other critics. However, scholars such as Mitchell now invoke the spectre of medium specificity as reason to avoid any formal considerations or definitions, including the distinction between genre and medium. Attempts to build hermetically sealed, exceptionalist definitions of comics can quickly become counterproductive—as can attempts to come up with new, more academically acceptable names to replace "comics," although this hasn't stopped Mitchell from trying—but these have nothing to do with acknowledging basic differences between medium, genre, and form, differences that are hardly unique to comics. Recent genre theory suggests that genre is not defined by form at all, much less medium, but is instead a dynamic system of classification shaped as much by social context as by textual patterns (Devitt 4–6, 9–13). Comics scholars, theorists, and practitioners have also attempted to disentangle genre, medium, and form, not to abolish the distinctions between these conceptual frameworks (McCloud 4–6; Horrocks 2).

Critical Inquiry might have avoided this entire line of argument, or at least advanced it in newer and more productive directions, had the editors and contributors devoted more attention to the scholarship that preceded them. Mostly unfamiliar with the work of comics studies, they painstakingly reconstruct debates that have occupied the field for decades—or that the field has already moved beyond. Scott McCloud's formalist analysis in his 1993 treatise *Understanding Comics: The Invisible Art* has prompted considerable objection and debate from scholars and fellow comics artists, but it has also shaped much of the academic discourse around comics for over two decades. Surely an obvious candidate for any conference on the philosophy and practice of comics, McCloud wasn't simply absent from the proceedings, he has been airbrushed out of the picture: the journal editors don't mention his name even while discussing ideas he popularized in North American comics scholarship, such as the role of the gutter or the relationship between time and space on the comics page (Chute and Jagoda 3–4). McCloud built *Understanding Comics* around Marshall McLuhan's observation that comics are a "cool medium" that prompts reader participation (McCloud 59), yet Chute and Jagoda restate this point without mentioning McCloud once (4).

Similarly, Mitchell's confusion over whether comics function as medium or genre might have been avoided had he consulted McCloud's work (or that of his many respondents) rather than turn to the questionable authority of Bill Ayers, the former Weather Underground militant turned educator, memoirist, and novice comics author. When Ayers adapted his book *To Teach* into comics form with artist Ryan Alexander-Tanner, he prefaced it with a two-page introduction explaining the communicative possibilities of comics. This brief passage contains nothing that isn't already found in McCloud, though it does open with a gag about Ayers's lack of familiarity with the preexisting discourse about comics, complete with a clichéd "Bang! Pow! Zoom! Comics Aren't for Kids Anymore" headline, which Ayers's cartoon avatar thinks he invented on the spot (xiv). Mitchell seems not to have caught the joke, as he goes on to repeat Ayers's oversights; after recapping the sequence, in which Alexander-Tanner teaches Ayers to recognize the distinction between medium and genre, Mitchell sides with Ayers's wife, Bernardine Dohrn, who dismisses the point as trivial ("Comics" 259). Tellingly, Mitchell denigrates and ignores the perspective of the practicing comics artist in favor of the uninformed academics (i.e., those characters whose positions most neatly parallel his own) in order to erase a distinction that has been broadly recognized by artists and scholars alike. When Mitchell asks, "What is at stake?" (259), he ignores the reception history of the very comics that he celebrates. What he terms, in a paraphrase of Pierre Bourdieu, the "heroic phase" (255) in comics—that is, their successful claims to artistic autonomy and their belated recognition by cultural institutions—has only been possible because artists taught audiences to recognize distinctions between genre, medium, and form, opening a space for comics that are not associated exclusively with children. This expansion of possibilities, a project enacted by generations of artists and scholars, was perhaps the most important prerequisite for the development of comics studies. Only now, after their apparent success, can W. J. T. Mitchell join the conversation and wonder what all the fuss was about.

For all that Mitchell might appear to present a radically different and unabashedly elitist vision of comics studies, however, his statements in *Critical Inquiry* aren't so different from those of Henry Jenkins in "Should We Discipline the Reading of Comics?" True, Jenkins scoffs at the desire to turn comics into a middlebrow literature composed of memoirs, testimonials, and other respectable genres, and the gathering of artists at the Chicago conference represents precisely the sort of exercise in canon formation that he rejects. Beneath their divergent tastes in comics, however, some common assumptions underwrite both scholars' arguments. Both discount the larger field of comics scholarship, minimizing its contributions when they don't neglect it entirely. Although he speculates about an "alternative history" of comics studies stretching back to the 1920s (2–4), a history well preserved in volumes like Heer and Worcester's *Arguing Comics*, Jenkins nevertheless titles his next section "Mapping a Field Which Doesn't Yet Exist" (4–6)—a curious introduction to a casebook of critical approaches to comics drawn from existing scholarly discourses and written by practicing comics scholars. Jenkins and Mitchell both promote the idea that comics studies is not simply undisciplined but unmade, awaiting a heroic generation of founders who will build a discourse (and perhaps name a form) that already exists; Mitchell and his fellow editors are simply more thorough in writing the traces of that discourse out of their journal.

When they turn to discuss individual comics artists or texts, both scholars are more descriptive than analytical. (Nor are the artists they discuss so different; Kim Deitch wouldn't have been at all out of place at the Chicago conference.) Both issue edicts about the proper way to read comics, or the kinds of questions such readings should properly consider, without showing what those readings would yield for our understanding of individual texts or the form as a whole. Both are highly skeptical of attempts to define the medium specificity of comics, and with good reason, though only Mitchell uses them to dismiss any considerations of form. Most troubling of all, both scholars describe comics as an illicit, disreputable, and above all juvenile pleasure, patronizing the artists and texts they purport to celebrate. Jenkins is more openly derisive of academic reading practices and Mitchell far more sweeping in his disregard for established comics scholarship, but both exalt fannish modes of reading and talking about comics over more scholarly methods. Although they come from very different disciplinary backgrounds, Jenkins and Mitchell demonstrate that the cultural-populist and literary-critical approaches to comics are not so different as they first seem. Both can slip all too easily into a common posture of unquestioning praise that celebrates their preferred comics artists (however widely they choose to cast the net) while ignoring or dismissing other critical perspectives. It is this mode of reading—never simply populist or elitist, but adopting anti-intellectual strains from both discourses—that I hope to challenge.

BREAKING THE FRAMES

While this book suggests the necessity for alternative practices in the study of comics, I have no interest in prescribing a single methodology or disciplinary framework as a model for all comics scholars, even under the guise of presenting a "radically undisciplined" approach. Comics studies benefits greatly from its multidisciplinary and interdisciplinary character and should encourage an even greater diversity of perspectives. However, I hope more scholars will embrace the most exacting professional standards of their chosen disciplines, contributing to a comics studies that is both methodologically varied and academically rigorous in all its forms. I also hope comics scholars will continue to interact with comics fans, journalists, and practitioners, learning from their critical language and expertise without ceding our own. But work produced in academic venues, for audiences of other academics, must uphold academic practices of research, analysis, and evidence. Those practices should include first and foremost an obligation to read and respond to other relevant work in the field, no matter what its disciplinary origin. Without that standard, comics studies will be forever reinventing the wheel, caught up in endless arguments over naming and definition instead of expanding its field of knowledge.

The methods I follow in this book are primarily those of literary criticism, including close reading, historical contextualization, and engagement with various strands of critical theory. These methods have value not because they are part of some venerable and unitary tradition—indeed, they arise from different moments in critical history and have sometimes been bitterly opposed to one another—but because they continue to perform important intellectual work. For all their abuses (many of which are charted in this book), the practices of critical reading serve an oppositional function in a society that desperately needs them, encouraging readers not to take textual claims or their own assumptions for granted but to evaluate each argument as they come to it. Paired with the tools of close reading, they also serve a verifying, authenticating function; by requiring us to examine and reconsider our sources, both primary and secondary, critical reading obliges us to check our own work and ensure that it always makes reference to sources and viewpoints external to itself. That commitment to referentiality must also include an awareness of the world outside the text. One of the recurring themes of this book, possibly its primary one, is the urgency of recovering history as both method and discipline—that is, the importance of history not simply as the context in which a work is created or received (although that too has been absent from too much comics scholarship) but as a process for sorting through the archives of the past, organizing their contents into narratives, and evaluating the claims those narratives make for their accuracy and explanatory power. This sense of history has perhaps been the most neglected and devalued critical apparatus in comics scholarship, whether that scholarship originates in cultural studies or literary criticism.

Because this book interrogates two different schools of comics studies, it necessarily takes a two-part structure. The first half focuses on academic writing about superheroes and related popular genres, with particular regard to critics' rationalization or neglect of various models of history. Chapter 1 opens with a reconsideration of one of the most influential essays ever written about superhero comics, "The Myth of Superman," by Umberto Eco, which argues that the genre suspends the passage of time as a means of balancing narrative development and stasis. While Eco's piece is itself less timeless and more historically contingent than he acknowledges, some contemporary comics scholars have attempted to contain, contradict, or simply misrepresent his arguments in order to claim that modern superhero comics depart substantially from the oneiric model he describes. Maintaining that contemporary practices of multiplicity, intertextuality, and self-reflexivity are both narratively transformative and politically liberatory, these scholars rely on the formulas of cultural populism even if they must misread Eco to do so. A reappraisal of "The Myth of Superman" shows that these practices aren't so novel as their promoters claim, nor is Eco's model so outdated.

Chapter 2 expands the discussion to address the role of history in contemporary superhero comics more broadly. While critics have expended a great deal of time and energy attempting to periodize the history of the superhero genre, these accounts tend to erase historical and material contexts in favor of a self-referential model of genre formation. The critical readings informed by this historiography similarly tend toward dehistoricized annotations as scholars track down intertexts and trace allusions to other comics, particularly when discussing the revisionist superhero comics and their successors—a highly self-conscious and self-critical phase in the genre's development. These discussions essentially register postmodernism's impact on the genre without acknowledging its larger transformations in the production of culture (and, in some cases, while actively resisting the postmodernist label). This chapter argues that narrow, genre-centric interpretations of history have also been used to foreclose on more skeptical or ideological readings, with specific reference to comics by Warren Ellis and John Cassaday, Frank Miller, Alan Moore, and Mark Waid and Alex Ross. The revisionists and their heirs call out for more historicized readings that are attentive not simply to larger cultural trends but also to the production processes that shape the comics.

Chapter 3 sets out to demonstrate the potential applications and benefits of such readings by connecting the comics industry's legal and economic practices to the narrative and ideological structures they reproduce. As a series that is owned by its creators yet was initially produced through the corporate publishing system, Alan Moore and Kevin O'Neill's *The League of Extraordinary Gentlemen* is constrained by industry ownership practices as well as by copyright law. Moore and O'Neill respond by working these constraints into their narrative, transforming them into recurring themes of creative independence and control. Primarily featuring characters taken from late Victorian and early twentieth-century literature, *League* is also well suited to comics scholars' interests in intertextuality and self-reflexivity. Where most scholars argue that Moore is critical of Victorian ideology, however, I suggest that he vacillates between condemnation and idealization in a manner that proves inextricable from his similarly ambivalent relation to the practices of ownership and appropriation that define his series. *The League of Extraordinary Gentlemen* is therefore an ideal case study for more materially and historically engaged modes of critical reading.

The second half of the book turns to criticism that prioritizes domestic fiction, memoirs, and histories, prescribing realism as the preeminent mode for culturally legitimated comics. Chapter 4 examines the implementation of this realist aesthetic in comics produced and edited by Chris Ware, particularly the anthologies *Best American Comics 2007* and *McSweeney's Quarterly Concern* issue 13, which attempt to consolidate the emergent canon of literary comics and set the direction for its critical interpretation. In the process, however, Ware also reinforces some of the same aesthetic hierarchies that once dismissed all comics as juvenile trash; his selections are ready for admission to the literary canon largely to the degree that they do not trouble its values. In addition to promoting this aesthetic in his anthologies, Ware has also incorporated it into his own work with increasing transparency. This chapter concludes with a discussion of Ware's *Building Stories*, which self-consciously advertises the ambitions and stylings of realistic fiction produced by and for creative writing workshops even as that fiction occupies an increasingly contentious place in American literary culture.

The focus on canon formation and literary authentication continues into chapter 5, which discusses the critical reception of Marjane Satrapi's *Persepolis*. Although Satrapi wrote and drew *Persepolis* in France and published it with a French comics cooperative, the book's translation into English has done much to drive the growing critical acceptance of comics in North America; along with *Maus* and *Fun Home*, *Persepolis* unquestionably sits at the center of the English-language canon of literary comics. To secure its place in that canon, however, journalists and scholars have removed *Persepolis* from the original contexts of its creation and production in the world of French comics. Relocating *Persepolis* outside the comics world has also obscured its departure from the conventions of other autobiographical comics, confounding the ways scholars normally interpret this genre. Reading Satrapi's book within these contexts highlights the heroic individualism and cosmopolitan consumerism that mark *Persepolis* as an expression of neoliberal values and not simply the critique of Western culture claimed by some of its critics. While earlier chapters argue for reading comics against a broader historical framework, this chapter makes the case that we must also read them within their original generic, material, and cultural contexts—that is, we must read them as comics and not as some rarer and more elevated form with no connection to their own history.

All the concerns that animate this book come together in chapter 6, which examines Kyle Baker's *Nat Turner*, a comic that dramatizes historical personalities and events while drawing from the visual iconography of heroic fiction. Although Baker takes the historical Nat Turner and the 1831 Southampton slave rebellion as his starting points, he extrapolates, transplants, or invents enough material—and his graphic style is indebted enough to superhero comics—that *Nat Turner* creates a romanticized, mystified version of history. However, the scholarship on *Nat Turner* has generally opted to ignore, excuse, or defend Baker's blend of history and myth, typically either by characterizing his comic as a work of historiographic metafiction that is not intended to be taken literally or, conversely, by claiming that its depiction of slavery is more accurate than historical sources, even those written by former slaves. Contradictory as they are, both of these arguments dismiss textual and historical evidence in favor of the celebratory impulse that currently governs the field of comics scholarship.

In this respect, the discourse on *Nat Turner* not only typifies the major schools within comics studies, it manifests a larger suspicion of referentiality within both literary and cultural studies. In a brief afterword, I situate comics studies in relation to these hermeneutics of suspicion and to the modes of reparative, restorative, or "postcritical" reading that have recently emerged in reaction to them. While the proponents of postcritical reading offer important challenges to prevailing customs in academic writing, their critique of critique has also indicted humanistic scholarship more broadly, often in ways that reinscribe the critiques of the humanities already leveled by the hermeneutics of suspicion. The end result is a renunciation of not only the methods of criticism but the scholarly mission and purpose of the humanities. The afterword argues for the continued professional, intellectual, and civic benefits of the humanities and the merits of academic disciplines that sustain rather than destroy their commitment to the values of evidence, expertise, and critical analysis. Without claiming these values are the only ones that should guide comics scholarship, this book suggests what they can contribute to the field—and what it has already lost in their absence.

Just as comics studies incorporates many academic disciplines and methodologies, so, too, can it expand to consider new subjects. As the field outgrows the tastes of comics fandom and literary culture that have defined it thus far, comics scholarship must broaden its focus beyond superheroes and alternative comics. Recent studies such as Bart Beaty's *Twelve-Cent Archie* and Deborah E. Whaley's *Black Women in Sequence: Re-inking Comics, Graphic Novels, and Anime* have already begun to devote more attention to neglected genres such as romance, humor, and children's comics, and to creators who have been excluded from the comics canon. Unfortunately, such expansions are not a part of this book, which takes as its primary subject comics scholarship in its present form. The comics I discuss here are those that have most preoccupied scholars to date: superheroes, memoirs and nonfiction comics, and realistic fiction. The structure of this book therefore replicates some of the blind spots that currently limit comics studies—for example, the discussion of female comics artists primarily in terms of the genres of autobiography and memoir, a practice I challenge in chapter 4's discussion of canon formation. The genres examined here are not the only ones that define comics, and they should not remain the only ones that delineate the field of comics studies. However, this study proceeds from the observation that the field needs more rigorous and varied critical frameworks just as much as it would benefit from a more inclusive canon.

Finally, I don't wish to argue that comics, either collectively or in any individual genre, are somehow entitled to more academic prestige or cultural clout. On the contrary, comics currently enjoy unprecedented levels of respect in both the academy and American culture as a whole—enough that scholars such as Andrew Loman, Ian Gordon, Bart Beaty, and Benjamin

Woo have begun tracing how this newfound status has developed, what forms it has taken, what it includes, and what it leaves out.[5] That stature is also the subject of this book, though I am less interested in its historical formation than in the disciplinary and ideological assumptions that underwrite its scholarly face. Those assumptions have resulted in a set of scholarly discourses—primarily two discourses, largely separate and perfectly mirrored—that seek either to exalt favored artists and genres or to exclude others from consideration as they jointly promote a model of comics studies that is overly restrictive, almost uniformly laudatory, and hostile to other critical perspectives.

Respect, then, is a quality I find simultaneously overvalued and underpracticed in comics studies. It's time for comics scholars to stop demanding respect from others and start treating our own discipline as an academic discipline. It's time to take the chip off our collective shoulder and focus on producing the same high quality of work that would be expected in any other field. Having successfully made the case that comics deserve serious consideration as art or literature, history or ideology, culture or commerce, it's time we commit to reading them that way.

CHAPTER 1

THE MYTH OF ECO

COMICS, CONTINUITY, AND CULTURAL POPULISM

Comics studies wasn't always so deferential. Earlier generations of scholars, working in academic environments far less favorable to the study of popular culture, understood that explaining the formal operations or social functions of comics didn't require shielding them from criticism. Far from disqualifying comics as objects of academic study, this more critical approach informed one of the earliest and most famous essays ever written on superhero comics, Umberto Eco's "The Myth of Superman." Initially published in 1962 as "Il mito di 'Superman' e la dissoluzione del tempo," the essay was translated into English by Natalie Chilton in 1972. Although Eco revised his work substantially for the translation, both versions of "The Myth of Superman" argue that Superman comics, and by extension any popular serial narratives, are caught in a temporal paradox as they attempt to combine the stasis and timelessness of mythic characters with the progressive development of the modern novel. To manage or hide this contradiction, Eco explains, serial comics create an "oneiric climate" that suspends the passage of time, with each new installment starting exactly where the previous episode began ("Myth" 17). Eco develops this idea further in the 1972 translation, arguing that the static narrative structure reinforces an equally stagnant ideological structure in which large-scale political action is neither possible nor necessary. While these observations once garnered implicit and almost ubiquitous acceptance among comics scholars, however, they have more recently prompted modification, contextualization, and criticism. Contemporary superhero comics no longer maintain the episodic structure that governed Eco's oneiric climate, but instead build extended narratives with rich intertextual connections and shared histories, a system of organizing principles that comics fans and scholars term "continuity" (Goodrum 98–99). These comics may include multiple variations on the same iconic characters or eclectic pastiches that incorporate other genres and other media. The narrative practices of superhero comics have changed over the last fifty years, and any essay of that vintage would benefit from modernization, recontextualization, or critical intervention.

Some of these interventions, however, serve other critical concerns. Eco's characterization of superheroes as defenders of the status quo runs counter to the populist tendency in cultural studies, which, as articulated by John Fiske, maintains that popular culture is always made by subordinated people to contest or evade dominant cultural formations (1–2). Other media studies scholars such as Timothy Gibson have critiqued this doctrine for confusing audience engagement with political resistance (256–258); even Matthew A. Cicci, who endorses Fiske's claims, must concede that many of the fan communities he surveys "seem uninterested in challenging the status quo" and instead merely "seek to consume the things they enjoy" (98–99, 111). But most of the comics scholars who subscribe to the resistant-audience model devote surprisingly little attention to the behaviors of actual audiences. They instead reconcile this contradiction between cultural theory and commercial practice by arguing that the comics they study are already subversive, shifting the site of engagement from the text's reception to its production. Even if most superhero comics don't question social hierarchies or power structures, they can usually be shown to challenge their own genre conventions or narrative forms. The populist turn in comics scholarship therefore contends that comics are inherently transformational, if not in their historical forms then certainly in their contemporary manifestations.

Reading superhero comics in this manner requires updating or refuting Eco's claims. Regrettably, many of Eco's critics also misinterpret his arguments or misrepresent contemporary superhero comics as they seek to challenge his evaluation of the genre. Their portrayal of these comics and related media typifies the methodological problems in the populist approach: critics read popular texts outside their material or generic contexts, ignore fundamental compatibilities with older conventions in favor of superficial differences, and characterize those differences as radical or transformational gestures absent any larger social or generic criticisms. These problems are compounded by the populist response to Eco, which reads him selectively or in isolation, assigns him views he doesn't hold, and rejects his claims whenever they contradict the theoretical assumptions of cultural studies. This celebratory and populist mode of reading does the comics no favors, exempting them from critical scrutiny and ignoring or misreading their critics if not dismissing them out of hand. But before turning to Eco's interlocutors we must first revisit "The Myth of Superman," an essay that is frequently cited and just as frequently misunderstood.

MYTHS OF CONTINUITY

Comics scholars have no shortage of reasons to challenge Eco's essay. He examines one particular moment in the development of the superhero genre, the Superman comics of the 1950s and early 1960s, yet his structuralist methodology and universalist language extrapolate his observations far beyond the texts that inspire them. Obviously he can't account for the comics that followed this era—although his revisions for the 1972 English translation have somewhat obscured the essay's historical provenance—but neither does he account for those that preceded it. In the final section of the 1972 essay, Eco describes Superman as "a perfect example of civic consciousness, completely split from political consciousness," a faithful defender of private property who is "busy by preference, not against black-marketing drugs, nor, obviously, against corrupting administrators or politicians, but against banks [*sic*] and mail truck robbers" (22). Yet this claim is neither obvious nor historically accurate. Eco overlooks the character's earliest stories, written by Jerry Siegel and drawn by Joe Shuster in the late 1930s, when Superman fought corrupt politicians, arms dealers, mine owners, and construction contractors and championed "a version of New Deal politics for juveniles" (Gordon, *Comic Strips* 134; see also Saunders 22–24). The Superman that Eco describes is the Superman of the 1940s, 1950s, and 1960s, after publishers stifled the political commentary in response to a moral panic over comic books and to Superman's increasing value as a commodity (Saunders 24–25; Gordon, *Comic Strips* 133–135).

Some critics argue that the narrative continuity of those Superman comics is also more complex and dynamic than Eco acknowledges. Although Tom De Haven endorses Eco's model of the oneiric climate (114), he nevertheless observes that the comics produced under the supervision of longtime editor Mort Weisinger, particularly those published in the late 1950s and early 1960s, expanded Superman's history, culture, and supporting cast

(115). If these comics were barred from advancing the storylines into the future, they could at least develop a rich past for their characters; De Haven even suggests that the internally consistent mythology of the Weisinger books presaged and initiated the type of inter-title continuity later seen in Marvel comics (136–137). However, these stories didn't allow Superman to age or change after he reached maturity, and the amount of time that passed between stories was vague to nonexistent (Hatfield, *Hand of Fire* 127). Eco himself acknowledges that two narrative devices common in the Weisinger era, the "Imaginary Stories" (speculative pieces that imagine definitive endings for Superman, but only for one issue) and the "Untold Tales" (flashbacks to previously unrepresented episodes in Superman's past), both serve to satisfy readers' desires for progress and change without allowing any temporal progression in the present-day storylines ("Myth" 18). Indeed, the very label "Imaginary Stories"—with its preposterous implication that any other Superman story could be any less imaginary—indicates how Weisinger and his writers attempted to contain these intrusions of progressive temporality and prevent them from infecting or advancing the main continuity.[1] The increasingly elaborate histories and noncanonical futures of the Weisinger era confirm rather than dispel Eco's oneiric climate.

Finally, many critics have noted that Eco's essay fails to account for later developments in superhero comics, particularly the ongoing serial narratives and intertextual connections between titles that developed in the Marvel comics of the 1960s and beyond (Hatfield, *Hand of Fire* 126–128). This oversight might seem to be the most pardonable one since Marvel didn't fully develop its elaborate narrative continuity until later in the 1960s, and Eco can hardly be faulted for failing to anticipate developments that occurred after he wrote "Il mito di 'Superman'" in 1962. A consultation of the original essay, however, reveals the substantial additions, deletions, and changes in the 1972 English translation. Its final section, "Civic consciousness and political consciousness" (21–22), does not appear in "Il mito di 'Superman'" and is original to the 1972 essay. In this section, Eco argues that his observations on the politics of superheroes are equally applicable not only to Superman and his contemporaries like Batman and Robin, but also to "the more recent Fantastic Four, Devil[,] and Spider Man, where the literary 'genre,' however, has acquired a more sophisticated form of self-irony" (21–22). Eco refers to the superheroes of Marvel Comics—in reprinting the Chilton translation in *Arguing Comics*, Jeet Heer and Kent Worcester alter "Devil" to "Daredevil" (162)—and names two that postdate his 1962 essay.[2] These references reveal that Eco was aware of recent developments in superhero comics in 1972, but he attempted to categorize Marvel's characters with the earlier DC heroes rather than adjust his arguments to accommodate them.

The arguments in "Civic consciousness and political consciousness" focus on the ideological valences of superhero comics rather than their models of time and narrative, but Eco doesn't acknowledge how Marvel deviated from prior conventions in both areas. Marvel's heroes routinely displayed political consciousness and took action at the national or global level, from the strident anticommunism of the early 1960s to the liberal centrism and antiwar stances of the later 1960s and early 1970s (Wright 220–223, 234–243). Marvel was also famous for creating outlaw heroes, ranging from monsters like the Hulk, who was more likely to smash private property than defend it, to persecuted minorities like the X-Men, who sometimes fought to overcome prejudice rather than preserve the status quo (Wright 207–209, 215–219). At the same time Marvel was realigning the ideology of its superheroes, it was also developing an intricate narrative continuity that linked all of its titles into a single setting with a shared memory. While these practices would accelerate in later decades, they had already begun by the early 1970s (Hatfield, *Hand of Fire* 122–124). Greater attention to recent developments in comics might have given Eco fair warning: not every hero is such an ardent champion of the social order, and the timeless myths he describes turn out not to be so timeless after all.

To be fair, Eco's oneiric climate is not a simple state of timelessness so much as it is one strategy for managing a contradiction faced by any character in a popular serial narrative: the contradiction between the stasis characteristic of mythological characters and the open-ended, unpredictable, progressive, but ultimately finite development of the modern novel ("Myth" 15). The oneiric climate is merely the method that Weisinger's Superman comics (and, more broadly, most superhero comics from the 1940s through the early 1960s) used to present the illusion of action, development, and novelty while preserving the characters in their most archetypal, recognizable, and commercially viable states. While most contemporary scholars observe that comics have shifted to other modes of storytelling, they rarely acknowledge that these strategies still confront the same temporal dilemma—and often do so in ways that are remarkably similar to Eco's oneiric climate. In "'Just Men in Tights': Rewriting Silver Age Comics in an Era of Multiplicity," Henry Jenkins observes that superhero comics have moved away from the self-contained stories and iterative logic Eco describes, first to a mode of serial and intertextual continuity between stories, and then more recently to a mode of multiplicity that features several different versions of the same characters in separate continuities (20–21). Although Jenkins doesn't consider how this multiplicity faces the same tensions between progressive time and static time, he does recognize that it frequently reconfirms the same timeless, oneiric versions of the characters that it duplicates.

Two of Jenkins's examples of this propensity to multiply and revise characters across different titles, Darwyn Cooke's *DC: The New Frontier* (2004) and Mark Waid and Barry Kitson's *JLA: Year One* (1997–1998), both explore the formation of the Justice League of America. The JLA debuted in *The Brave and the Bold* issue 28, cover-dated March 1960, but *JLA: Year One* depicts its heroes with modern, psychologistic characterization and locates them in an updated (if conveniently unmarked and timeless) setting. Jenkins notes that "Waid has little interest in placing these stories in the historical context of the early 1960s; locating these events within the continuity of the superhero's [*sic*] careers is central to his efforts to revive the spirit of the Silver Age, but situating them in a precise historic period is not" (33). But this example demonstrates how shared continuities are still subject to the pressures of time: if Waid and Kitson did situate the Justice League of America within its original historical context, if their characters first appeared in 1960, then they would have been ready for retirement by the time *JLA: Year One* was published in 1997. The ongoing publication of their present-day adventures would be invalidated and their story would be approaching its end—precisely the dilemma that the oneiric climates and iterative schemes of the Weisinger era were designed to avoid.

Other treatments of the same characters, such as *DC: The New Frontier*, are more willing to locate their heroes within historically specific settings because they tell finite stories that are isolated from the primary continuity, but even these series tend to reconfirm rather than reinvent the primary attributes and histories of their subjects. As Jenkins explains in an interview with Sam Ford, these alternative versions of established characters "can also be deeply conservative," both because they are "hermetically sealed from the main continuity," thus limiting their ability to rewrite the franchise, and because so many of them "reaffirm the underlying logic to these characters" (Ford and Jenkins 308) by reinscribing their origins, powers, and personalities.[3] No matter what the setting, Superman's home planet will still explode and Batman's family will still be murdered. In many respects these contemporary variations are less radical than Weisinger's Imaginary Stories, which could at least depict new developments and final endings for these characters, if only for the duration of a single issue. Jenkins concedes, "The more we change, the more it is clear that the world depicted in the normal continuity has to be what it is because of the core integrity of these characters" (308)—or, as Eco would put it, because of their mythological character.

Comics organized around continuity or multiplicity may displace Eco's iterative resolution from the individual story to the story arc, the individual creator's tenure on a title, or even an extended continuity that can span multiple creators and many years, but sooner or later the most popular superheroes will inevitably find themselves reset to their most familiar forms. In the Ford interview, Jenkins praises Marvel Comics' *Civil War* crossover event (2006–2007) for "transforming the rules of the genre (through events such as Spider-Man's unmasking or Captain America's death, which will have a lasting impact)" (306). By the time this interview was published in 2009, Marvel had already undone Spider-Man's unmasking, erasing it from continuity scant months after *Civil War* concluded—so much for lasting impact. Just two months after the interview was published, Marvel began releasing the miniseries that would restore Captain America to life.[4] Jenkins drastically overstates contemporary superhero comics' break from their past practices; the difference between the oneiric reiteration of the Weisinger era and the more protracted continuity resets of the present is a difference of duration and self-conscious attention rather than kind. The dreams may last longer, but the oneiric climate still persists.

MYTHS OF REFLEXIVITY

My point is not that the oneiric climate remains the best tool for interpreting superhero comics or that other critics should follow Eco's structuralist approach, but rather that most contemporary superhero comics are far less radical than their supporters claim, and that Eco's arguments are both more relevant and more subtle than many of his critics acknowledge. Angela Ndalianis, for example, provides a generally accurate summary of the oneiric climate in her essay "Enter the Aleph: Superhero Worlds and Hypertime Realities," but in the course of arguing that contemporary popular culture is just as sophisticated as the late modernist art Eco praises in "The Myth of Superman," she misreads other parts of his essay. Ndalianis is clearly correct that popular culture is just as capable of provoking critical and self-reflexive reading practices as the avant-garde novels and art-house films of Eco's day (273), yet her primary example doesn't support this claim. Her essay centers mostly on *Smallville* (2001–2011), a television series on the WB and CW networks about Clark Kent's early years before he became Superman. As she inventories the show's many allusions to and deviations from the Superman comics, Ndalianis describes a series that, far from offering viewers opportunities for critical reflection on their world, provides them with little more than a set of intertextual references to the familiar elements of Superman continuity. When Ndalianis notes that "Lois [Lane] appears in Smallville and meets Clark *before* they meet at the *Daily Planet*" (276, her emphasis), she suggests that this minor variation on the Superman canon refutes Eco's arguments that causality can't be altered without dispelling the mythical value of the characters.[5] Perhaps it does refute these arguments—but Eco never makes them.

A comparison of Ndalianis's citation of Eco to Eco's statements in "The Myth of Superman" proves instructive. Ndalianis writes,

> "*Before* causally determines *after*, and the series of these determinations cannot be traced back" otherwise, says Eco; the myth is disrupted, falters, or is radically revised and undermined (Eco 1972, 16). *Smallville* continuously confronts the audience with this possibility. (276)

The passage she quotes, however, says nothing about temporality and myth. It comes from the section titled "Temporality and 'consumption'" and it outlines the model of linear, unidirectional chronology formulated by Aristotle and Kant and refined (in very different terms, for very different contexts) by Einstein's physics, Sartre's existentialism, and Husserl's phenomenology (Eco, "Myth" 16–17). This is not Eco's articulation of the myth of Superman; it is his summary of the absolute, inexorable, progressive time that he says modernist novels and Superman comics both defy. When Eco next mentions Superman, in the first sentence of the next section, he does so in strikingly different terms:

> If contemporary discussions which involve man in meditation upon his destiny and his condition are based on this concept of time, the narrative structure of Superman certainly evades it in order to save the situation [i.e. stasis, inconsumability] which we have already discussed. In Superman it is the concept of time that breaks down. (17)

Ndalianis praises *Smallville* for its trivial defiance of the claim that "*Before* causally determines *after*," yet Eco has already argued that Superman comics defy causality to preserve their hero's mythic character. The myth sustains itself precisely by breaking down the temporal relations of before and after; Eco says exactly the opposite of what Ndalianis claims he does.

She nevertheless continues to oversimplify Eco's arguments while exalting *Smallville* for confounding her oversimplifications. Ndalianis claims, "In *Smallville*, the anticipated metanarrative [of Superman canon]—Eco's mythic layer—is *both* worshipped as static entity *and* revealed to always be in a state of process, an interplay that problematizes Eco's distinction between the mythic and the serial" (276, her emphasis). But Eco's oneiric climate already problematizes and manages this distinction through an interplay of stasis and progress, adding new elements to the myth while restarting the story anew with each new installment ("Myth" 17–18). Later, Ndalianis describes *Smallville*'s repackaging of familiar tropes in marginally new configurations as "a mythology that is *both* already said *and* which is in the process of being said; this is not only something that unsettles Eco's schema but it also calls into question his assertion that the myth value of the superhero collapses when the myth layer succumbs to serial logic" (284, her emphasis). But, again, this simultaneous logic of familiarity and novelty, repetition and addition, does not unsettle Eco's schema—this *is* Eco's schema, his account of how superhero comics balance the timelessness of myth with the progressive development of the modern novel. Eco does state that the novel's quality of unpredictability (not, as Ndalianis claims, seriality) "sacrifices for the most part the mythic potential of the character" (15) since myths have already reached a known and eminently predictable ending. This leaves serialized comic book characters in a paradoxical position: they must be archetypal, emblematic, and static, but they must also appear to be subject to the possibility of progression and change in an unpredictable narrative. This is the contradiction that Eco's oneiric climate and his iterative scheme attempt to resolve, allowing static characters to repeat stories again and again without aging or advancing toward an ending, protecting the already said while presenting it in the process of being said again. Far from collapsing the mythological value of Superman, Eco's iterative seriality preserved it for decades.

Since Ndalianis restates, rather than refutes, Eco's narrative model, her only remaining point of contention is to dispute his distinction between the paradoxical, discontinuous temporality of late modernist novels and films and the oneiric temporality of Weisinger-era Superman comics. Eco observes that those comics disrupt time in a manner not wholly dissimilar to the novels and screenplays of James Joyce and Alain Robbe-Grillet, but he seeks to limit this comparison by stating that in Joyce and Robbe-Grillet "the breakdown of familiar temporal relations happens in a conscious manner, both on the part of the writer and of the one who derives aesthetic satisfaction from the operation" ("Myth" 19), that is, the reader or viewer. Eco claims this breakdown "tends to furnish the reader with imaginative models capable of making him accept situations of the new science" (19)—that is, modern, post-Einsteinian physics—and helping them envision new ways of understanding both the universe and humanity's place within it. By contrast, Eco argues, the temporal breakdown caused by Superman's oneiric climate happens unconsciously and invisibly, and, if noticed by the reader, would lead not to new ways of imagining physics or metaphysics but instead to the disruption of the oneiric climate that sustains the mythic narrative (19).

Ndalianis contends that contemporary media culture no longer supports this distinction, but her argument once again turns on a misreading of Eco. She notes that while Weisinger's Superman comics manipulated time invisibly and without any greater critical purpose, comics and television series now routinely draw attention to their intertextual references and highly self-conscious manipulations of continuity (273–278). Yet, as this summary should indicate, Ndalianis has already changed the terms of the comparison from the representation of time to the self-consciousness of representation. For Eco, the signal difference between Robbe-Grillet and Weisinger is not that Weisinger concealed his comics' breakdown of temporality but that he broke down temporality only to sustain the audience's willing suspension of disbelief in his characters rather than to describe humanity's changed understanding of the universe. Eco's late modernist narratives offer their audiences symbolic representations of new models of time, "a kind of symbolic suggestion or allegorical diagram of that absolute which science has resolved [. . .] in a possible way of establishing our relation with the world and, therefore, in a possible way of describing the world" ("Myth" 19).

Ndalianis doesn't attempt to compare modernist art and popular culture in these terms. In her reading, texts like *Smallville* might manipulate their metanarratives or allude to their intertexts in full view of the audience, but they don't offer an alternative understanding of time, let alone any larger arguments about humanity's place in the universe. This, of course, is exactly what Eco found missing in the comics of Mort Weisinger. *Smallville* may be more transparent in its intertextuality—although features such as the Imaginary Stories and Untold Tales certainly display their own self-conscious manipulations of the Superman canon—but it deploys this arch reflexivity primarily to tweak its audience's desire to see familiar elements from the Superman mythology (Ndalianis 274), not to comment on matters external to that mythology. *Smallville* may work through allusion and revision rather than oneiric iteration, but its mission to tell new stories about familiar characters by starting over from the beginning is merely one more variation on the model Eco describes.

When *Smallville* does reach outside superhero comics, it generally looks no further than other popular films or television series, although Ndalianis attempts to equate these intertextualities with more sophisticated critical strategies in more venerated works. "Recalling the film strategies of the French New Wave," she writes, "these new breeds of superhero media are as much about the *process* of meaning construction as they are about the stories they deliver" (282, her emphasis), by which she means *Smallville* is filled with references to horror films such as *Saw* and television series such as *The Dukes of Hazzard*—references that, even in Ndalianis's own descriptions, are devoid of any commentary or critique on their source material, let alone on the processes of constructing meaning. She argues that these allusions "threaten to collapse the fictional reality of the Supermanverse" (282), yet her examples amount to little more than in-jokes, homages, or derivative imitations. Where Eco drew distinctions between the art-house films of Alain Resnais and Alain Robbe-Grillet and the superhero comics of Mort Weisinger, Ndalianis simply equates *Smallville* to the New Wave without considering that these creators apply their self-reflexivity and intertextuality to very different purposes.[6]

At other points in her essay, however, Ndalianis makes curiously exceptionalist arguments that seek to distinguish superhero comics from other genres and other media. She not only claims that the temporal contradictions of Superman continuity are original to superhero comics, she enlists Eco in this claim when she says he "makes a further clarification about the uniqueness of the narrative phenomenon that the superhero comics introduced into popular culture" (272–273). But Eco never says the oneiric climate is unique to comics. In his discussion of the iterative scheme, he demonstrates how other popular serials (most notably Rex Stout's Nero

Wolfe novels) similarly ignore the passage of time by starting anew with each new installment; he also traces this mode of storytelling at least as far back as the Fantômas novels of Pierre Souvestre and Marcel Allain ("Myth" 19–21). Nevertheless, Ndalianis invokes Eco to support her claims for the originality of superhero comics, just as she rejects him when he suggests that the comics of his day don't compare favorably to more consecrated art forms. Superhero comics and their spin-offs are just like other media when their worth is in question and different from all other media when that would increase their stature. These shifting tactics suggest a greater dilemma in comics scholarship and in cultural studies at large, one that is hardly limited to critics' readings or misreadings of Eco; like many other scholars of popular culture, Ndalianis doesn't analyze or interpret her subjects so much as she celebrates them.

MYTHS OF POSTMODERNITY

Appeals to the sophistication, subversiveness, or exceptionalism of popular media are the cornerstones of cultural populism. One of the major points of that tradition's entry into the field of comics scholarship is Jim Collins's 1991 essay "Batman: The Movie, Narrative: The Hyperconscious," which is cited by Ndalianis, Jenkins, and two other scholars in Ndalianis's collection *The Contemporary Comic Book Superhero*. Written at the moment of cultural studies' ascendancy within the academy, the essay focuses on what Collins identifies as "the distinguishing feature of recent popular narrative, namely its increasing hyperconsciousness about both the history of popular culture and the shifting status of popular culture" (165). While he notes that a similar self-consciousness pervaded the elite culture of modernism and postmodernism, Collins argues, much as Ndalianis would nearly two decades later, that this hyperconsciousness has newly migrated to popular culture—yet he also acknowledges that popular culture has already been self-reflexive for several decades. Just what is it, then, that makes today's hyperconsciousness so different, so appealing? Collins maintains that contemporary popular culture doesn't restrict itself to reworking the conventions of a single genre but instead works "across genres, mixing different forms of discourse as well as different media," finding new forms of circulation and new audiences (165).

Like the paradoxical temporality of superhero comics, the hyperconsciousness of popular culture proves to be neither so recent nor so distinctive. To stay with Superman for a little while longer, the Man of Tomorrow was initially conceived as "a hodgepodge of elements" borrowed from science fiction novels, adventure pulps, and comic strips (De Haven 39), and the canon that formed around him is as much a product of radio, film, animation, television, and prose novels as it is of comics. Many of the elements that are indelibly associated with Superman, from Perry White and the *Daily Planet* to radioactive kryptonite to the character's distinctive mottos and taglines ("Look! Up in the sky!"), first appeared on his radio serial, *The Adventures of Superman,* and later were integrated into the comic books (De Haven 95–96; Bridwell 9–12). Nor were those other media themselves absent from the comics: in "Superman, Matinee Idol" (credited to Jerry Siegel and Joe Shuster and published in *Superman* issue 19, 1942), Clark Kent and Lois Lane go to the movies and watch a cartoon much like the animated short films Max and Dave Fleischer had begun producing for Paramount Pictures in 1941. The comic mimics the style of the cartoons, replicating their silent compositions and silhouetted costume changes and reusing the mad scientist villain from the first short; artist Joe Shuster (or, more likely, his finisher and ghost artist Ed Dobrotka) goes so far as to decorate the panel borders to resemble the sprocket holes on a reel of film (figure 1.1). That same issue of *Superman* features yet another cross-media homage in "Case of the Funny Paper Crimes," where Superman battles a gallery of criminals from the newspaper comic strips. Incorporating parodies of crime, cowboy, fantasy, and science fiction comics, the story fuses as many genres as the more recent works that Collins describes.

These stories are as self-reflexive as they are intertextual. When the lead villain in "Case of the Funny Paper Crimes" is unmasked as a frustrated cartoonist (figure 1.2), Dobrotka draws him to resemble writer Jerry Siegel (Murray 203), who had in fact tried and failed to get Superman accepted for newspaper syndication before he settled for the comic books (De Haven 40). "Superman, Matinee Idol" is even more self-conscious about its conventions and their transmission across multiple media: in this story, *Superman* comics and the Fleischer brothers' cartoons both exist within Superman's world, to the point that Clark must distract Lois whenever the cartoon is about to reveal his secret identity. This open secret could never be sustained in the ongoing continuity of the Superman comics, of course, and later reprints would label "Superman, Matinee Idol" as "Our Very First Imaginary Story" (Gordon, *Superman* 150). Regardless of their questionable continuity, these highly self-reflexive stories from 1942 demonstrate that hyperconsciousness

FIG. 1.1. *Jerry Siegel, Joe Shuster, Ed Dobrotka, and John Sikela, "Superman, Matinee Idol,"* Superman *issue 19 (DC Comics, 1942), p. 6.*

FIG. 1.2. *Jerry Siegel, Ed Dobrotka, and John Sikela, "Case of the Funny Paper Crimes,"* Superman *issue 19 (DC Comics, 1942), p. 13.*

and the combination of different genres and media discourses were nothing new when Collins published his article in 1991.[7]

Unlike Ndalianis, however, Collins evaluates his chosen texts for more than their references to other media or other genres. His essay features perceptive close readings of visual narration in Frank Miller, Klaus Janson, and Lynn Varley's *Batman: The Dark Knight Returns,* intertextual narration in Alan Moore and Dave Gibbons's *Watchmen,* and competing styles of image manipulation in Tim Burton's film *Batman,* marshaling these interpretations to argue that postmodern hyperconsciousness is more nuanced and more complex than earlier manifestations of intertextuality in popular culture. To cite just one example, Collins contends that the eclectic visual pastiche of the final confrontation in Burton's *Batman* confuses and "deforms" the highly conventional narrative in which the hero fights the villain to save the girl (168). While he ably demonstrates how the climactic battle atop a cathedral references works from Alfred Hitchcock's *Vertigo* and *North by Northwest* to Antoni Gaudí's Sagrada Família, Collins never articulates how this pastiche complicates (let alone deforms) the hackneyed narrative resolution. He instead shifts arguments, claiming the pastiche of *Batman* is "in many ways even more complicated" than the Sagrada Família because Gaudí's basilica merely assembles "a repertoire of architectural styles," whereas Burton's film builds "a hybrid repertoire" drawing on comics, film, architecture, and so forth (169). He overlooks both the differences between architecture and film—the more narrative and temporal aspects of the latter providing additional sites for allusion and intertextuality—and the many types of media that combine in a church, including architecture, sculpture, painting, stained glass, and the music played during services. The larger question, however, is why he assumes contemporary popular culture is necessarily more complex than either its canonical counterparts or its own popular precursors.

In making this assumption, Collins positions himself against Eco, though not specifically against "The Myth of Superman." In "*Casablanca*: Cult Movies and Intertextual Collage" (1984), Eco establishes that the celebrated 1942 film is as eclectic a pastiche as any recent work Collins could name. Collins takes issue with Eco's attempt to privilege the improvisational, supposedly ingenuous pastiche of *Casablanca* over the knowing referentiality of retrospective, nostalgic films such as *Raiders of the Lost Ark*, but his own attempts to distinguish between these works are remarkably similar to Eco's. Collins argues that films like *Casablanca* and *Batman* operate within different cultural contexts and negotiate different semiotic environments (169), which isn't so different from Eco's contention that *Raiders of the Lost Ark* is "conceived within a metasemiotic culture, [. . .] Spielberg and Lucas are semiotically nourished authors working for a culture of instinctive semioticians" ("*Casablanca*" 210). Both critics observe that the popular culture of the 1980s is steeped in self-consciousness, producing works that respond to this semiotic saturation.[8]

Later in his essay, Collins challenges another appeal to the virtues of ingenuousness, Eco's comparison of John Huston's film adaptation of *The Maltese Falcon* to Wim Wenders's *Hammett*. This comparison originates in yet another Eco essay, "The Multiplication of the Media" (1983), and if Collins had taken Eco's remarks within the full context of that piece he once again would have found much to agree with, as Eco specifically renounces the Frankfurt School theories of mass culture that Collins finds "ideologically repugnant" (181n2). Eco writes that

> we were all (perhaps rightly) victims of a model of the mass media based on that of the relationship with authority: a centralized transmitter, with precise political and pedagogical plans, controlled by Authority (economic or political), the messages sent through recognizable technological channels [. . .] to the addressees, victims of ideological indoctrination. ("Multiplication" 148)

Dismissing this model, Eco outlines a changed media landscape much like the one Collins describes, an "incontrollable plurality of messages that each individual uses to make up his own composition with the remote-control switch" (148). He argues that old distinctions between elite and mass culture have become distorted and blurred, if not erased, and he repeatedly suggests that comics can no longer be separated from the world of the fine arts (146–147). Once again, however, Collins limits his comments to those areas where he disagrees with Eco rather than engage with the many places where Eco might endorse his views.[9]

Those disagreements stem from a profound difference in opinion, not on the Frankfurt School mass culture critique, but over the role of mass culture itself. While Eco concedes that the new media landscape may offer the audience an "incontrollable plurality of messages," he argues that this cornucopia of texts has not truly liberated them: "The consumer's freedom may not have increased, but surely the way to teach him to be free and controlled has changed" ("Multiplication" 148). If Eco dismisses the authoritarian reductionism of the Frankfurt School, he is equally skeptical about Birmingham School models of the resisting reader or textual poacher. Consumers may be able to construct their own texts or even form their own identities from the array of options that contemporary culture provides them, but they are still consumers, no more free than they were under the Frankfurt School models of a controlling culture industry; and if the newer, more pluralized culture teaches them how to be free, it also teaches them how to be controlled. Eco implies there is no difference between the two.

These arguments are anathema to Collins and other cultural populists. In the course of attempting to identify when and why popular culture changed from ingenuous pastiche to knowing hyperconsciousness (a question he never quite answers), Collins says that

> it is answerable only if we begin by rejecting the notion that texts are "interesting" semiotically only when they can be decoded/re-encoded by an analyst capable of exposing the hidden textual mechanisms. The foregrounding of the citations, the explicitness of the calling-up/cutting-up process reflects a different dynamic in the exchange between producer and audience, one based on the sophistication of both parties, each possessing knowledge formerly (and allegedly) accessible only to the semiotician. ("Batman" 170)

Eco acknowledges the sophistication of producer and audience alike in "The Multiplication of the Media," yet he doesn't see this interpretive model as any more liberatory than the old Frankfurt School model of ideological indoctrination. This lack of faith in the liberating power of audience consumption violates one of the primary tenets of cultural populism, which maintains that popular reception is always subversive (McGuigan 72–73). Scholars who depart from these assumptions or criticize popular media—or, like Collins's hypothetical semiotician, simply believe they possess interpretive tools necessary for reading popular texts critically—are branded as elitists and accused of being out of touch (T. Frank 282–283). As Jim McGuigan notes, such readings produce "a simple inversion of the mass culture critique at its worst," an equally dogmatic formula that reduces cultural studies to "a kind of subjective idealism" in which popular receptions are conveniently aligned with the scholar's progressive values (71–72).

Determined to renounce the economic reductionism of the Frankfurt School, the cultural populists overcompensate by avoiding material contexts more generally (McGuigan 40–41). This lack of attention to political economy should constitute one more commonality between Eco and his critics. In addition to overlooking Superman's historical development, "The Myth of Superman" scarcely considers that his publishers might have wished to keep him static and unchanging for economic reasons as well as mythical ones: in the 1950s, when the oneiric climate reached its peak, each issue of *Superman* sold more than one million copies (De Haven 85; J. Miller). Eco's populist challengers have proven equally reluctant to engage with the material history and production contexts of the comics they study. Collins observes that comics and graphic novels "until quite recently enjoyed virtually no advertising support, and were seldom seen in mall bookstores where they are now so prominently displayed," offering this sudden visibility as proof that economic factors (which he reduces to mere "force of advertising") can't wholly account for the postmodern turn toward hyperconscious popular culture ("Batman" 171). Yet those graphic novels only became so prominent in the mall bookstores because of material changes in production and distribution as well as marketing. While the term "graphic novel" had been in circulation among comics fans and creators since the 1960s, the format didn't break into bookstores until the late 1980s with the publication of collected editions of Art Spiegelman's *Maus*, Frank Miller's *Batman: The Dark Knight Returns*, and Alan Moore and

Dave Gibbons's *Watchmen* (Hatfield, *Alternative Comics* 29–30). This sudden popularity was predicated on both a critical mass of comics written for adults and a publication format that could reach new audiences in new venues outside the usual comics stores and spinner racks, but these factors appear nowhere in Collins's history of hyperconsciousness.

If cultural populists don't account for even the most mundane production practices, then it isn't surprising that they also dismiss more overtly economic theories of cultural production. When Collins asks what factors produced the dramatic changes between the popular culture of the 1940s and that of the 1980s, he almost immediately rules out any economic influences:

> The emergence of this "meta-pop" in the eighties is due to a number of interconnected factors, but its all-pervasiveness in so many different media cannot be fully accounted for by the usual explanation that "retro" culture is simply "late" capitalism's way of recycling old merchandise as new for guaranteed audiences, an explanation that carries with it the usual one-dimensional indictment of nostalgia. ("Batman" 170–171)

Collins appears to refer to materialist theories of postmodernism formulated by scholars such as Fredric Jameson, although his critiques are presented with such ironic, scare-quoted detachment that they can be difficult to source. In any case, as with Eco, greater attention to the writings of materialist critics like Jameson would reveal more nuanced explanations. Jameson proposes that postmodernist historicism, pastiche, and nostalgia culture are not simply commercial means of dredging up old material for new audiences, but rather artistic responses to new economies of multinational capital and the new communications and information technologies that accompany and enable them—computers, televisions, and other media-delivery devices that demand new strategies of representation (37). For Jameson, postmodernism itself arises as a cultural response to and an expression of life in a more decentralized and abstracted mode of capital that is increasingly built around the circulation and recirculation of information.

Even as Collins concedes that his abbreviated materialist explanation "has its obvious merits" and recognizes that postmodernist hyperconsciousness "may be unimaginable outside of corporate capitalism" (171), he falls back on routine appeals to the sophistication of creators and audiences, maintaining that hyperconsciousness "depends upon a simple realization on the part of both the producer and the audience: popular culture has a *history*; earlier texts do not simply disappear or become kitsch, but persist in their original forms as well as diverse reactivations" (171, his emphasis). While the longevity and reach of popular media have no doubt intensified since Collins wrote his essay—amplified by instantaneous global telecommunications, ongoing media consolidation, and almost limitless digital storage—these material and technical considerations were already present in the early 1990s. Collins nevertheless assumes that producers and audiences, working on their own volition, are entirely responsible for the self-reflexivity and historicism of postmodern culture. He doesn't explore the reasons why popular culture, once regarded as disposable and ephemeral, has achieved such persistence or why contemporary artists and audiences are so preoccupied with their antecedents, except to note that these traditions operate "outside the realm of the academy (and the traditional mechanism responsible for the canonization of privileged works)" (172). In other words, these traditions are assembled purely within the marketplace of popular culture yet somehow remain independent of any economic determinations. As I will discuss in the next chapter, David Harvey, Simon Reynolds, and other materialist critics provide very different explanations for these transformations in popular culture, but such explanations remain out of bounds for Collins and other cultural populists, who can only credit the infallible tastes of the people.

MYTHS OF PROGRESS

The narrative practices of superhero comics have changed considerably since the publication of Collins's essay, much less Eco's "The Myth of Superman." Those practices now include multiple story universes scattered across diverse media forms, countless reiterations of the same handful of popular characters, and a seemingly endless series of continuity resets and reboots, most of which take continuity itself as their primary subject matter. Arguably, the comics are more hyperconscious than ever before, so much so that this observation has migrated from cultural and media studies to other, more formally minded disciplines such as narratology. Even this mode of scholarship, however, shares the populists' assumptions that comics organized around intertextuality or multiplicity constitute a wholesale departure from their predecessors. In "Navigating Infinite Earths: Readers,

Mental Models, and the Multiverse of Superhero Comics," Karin Kukkonen suggests that the multiple parallel universes of shared superhero continuities challenge a classical cosmology that presumes we inhabit a single reality. However, the examples she offers are, like Ndalianis's readings of *Smallville*, more concerned with navigating the hierarchies of these fictional worlds than offering any insights into the cosmologies through which we apprehend our own. Unsurprisingly, Kukkonen also maintains that these elaborate continuities and parallel storyworlds have superseded Eco's oneiric climate (48–49), essentially duplicating Jenkins's arguments about multiplicity—and like Jenkins, she relies on examples that have themselves been superseded by those storyworlds' ceaseless and convulsive reversions to the mean.

One of Kukkonen's primary examples is the Flash, the hero who introduced the DC Comics multiverse in the 1961 story "Flash of Two Worlds" and whose various forerunners, counterparts, and successors serve as a visual index of the different storyworlds or stages of DC continuity (49–50). By the time her article saw print in 2010, however, that index was already out of date: Barry Allen, who fought crime as the Flash from 1956 to 1985, had been pressed into service once again in a 2009 revamp. This change has little impact on Kukkonen's description of comics storyworlds, but it proves highly instructive in demonstrating the limitations of any argument that assumes superhero comics have changed so much as to render Eco's observations useless. That's because for nearly twenty-five years, Barry Allen had been one of the few heroes to defy Eco's oneiric climate. His story reached its apparent end when he died in *Crisis on Infinite Earths* (1985), along with the original Supergirl and a host of other, less popular heroes. Allen's former sidekick, Wally West, took up the scarlet mantle of the Flash, and the shared story of the DC universe advanced in the sort of absolute and irrevocable progression Eco had once deemed impossible. In an industry run by fans turned professionals, however, change is only as permanent as the sentiments of the creators or the fluctuations of the audience. When sales plummeted after an abortive 2006 attempt to replace Wally West with yet another Flash, DC brought Barry Allen back to life. They were simply following a trend: Supergirl, who was not only killed in the Crisis but erased from DC continuity shortly thereafter, was restored to more or less original form in 2004; the second Robin, Jason Todd, saw his ignominious death at the hands of a 1988 telephone poll reversed in 2005; and that same year, Bucky Barnes, the former Captain America sidekick who had been declared dead in 1964 (dated retroactively to the end of World War II), found himself resurrected as the Winter Soldier.[10] Though he and Jason Todd both assumed new identities, the finality of their deaths had been erased in favor of the type of never-ending seriality that is still the norm in superhero comics.

Nor is death the only condition that can be undone. In a line-wide relaunch in 2011, paradoxically branded "the New 52," DC Comics reset several characters back to the versions that were most familiar to the general public. Barbara Gordon, who had been one of comics' most prominent disabled superheroes as the hacker Oracle, miraculously regained full mobility so she could patrol the streets of Gotham City as Batgirl; Superman, who had been married to Lois Lane since 1996, found himself young and single once again, restoring the eternal Clark-Lois-Superman love triangle to something Eco might have recognized in 1962. (Some of these developments would prove no more lasting; in 2016 DC relaunched their relaunch, killing off the young, single Superman and restoring the one who was married to Lois. Rather than advance in new directions, the franchise remains caught between a twenty-year-old status quo and an eighty-year-old one.) Desperate to recapture old readers or simply retain current ones, superhero publishers will revert any character to their past glories, no matter what the obstacle. The same holds true for entire multiverses: worlds are destroyed and reborn, continuities are purged and restored, and the only constant amid the constant change is the certainty that any character eventually will be returned to their most popular and durable form. Supported by nostalgic creators and fans and supporting lucrative licenses in turn, the dream always wins in the end.

Certainly Collins is correct when he maintains that postmodern popular culture is qualitatively different from that of earlier periods. Its history, conventions, and contexts have become its most frequent subject matter, saturating popular culture to an extent that far surpasses modernist pastiches like "Superman, Matinee Idol" or *Casablanca*. Ndalianis is equally right to suggest that the artifacts of popular culture are just as capable of prompting critical awareness as the late modernist works Eco exalts, even if her examples don't support her sentiments, and Jenkins and Kukkonen accurately observe how the narrative practices of superhero comics have changed since the 1950s, although today's serialized comics still face the same temporal contradictions. However, all these scholars go well beyond these claims to argue that the texts they study possess subversive or transformational qualities that upend the judgments of earlier critics such as Eco. Too often, these arguments misrepresent Eco's criticisms while they compound his neglect of historical and material contexts, relying instead on axiomatic assumptions about audience agency or textual sophistication. For better or for worse, Eco and the cultural populists make many of the same arguments, yet these similarities are occluded by the most fundamental difference between them: he reserves the possibility, even the necessity, of criticizing popular texts, and they do not.

McGuigan worries that an uncritical cultural populism, one that interprets popular texts but doesn't account for the material factors or power relations that shape them, can't adequately explain the cultures it purports to celebrate (244). Indeed, Collins, Ndalianis, Kukkonen, and Jenkins all either overlook or oversimplify the production contexts and political economies that influence their subjects, but their approach is even more problematic than McGuigan recognizes: the populist mode of interpretation often fails even to interpret the comics, films, and television series it selects for study. These scholars may champion their chosen texts or explain how those texts produce meaning, but they rarely try to determine what they mean (as Eco does, in his universalist and ahistorical manner), other than to arrive at the predetermined meanings of cultural populism, the foundational assumptions that double as conclusions, the reflexive assertions not simply of the complexity and worth of popular culture but also of its radicalism or exceptionalism. By shielding popular texts from the type of critical scrutiny that academics routinely apply to other works, the cultural populists undercut their own arguments for the importance of popular culture. By dismissing or misrepresenting the views of critics such as Eco, they miss opportunities to refine their own arguments and increase our understanding and appreciation of our culture. A comics scholarship that is confident in its judgments and clear in its academic mission can afford to read the comics and their critics with more care.

CHAPTER 2

THE ABUSES OF HISTORY

POSTMODERNISM AND CONTEMPORARY SUPERHERO COMICS

Theories of hyperconsciousness or multiplicity may license populist appeals to a largely notional radicalism of form, but as descriptions of contemporary superhero comics, they are perfectly accurate. Since the 1980s, the genre has devoted increasing attention to its own conventions, characters, and especially its history in projects ranging from continuity-obsessed crossovers to revivals of forgotten heroes. Some of these comics offer criticisms or appraisals of the superhero genre; others merely repeat familiar histories or imitate other, more famous comics. Most critical accounts of these projects have been equally imitative, annotating their references or echoing their arguments without question, yet only a few attribute this self-conscious and historicist turn to the rise of postmodern culture more broadly. Whether they claim the mantle of postmodernism for their subjects with enthusiasm or dismiss the very concept as absurd, these scholars all address postmodernism's ascension in the superhero genre—but, much like the cultural populists, they do so primarily to validate the comics they study, not to relate them to this larger cultural transformation.

In referring to postmodernism, I don't mean simply to describe a set of artistic practices or aesthetic features. As noted in the previous chapter, superhero comics were using self-reflexivity, intertextuality, and similar techniques in the early 1940s, but this doesn't mean those comics were postmodern; quite the contrary, they were produced outside the institutions and value systems that generated both modernism and postmodernism (and, by most definitions, they preceded the development of postmodernity by a matter of years if not decades). Taking my cues instead from critics such as David Harvey and Simon Reynolds, I approach postmodernism as a cultural movement shaped by economic practices, technological developments, and other material factors that led to a fundamental transformation in the culture of the late twentieth century. In this broader, more historical sense, one of postmodernism's earliest and most significant impacts on the superhero genre came with the revisionist comics of the 1980s. These comics, best exemplified by Frank Miller, Klaus Janson, and Lynn Varley's *Batman: The Dark Knight Returns* (1986) and Alan Moore and Dave Gibbons's *Watchmen* (1986–1987), were postmodern not only in their self-conscious interrogation of the genre's conventions but in their enthusiastic reception by journalists, academics, and other cultural gatekeepers; Roger Sabin suggests that "the growth of cultural studies in tertiary education and the fashionableness of post-modernist theory" (*Adult Comics* 92) eroded divisions between elite and mass culture, making it acceptable or even desirable to accord comics the same respect once reserved for "serious" literature.

However, these breakthrough titles were followed by a wave of derivative comics that intensified the graphic violence and sexuality at the expense of sophisticated storytelling and social commentary (Sabin, *Comics, Comix* 167, 174). Those imitations arguably culminated in the debut of Image Comics, although the early Image artists tended to emulate the narrative and visual styles of mainstream Marvel Comics superhero books, where most of them had worked before leaving to form their own company in 1992. The Image books were wildly successful at first, prompting DC and Marvel to make their own heroes more violent still (Bukatman 50). Just as the first boom in revisionist superheroes was supported by (and helped create) the growth of the bookstore market for graphic novels (Sabin, *Adult Comics* 93–95), so were the Image-style heroes nourished by an explosive market in speculative comic book collecting (Gabilliet 148–152). The speculator market's abrupt collapse in the mid-1990s depressed sales and cleared the field for a counterreaction against the escalating violence, hypersexualized characters, and amoral protagonists. Comics such as Kurt Busiek and Alex Ross's *Marvels* (1994), Busiek and Brent Anderson's *Astro City* (1995–present), and Mark Waid and Ross's *Kingdom Come* (1996) reaffirmed the old conventions while expressing their creators' nostalgia for the morally upright heroes of previous decades. Filled with allusions, analogues, and homages to other characters and continuities, these books created pastiches of comics history, a practice that has continued into the new millennium in series such as Warren Ellis and John Cassaday's *Planetary* (1999–2009). Peter Coogan, Geoff Klock, and other critics have characterized this movement, sometimes dubbed "reconstructive" or "retro" comics, as a rebirth of the superhero genre, one they define in opposition to the revisionist comics despite some obvious similarities in technique and subject matter. Both movements are highly self-aware; both explore the genre's history even as they subject it to revision and reinterpretation; both respond to the genre's exhaustion of narrative conventions and its surplus of old stories and styles. In short, both are postmodernist, although they approach the superhero genre from very different critical and ideological stances. However, many of the critics who study these comics are invested in fan narratives and fan histories that highlight the differences while overlooking the similarities.

Other scholars, such as Karin Kukkonen, approach these comics through the language and methods of critical theory, yet they focus so exclusively on retracing the intertextual references that they forgo any interpretive work. In most cases, the pastiches are so transparent and so limited to recapitulations of genre history that the resulting critical discussion is more descriptive than analytical. The scholars who compile these annotative readings are particularly reluctant to engage in ideological interpretations, especially oppositional ones. Sean Carney, for example, departs from his peers by reading these texts not as commentaries on comics history but as allegories of history itself, yet his approach specifically rules out ideological readings. This shared neglect of ideology means that most scholars haven't addressed the reactionary element that is implicit (and sometimes explicit) when superhero comics call for a return to the genre's idealized past. Ironically, the critical readings most likely to construct historical narratives around contemporary superhero comics are often the least historicized, both materially and ideologically.

THE LOGIC OF THE AGES

Many of these scholars use a historiographic template so specific to superhero comics that it can't account for other genres, let alone larger cultural or economic influences. This template follows the pattern established by fans and collectors who have divided the genre's history into a system of loosely defined ages. The "Golden Age" refers to the period that saw the initial creation of the comic book format in the 1930s, the dramatic explosion of the superhero genre after the debut of Superman in 1938, and the superheroes' growing popularity during World War II. The genre waned after the war and most superhero titles were canceled by the early 1950s, only to rebound in the wake of the anti-comics crusade and the formation of the Comics Code

Authority in 1954. The appearance of a redesigned and revitalized Flash in 1956 initiated a new popularity that would last through the 1960s, a period now commemorated as the "Silver Age." Most fans recognize the period that followed in the 1970s and early 1980s as a "Bronze Age" marked by the consolidation of continuity and by attempts to branch out into other fantasy genres, a response to another downturn in the comics market. After that point the labeling breaks down as fans have proposed any number of names and definitions for the modern era, although most accounts divide this period into revisionist and reconstructive movements (Lewis 302–303).

While these ages provide a useful shorthand for denoting different periods in the history of the superhero genre, their value as analytical or historical tools is limited. Fans have reached no consensus on when these periods begin or end, what features define them, or even, in the later stages, what to call them, nor are these labels applicable to any other genre (Woo 269–271). Nevertheless, these problems haven't prevented some scholars from attempting to rationalize the system of the ages. A. David Lewis tries to organize them, somewhat reductively, around superhero moral codes and the Comics Code (305–308), while Peter Coogan adapts them to film scholar Thomas Schatz's model of genre evolution (193–230). Schatz argues that all genres pass through an experimental stage, in which conventions are established; a classic stage, in which artists and audiences reach a mutual understanding of these conventions; a stage of refinement, in which the conventions are tweaked and embellished; and finally a baroque, mannerist, or self-reflexive stage, in which the genre becomes its own primary subject (36–38). Coogan maps these stages onto the Golden, Silver, Bronze, and Iron Ages, respectively—the latter being his name for the revisionist comics and their contemporaries—and then adds a "Renaissance Age," in which the genre reconstructs and reestablishes its conventions (193–194).

These efforts are not without their inconsistencies. Coogan's attempt to date the beginnings and endings of each age to specific comic books leads him to some unsustainable conclusions—for example, his Renaissance Age purportedly begins at DC Comics in 1987 (while issues of *Watchmen* were still being published) but doesn't arrive at Marvel for another thirteen years (long after the publication of *Marvels*). Defining each age through a narrow set of genre conventions and thematic preoccupations, Coogan's principles of inclusion can often seem arbitrary or incomplete. Beyond these details, however, the underlying logic and assumptions of his evolutionary approach to genre history also raise some serious problems. As Benjamin

Woo notes, the ages model "proceeds from a conception of history that is simultaneously nostalgic and teleological": nostalgic because the declining scale of the metals, redolent of the mythical ages of man, suggests a fall from an idyllic past; teleological because the evolutionary model implies a progress toward the present (272). Woo brands the latter implication "pure Whiggishness" (272), though he could just as easily note the Tory strain in the system's logic of decline. In Woo's view, the system is both totalizing and essentializing, and because it implies that all comics produced during an age must share the same features, "the periods are elevated to an ontological status" (273). Certainly no period has been more ontologized than the revisionist comics and their contemporaries, often branded as a "Dark Age" for their violent antiheroes (Lewis 307; Kidder 78; Yockey 364). This ideologically and aesthetically freighted label not only condemns the comics it seeks to describe, it confuses the moral critique of some pioneering revisionist works with the amoral violence of their imitators.

But this confusion is a necessary pretext for the next stage: every dark age must summon forth a renaissance. Following the precedent of the early modern scholars who proclaimed the time between the fall of Rome and their own era to be a "dark age," some comics scholars and fans have been eager to apply the same label to the revisionists—the better to set apart their successors. Coogan calls the current era the "Renaissance Age" because "we seem to have come out of the darkness of the Iron Age and because of the promise it seems to hold" (198). If the prospect of a historical schema that moves from the Bronze Age to the Iron Age before leaping forward to the Renaissance is too much for some readers, Coogan also identifies this period as a "reconstructive stage" in which the conventions that were exploded in the baroque stage are rebuilt or reaffirmed. Coogan derives this label from a 1995 *Astro City* letter column in which author Kurt Busiek says, "I prefer the term 'reconstructionist,' because after over a decade of deconstruction being the mode in superhero comics, I think it's time to build some of that sense of wonder back up and see what we can do with it" ("Greetings" n.p.; qtd. in Coogan 198).[1]

Upon closer examination, however, the revisionists and the reconstructionists aren't as different as they might seem. Busiek offers the reconstructionist label in response to a letter from reader Julian Bukalski asking, "Is *Astro City* a revisionist superhero work?" ("Greetings" n.p.). Bukalski notes that the case is ambiguous, largely because he associates the comic's nods toward realism with the revisionists, but the fact that such ambiguities should appear in Coogan's primary example of reconstructive comics suggests these movements are more similar than he acknowledges. Reconstructive comics turn out to be as baroque and mannered as their revisionist predecessors, and both movements pay self-reflexive attention to their genre's history and conventions; both are manifestations of postmodernism in the superhero genre. Unfortunately, the evolutionary model of the superhero ages, which focuses on minute differences within the genre, tends to shut out these larger currents of cultural history. Scholars who rely exclusively on that model have neglected to account for either the business practices or the historical developments that have shaped the superhero genre over the last thirty years.

Even Coogan's attempts to catalogue the features that distinguish reconstructive comics end up demonstrating their continuity with revisionism. According to Coogan, comics such as *Astro City* and *Kingdom Come* begin with elaborate histories and story universes (i.e., continuity) already in place; they incorporate real historical events alongside events from the history of the superhero genre; they allow the passage of time and the aging of characters; they depict superheroes as celebrities; they draw on familiar character types and pay homage to other superheroes; they revive discarded conventions such as secret identities, costumes, and heroic motivations; and they present more realistic, less formulaic origins and characterizations (221–229). Yet we can observe every one of these rebuilt conventions in no less revisionist a work than *Watchmen*. Coogan himself claims that the incorporation of historical events in superhero comics became prominent with *Watchmen*'s use of Richard Nixon and the Vietnam War (221), but the book also displays all the other conventions, from the expansive fictional history to the aging characters. The protagonists are based loosely on the Charlton Comics line of Action Heroes, but they occupy archetypal roles that recall more famous heroes like Superman and Batman (Klock 65–66). And while Coogan suggests that the construction of the superhero costume is foregrounded in the Renaissance Age, no comic foregrounds it more than *Watchmen*, which ventures so far as to consider the impracticalities of urinating while in uniform (Moore and Gibbons 8.20).[2] Origin stories, super-vehicles and equipment, and secret identities receive similar attention, depicted with minute and pragmatic attention to detail but always left intact.

We could find similarly reanimated genre conventions in *The Dark Knight Returns*, Alan Moore and Garry Leach's *Marvelman*, and other revisionist works.[3] These comics may contest the values and ideology of the superhero genre, but they still display all of its semantic elements, often in ways that restore novelty or plausibility to conventions that had become dulled through overuse. Richard Reynolds comments that *Watchmen* and *The Dark Knight Returns* "do not by and large break the rules" that govern superhero costumes but instead "play a knowing set of variations" on the audience's expectations (30). Or, as Moore says in his introduction to *The Dark Knight Returns*, Frank Miller has

> managed to dramatically redefine that character without contradicting one jot of the character's mythology. Yes, Batman is still Bruce Wayne, Alfred is still his butler and Commissioner Gordon is still chief of police, albeit just barely. There is still a young sidekick named Robin, along with a batmobile, a batcave and a utility belt. The Joker, Two-Face, and the Catwoman are still in evidence amongst the roster of villains. Everything is exactly the same, except for the fact that it's all totally different. ("Mark of Batman" n.p.)

This blend of familiarity and innovation explains Sabin's observation that "instead of being 'the last word in superhero comics,' as some pundits had suggested, *Dark Knight* and *Watchmen* had completely revitalized the genre" (*Adult Comics* 98).

The revisionist projects mentioned above share one more important feature with most reconstructive comics: they all take place outside the regular narrative continuities of the major superhero publishers. Comics such as *Watchmen* and *Astro City* feature original characters who serve as analogues or archetypes for more continuity-bound heroes; *The Dark Knight Returns* and *Kingdom Come* use the most prominent DC Comics heroes but place them in alternative futures. Even in-continuity series such as Frank Miller and Klaus Janson's *Daredevil* (1979–1982) and James Robinson and Tony Harris's *Starman* (1994–2001) feature less popular characters and occupy new or neglected corners of their shared universes, affording their creators more room for experimentation. In each case, the relaxation of continuity (combined with the finite nature of many of these stories) affords creators the freedom to age, transform, corrupt, or even kill their characters since none of them have to support a major commercial franchise in perpetuity. While the main DC and Marvel universes would eventually absorb elements of the revisionist and reconstructive styles, both movements were nourished by their initial isolation from continuity.

What separates the revisionists from their successors, then, is not the rebuilding of genre conventions but rather their more critical attitude toward those conventions, the values they convey, and the social order they support. Traditionally, as Richard Reynolds notes, most superheroes have fought to preserve or restore the status quo even at the cost of breaking the law (14–16, 77). Revisionist comics not only question the heroes' motives, morals, and legal authority, they often ask whether the societies the heroes defend are worth preserving. Reconstructive comics typically pull back from this critique, asserting the basic decency not only of the superhero but of society itself. Coogan positions this reaffirmation as a direct response to *Watchmen* and its peers (226), and it is the convention that is hardest to reconcile with the revisionists. Even so, he praises the reconstructive comics for their realism, a term more commonly used to describe their revisionist predecessors. Fans apply the realist label to describe the purported verisimilitude of the revisionists' hard-boiled violence and frank sexuality (Kidder 81), though critics such as Geoff Klock and Andrew Hoberek argue for a more expansive definition of realism that includes the use of real-world locations and political figures, the interrogation and explanation of longstanding genre conventions, the introduction of the passage of time, and the use of formal and technical innovations to represent subjectivity (Klock 29–30; Hoberek 19–21). Coogan applies the same term to the reconstructive comics, suggesting that they use more complex characterization to "make the heroism of the superhero realistic and workable for readers already familiar with sixty years of formulaic fisticuffs" (227). In his description, reconstructive comics not only repair the damage done by the revisionists, they undo the exhaustion of old conventions by examining them in a new light—but that project is inherited from the revisionists, who set out to redefine old superheroes to suit modern sensibilities, as Moore describes in "The Mark of Batman." Coogan's realism is strictly a matter of character and psychology, not the more wide-ranging social critiques or representational strategies of the revisionists, but his language suggests these movements are more alike than most accounts admit.

That should not imply they are identical. Beyond their more celebratory attitude toward the genre, reconstructive comics also stand out for their narrative logic of multiplicity. Henry Jenkins identifies the transition from shared continuity to transmedial multiplicity as beginning in the late 1980s and early 1990s ("'Just Men'" 22), at the very moment when revisionist comics began departing from or rewriting established continuity, but most of his examples date to the new millennium and Coogan's reconstructive movement. As noted in the previous chapter, the shift to multiplicity doesn't negate the old commercial incentives, nor does it erase the narrative tactics adapted in response to them; publishers have always converted popular heroes into spin-offs, counterparts, and entire families of derivative characters. However, those publishers now present multiple and contradictory versions of their heroes in out-of-continuity projects or subsidiary imprints like Marvel's Ultimate line, to say nothing of the many unlicensed analogues and homages published by other companies. Fan audiences who prefer familiar properties to new characters and major publishers that refuse to allow artists to share in the ownership of their creations have further encouraged the duplication of existing heroes rather than the development of new ones (Falconer).

This multiplicity extends to the comics' knowing incorporation of their past. Matt Yockey suggests that the superhero genre as a whole is "primarily concerned with representing its own convulsive history" (361), but surely it's no coincidence that most of his examples come from the twenty-first century. If superhero comics in the late 1980s were either obsessed with streamlining their continuity or else carefully bracketed off from it, the reconstructive comics pride themselves on recovering forgotten pieces of comics lore. Series such as *Astro City* offer pastiches of long-running superhero universes, creating their own instant continuity. In *Supreme* (1996–2000), Alan Moore and Rick Veitch meticulously restored all the Silver Age oddities that DC had purged from the Superman canon in John Byrne's *The Man of Steel* (1986), while their collaboration with Steve Bissette in *1963* (1993) re-created the energy and humor of early sixties Marvel comics at a moment when that company seemed to have abandoned its history. Other titles such as Busiek and Ross's *Marvels* and Grant Morrison and Howard Porter's *JLA* (1996–2000) conducted this recovery within the narrative continuities of Marvel and DC; Morrison's comics from this period went so far as to proclaim a new age of superheroes and laud its retro sensibility (Singer, *Grant Morrison* 137–138). History became multiple as the reconstructive comics incorporated not just the present continuity but all past continuities; Coogan comments that *Astro City* "reconstructs the history of the superhero genre because it contains all of the past" (222). As he concludes his description of these comics, however, Coogan ponders whether the genre will begin a new cycle of innovation or simply linger in the reconstructive stage forever. He notes that other once-popular genres that initiated self-conscious revivals (the western, the musical, and so on) have not progressed beyond them, and suggests that "in the reconstructive stage, all the past stages become available for story telling, and the audience and producers therefore can play at will with the genre's past" (230) rather than advance in new directions. There appears to be some recognition that this type of nostalgic self-reflexivity might be an evolutionary dead end. This is the contradictory telos that Woo describes in his critique of the ages system: superhero comics are "reborn" into a terminal stage where they can only look back on past glories.

Simon Reynolds describes the long reach of the past in far less positive terms in *Retromania: Pop Culture's Addiction to Its Own Past*, which laments nostalgia's dominance over pop music and popular culture as a whole in the new millennium. Citing the popularity of reunion tours, tribute albums, revival movements, and mash-ups, along with a general dearth of new musical genres, Reynolds asserts that

> in the 2000s the pop present became ever more crowded out by the past, whether in the form of archived memories of yesteryear or retro-rock leeching off ancient styles. Instead of being about itself, the 2000s has been about every other previous decade happening again all at once: a simultaneity of pop time that abolishes history while nibbling away at the present's own sense of itself as an era with a distinct identity and feel. (x–xi)

Unlike Coogan, however, Reynolds traces this retromania across multiple genres and identifies its origins in a network of cultural, technological, and economic factors, not just theories of genre cycles. He attributes its rise in part to new modes of recording and transmission such as MP3s, which enable the storage and sharing of music on a massive scale, and streaming video, which ensures that virtually any recording can be viewed by anyone with an internet connection. These innovations have given music (and film, and any other media that can be digitized) a presence and a permanence quite at odds with the ephemerality, scarcity, and difficulty of access that once defined most fan subcultures.

The same has been true of comics. Even before comic book archive files made comics as shareable as MP3s, the explosive growth of the bookstore market encouraged publishers to collect old material in trade paperbacks, making those comics available to fans who had missed their initial publication. When I started reading comics in the late 1970s, storylines such as the Avengers' search for the Celestial Madonna or Captain America's battle against the Secret Empire loomed large in Marvel continuity but were only legible through the flashback panels and asterisked footnotes that dotted the continuity-minded comics of the day. A few popular stories received the occasional reprint series, but those reprints themselves went out of print as soon as they left the comic-shop shelves and drugstore spinner racks. To read an old storyline, a fan would have to track down all the back issues and pay whatever prices the collectors' market demanded for them. The growth of online trading markets (first through bulletin boards and Usenet groups such as rec.arts.comics.marketplace, then through auction sites such as eBay) made the process easier by expanding the geographical limits of the search. Nothing could be more convenient, however, than heading down to the bookstore and purchasing a trade paperback or hardback omnibus that collects every issue—unless it's clicking over to an online subscription service or illegal file-sharing site and downloading the entire series. Now any fan can read the Celestial Madonna or Secret Empire storylines and decide whether they live up to the decades-long buildup they received in Marvel's shared memory.[4]

But accessibility and the ever-expanding cultural archive aren't the only reasons for the past's dominance over the present. Simon Reynolds also locates retromania within the Western economies' larger transformation from the manufacture of goods to the manipulation of information—a tectonic shift from material production to postproduction (415–422). He notes that this shift is mirrored in pop music's evolution from the physical playing of instruments (often by musicians who themselves came from cultures and regions oriented around agricultural or industrial production) to the digital editing of other people's music (418–419). The same processes are at work in comics, from the growth of computer-generated coloring, lettering, and art to the vogue for recycling familiar characters and storylines. Reynolds echoes Fredric Jameson's assertion that these phenomena are connected, that postmodernism is the cultural logic and expression of this transformation in capitalism, although he says Jameson "never quite pinpoints [. . .] the actual mechanics of the link between an economy dominated by financial speculation and a culture oriented around recycling" (421). Reynolds identifies the fashion industry as the point of overlap and suggests that its "artificially accelerated metabolic rate, its rapid cycles of engineered obsolescence" drive postmodern culture's surplus of abandoned and reclaimed styles (421).

In fact, another exponent of the material basis of postmodernism makes this exact connection, though he doesn't describe it solely in terms of fashion. For David Harvey, writing in *The Condition of Postmodernity*, the mechanisms that link economy and culture in the postmodern era go by the names of flexible accumulation (147) and accelerated turnover time (285), but they describe the same cycles of production and consumption. Innovations in transportation, communications, and distribution have allowed businesses to circulate commodities (whether real or, in the case of the financial industry, largely virtual) with ever-increasing speed. Harvey observes that this has resulted in increased volatility and ephemerality across the culture, from labor practices to intellectual production (285). These same developments also contribute to an increase in "time-space compression" (240), the overcoming of distances and shrinking of time horizons that Harvey sees as one of the main drivers of modernity. He names fashion as one of the primary means used to hasten the pace of consumption (285) and cites popular music alongside postmodern fiction as some of the most visible sites for the ensuing eclecticism (301–302). Like Reynolds, Harvey views historicism, nostalgia, and pastiche as manifestations of postmodern capitalism, markers of a culture defined by its surpluses of cultural production.

Contemporary superhero comics display a strikingly similar eclecticism, at least with regard to their own history. Unlike Simon Reynolds, however, most comics scholars are content to ignore the business practices, economic factors, and cultural trends that inform these recirculations. If they take note of postmodernism at all, they either regard its application to comics as "tedious" (Klock 3) or refer to it chiefly as a set of stylistic gestures, as when Coogan avows, "Postmodernism's intertextuality and the Iron Age's baroque self-reflexiveness coincidentally combined in the superhero's generic evolution" (216). There is no acknowledgment that baroque self-reflexivity is itself one of the features of postmodernism, or that postmodernism's ascendance within comics could be anything other than an accident of history. Indeed, history itself, outside the confines of the genre and its conventions, is largely absent from his model. This oversight, not the details of when the ages began or ended, is the major flaw in most fan narratives and far too many scholarly accounts of the superhero genre. Viewing the pastiches of contemporary superhero comics solely through the lens of genre development, they overlook the larger historical factors that produce a cultural shift toward plurality and historicity.

THE ARCHAEOLOGY OF INFLUENCE

Nostalgia, pastiche, and all the other surface manifestations of postmodernism are on full display in *Planetary* (1999–2009), by Warren Ellis and John Cassaday. The series dispatches a team of superhuman investigators to uncover what characters and critics both term the secret history of the twentieth century: a history of Victorian monsters, pulp heroes, Golden and Silver Age superheroes, Japanese kaiju, Hong Kong police detectives, and other figures familiar to comics and movie fans worldwide. In "Warren Ellis's *Planetary*: The Archaeology of Superheroes," Karin Kukkonen says the cast and setting "amount to nothing less than the main story worlds and characters of the 20th century's popular fiction" (154); she might just as easily have said they amount to little more, but such criticisms are all but unheard of in comics studies. Scholars of *Planetary* and other contemporary superhero comics are generally content to itemize their references, unpack their allusions, echo their criticisms or appreciations of other comics, or endorse their bids for authority within the superhero genre. Taking series such as *Planetary* on their own preferred terms, these scholars repeat the comics' commentaries instead of developing their own. They may draw on the interpretive frameworks of critical theory—typically just a single theorist—but they use them to foreclose on more resistant readings while making exorbitant claims for their subjects' sophistication.

Kukkonen, for example, invokes Michel Foucault's "archaeology of knowledge" on the grounds that the Planetary team identify themselves as "mystery archaeologists" (Kukkonen 155). However inviting the comparison may be, Kukkonen's application of Foucault obscures rather than illuminates the comic's use of historical references and discourses:

> As *Planetary* relates their story to their contemporary contexts so closely, the Silver Age superheroes seem to lose part of their fictional status. As statements in a discourse formation, the distinction between fiction and reality becomes almost irrelevant, because from the discourse perspective events in the real world and fictions both exist on the same ontological level as "statements." According to Foucault they are coexistent rather than one being an expression of the other, and therefore he rejects the notions of interpretation and of structure (Foucault 1972, 137). (Kukkonen 160)

The cited page unfortunately says nothing about fiction, reality, or the notions of interpretation or structure, being instead a description of the history of ideas, from which Foucault distinguishes his archaeology of knowledge (138–140). In the course of that distinction he does indeed reject interpretive disciplines that regard discourses merely as expressions of hidden meanings (138–139), but he never claims that the distinction between fiction and reality is irrelevant. Elsewhere he declares that statements have a material existence (100), but this simple point—that statements exist as words, sounds, or images, and therefore can be described as objects in their own right—doesn't support Kukkonen's implication that superheroes and their stories somehow become ontologically equivalent to real-world events. The *statements* are real; their fictions are still fictional.

By equating the two, Kukkonen evokes a conception of postmodernism as vulgar and oversimplified as the version she rejects in her opening summary of the metafictional gambits that *Planetary* supposedly surpasses:

> The direct gaze out of the panel, as characters address readers directly; the parody through subversion, as the hero is reduced to a dupe: these postmodern tricks that attempt to achieve a complicity with readers, to make them part of the sophisticated crowd that looks through the myths and constructions of traditional storytelling, often result in little more than an "ironic gag." (154)

Kukkonen attempts to set *Planetary* apart from prior superhero comics such as Grant Morrison and Chas Truog's *Animal Man* (1988–1990), but it's worth noting that Ellis and Cassaday don't really break from the model she describes; *Planetary* achieves complicity with its readers and flatters their sophistication through its obvious, unmissable intertextual references rather than through more overtly metafictional games. With little to distinguish her chosen text, Kukkonen can only argue that *Planetary* achieves a deeper engagement with postmodernism by reducing postmodernism to a series of stylistic gestures. The relentless intertextuality of *Planetary* may indeed be postmodern, but in the absence of any relation to postmodernism's historical origins or material instantiations it is postmodern only in Fredric Jameson's highly critical sense of postmodern pastiche as "blank parody" (17), of postmodern architecture as a "complacent eclecticism" that cannibalizes and recombines the styles of the past with no guiding principle or purpose (18–19). *Planetary* might well exemplify this strain of postmodernism, but the series does little to engage with it on a critical level.

Ellis's pastiches are not wholly devoid of argument, but that argument rarely extends beyond jockeying for his own artistic status as he recapitulates the styles and arguments of other comics. Sometimes the imitation is so perfect that it becomes impossible to distinguish *Planetary* from the comics the series ostensibly defines itself against. This is driven home in issue 7, "To Be in England, in the Summertime," which indulges in more than a few ironic gags of its own. The issue both parodies and echoes the revisionist comics produced during the "British Invasion" of the American comics industry in the 1980s and later published by DC's Vertigo imprint in the early 1990s. The story revolves around the apparent demise of the chain-smoking British occultist Jack Carter, who serves as a proxy for Alan Moore's chain-smoking British occultist John Constantine. (No reader ever had to work to figure out a Warren Ellis allusion.) His funeral is attended by proxies for other DC and Vertigo characters from the 1980s and early 1990s, including Swamp Thing, Animal Man, Morpheus, Death, and so on; the bearded, pot-smoking officiant is a stand-in for Alan Moore himself (Ellis and Cassaday 7.5–7). Orion Ussner Kidder admits that these figures are "not much more than meticulously rendered arrows that point directly at their originals" (90), but he maintains that the Constantine analogue delivers more commentary than the others. The issue attempts to lay the revisionist comics to rest by burying one of their most iconic characters; even though Jack Carter turns out to be very much alive, he discards his Constantine-style trench coat for a new look that's equally derivative of one of Ellis's own characters, the gonzo journalist Spider Jerusalem, who was appearing contemporaneously in *Transmetropolitan* (1997–2002). Carter tells the Planetary team, in Ellis's typically didactic fashion, "The eighties are long over. Time to move on" (7.21).

Even as Ellis buries the revisionists, however, he also repeats their critiques of both superhero comics and British culture. Carter was ostensibly killed by an unnamed superhero who is outraged over having been revised from a noble, upright guardian into a psychologically conflicted, sexually deviant fascist. The series becomes unabashedly ironic and metafictional as Ellis allows the hero to lament his fate before Carter, alive and well, dispatches him with a shotgun (7.19). Tellingly, the only character killed in this funerary issue is the square-jawed Silver Age superhero, not the revisionist who did him in. This shouldn't be surprising as *Planetary*, for all of Ellis's and Kukkonen's protestations to the contrary, participates in the revisionist project. The next issue, "The Day the Earth Turned Slower," does exactly for fifties science fiction movies what Jack Carter did to the murderous superhero: take a child's genre and relocate it within a putatively adult context of violence, exploitation, and cynicism. Most of the genres visited in *Planetary* are subject to similar treatment. Ellis chides Carter (and by extension the revisionists) for taking a classic superhero and turning him into a pedophile with a racist past, but this isn't so different from taking the Fantastic Four and turning them into Nazis—which Ellis had done in the previous issue. The Vertigo parody reads less like a critique of the revisionists than a latecomer's desperate bid to join their ranks.

Comics scholars identify another context for this issue, and an argument that extends beyond Ellis's attempts to claim affinity with the revisionists while mocking the surface trappings of their style, when they note that the story connects the revisionist comics to the historical circumstances of their creation in the 1980s (Kukkonen 159; Kidder 91; Klock 160). But this theme requires no special critical intervention to bring it to light; what it amounts to, in practice, is a few pages in which Planetary member Jakita Wagner attributes the revisionist heroes' stylistic excesses to the context of life in Margaret Thatcher's Britain. When she lists the miseries suffered under Thatcher's government, she does so in terms that were already perfectly explicit in the revisionist comics. Wagner tells team leader Elijah Snow that Jack Carter told her (any given issue of *Planetary* consists mostly of expository lectures) that Thatcher "wanted concentration camps for AIDS victims, wanted to eradicate homosexuality even as an abstract concept" (7.7). This language should be familiar to anyone who has read Alan Moore's introduction to the first American publication of *V for Vendetta*, where he laments the authoritarianism and bigotry of Britain in the 1980s: "the tabloid press are circulating the idea of concentration camps for persons with AIDS. [. . .] The government has expressed a desire to eradicate homosexuality, even as an abstract concept" (Moore and Lloyd 6). Ellis has not revealed the historical origins and contexts of revisionism so much as he has restated them, word for word.

Klock maintains that contemporary superhero comics stage a self-conscious battle for priority over and independence from their predecessors, a Bloomian anxiety of influence. It's easy to see why he likes *Planetary*, which advertises this anxiety at every turn and plays out its intergenerational struggle in the most histrionic of terms. Klock notes, "The four-member exploratory Planetary team are clearly in debt to Stan Lee and Jack Kirby's Fantastic Four, so the Fantastic Four are reconceived as the

Planetary's Nazi foes" (159), suggesting that Ellis's recognition of his own influences has inspired his most cynical revisions. The series provides easy fodder for Bloomian readings, yet such exercises can only annotate a series that already annotates itself. Hence Klock's protracted descriptions of allusions that barely qualify as allusions, of references that are obvious to anyone who has ever read a comic book: "the woman warrior is Wonder Woman; the crouching figure in the dark cape is Batman;" etc.; etc. (157; see plate 2). A similar impasse is reached in Kidder's exhaustive close reading of a page from an issue inspired by wuxia films, which reaches the only reasonable conclusion that Cassaday's art has incorporated elements from wuxia films (88–89)—but Kidder recognizes that *Planetary* has few goals other than depicting "the cluster of influences that gave rise to it and continues to shape it" (82), a perfectly apt summary of a decidedly unambitious series. Despite the best efforts of its boosters, *Planetary* amounts to little more than a history of the already known, an archaeology of texts that are still present and in plain sight, a tabulation of the influences on a comic dedicated primarily to tabulating its influences.

If any allusion in *Planetary* amounts to more than a blatant copy or a blank parody, it would have to be the Four. The dark reflections and main antagonists of Ellis's investigators, the Four are also a warped version of the Fantastic Four, a family of explorers who gained superhuman powers after they piloted an experimental rocket in *Fantastic Four* issue 1 (1961). Ellis's Four are a quartet of astronauts who seek to possess and exploit the wonders they discover; he traces their origins back to the Nazi rocket scientists brought to the United States after World War II (6.2). Kukkonen notes that *Planetary* brings the Fantastic Four back into their original historical contexts in the Cold War and the space race (159–160). However, when she asserts that "the Apollo program and the Silver Age superheroes are all statements of the same discourse formation" (160), she overlooks the many institutions and power relations that distinguish the military and technological applications of that discourse from the strictly cultural ones. She also ignores the possibility that a cultural text could rework or transform its historical discourse, or respond to multiple discourses at once. The early *Fantastic Four* was as much antifascist as it was anticommunist: Mister Fantastic and the Thing were both World War II combat veterans, as was artist Jack Kirby, and one of the early villains, the Hate-Monger, was revealed to be a clone of Adolf Hitler in *Fantastic Four* issue 21. *Planetary* recontextualizes the Fantastic Four's origins within a more modern understanding of the history of the Cold War, but it also fundamentally alters the characters and wrenches them out of their initial discourses. This revisionism complicates any easy historicist interpretation.

Ellis nevertheless attempts to mount such an interpretation of the Fantastic Four himself. His heroes castigate the Four for their Cold War mentality of "arrogance and righteousness and the individual American way" (6.6), a critique that might easily be extended to the superhero genre in general. However, neither Ellis nor his critics acknowledge that it could just as easily be applied to the nominal heroes of *Planetary*. They may despise the Four for hoarding their amazing discoveries, but the Planetary team doesn't share them either until the final issue, at which point the series is over and Ellis no longer needs to maintain the appearance of the real-world setting that *Planetary*, like *Fantastic Four* and most other superhero comics, depends on. What prevents the Fantastic Four from sharing their discoveries is not some ideological failing on the characters' part, but rather their publisher's desire to print their comic in perpetuity, placing firm limits on how much the heroes or their setting can change. (Once again, Eco's oneiric climate remains relevant.) Ellis's superficially historicist revision of the Fantastic Four only works by removing the comics from their historical and material contexts. He takes aim at a structural convention of serial comics and passes it off as an ideological critique of characters who, in their original forms, don't express the ideology he critiques them for.

Conversely, the Planetary team displays plenty of "arrogance and righteousness" of their own. Their founder and leader, Elijah Snow, is a swaggering bully who boasts of his power and knowledge while he berates his teammates. Threats to anally violate the Drummer with his own drumsticks are a particular favorite, as are kicks to the groin and other obvious bids for masculine dominance. The ultimate proof of this dominance comes when Snow tortures one of the Four, a brutal violation of human rights and legal norms that Ellis justifies by falling back on the tropes of post-September 11th torture narratives such as the Fox television series *24*. He presents the torture both as a necessary measure for stopping the Four and as righteous vengeance for past losses suffered at their hands; the Drummer defends Snow's actions on the grounds that he's only doing it to save his people (*Planetary* 23.3, 23.22), the same justification offered in the ticking time-bomb fantasies of *24* and in the legal rationales of the George W. Bush administration. Like Jack Bauer of *24*, Snow promotes the myth of the hard man who violates society's moral boundaries in order to protect it.[5] *Planetary* not only sustains the ideological justifications of the superhero genre it claims to criticize, it extends them even to the point of torture and murder.

Torin Monahan observes that *24* presents these actions not as choices but as necessities; the series suggests that its characters can't be morally culpable if they are stripped of their autonomy (112–113). Ellis replicates this logic when he allows Snow to describe himself as one of Earth's "protective systems," or "machines constructed by life's invisible defensive systems to do a job" (24.4, 24.5). Snow effectively disavows any agency over his actions while claiming nature itself licenses him to do what he does. Only Jakita Wagner objects to the torture, until the Four destroy a Planetary skyscraper and all the people inside it, at which point she drops her protests and demands that Snow give her an opportunity to hunt down the attackers (24.21). Ellis restages the September 11th attack on the World Trade Center to give the Planetary team a supposedly unimpeachable rationale for breaking any law, any moral code in their mission to punish the Four. Never mind that in this narrative, the torture came first; the tragedy simply removes Wagner's objections and renders her principles irrelevant.

Despite their moral posturing, the Planetary team are barely distinguishable from the Four—a point Ellis himself acknowledges in the *Planetary/JLA: Terra Occulta* crossover, where Snow and his people adopt the role of the Four (Carney, "Function" 114). Even in the regular series, the rival teams differ chiefly in the type of authority they embody. The Planetary organization is a global corporation with offices around the world, private military contractors and vehicles, secret spaceships and alien visitors (hidden from the rest of the world, just like the Four's discoveries), and undisclosed torture sites, all funded through Snow's personal wealth, which has no apparent source or limit. Their struggle with the Four pits the arrogance of the Cold War military-industrial complex against the arrogance of the borderless postmodern corporation, and Ellis comes down unequivocally, enthusiastically on the side of the latter. When the Planetary organization and their allies in the Hark Corporation finally release the Four's trove of technology, they do so "non-commercially" (27.2), a dream of corporate philanthropy at least as outlandish as anything in the derivative storyworlds the Planetary team visit.

That dream rests on a deeper fantasy of untrammeled personal power: Elijah Snow and Anna Hark are motivated not by profit but by a sort of genetic noblesse oblige. Snow is a "century baby," one of a select group of people whose birth on the cusp of the twentieth century bestowed them with special powers and abilities. Hark is the daughter of a different century baby, Jakita Wagner the child of still another, and the Drummer is similarly endowed by his own rare bloodline. The Four, on the other hand, are normal humans who have sold the Earth to extradimensional gods in exchange for their powers; Snow calls their leader "one of the little people" and says he "had to sell out the planet Earth to gain what the likes of us were born with" (26.5, 26.6). While the first comment is part of a ploy to goad the Four into a trap, the latter one is shared only with Snow's associates and presumably reflects his actual beliefs. The comic boils down to a struggle between those who were born to rule the world and those who have usurped their rightful place. Ellis favors the natural corporate aristocracy over the twisted social climbers empowered by the state, creating a profoundly antidemocratic narrative that celebrates absolute power so long as it's exercised by the right sort of people.

STRANGE HISTORIES

Unfortunately, ideological readings of this sort are almost entirely absent from the critical examinations of *Planetary*. In his essay "The Function of the Superhero at the Present Time," Sean Carney argues that the Planetary team's mission is to deliver humanity from ideology, to liberate us into a narrative multiplicity and totality that exists "outside of ideological consciousness" (114). Carney extrapolates this from the book's motto and mission statement, "It's a strange world. Let's keep it that way" (1.24), which is repeated with minor variation in nearly every issue of the series. For Carney, this statement marks the Planetary team as heroes whose purpose is to strip superheroes of their ideological dimension and restore them to a state of mystery and wonder. In his allegorical reading of the series, the Four (figures of the Silver Age) destroy the wonder of the Golden Age by remaking superheroes into ideological myths that naturalize the values and authority of the Cold War state; the Planetary team undoes this, making the heroes strange and wondrous again by rendering them ideologically incoherent. Yet, as Carney notes, neither comic book history nor *Planetary* itself supports this reading: Ellis's revisionism is "creatively false" ("Function" 113) as the Golden Age heroes were also openly ideological (and typically even more patriotic than their successors), and the Planetary organization, as already noted, is not as different from the Four as Ellis claims. Carney recognizes this continuity, not just between the Planetary team and the Four, but between the terms of his own opposition: "the ideological and the strange or historical are not opposites but two sides of a coin, or two separate moments in a single narrative process or substance" (114). The strangeness celebrated in *Planetary*—which is, in the end, nothing more than a recitation of familiar genre tropes and an exhortation to regard them with abject awe—does not liberate the human race from ideology, but it is a convenient means for placing the superheroes beyond ideological critique.

Carney's distinction between the ideological and the historical rests on an elaborate allegory drawn from the history of the superhero genre. He suggests that prior to the revisionist comics of the 1980s, superheroes functioned as myths in the Barthesian sense—that is, as discourses that naturalized history, culture, and ideology (Barthes 142–144). Revisionism, Carney argues, imbued the heroes with an ambivalence that transformed them into "allegorical figures for humanity's relationship to its own history; they are allegories for the human ability to create forms that are larger than humanity itself, and that humans then need to struggle with and repossess as their own agency" ("Function" 102). Superheroes like the Four, limited to a single ideological function, cannot allegorize humanity's ambivalent relation to its own history. Yet by creating this false opposition between ideology and history—and by declining to read the ambiguous, conflicted, or apolitical postures of revisionist heroes as ideological stances in their own right—Carney essentially locks ideology out of his readings. In practice, he places the revisionist superheroes beyond any human judgment or criticism because they aren't human, nor even superhuman, but instead become figures for history itself.

Carney's discussion of *The Dark Knight Returns* is instructive. He argues that Miller criticizes traditional, pre-revisionist superheroes (typified in the comic by Superman) because "they function as conservative myths which solve, in an imaginary manner, humanity's real social problems" ("Function" 103). But Miller's Batman—or, rather, Carney's Miller's Batman—can't be pinned down so easily. His longtime ally Commissioner Gordon essentially places him beyond interpretation through an analogy to the conspiracy theory that Franklin Delano Roosevelt allowed the Japanese navy to attack Pearl Harbor because it would provoke America to enter World War II. Gordon says he was shocked by the allegation, but he realized he "couldn't judge it. It was too big. He was too big" (F. Miller 2.40) in a manner that obviously parallels his view of Batman. Carney suggests that this view places Batman beyond mythology, beyond human ideology or understanding, though not beyond the contradictions of history, and Gordon "can only suffer the contradiction unhappily. This is the only position of truth a human can take in relation to the modern experience of history" (104). But Miller's Batman also proposes imaginary solutions for humanity's real social problems—first vigilante justice, then mob vigilance, and finally a radical underground, all of which imply ideological positions. A similar contradiction arises between Carney's readings of the comics and his theoretical model, derived from Georg Lukács, in which history is a product of human actions, not transcendental forces: "The problem with traditional superheroes," Carney argues, "is that their narratives imply readers who will imaginatively abdicate responsibility for human actions to these heroes, in the same way that humans abdicate responsibility for their actions to something they call 'history'" (102). Yet Gordon abdicates his responsibility to both in precisely this manner. To place Batman's actions outside the frame of human understanding is to imply that we cannot evaluate them, only accept them (however unhappily)—in other words, resign ourselves to Miller's ideology and place it outside the bounds of the ideological, naturalizing it not as myth but as history. The only proper position to take toward such heroes, in Carney's allegorical reading, is one of abject deference.

By extension, this becomes the only proper position to take toward their texts as well. Carney dismisses ideological readings of *The Dark Knight Returns*, especially those that interpret it as "a reactionary condemnation of American society's moral decay" ("Function" 102), by implying they take the comic too literally. He waves away the book's broad political caricatures by insisting that "the heavy-handedness of these portrayals in the book, combined with Miller's simple, iconic style of illustration, caution the critic against literal interpretations" (102)—as if the book's very didacticism were proof that we can't take Miller at his word. Later, he acknowledges that his allegory of history "necessitates that the conclusion of the narrative not be read literally, as the forming of an underground militia" (104) even though the narrative ends with Batman forming an underground militia that will seek to topple a corrupt and incompetent federal government. Per Carney's argument, this ending does signal Batman's final break from the conservative social function of the traditional superhero, but that doesn't mean he has moved beyond any ideology or social function. He remains the heroic outsider who defies the law in order to save society from menaces both internal and external, who seeks a justice the authorities are either unwilling or unable to enforce. Miller has not broken from the Batman myth so much as he has magnified it to new scales, from local law enforcement to national politics.

Carney spends a substantial portion of his short discussion stressing all the ways we must not read *The Dark Knight Returns*. We can't read it literally, but we also can't read beyond the ending, as that would require speculating about what Batman is going to do with his underground militia and therefore imagining the type of ideological function Carney says he no longer fulfills. Carney prefers to keep Batman's ideology opaque and ambivalent, as he prefers to keep Planetary's incoherent and strange; the ambiguity forestalls more oppositional or ideologically specific readings and allows him to maintain his allegories of history. Although Carney opens his essay with a mild criticism of the "depoliticizing gestures" of Klock's analysis ("Function" 101), Klock at least acknowledges the reactionary elements of Miller's narrative and considers them at length (39–50). Carney defers or redirects any discussion of ideology on any but the most abstract of levels. Like Klock and so many other scholars of contemporary superhero comics, he reads the comics allegorically to save them from themselves.

Carney's article "The Tides of History: Alan Moore's Historiographic Vision" elaborates on these allegories while drawing from a broader theoretical base and a richer body of material; Moore's comics give him more to work with, historically speaking. Nevertheless, Carney remains overly generous in accepting their ideological claims—sometimes more generous than the comics themselves. His discussion of *Marvelman* (a British serial reprinted and then continued in the United States as *Miracleman*) is a case in point: Carney's description of the conclusion of Moore's run on the title, in which Miracleman and his superhuman allies take over the Earth and establish a utopian society, is almost wholly at odds with what is shown in the comic.

> Although Neil Gaiman, who took over the scripting of Marvelman from Moore, went on to explore the existence of discontent within this new utopia, the fact that Moore completed his own interest in the story with the achievement of a perfect world indicates that the creation of an unambiguous, simple utopia was his ultimate goal: *Marvelman* stands, then, as a critique of the very absence of such utopian thinking in the West, particularly in the Conservative Thatcherite government which is pushed gently aside for Marvelman to usher in a new Golden Age. ("Tides" par. 6)[6]

Carney glosses over Moore's many indications that this new society is far from perfect. In Moore's final story, *Miracleman* issue 16, demonstrators across the political spectrum protest the superhumans' assumption of absolute power, separatists huddle in fortified enclaves, and disaffected youth adopt the appearance of mass murderer Johnny Bates to signal their alienation from the new world order. Most personally, Liz Moran (the estranged wife of Mike Moran, Miracleman's human counterpart) refuses Miracleman's offer to build her a superhuman body so she can join him in his new home on Olympus. As the issue draws to a close, Miracleman sits on the ramparts of Olympus and ponders this rejection of the eugenic hierarchy that is one of the cornerstones of his utopia—but it doesn't trouble Carney's reading. While he recognizes that other Moore comics such as *Watchmen* are highly critical of utopianism, Carney doesn't extend this critique to *Miracleman*, which implies its heroes have lost all connection to the humans they seek to perfect through loving rule. The series could provide ample support for Carney's contention that Moore's comics express a deeply ambivalent view of historical progress ("Tides" par. 3), but instead he interprets it to confirm his own views on the importance of utopian thinking. The details of the text have been subsumed to the historiographic thesis.

Moore's comics, as Carney notes, envision a history shaped by multiple forces and actors—material and ideal, societal and individual, progressive and reactionary, a complexity that allows Carney to explore the comics and his own historiographic models in greater detail. He observes that *From Hell* (1989–1998), by Moore and Eddie Campbell, can't fully support the Lukácsian theories that preside over "The Function of the Superhero at the Present Time" as Moore's view of history is "neither wholly materialistic nor utterly abstract and metaphysical, but an aspired-to identity between the two. In this, Moore resists the metaphysical fallacy to which Lukács succumbs, which is to imagine the working class as the earthly manifestation of Hegel's *Geist*: the identical subject-object of history" ("Tides" par. 27). In this act of rhetorical judo, Lukács's historical materialism becomes the very quality that inspires his metaphysical fallacy (when we might observe instead that metaphysics comes into play precisely through those parts of Hegel he has not rejected, his reductionism and his teleology). In using *From Hell* to challenge that materialism, however, Carney articulates a model of history that is itself almost wholly divorced from material causes.

From Hell displays its own profound reliance on the metaphysical, both in the magical workings and eternal recurrences that Moore maps onto the historical record and in his ultimate conclusions about the identity of Jack the Ripper. In letters, interviews, and the text of *From Hell* itself, Moore observes that "Jack the Ripper" is not simply the unknown person who murdered five women in 1888; he is also a fiction created by opportunistic journalists, crank-letter writers, a panicked public, flummoxed police, and subsequent generations of researchers, writers, fabulists, and conspiracy theorists, including Moore and Campbell themselves. In his most Platonic explication of this theme, part of a 1998 correspondence with Dave Sim, Moore proclaims that "Jack the Ripper, in a very real sense, never actually had a physical existence. He was a collage-creature, made from crank letters, hoaxes, and sensational headlines. He exists wholly in Idea Space, looming forward from our books of theory and our fictions" (Moore and Sim 321). José Alaniz raises the obvious and necessary objection:

> The amoral notion of a vicious killer or killers called JTR amounting to nothing more than some Baudrillardian simulacrum, bereft of any physical existence beyond that provided by an economy of signs [. . .], invites a critique of Moore's tidy formulation, if for no other reason than that JTR was real enough to the five women he/they eviscerated, strangled and killed. (147)

Carney claims that this argument "falls prey to the binary thinking Moore seeks to avoid" ("Tides" par. 24), and indeed, Moore does seek to avoid it. (So does Alaniz, who notes that *From Hell* reminds us of the materiality of the murders through its unflinching attention to the bodies of the victims.) In the "Epilogue" to *From Hell*, the spiritualist Robert Lees voices Alaniz's concerns:

> ABBERLINE: It's all just stories when all's said and done.
>
> LEES: But that's just the thing, it isn't just stories. Those women really died. And poor Druitt, caught up in something he could never understand.
>
> ABBERLINE: That's all done with, though. That's all gone. All that's left is what people can read about. Chapbooks and tombstones, Mr. Lees. Chapbooks and tombstones. (Moore and Campbell "Epilogue" 5)

Abberline reasserts Moore's narrativist conception of history, but that concept has already crept into Lees's objection. Montague John Druitt was a schoolmaster and barrister who committed suicide in December 1888, less than a month after the final Ripper murder. The timing and other circumstantial evidence led to his identification as a suspect in the killings, but in Moore and Campbell's version of events he is an innocent man killed by a Masonic conspiracy to deflect attention from the true murderer. If this story is avowedly fictional, the case for naming Druitt as the killer is almost as suspect. His drowning alone is certain; everything else is just a story.

Carney calls this "the central theme of *From Hell,* which is how fiction is constitutive of history, how the two are *identical*" ("Tides" par. 27, his emphasis). But it's one thing to suggest that fiction can inform or become history and quite another to claim that they are identical, or that acts of "social magic"—which is to say, symbolism—are "the material substance of history itself" (par. 29). Philosophers of history such as Hayden White recognize that histories are narratives, organized and emplotted with the structures we more typically associate with fiction (96–99). In Carney's formulation, however, those narratives aren't just records or interpretations of past events but are themselves the raw material of history; he argues that *From Hell* "is not interested in the relationship between history and the meaning made from history, but in meaning as history, meaning as where humanity cannot but locate itself" (par. 24). Pushing beyond the observation that history is narrative, Carney articulates a concept of history almost wholly disconnected from material forces or events except insofar as those events are themselves shaped by human thought or meaning-making. This Hegelian formulation—surely as metaphysical as anything in Lukács—is a perceptive reading of *From Hell,* but it requires Carney to disavow or at least ignore materialist accounts of history and culture, even among his own sources. He quotes Jameson several times and he seems familiar with Harvey's work, alluding to time-space compression (pars. 16, 28) and paraphrasing the title of *The Condition of Postmodernity* no less than seven times. Nevertheless, these citations are largely confined to Jameson's and Harvey's descriptions of the psychic experience or the artistic representation of postmodernism, paying only lip service to their arguments about its origins in postindustrial capitalism. Carney's allegories presume a purely ideal history, one almost as exaggerated as Kukkonen's caricature of vulgar postmodernism.

Those allegories display a similar indifference to ideological readings, particularly with respect to representations of gender and race. This becomes especially apparent in Carney's analysis of Moore, J. H. Williams III, and

Mick Gray's *Promethea* (1999–2005), a series largely given over to illustrated lectures that explain Moore's magical and spiritual beliefs. The titular character is a spirit of the imagination who bonds with a series of mortal women (and one man) to form a long line of mythical heroes. Carney interprets her as "dialectical epiphany, the substance of history itself" because she is "both the madonna and the whore, because she is the identity of the sacred and the profane" ("Tides" par. 35). This is a depressingly literal description of *Promethea* issue 21, in which the protagonist, in the middle of a journey up the mystical Tree of Life, travels to the sphere of Binah, home of the feminine principle, where she encounters a spirit that is at once the Whore of Babylon and the Virgin Mary (21.14–21). Promethea is stunned by the revelation that the madonna and the whore are one and the same, yet for all that Moore attempts to collapse the terms of this ancient binary, he does nothing to suggest that femininity might take other forms. In providing a meticulous visualization of the medieval mystic philosophy of the Kabbalah, Moore also re-creates its medieval gender politics: the highest feminine principle is the font of compassion and lust, the highest masculine principle the seat of wisdom and energy (22.12). Promethea herself may perform a symbolic unification of these male and female aspects, enacting Carney's dialectic, but in the process Moore tacitly endorses the logic of patriarchy by concretizing and naturalizing its freighted binaries.

Issue 22 enacts that logic in even more grotesque terms. Visiting Chokmah, the sphere of the masculine principle, Promethea discovers the source of all existence, which Moore and Williams allegorize as the nature god Pan raping the moon goddess Selene. Promethea tells her guide (in one of the moments of didactic self-annotation that distinguish all these pastiche comics) that they are witnessing "The myth, where Pan rapes her, although . . . it's almost like she wanted that. Like he had to" (22.16).[7] Carney cites this scene as evidence that Moore is aware of "the threat of violence" in history ("Tides" par. 44), but he doesn't address the implications of basing an entire cosmogony around an act of rape—let alone the implications of Promethea's attempt to justify that rape. He reads the assault simply as another trope for the dialectics that structure history: "This is a vision of libidinal history, of the origin of creation as a cosmic rape: as profane, it is a rape, as sacred, it is an act of 'godsex'" (par. 44). Carney renders the rape as nothing more than a term in an equation, the base half of the dyad, notable only as a laudable reminder of the capacity for violence within history and not as a scripting of that violence and misogyny onto the very structure of the universe. In this reading, as in "The Function of the Superhero," Moore's texts are not to be examined and critiqued, only explained—or fitted to illustrate Carney's more genteel allegories.

Carney commits a similar (if less extreme) oversight in his discussion of Moore and Rob Liefeld's *Judgment Day* (1997), in which a black superhero named Sentinel is revealed to be a fraud who invented his own heroic identity by writing his destiny in a magical book that both contains and creates all the stories of the human race. Stumbling across the book in 1958, young Marcus Langston discovers he is destined to die at age nineteen while robbing a liquor store to pay his heroin dealer. Langston crosses out this story and writes a new one in which he becomes the first prominent superhero to emerge after the 1960s, but he doesn't stop there:

> He decides to write a nastier, shadowier and more violent world for himself . . . and for everybody else. Our entire reality changed and darkened. Gone was the naive wonder of the 'forties, the exuberance of the 'fifties and the nobility of the 'sixties. Working a dreadful reverse alchemy, Marcus Langston let our world slide from a Golden Age to a Silver Age, and finally to a Dark Age. Now, heroes motivated only by money or psychopathology stalked a paranoid, apocalyptic landscape of post-nuclear mutants and bazooka wielding cyborgs. (3.20)

The art for this chapter, by Ian Churchill and Norm Rapmund, reinforces Moore's nostalgic and pessimistic logic of the ages. One panel shows Sentinel leaping in a pose virtually identical to the one Batman strikes on the cover of the first issue of *The Dark Knight Returns*; the next shows Sentinel fighting alongside his teammates from Liefeld's *Youngblood*, the first series published by Image Comics in 1992 (figure 2.1). The criticism of revisionist superhero comics and their successors, the violent Image-style books of the 1990s, is unmistakable, turning *Judgment Day* into an "allegory for its own history" that charts the increasing (if largely gestural) realism of superheroes after the 1970s as "a fall from grace or loss of innocence" (Carney, "Function" 110).

To his credit, Carney doesn't simply annotate or repeat this allegory; he interprets it as another window onto Moore's philosophy of history, an ambivalent narrative that charts a genre's purported decline but also allows for human agency within history through the poetic device of the rewrite. Carney suggests that Langston's revisions to his own biography "began as

FIG. 2.1. *Alan Moore, Ian Churchill, and Norm Rapmund,* Judgment Day *issue 3 (Awesome Entertainment, 1997), p. 20.*

a progressive action: the creation of a more human world where an urban black youth was not pre-destined to die robbing a liquor store. Thus for Moore, this fall from grace is not to be lamented nostalgically but employed productively, for the new perspective on history it makes possible" ("Function" 110). He reads the emergence of Sentinel, and of black superheroes more broadly, as an allegory for the civil rights movement and a reflection of a changing American society "which by changing was itself attempting to 'rewrite' the so-called foretold end for African-American lives" (109). Unfortunately, Carney doesn't consider the political valences of making Sentinel pull double duty as an allegory for both the fight against racism and the revisionist degradation of the superhero. It would be all too easy to conclude that *Judgment Day* identifies the increasing diversity of superhero comics after the 1960s as the beginning of the genre's fall from grace, the first step toward the debased violence and realism of contemporary comics; it would be still more troubling if we assume the series maps this narrative onto the nation as a whole.

However, Carney's allegories rest on a pair of historical claims that don't hold up under scrutiny. Carney states that Sentinel begins his career in the 1970s, at the moment of the "actual arrival of the African-American superhero," and observes that Marcus Langston finds the magical book "in 1958, just as the American civil rights movement was about to explode into action" ("Function" 109). In fact, the first black superheroes appeared in the 1960s (the African Black Panther in 1966, the African American Falcon in 1969) and the postwar civil rights movement began well before 1958, with events such as *Brown v. Board of Education* (1954), the Montgomery bus boycott (1955–1956), the formation of the Southern Christian Leadership Conference (1957), and the integration of Little Rock Central High School (1957) all preceding Carney's anachronistic and ahistorical cutoff point. With the dates of Sentinel's career rendered as more or less arbitrary, Carney's allegory is sustained not by his reading of Moore's comic but by his reading of the civil rights movement as a "rewriting" of African American fortunes—in effect, he turns the civil rights movement into an allegory for *Judgment Day*.

Even if we set aside the spurious historical interpretations, Sentinel remains a problematic character. Beginning as one stereotype (the black junkie and criminal) before transforming into another (the hypermasculine action hero), he relapses into crime when he murders a white superhero so he can steal back the book that changed his destiny, the book that was her birthright—hardly a positive portrayal of the civil rights movement or the emergence of black superheroes. Any allegory for comics history that rests upon him is one that implies a correlation between the diversification of superhero comics, the popularity of revisionism and its successors, and the erosion of the genre's moral codes. While *Judgment Day* does not fully articulate this reactionary narrative, other reconstructive comics were more willing to shoulder the burden.

INSERT PRETENTIOUS BIBLICAL EPIGRAPH HERE

Kingdom Come, by Mark Waid and Alex Ross, exemplifies all the problems of reconstructive comics: the nostalgic telos, the reactionary ideology, the ambivalent relationship with its revisionist precursors, and the failure of the existing critical discourse to note any of these problems. Waid and Ross depict a possible future in which Superman and his colleagues from the Justice League of America must come out of retirement to police their unruly successors, whose aimless and excessive violence threatens to destroy the world. This explicit call for the restoration of traditional superhero morality has led scholars to characterize the series as a direct response to *Watchmen* and *The Dark Knight Returns* (Klock 94–97; Coogan 226), yet Waid and Ross are deeply indebted to these texts and to the revisionist style more generally. *Kingdom Come* denounces its revisionist forebears while crowning itself as their heir, not unlike the wild young heroes it condemns.

The plot echoes the revisionist comics at every turn. The series opens with the heroes of the Justice League in self-imposed exile, much as they are in *The Dark Knight Returns*, and Batman feuds with Superman and forms an underground alliance with Green Arrow, just as he does in Miller's series. The references to *Watchmen* are even more explicit. The story begins in earnest when a nuclear blast is triggered by a team of superheroes composed primarily of Charlton characters, including Captain Atom, Nightshade, Thunderbolt, and the Peacemaker (1.27), all of whom served as templates for the heroes in *Watchmen*. (Their leader, Magog, is designed to resemble Rob Liefeld's Cable, a confusion of influences that makes it impossible to distinguish between the moral critique of *Watchmen* and the amoral Marvel- and Image-style antiheroes.) Superman learns of the disaster by viewing a tower of television screens reminiscent of the "cathode mosaic" of televisions that displays the aftermath of the explosion Ozymandias engineered in Manhattan (Moore and Gibbons 11.1, 12.19). If these allusions weren't clear enough, Ross visually cites Hollis Mason's autobiography and the "Who watches the watchmen?" graffiti in the first issue (1.7) and wheels Rorschach himself onstage for a highly out-of-continuity cameo in the second issue (2.26, 2.29).

These citations serve to establish the future of *Kingdom Come* as the world of the revisionists and their inheritors, and to position revisionism as an object of critique. Even as they castigate the revisionist superheroes for their violence, however, Waid and Ross never quite depart from the revisionist model. In its broadest strokes, the plot of *Kingdom Come* isn't so different from Alan Moore's unused proposal for "Twilight of the Superheroes," a crossover that would have pitted the DC Comics heroes against one another in a near-future dystopia. That proposal is filled with the worst excesses of the revisionists: in the most vivid and memorable plot twist, the Martian Manhunter poses as a dominatrix so he can murder Billy Batson, Captain Marvel's youthful alter ego, in the midst of a sexual liaison gone horribly wrong (Moore, "Twilight"). Waid and Ross pull back from Moore's most cynical reinterpretations, yet they still portray the superheroes as flawed and fallible beings locked in pointless conflict. The older heroes are not exempt from this criticism; *Kingdom Come* depicts them as fascists who impose their will without any legal authority and gods who have lost all connection to humanity. But this too is a quintessential revisionist plot, in which superheroes set themselves above humanity as rulers or dictators (Coogan 216). The series culminates in yet another nuclear explosion that wipes out the vast majority of the world's superhumans, recalling similar cataclysms in the finales of *The Dark Knight Returns* and *Watchmen* (Klock 96). As the prospects of a nuclear holocaust were somewhat less imminent in 1996 than they had been a decade earlier, *Kingdom Come* seems to be replaying the fears of its predecessors rather than animating new ones.

This debt extends to the comic's paratextual markers as well. In a transparent bid for thematic depth and literary respectability, the first three issues each end with a black page that contains only a quote from the book of Revelation, echoing the black panels that closed each chapter of *Watchmen* with quotes ranging from the book of Genesis to Elvis Costello. Within the text, Waid's narration mimics Alan Moore's penchant for summing up his characters in pithy metaphors, if not his facility with them; Waid's description of the Flash as a hero who "lives between the ticks of a second" (1.31) is at once too close and not nearly close enough to Moore's more tangible description of "a man who moves so fast that his life is an endless gallery of statues" (Moore, Bissette, and Totleben 24.1). Both attempt to capture the awe and wonder that a normal human might feel in the presence of the superheroes, a hallmark of the reconstructive comics (Coogan 198) yet also, as Moore's line illustrates, a key ingredient of the revisionist style. Ross's painted art similarly follows in the footsteps of high-profile revisionist projects like Bill Sienkiewicz's *Elektra: Assassin* (1986–1987) or Dave McKean's *Arkham Asylum* (1989). Ross's style, invested in the heroic figure to the point that it flirts with fascist aesthetics, looks nothing like Sienkiewicz's and McKean's expressionistic collages, but in all three cases the use of paints rather than pencils, inks, and flat colors advertises the projects as serious comics aimed at adult audiences. So, too, does *Kingdom Come*'s publication in DC's Prestige Format, a line of comics printed on glossy paper with square bindings and heavy cardstock covers. This was the format of *The Dark Knight Returns*, Alan Moore and Brian Bolland's *The Killing Joke* (1988), and other revisionist comics before it came to be used for any high-priced superhero comic. The script, art, paper, cover, and binding all position *Kingdom Come* as an adult comic in the revisionist mold, another reminder of the unrecognized continuity between these movements.

Published at a moment of transition between revisionism and reconstruction, *Kingdom Come* also exhibits all the hallmarks of the nostalgic style that would emerge in its wake. Early in the series, viewpoint character Norman McCay visits Planet Krypton, a Planet Hollywood–style theme restaurant built around DC's superheroes and filled with relics from every period of the company's history (1.8–9). A model of the original Batplane from the 1940s hangs from the ceiling, a case displays the Batman costume worn by Adam West in the 1960s, and a waiter is dressed as the Carrie Kelley Robin from *The Dark Knight Returns* (plate 3). Never mind that these objects couldn't possibly coexist in a world where Batman and his first Robin, Dick Grayson, are still alive and fighting crime sometime after 1996; Planet Krypton is a pastiche without any organizing historical principle, the very definition of Jameson's complacent eclecticism. Nor is the rest of *Kingdom Come* any different. Faced with the prospect of designing a small army of new heroes for the retirees to discipline, Waid and Ross have opted to base many of them on old DC characters rather than the Image-style heroes that inspired the book's critique. This decision leads to ludicrous juxtapositions such as a grim and gritty, gun-toting version of Mr. Terrific, the Golden Age hero who fought crime with the words "FAIR PLAY" splayed across his abdomen. In isolation, this redesign provides a succinct and parodic illustration of the decline of the heroes from their Golden Age ideals; repeated a few dozen times over the course of the series, it shows an inability to imagine the type of heroes or the type of comics the book wants to censure. *Kingdom Come* is instead littered with Easter eggs, in-jokes, and *Mad* magazine–style "chicken fat" depicting obscure characters from DC's past. When the visual references reach beyond comics, they rarely venture farther than classic rock albums, *Star Wars* characters, and other totems of Ross's childhood and adolescence. Coogan may claim that the series represents a rebirth for the genre (230), but like so many of its reconstructive peers, *Kingdom Come* spends most of its time looking backward.

The traditionalism isn't limited to the comic's self-conscious allusions or its preferred moral code; its nostalgia and its investment in the logic of decline also reinforce some of the genre's less palatable traditions. Because Waid and Ross stock Superman's team with the original members of the Justice League and Justice Society, characters who were created in the decades before the comics industry took its first tentative steps toward greater diversity, Superman's group consists almost entirely of white heroes. Even after they begin enlisting younger allies, Waid and Ross depict only a single black recruit, Victor Stone, a.k.a. Cyborg—although as Victor is never named at any point in the series and his body now consists entirely of golden metal, any readers without access to Jess Nevins's comprehensive annotations may have difficulty discerning his identity, let alone his race (Nevins, "*Kingdom Come*" note to issue 2 cover). Androids, bird-men, and alien visitors from the future have better representation on Superman's Justice League than most real-world racial and ethnic groups do. Considerably more diversity can be found among the Justice League's violent replacements in the next generation of superhumans. Many of these characters simply adopt the aliases of minor white superheroes from the 1940s such as Johnny Thunder or the Star-Spangled Kid; those with new designs bear ethnically marked names such as "Tokyo Rose," "Kabuki Kommando," "Kongo," "Kabrini" (a green giant, after Cabrini-Green, the notorious Chicago housing projects), "Shiva the Destroyer," and "Buddha" (Nevins, "*Kingdom Come*"). The visual representations are equally stereotyped—notably Kabrini, a hulking brute with cornrows and massively swollen lips (plate 4). A handful of black and Asian heroes (all based on older white characters) join Batman's more principled group of covert agents, but the new, racially caricatured vigilantes remain unrepentant to the end. There is no evidence to indicate that Waid or Ross intended this racial subtext, but intentions hardly matter when the finished product is so clear: sorting its characters by race as well as by virtue, *Kingdom Come* is the story of a group of angry white senior citizens who battle and imprison their young, multicultural, and generally unworthy inheritors. The comic makes explicit what was latent in *Judgment Day*, implying that the diversification of the superhero genre has gone hand in hand with its decline. *Kingdom Come* is perhaps the most stark example of how the traditionalism and nostalgia of reconstructive comics can shade into a deeply reactionary politics.

More than twenty years after its release, *Kingdom Come* no longer stands at the vanguard of superhero comics. One of the current trends in the genre is the introduction of new and diverse young heroes such as Kamala Khan (Ms. Marvel) and Miles Morales (Spider-Man), not as antagonists but as noble heirs to proud heroic legacies. (Some of the comics featuring these characters, such as Marvel's *Champions* or the aggressively overbranded *All-New All-Different Avengers*, are written by Mark Waid, and the latter sports covers by Alex Ross.) But the underlying narrative logic of the reconstructive comics remains largely intact as superhero publishers continue to revisit their own history, explore their shared continuity, and multiply every available franchise into profusions of derivative titles and characters. Similarly, postmodernism's claims to contemporaneity have been contested as the rise of new production and distribution technologies has prompted calls for the development of new critical terminologies. As Simon Reynolds notes, artists and cultural theorists have proposed any number of names for postmodernism's successor—digimodernism, altermodernism, superhybridity, postproduction (412–417)—yet these terms don't suggest a break from postmodernism so much as an intensification of its practices, what Reynolds, quoting artist Seth Price, calls "a 'more and faster' version of postmodernism" (412). Judged by its cultural production and not the claims of its proponents, this accelerated phase of postmodernism doesn't offer a new era of postproductive plenitude, only the endless recirculation of the same genres and styles that were present at or just prior to its inception, exacerbated by hypertrophied versions of the same economic practices that produced them in the first place.

Comics studies, or any other facet of cultural studies, therefore needs scholarship that recognizes historicism, hybridity, and hyperconsciousness not as relics of a short-lived fad or monuments to a vanished age but as evidence of an ongoing transformation in the production of culture. A robust and contemporary criticism must be able to connect these cultural practices to the commercial structures that support them and the ideologies they promote in turn. Unfortunately, those discussions have been crowded out by the transcription of intertextual references and the construction of elaborate allegories that serve to insulate superhero comics from their own politics. These comics warrant renewed examination as material and ideological texts in their own right, not simply as metacommentaries on their genre. Without such examinations, superhero scholarship will remain trapped in an annotative and nostalgic mode, much like the comics it studies.

CHAPTER 3

PROPERTIES OF THE IMAGINATION

COPYRIGHT AND EMPIRE IN *THE LEAGUE OF EXTRAORDINARY GENTLEMEN*

If any comic should thrive under a discussion of intertextuality, nostalgia, and postmodern cultural memory, it's *The League of Extraordinary Gentlemen*. Written by Alan Moore and drawn by Kevin O'Neill, the series features a diverse cast of fictional characters—that is, characters who have already appeared in other works of fiction, such as Sherlock Holmes or Emma Peel—and places them in stories that range from the final years of Queen Victoria's reign to the first decade of the twenty-first century. As the first title published by Moore's America's Best Comics imprint, the series began as a contemporary of *Promethea* (1999–2005) and other self-consciously nostalgic superhero comics (Klock 98–100), though its frame of reference reached beyond the superhero genre to the classics of Victorian fantasy and science fiction. Most critical discussion of the series has gravitated toward its representations of these literary predecessors, with scholars typically arguing that Moore and O'Neill draw on the literature of the Victorians in order to criticize their values. In the later volumes, however, the focus changes to matters of creative ownership, artistic independence, and fiction's relationship to the societies that produce and consume it, a shift that is both accompanied and provoked by the narrative transition to more recent periods whose characters are still held under copyright. *The League of Extraordinary Gentlemen* therefore makes an ideal test case for more materially, institutionally, and ideologically engaged modes of comics reading; any consideration of the series as a whole must examine its ambivalent and conflicted representation of Victorian culture alongside its reliance on preexisting characters, its dependence on copyright law, and its self-conscious struggles for creative autonomy.

The early volumes published by America's Best Comics take both their casts and their subject matter primarily from Victorian popular fiction. Volume 1 (1999–2000) assembles a quintet of characters—Captain Nemo, the Invisible Man, Dr. Jekyll (a.k.a. Mr. Hyde), Allan Quatermain, and Mina Murray (formerly Mina Harker from Bram Stoker's *Dracula*)—and drops them into the middle of a war between the criminal masterminds Professor James Moriarty and Dr. Fu Manchu. Volume 2 (2002–2003) pits the League against the Martian invasion from H. G. Wells's *The War of the Worlds*, a conflict that ends with the team's dissolution. *The League of Extraordinary Gentlemen: Black Dossier* (2007), a graphic novel published as an interlude between volumes, jumps forward sixty years to show Allan and Mina (both rendered young and immortal as a result of their adventures) on the run in a 1950s Britain that is only beginning to recover from the totalitarian regime of George Orwell's *Nineteen Eighty-Four*; however, the contents of the titular Black Dossier, which are included in the comic that bears its name, detail the history of the League and its forebears. With its publication, Moore and O'Neill dramatically expanded their source material to encompass virtually any fiction, from any period, in any medium.

Black Dossier would be the last volume published by America's Best Comics. Moore had initially formed the imprint in partnership with WildStorm Productions, a comics company founded by Image Comics artist Jim Lee. Shortly before the imprint launched in 1999, WildStorm was purchased by Moore's former employers at DC Comics, whom he had refused to work with following a series of creative and contractual disputes in the late 1980s; Moore tolerated the arrangement until new arguments over the publication and adaptation of his work led him to separate himself from the company for good (Khoury 174–176, 199–205). While DC Comics owns the other ABC titles, Moore and O'Neill hold the copyright to *League* and have been free to take it to other publishers. *The League of Extraordinary Gentlemen Century* (2009–2012), also identified as *The League of Extraordinary Gentlemen*, volume 3, was published by Top Shelf Productions in the United States and by Knockabout Comics in the United Kingdom. A trilogy of comics, *Century: 1910* (2009), *Century: 1969* (2011), and *Century: 2009* (2012) follow the surviving members of the League—Mina, Allan, and Orlando (a transgender immortal loosely based on the main character of Virginia Woolf's *Orlando*, but with an even more vast history)—as they adjust to the twentieth century and to their own immortality. Moore and O'Neill then released another trilogy of books about Captain Nemo's daughter: *Nemo: Heart of Ice* (2013), *Nemo: The*

Roses of Berlin (2014), and *Nemo: River of Ghosts* (2015). The series now spans two decades and three publishers, with a fourth and final volume of *League* scheduled for release in 2018.

Despite their period setting and their omnivorous literary pastiche, the early volumes of *League* are constructed according to the syntax and conventions of superhero team books, with all the stock characters and plot devices that implies (Klock 100–102). Indeed, many critics can't resist the comparison, branding the team a Victorian Justice League (see Klock; Jones; Torner; Goldman; Halsall)—although given the outlaw status of most of the members, the Suicide Squad might be the more apt comparison. These similarities extend beyond generic formulas to include some of the legal constraints under which the series was produced: like most long-running superhero comics, *The League of Extraordinary Gentlemen* chronicles the adventures of characters created long ago by other writers. Unlike those series, it isn't produced under the work-for-hire conditions common to the major superhero publishers because it relies largely on characters who have passed into the public domain; paradoxically, the only ABC title Moore owns is the one in which he did not create the vast majority of the characters. Nevertheless, copyright law does place limits on which characters Moore and O'Neill can use and how they can use them, especially once the narrative advances into recent decades whose characters no longer fall under public domain. Copyright not only restricts the narrative possibilities of these volumes, it dictates one of their major themes as the League struggles to escape the authority of the law and Moore argues that art should not be bound by such materialistic concerns.

Most of the scholarship on *The League of Extraordinary Gentlemen* overlooks these copyright issues, however, focusing instead on the early volumes' representation of the Victorians and their ideology. Like the self-reflexive superhero comics discussed in the previous chapter, *League* has been read primarily as a literary-historical critique, albeit one whose concerns extend well beyond genre history. Novelist Michael Moorcock suggests that *League* "inhabits the world of late Victorian and Edwardian imperialism only to examine it, confront it, subvert it and so cast a cold eye on contemporary imperialism" (52). He wrote these words for a tribute volume published on the occasion of Moore's fiftieth birthday, where we might expect the generous praise to go unleavened by criticism, but Annalisa Di Liddo endorses his reading in her appraisal of Moore's work (*Alan Moore* 103–104). Di Liddo also praises the series for its treatment of gender, describing Mina Murray, the chief protagonist, as a prototype of the independent "New Woman" (108–110). Laura Hilton shares this assessment but adds that Moore's Mina is even more independent than Stoker's (199–204), while Alison Halsall suggests that the series inverts and parodies Victorian discourses of gender and empire (256). These scholars offer only fleeting acknowledgment, if any, of the sexual violence, racial stereotypes, and reactionary ideologies that pervade the series; when they do address these subjects, they regard them only as objects of Moore and O'Neill's critique. Certainly, the series appropriates some characters in order to criticize their ideology, yet it is just as likely to replicate the assumptions and values of their creators—or to do both at once. In fact, the later volumes are far more critical in their assessment of contemporary mass culture while they articulate a nostalgic and romanticized view of Victorian society.

While these might seem to be two separate issues—the narrative constraints enforced by copyright law and the comic's shifting and conflicted attitude toward the characters and cultures it represents—Moore's appropriation of older characters is directly tied to his reproduction of their ideologies. In his copious interviews and commentaries, as well as in the pages of *League* itself, Moore attempts to assert his artistic freedom, including freedom from any critical interpretations, while simultaneously defending his creative decisions by claiming that they are true to their sources and to their historical subjects. He contends that art should exist independently of legal authority and commercial exploitation while writing a book whose very premise is built on adapting other writers' characters within the parameters of copyright law; he argues for fiction's positive influence on readers and their societies while blaming those same societies for any controversial elements that appear in his own work. We cannot understand the ideology of the series without examining its struggles for legal ownership and creative control, for in *The League of Extraordinary Gentlemen* these issues are always intertwined.

WHAT KEEPS ART ALIVE

Copyright exerts less influence over the first two volumes than it does over their successors. With the exception of Sax Rohmer's Dr. Fu Manchu, who is never identified by name but is instead referred to as the "devil doctor," these early volumes largely feature characters who have passed into the public domain. As its stories have expanded into the twentieth and twenty-first centuries, however, *League* has begun to incorporate more characters who are still covered by copyright. Sometimes they are used for parodic purposes that fall under the provisions of fair use, as when P. G. Wodehouse's Jeeves and Wooster meet creatures from H. P. Lovecraft's Cthulhu mythos (*Black Dossier* 108–111).[1] More typically, Moore works around copyright by omitting or obscuring the names of these characters, as he did with Fu Manchu: in *Black Dossier*, James Bond is named only as "Jimmy," although he remains easily identifiable by his predilections for vodka martinis, pen-sized rocket launchers, and women with brazen double entendres for names. Emma Peel from the television series *The Avengers* also turns up, though she still uses her maiden name in 1958—and Moore has changed the spelling from "Emma Knight" to "Ema Night," one of many such fig-leaf protections that adorn the later volumes.

Sometimes these prohibitions become productive constraints, forcing Moore to evade copyright with methods that are more creative than if he enjoyed unfettered access to the original texts. *Century: 1910* appropriates Bertolt Brecht and Kurt Weill's *The Threepenny Opera* (1928), with characters bursting into song and addressing the reader directly in Brechtian distancing effects that dispel any pretenses to illusionistic realism. Most of the characters in *The Threepenny Opera* are in the public domain as they are themselves adapted from John Gay's *The Beggar's Opera* (1728), but the songs remain under copyright. Moore neatly sidesteps this restriction by rewriting the lyrics in his own words while largely preserving their rhythms. The meter remains the same, yet because comics are a silent medium the melody goes unheard (except in the heads of any readers familiar with these popular songs); the lyrics have been altered and should no longer require permissions or royalties. Moore performs the same trick with the Rolling Stones' "Sympathy for the Devil" in *Century: 1969* and follows it up for good measure with a rewrite of Percy Shelley's *Adonais* even though Shelley's 1821 poem requires no such evasions—but by that point the fictional simulacra have become so all-encompassing that every poem, song, or work of art receives its own pastiche, legally mandated or not.

These rewrites are no mere exercises in substitution. While Moore sometimes preserves the original meaning of Brecht's lyrics (his rewrite of "What Keeps Mankind Alive?" even includes verses rarely performed in English), he more often changes the songs to fit the demands of his narrative. *Century: 1910* reassigns "Pirate Jenny" to Suki Tawdry, changing the song from a first-person fantasy of revenge to an onlooker's dire prediction of impending doom, and alters "The Ballad of Mack the Knife" to imply MacHeath was Jack the Ripper.[2] Despite these alterations, however, the two subsequent chapters of *Century* and the Top Shelf Productions web page for *1910* are careful to credit Brecht and Weill for inspiring the lyrics and to thank their estates for granting permission to be inspired by them. Legitimizing the musical games in this manner takes some of the fun out of them, but Moore had little choice as Brecht and Weill's publisher, Warner/Chappell Music, objected to the unlicensed adaptations. Moore told *Mustard* magazine, "We did have a contretemps with the owners of Brecht and Weill's music [. . .] despite the fact that all the words are different and, y'know, you can't actually hear music in a comic" ("Alan Moore"). At least this explains why Mick Jagger and Keith Richards don't receive a similar acknowledgment in *Century: 1969*—their lawyers didn't send a threatening letter.

These struggles over copyright expand beyond mere technical challenges or legal obstacles to become one of the major themes of the series beginning with *Black Dossier*, which revolves around the ownership of the League and fiction more broadly. The plot sees the surviving members of the League, who fled Britain in the 1940s in advance of its takeover by Big Brother and his Ingsoc party, return to retrieve the eponymous Black Dossier that contains information on all of the League's incarnations and allies. Notes in the margins of the dossier, scrawled by the Ingsoc leadership, express disbelief in its contents and note that it "makes references to parties such as the Holmes brothers who have since been classified as unpersons" (17). This ominous comment recalls a conversation a few pages earlier:

> MINA: I mean, when we broke from British intelligence after the war, they must have assumed we were dead.
>
> ALLAN: Mm. Or that we'd never existed. "Unpersons." Wasn't that what the regime called people like us? People they'd revised out of history, like characters written out of a story. (14)

The metafictional joke, of course, is that Allan, Mina, and the Holmes brothers (Sherlock and Mycroft) never existed except as characters in a story. Moore's Big Brother hasn't simply written dissidents out of history, as Stalin airbrushed commissars out of photographs or Orwell's Ministry of Truth rewrote historical records. He has attempted to police the boundaries of the real and the fictional—or rather, between realistic fiction and fantastic fiction, since Big Brother is no more real than Sherlock Holmes. In this sense, unpersonhood is less a political classification than a generic and aesthetic one, as Big Brother and his followers consign any character more fantastic than themselves to unreality and deem their adventures "unbelievable rubbish" (17).

This purge serves as a fictitious restaging of the postwar ascendancy of realistic fiction and the concurrent devaluation of what has been termed "genre fiction." As novelist Michael Chabon observes in his introduction to an issue of *McSweeney's Quarterly Concern* collecting original genre fiction, prior to the postwar era respected literary magazines and anthologies published stories across a wide range of genres, including "the ghost story; the horror story; the detective story; the story of suspense, terror, fantasy, or the macabre" (7), and so on, before those genres were displaced by "the contemporary, quotidian, plotless, moment-of-truth revelatory story" (6) of realistic fiction. Moore himself offers a similar lamentation to Jess Nevins:

> But there are a lot of such jewels that lie ignored in our literary past because these things that I'm talking about are largely genre fiction, which is still by and large despised by the literary elite. [. . .] But the treasures amongst our lower classes of literary status that are in danger of completely slipping between our fingers, that are no longer available in print, that are more or less forgotten—these are the real, like I say, the endangered species of the literary world that I've got a particular fondness for. (Nevins, *Heroes* 236)

Moore describes canon formation as a kind of literary unpersoning, an erasure not by overt censorship but through the imposition of taste and the assignment of cultural capital. Against such hierarchies, *League* gleefully collapses the social distinctions between high and low culture just as surely as it ignores the authorial boundaries between the texts themselves (Thoss par. 2).

Expulsion from the canon is only one possible fate for Moore's fictions; another, more pernicious one is their commodification. *Black Dossier* presents a number of different cheap knockoffs of the League as a sly protest against their commercial exploitation. These include the Warralson team of 1946—a cynical and failed attempt to duplicate the original team from volumes 1 and 2—and a floating replica of Captain Nemo's *Nautilus*, a tourist attraction that O'Neill initially draws to resemble the submarine from the Walt Disney film *20,000 Leagues Under the Sea* and subsequent theme park ride (99) before modifying it into a crude parody of his own design for Nemo's craft in *Century: 1910*. Moore also slips in some wry digs at the critically reviled 2003 film adaptation of his own comic. When his characters visit a spaceport and marvel at the rockets in the X-L series (for "extra-large"), Mina quips that they would have to be American made: "Who else thinks 'extra' starts with an X?" (118). The joke nods to the Twentieth Century Fox media campaign for *The League of Extraordinary Gentlemen*, which did in fact abbreviate the film's title to "LXG." Moore is notoriously disdainful of most film adaptations of his comics, particularly that of *The League of Extraordinary Gentlemen*, which marked the beginning of his final separation from DC Comics and the film industry (Khoury 199–205). These derisive references to the replication and dilution of his work suggest that *Black Dossier* is in large part the story of his own comic's exploitation: the League's efforts to escape the control and scrutiny of MI5 parallel Moore's own attempts to remove *League* from corporate ownership and imitation.

That parallel is made abundantly clear when Prospero, Duke of Milan, protagonist of Shakespeare's *The Tempest* and the League's founder and benefactor, delivers his final soliloquy in the closing pages of *Black Dossier*. Speaking in iambic pentameter, Prospero extols the virtues of fiction, affirms its power to influence humanity, and asserts that it should be "Untarnished by all subterfuge or spies, unshackled from mundane authorities" (183). Prospero directs the League from his home in the Blazing World, Margaret Cavendish's utopian realm, which Moore turns into a refuge for fictional characters; as Prospero explains, "Here champions and lovers are made safe from bowdlerizer's quill, or fad, or fact" (183). It's only fitting that Prospero should disdain the work of Thomas Bowdler, the nineteenth-century publisher who sanitized Shakespeare's plays, but these lines apply just as well to Moore's own experiences with America's Best Comics. Although he had been promised that DC would not interfere with the America's Best line when they bought WildStorm, several of his stories were subject to editorial oversight and censorship. DC Comics president and publisher Paul Levitz refused to publish a Cobweb story that alluded to L. Ron Hubbard and the Church of Scientology (Khoury 204), and he pulped the entire first printing of *The League of Extraordinary Gentlemen*, volume 1, issue 5, because it included a vintage advertisement for a Marvel vaginal syringe (Khoury 176); evidently Levitz didn't want to offend his rival publishers at Marvel Comics. The interference only increased during the production of *Black Dossier* as DC insisted on art and story changes while reneging on their plans to publish an oversized hardcover with a seven-inch record single and other inserts (Khoury 203; Amacker, "Opening" pt. 1). Given the increasingly acrimonious relationship with DC, it's hard not to read Prospero's parting soliloquy as a comment on Moore's own imminent separation from his publisher.

The speech makes for a stirring resignation letter, but as a defense of the merits of fiction, it may prove too much. For Prospero, fiction offers more than simple inspiration or escape:

> And more, the very personality that scrys this epilogue was once unformed, assembled hastily from borrowed scraps, from traits admired in others, from ideals. Did fictional examples not prevail? Holmes' intellect? The might of Hercules? Our virtues, our intoxicating vice: while fashioning thyself, were these not clay? If we mere insubstantial fancies be, how more so thee, who from us substance stole? [. . .]
>
> On dream's foundation matter's mudyards rest. Two sketching hands, each one the other draws: the fantasies thou've fashioned fashion thee. (182–183)

Prospero and Moore envision a reciprocal relationship between fiction and reality, each one shaping the other—much as Moore scripts the words for that other, fictional magus, yet is also influenced by his rich literary history. While arguing for the power of the ideal, however, Moore ignores the full implications of these insights. Prospero makes the briefest acknowledgment that fictional characters may model vices as well as virtues (Holmes's arrogance? the rage of Hercules?), but doesn't recognize that fictions may also serve the interests of mundane authorities or repressive ideologies precisely because they are unshackled from facts; what's good for *The Tempest* is good for *The Turner Diaries*. In an interview with Kurt Amacker, Moore mentions that "the Nazi regime in the 1930s was inspired by Heinrich Himmler's bizarre Arthurian fantasies" ("Opening" pt. 2), but no such admission troubles Prospero's assertion that fictions "are life's secret soul. Its guiding lantern principle, its best" (183). Prospero praises a fiction that can shape the world but is never shaped by it, and never shapes us in ways that are not admirable. This is a curious omission in a comic that has already gone to great lengths to highlight Bulldog Drummond's reactionary politics and James Bond's misogyny. But those characters are not admitted into the Blazing World, which harbors only those fictions that Moore approves of—or whose troubling aspects he refuses to see.

1. *Robert Crumb, rejected cover for the* New Yorker *(2009).*

2. *Warren Ellis and John Cassaday,* Planetary issue 1 *(WildStorm Productions, 1999), p. 19.*

3. *Mark Waid and Alex Ross,* Kingdom Come *issue 1 (DC Comics, 1996), p. 9.*

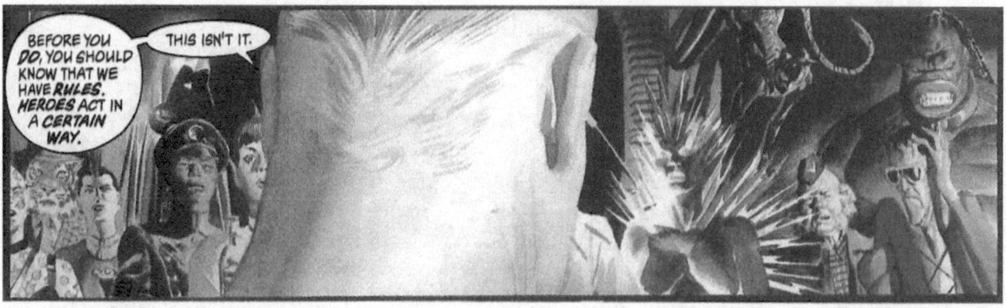

4. *Kabrini (far right). Mark Waid and Alex Ross,* Kingdom Come *issue 2 (DC Comics, 1996), p. 28.*

5. *Alan Moore and Kevin O'Neill,* The League of Extraordinary Gentlemen, *vol. 1, issue 1 (America's Best Comics, 1999), front cover.*

6. *Alan Moore and Kevin O'Neill,* The League of Extraordinary Gentlemen Century: 2009 *(Top Shelf Productions/Knockabout Comics, 2012), n.p.*

7. *Florence K. Upton and Bertha Upton,* The Adventures of Two Dutch Dolls and a Golliwogg *(1st US ed., DeWolfe, Fiske, 1897), p. 48.*

8. *Alan Moore and Kevin O'Neill,* The League of Extraordinary Gentlemen: Black Dossier *(America's Best Comics, 2007), p. 158.*

9. *Chris Ware, "Comics: A History,"* McSweeney's Quarterly Concern *issue 13 (2004), p. 11.*

The idea of an otherworldly repository for fiction is not a new one in Moore's work. "In Pictopia!" (1986) presents a city inhabited by every character from American comic strips and comic books; *Supreme* (1996–2000) introduces the Supremacy, which holds all the characters from Moore's fabricated history of the Supreme comics (in other words, pastiches of every period in Superman's history); and *Promethea* (1999–2005) features the Immateria, which contains every myth, symbol, and idea ever conceived by humanity. In the final issue of that series, Promethea declares that imagination guides us into the future (32.20) and inspires us through heroes of our own creation (32.3), just as Prospero asserts at the conclusion of *Black Dossier*. However, she also proclaims that "consciousness, modern theory maintains, is built on language" (32.13). Presumably that theory is poststructuralism, a set of discourses that inflects much of Moore's later work. He echoes the strongest poststructuralist formulations when, speaking through a narrative caption, he states, "The only reality we can ever truly know is that of our own perceptions, our own consciousness, while that consciousness, and thus our entire reality, is made of nothing but signs and symbols. Nothing but language" (32.13). Here Moore turns from the conventional (if hardly uncontested) idea that consciousness is shaped or even produced by language to the assertion that reality therefore consists entirely of language—the belief, as Promethea says later in the issue, that "We conjured all reality with intricate, snaking words" (32.27). Where poststructuralism begins with the claim that language does not and cannot enjoy an absolute relationship to its referents, Moore assumes its primacy over them. Willfully confusing material reality with the consciousness that perceives it and the language that frames it, Moore presents an idealist and idealized poststructuralism akin to the vulgar postmodernism of so many contemporary comics and their critics; both refuse to distinguish between fiction and reality.[3]

This philosophy forms a striking contrast with Moore's sentiments in *Lost Girls* (1991–2006), a serial he produced with underground comix artist (and his future wife) Melinda Gebbie. Cited by Moore as one of the inspirations for *The League of Extraordinary Gentlemen* (Khoury 209), *Lost Girls* begins with a similar conceit, gathering three characters from children's literature to form an intertextual liaison. The series diverges in its frankly pornographic ambitions, presenting a series of sexual encounters far more explicit than even the raunchiest passages in *League*, and in its justification for those ambitions. In chapter 22, Monsieur Rougeur—pornographer, hotelier, and pederast—argues that pornographies conjure an ideal realm of the imagination that lies beyond the reach or control of the world's authorities. These "enchanted parklands" (8) don't sound so different from Prospero's Blazing World, but for Rougeur, fiction is wholly insulated from reality. Where Prospero and Promethea credit stories with everything from the formation of our personalities to the inspiration of our technological advances, Rougeur insists that his tales of incest and pedophilia can't be monstrous because "they are fictions. They are uncontaminated by effect and consequence. Why, they are almost innocent" (5). Moore is happy to claim fiction's most beneficial effects, but he is all too willing to disavow its reprehensible ones. "Fiction and fact," Rougeur says, setting aside Moore's imaginative determinism, "only madmen and magistrates cannot discriminate between them" (4).

Rougeur issues this manifesto shortly after having sex with a thirteen-year-old girl. In other narratives this act might call his judgment into question, but in *Lost Girls* it serves merely to authenticate his ideas. Moore, of course, knows that Rougeur is fictional and that by his own logic he too must be "almost innocent"—which is to say Moore has set up the metafictional exposition as a tacit demonstration and enactment of Rougeur's views on the pornographic imagination. As *Lost Girls* generally shares those views, there is no reason to separate Rougeur's stance from Moore's; even those critics who are inclined to defend *Lost Girls* have noted the didacticism of Rougeur's speech (Laity 148) and identified him as an "alter ego" for his author (Di Liddo, *Alan Moore* 161). As a forger who is adept at mimicking other writers' styles and an impresario who opens his hotel as a space where pornographic fantasies can play out, Rougeur makes almost as good a spokesman for Moore as Prospero, the bearded magus who directs the League's adventures and sends in a deus ex machina or two when they need the help. Neither authorial stand-in takes any responsibility for fiction's worst consequences, but only in Rougeur's case is that evasion made explicit.

DECLINE OF THE WEST

If *Black Dossier* argues for fiction's freedom from political censorship, subsequent volumes are just as self-conscious in their portrayal of its exploitation by commercial interests. In the opening pages of *Nemo: Heart of Ice*, Janni Nemo, the daughter and successor of Captain Nemo created by Moore and O'Neill for *Century: 1910*, steals cargo that had been under the care of Charles

Foster Kane, prompting the obsessive newspaper magnate to hire a trio of former boy adventurers to capture her. This group consists of Frank Reade Jr., Jack Wright, and Tom Swift (renamed "Swyfte" for copyright reasons), and together they constitute yet another knock-off of the League, a specifically and satirically American version. This team is brought together not by the state but by an industrialist, formed not for national defense and public safety but for revenge and the recovery of private property.

Significantly, these characters were also created under practices familiar to any veteran of the American comic book industry: work for hire and imitation verging on plagiarism. Frank Reade Jr. was the star of 179 dime novels in the boy inventor or "Edisonade" genre; Luis Senarens wrote these novels for publisher Frank Tousey after Harold Cohen, the creator of Frank Reade Sr., refused to write under the Tousey house pseudonym "Noname" (Nevins, *Encyclopedia* 734). Senarens also created Jack Wright in a series of adventures that are essentially identical to his Frank Reade Jr. stories, making Wright a copy of a copy (Nevins, *Encyclopedia* 966). The newest and most lasting of the three, Tom Swift was created by Edward L. Stratemeyer, the book packager who published several long-running series (including Nancy Drew and the Hardy Boys) written by anonymous freelancers working under common pen names. Though not a direct copy of another character, Swift was a latecomer in the Edisonade genre and no more original than either Wright or Reade. Moore incorporates this history of imitation into *Heart of Ice* when Reade Jr. is forced to admit that his father's "Steam Man of the Prairies" copied the original design, just as the first Frank Reade Sr. story copied Edward S. Ellis's "The Huge Hunter, or the Steam Man of the Prairies" (Nevins, *Encyclopedia* 734); Reade also confesses that he and his colleagues were inspired by Nemo and Robur, just as Senarens and the other Edisonade writers were inspired by Jules Verne (*Encyclopedia* 279). Moore takes Reade, Wright, and Swift to task for their chauvinism, racism, and greed, but he also uses them to parody the culture industry that produced such derivative heroes without giving adequate credit or compensation to their creators.[4]

The nominal hero of *Heart of Ice*, however, is scarcely any better. Janni Nemo may be the creation of Moore and O'Neill, but she is in many ways a copy of her famous father, with only the gender difference to distinguish her from Frank Reade Jr. She journeys to Antarctica to retrace one of her father's expeditions (which Moore had previously outlined in "The New Traveller's Almanac," the text feature that ran in each issue of *League* vol. 2) with the intention of surpassing the elder Nemo's accomplishments—a task at which she fails utterly. Virtually a bystander in her own book, carted to safety by her last surviving crewman, Janni writes,

> My father lived in a far larger world than I. [. . .] We have a flaw, we striding figures of our age. Our warmth to others wanes beneath the pack-ice of our legends. [. . .] The giants who were contemporaries of my father are no more. Jean Robur went down at the Somme, leaving an infant son. Mors died, and Cavor too. Now only Reade and his insipid ilk stand at the twilight of the science-champions. (n.p.)

The "scientific romances" of Jules Verne and H. G. Wells have yielded to the derivative genre of the Edisonades, which were themselves on the wane in the early decades of the twentieth century. This passage derives much of its elegiac charge from Janni's recognition that she, too, is an epigone who cannot hope to match her father's deeds—merely the latest in a series of latecomers.[5]

This irony exposes a deeper contradiction between Moore's palpable disdain for the corporate exploitation of intellectual properties and the very premise of his series, which, as Andrew Hoberek observes, depends on the adaptation and reimagination of characters created by other authors (90–92). *Black Dossier* and its sequels are organized around this tension, pitting the franchised avatars of corporate ownership (art as commercial property) against representatives of the artist's participation in and revision of prior traditions (art as common property or ideaspace). If the timeless freedom of the Blazing World emblematizes the latter, Jackson Ayres suggests, then the unhappy immortals and undead magicians who haunt the pages of *Century* stand for the former, serving as figures for the perpetual afterlife of postmortem copyright (149–154). This reading could easily be extended to Ayesha, the immortal tyrant and primary antagonist of the *Nemo* trilogy, who prolongs her life through artificial means to pursue her vendetta against Janni. Without limiting his characters to their allegorical functions, Moore suggests that the deathless, endless duration of these intellectual properties is both unnatural and inhibitive to creative expression.

A different facet of this conflict manifests in the profusion of robot duplicates and other technological simulacra that Janni encounters in the *Nemo* sequels. In *The Roses of Berlin* she confronts the android Maria from Fritz Lang's *Metropolis*, while in *River of Ghosts* she and her crew battle legions of cloned despots and glassy-eyed Stepford wives who are being cranked out on assembly lines and shipped to the United States as consumer goods. The volume places these androids in opposition to the ostensibly more authentic copies of Janni's crew, which consists mostly of the descendants of famous mariners, pirates, and criminals from literature and film. Unlike the clones and robots, however, the Nemo lineages are produced through traditional methods of marriage and reproduction—highly traditional, in fact, as the text feature at the end of *Heart of Ice* describes Janni's arranged marriage of her twelve-year-old daughter to cement an alliance with the Robur family. In a trilogy that always privileges the institutions of biological reproduction (the cloned Boys from Brazil in *River of Ghosts* are slaughtered when they inadvertently trespass upon the spawning grounds of the Creatures from the Black Lagoon), the Nemo-Robur lineage serves as both a natural aristocracy in the manner of Warren Ellis's *Planetary* and a rebuke of the mechanically reproduced, undifferentiated, and rather shoddy products of the culture industry—especially the bikini-clad fembots of *River of Ghosts,* who enter the narrative primarily to be assembled and then brutally disassembled in various stages of undress.[6] Against such disposable imitations, Moore and O'Neill present their heroes as legitimate heirs with the most impeccable pedigrees.

This conflict between literary royalty and the chaff of potboilers and exploitation films also continues a theme begun in *Black Dossier* and elaborated at length in *Century*—namely, Moore's belief in the decline of popular culture and modern society more generally. His defense of genre fiction is limited to the fiction of previous generations, and he regards contemporary culture as "a fairly bleak and barren modern landscape" (Banerjee). Moore is never shy about writing these opinions into his scripts: at the beginning of *Black Dossier,* Quatermain, appalled at Bond's attempted rape of Mina, kicks him and muses, "God, is this what it's come to? The British adventure hero?" (8). While Moore has long expressed his distaste for James Bond, criticizing the secret agent's misogyny as far back as "The Mark of Batman," his disdain is by no means limited to one character. *Century: 1969* and *Century: 2009* build on *Black Dossier* in presenting contemporary culture as corrupting and degraded. *Century: 1969* finds one of the Vril-ya, an advanced species from Edward Bulwer-Lytton's 1871 novel *The Coming Race,* performing in a seedy Soho sex show. Characters native to the 1960s fare no better: a half-dressed Pippi Longstocking is shown coming out of a strip club, and the walls of a phone booth are lined with advertisements for call girls who bear the names of British girls' comics—*Bunty* and *Mandy* and so forth.

The more recent characters who populate *Century: 2009* don't even require this sort of recontextualization to be made crass and unpleasant. When Orlando returns to London after a long absence, she is greeted by the sight of *Viz* characters "Sid the Sexist" and "Roger Mellie, the Man on the Telly," who is accosting a man raising funds for "obese children in need" (n.p.). The networks air shows like *Celebrity Rape-an-Ape*, a satire of reality television from Armando Iannucci's *Time Trumpet*, and the streets are plastered with advertisements for fictional films and bands that satirize a derivative and shallow popular culture (Ayres 160). Another peripheral gag shows the stars of the ITV television series *Minder* (1979–1994) assaulting the star of the unpopular 2009 remake. Ryan Bibb, one of the contributors to Jess Nevins's online annotations, suggests, "Maybe he's taking a beating for being a poor copy of the original. This would fit the cynical tone of LOEG2009, berating modern culture for its laziness and lack of quality, making pale imitations of old classics" (Nevins, "Annotations to *League*," note to p. 12). This is an eminently plausible reading of *Century: 2009*, but a very odd charge coming from a book that stars reimagined versions of Orlando, Mina Murray, and Allan Quatermain, characters first published in 1928, 1897, and 1885. While *Century: 2009* should in theory be the volume least dependent on the past, the comic instead advertises Moore's disconnection from twenty-first-century culture.

That disconnect can be measured by the musical numbers, which grow more anachronistic and antiquated as *Century* progresses. *Century: 1910* relocates *The Threepenny Opera* (first performed in 1928, but set during Victoria's coronation in 1837) to coincide with the coronation of George V, the better to fit within Moore's timetable.[7] Though off by nearly two decades, the music is a suitable match for the extreme class polarization of early twentieth-century London. However, the Brecht references become increasingly out of place as they persist through the sequels. The musical sequences in *Century: 1969* focus largely on the Rolling Stones, but an epilogue set in 1977 rewrites Brecht and Weill's "Ballad of Immoral Earnings" as the punk song "Immoral Earnings (in the U.K.)," performed with snarling ferocity by "Zuki and the Tawdries." *Century: 2009* abandons even that period drag when Allan and Mina perform a straightforward rendition of the "No They Can't Song," the first song to be performed nondiegetically since *1910* and the only time the protagonists sing anywhere in *Century*. Moore also recasts the "Cannon Song" as the "Cannon Rap," though his faithful transposition of Brecht and Weill's rhythms lacks the distinctive flow or wordplay of rap lyrics. The rap

FIG. 3.1. *Alan Moore and Kevin O'Neill,* The League of Extraordinary Gentlemen Century: 2009 *(Top Shelf Productions/Knockabout Comics, 2012), n.p.*

is performed by "goth icon Spooky Tawdry," who sports a severe, fetishistic appearance that looks completely incongruous among the dapper, predominantly black audience gathered in the "Drum 'n' Bassment" (figure 3.1). The confusion of goth, rap, and drum and bass suggests Moore has no idea what distinguishes these genres or which of them were even contemporary in 2009; their lyrical marginalization in favor of more rewritten Brecht suggests he has little interest in finding out.

The art and design are similarly confused. The trade dress for *1910* sports a vaguely Art Nouveau font, and the paratextual materials include period advertisements (real and fake) alongside allusions to Walter Sickert and the Cubists. The cover of *1969* exchanges these fine art trappings for the garish colors and bulbous, almost liquid letters of a concert poster, but *2009* is wrapped in a generic comic book cover image of Mina and Orlando facing down an amorphous menace; the jagged lettering wouldn't look out of place on a 1950s horror comic, but it does nothing to capture the visual culture of the twenty-first century. The interior art is somewhat more contemporary, featuring O'Neill's caricatures of television and film characters alongside his illustrations of women with exposed bellies, young people with sagging pants, and other bêtes noires of every angry old man in the developed world. The paratexts include a faux Kickstarter page, a frontispiece illustration of Britannia as a leather and PVC–clad dominatrix, and a fake iPad screen on the inside front cover—but that screen is filled, by its own admission, with "obsolete engravings" from Victorian publications. If the point is that twenty-first-century culture consists largely of collages and remakes of earlier periods, then Moore and O'Neill have landed a blow—but, again, *League* is hardly in a position to criticize as it has long indulged in the very qualities it mocks.

Prior to the conclusion of *Century*, Moore told Subhajit Banerjee that one of the themes of the volume is "a marked sense that culture is possibly contracting in certain areas. [. . .] That the range of characters and ideas to draw upon have nowhere near the same breadth that they seem to back in the day" (Banerjee). He overlooks one obvious reason why the later chapters of *Century* have so few new characters to draw upon: copyright law places most of them out of reach for all but the most fleeting cameos or parodies. The few modern-day characters of any importance are either creations of Moore's friends, like Iain Sinclair's Andrew Norton, whom Moore uses with permission, or else characters so familiar Moore doesn't need to name them, like Emma Peel, now recast as the head of MI5 in the manner of Judi Dench's portrayal of M in the James Bond films. This latter category includes perhaps the most famous character to appear in *Century*: a young wizard, marked with a scar on his forehead, who has recently concluded his studies at a magical boarding school. Though he is never formally named, this young man obviously stands in for J. K. Rowling's Harry Potter, and Moore's decision to cast him as the ultimate antagonist of *Century*—namely, the Antichrist—marks his most scathing attack on contemporary mass culture.

Moore wastes no opportunity to voice his scorn for Rowling's novels, whether he's unpacking their artificial but reassuring use of 1940s imagery, tracing their conventions to any number of literary predecessors, or scoffing at their "sloppily-defined magical principles" (n.p.), a charge that perhaps carries more sting for readers who consider themselves practicing magicians, as Moore does. The characters who confront the Antichrist directly are even more blunt in their criticisms. His mentor and tormentor, Voldemort (also Aleister Crowley; it's complicated), castigates him for his banality, while the woman who finally stops his rampage simply calls him "a dreadful little boy" (n.p.). That woman is P. L. Travers's Mary Poppins, and she tells the franchised Antichrist that she is "concerned regarding [children's] wellbeing, and the healthy development of their imaginations. I am concerned regarding their behaviour . . . and I'm afraid, young man, that I don't care for you at all" (n.p.). In delivering Moore's final verdict on the Harry Potter books—not simply unimaginative, but unhealthy—Mary

Poppins echoes Moore's own pronouncements that the novels are evidence of a culture in decline (Ó Méalóid, "Interview: Alan Moore").

Moore attempts to connect these literary judgments to a larger cultural critique when he locates the Antichrist's boarding school in "England's mythic dreamtime" (n.p.), a symbolic landscape now scarred by mass destruction. The Antichrist has murdered all his teachers and fellow students; Orlando specifically compares the killing spree to the school shootings that have now become appallingly regular occurrences in the United States, and the devastation in the neighboring village to the ongoing war in Q'mar (Moore's stand-in for Iraq). Yet she can't decide whether these fictional murders reflect events in the real world or shape them: "If our magical landscape, our art and fairytales and fictions . . . if that goes bad, maybe the material world follows suit" (n.p.). Hoberek suggests that Orlando's indecision points to Moore's characteristic refusal "to distinguish between the aesthetic and 'material' worlds" (104). One of the cornerstones of his magical practice, this refusal has allowed Moore to oscillate between idealistic assertions of fiction's ability to shape the world and defensive renunciations of any responsibility for the same, as seen in *Black Dossier* and *Lost Girls*. In this case, however, Moore finally considers the counterpoint to his argument about the power of ideas, the negative influence that Prospero ignores and Monsieur Rougeur denies—but the Harry Potter novels are a strange place to argue for this particular influence. While readers such as Julia Turner detect the tropes of terrorism and the security state in the later volumes of the series, arguing that "Rowling culls the scariest elements of modern life and uses them as a kind of shorthand, a quick way to instill fear," this is clearly a case of life inspiring art and not the other way around. For that matter, Moore himself culls the scariest elements of modern life and reduces them to a kind of shorthand, though less to instill fear than to claim a certain gravitas: *Century: 2009* features scenes of war in the Middle East, police brutality on the streets of London, and the 7 July 2005 London suicide bombings, yet its apocalypse boils down to nothing more than the tantrum of an angry wizard boy. The greatest threat in the book arises not from nuclear-armed terrorists or endless wars, but from a children's lit character gone bad. Moore's argument about the consequences of violent and apocalyptic fictions is long overdue but oddly misplaced. Ignoring the many material and ideological forces that have contributed to the violence that haunts its pages, *Century: 2009* abandons its pretenses toward social realism and blames the modern world's ills squarely on its mass culture.

NOSTALGIA AND EMPIRE

With this jaded portrait of modern culture comes a reevaluation of the past—or rather, a rebalancing of the tensions that were always present in earlier volumes' depictions of the past. In *Century: 2009*, Mina says the poverty and inequality of the Great Recession remind her of the Victorian era, but she later draws this distinction between her time and our own: "People were desperately poor in 1910, but at least they felt things had a purpose. How did a culture fall apart in barely a hundred years?" (n.p.). This complaint admits any number of responses—questioning whether that sense of purpose was as universal or beneficent as Mina imagines, for example, or noting that Moore's blithe dismissal of the postwar era's tremendous advances in health, public safety, social welfare, and civil rights is itself a form of decadence born of luxury and historical amnesia.[8] The most telling answer, however, is the one Moore provides for Orlando: "By becoming irrelevant, same as always." Taken literally, this would contradict Orlando's suggestion less than ten pages earlier that art and culture continue to influence the material world, but her statement says less about contemporary culture's relevance (to whom, exactly?) than about her own sense of alienation and displacement within it. Moore may cloak his critiques in the language of economic injustice, but these anxieties are strictly cultural, if not personal, fueled by changing mores and advancing years.

Mina's lament forms an odd contrast with earlier installments of the series, which offered a far less rosy view of the past. *Century: 1910* depicts a London in which the poor, especially women, live under perpetual threat of rape and murder while the police and security services work only to protect the upper classes. MI5 rushes to execute MacHeath without a trial so he can take the fall for a murder committed by the Earl of Gurney; after the earl insists on taking credit for all the Ripper murders, Mycroft Holmes pardons MacHeath with scarcely a thought for the women he did kill. MacHeath then joins Suki Tawdry and a cast of dancing prostitutes in a spirited performance of "What Keeps Mankind Alive?" from *The Threepenny Opera*. The singers tell the League and other wealthy do-gooders to feed the poor before presuming to rid them of vice—"First let us eat, then preach morality"—and remind them that "mankind is kept alive by monstrous deeds" at every level of the class structure (n.p.). Their indictment of the middle and upper classes rings hollow, however, when it's preceded by Suki telling MacHeath, "I'm glad you weren't hung for your murdering, Mac. Us girls need protecting" (n.p.)—an odd claim, as we have already watched him murder two women and rob another at knifepoint (to say nothing of the women he killed as Jack the Ripper, the earl's false confessions notwithstanding). Following Brecht and Weill's template, the ending is supposed to be a gross injustice that highlights the greater injustices of capitalism, yet the abrupt recasting of MacHeath from murderer to protector—celebrated by the very women he has victimized—suggests Moore is less interested in depicting the lives and experiences of the poor than he is in using them to score a vague political point.[9] They are props to be wheeled onstage when he wishes to indict a culture and shunted aside when their suffering is incompatible with his arguments.

The first two volumes of *League* are no less critical of Victorian culture, and no less ambivalent in their criticisms. Moore and O'Neill don't shy away from depicting the era's racism, sexism, xenophobia, and imperialism, nor do they fail to note its curious mixture of prurience and propriety. The cover to the first issue of volume 1 mocks all of these attitudes with a parody of the *Illustrated Police News* (Nevins, *Heroes* 110–113) that offers titillating headlines such as "Opium—A Heathen Curse on Christendom" and "An Affront to Womanhood in Foreign Parts" (plate 5). These sentiments carry over into the story proper, where they are maintained with such consistency that it's difficult to determine when they cease to be objects of parody and simply become the story. Every event depicted on the cover is addressed in the first issue and is treated in the same sensationalistic terms: Allan is found languishing in a Cairo opium den, where Mina is nearly raped by two men drawn in the same hook-nosed ethnic caricatures O'Neill uses on the cover (1: 1.5–8). This assault is far from unique in the annals of *The League of Extraordinary Gentlemen*. In the first issue alone, we learn that Edward Hyde has been murdering prostitutes, and Mina is menaced a second time when she dresses as a demimondaine and offers herself up as bait (1: 1.19–24). The second issue follows this threat with a comedic excursion to Miss Rosa Coote's Correctional Academy for Wayward Gentlewomen, where Hawley Griffin (the Invisible Man) has been raping the students under the pretext that his attacks are visitations from the Holy Ghost (1: 2.12–19). The scene is played for laughs, with references to pornographic characters such as "Lord and Lady Pokingham"; the final joke is that Griffin's last victim is Eleanor H. Porter's boundlessly optimistic Pollyanna.

Moore is fully aware how modern readers will interpret these scenes. In a 1998 interview in *Tripwire*, he defends them as satire:

> I think that when you take the sex scene with Pollyanna that takes place in the second issue, you'll see that there is a lighthearted element to it. The scene where the Egyptians try to rape Mina is nasty but comical though. Rape is serious, the idea of rape is a horrible thing and there's no intention of trivialising it. However, one of the unspoken pillars of Victorian fiction was the notion of "the fate worse than death." Human sexuality, screwed up as it is, is a big part of Victorian fiction, as is the racism. When you see the Arabs in the first issue and when you see the Chinese in #3, I'm sure they'll be portrayed in the same way. This is what we wanted. We're not talking about real Arabs, real Chinamen, or even real women.
>
> I suppose people could accuse me of wallowing in those elements under the guise of postmodernism and they'd probably be right. I don't think that you get an unpleasant atmosphere after reading the stories. It's more British attitudes that are being pilloried rather than the targets of those attitudes. What makes it funny is the absurdity of the Victorian vision, this idea of a supremacist Britain that ruled the entire world. (qtd. in Nevins, *Heroes* 58)

I am inclined to agree with Moore: he is wallowing in those elements under the guise of postmodernism. Many parts of *League* are satirical, skewering the imperialism, xenophobia, and misogyny of the present as well as the past (Nevins, *Heroes* 229–230). Sometimes, however, the humor seems to be directed not at the people who hold these attitudes, but at those who are victimized by them. Certainly Moore doesn't appear to have parody on his mind in this later confession to Nevins:

> I thought it was funny having the Invisible Man having sex with the girls. I know technically it was rape. I still thought it was funny, just because—it's a funny idea, people floating in space with their legs wrapped around nothing, gasping in rapture. That was funny [. . .]. It's a good visual joke. (*Blazing World* 273)

Whatever Moore's stated intentions in the *Tripwire* interview, he does trivialize rape by treating it as a source of comedy and minimizing it as only "technically" rape. Satire requires some degree of critical distance from its subject, but no such distance is visible here.

While Moore and O'Neill criticize the Victorians for subordinating women and dehumanizing foreigners, *The League of Extraordinary Gentlemen* subordinates and dehumanizes nearly all of the women and foreigners who appear in its pages. Moore and O'Neill partially counter this trend through their portrayal of Mina Murray and Captain Nemo as the most principled and capable heroes in the series, but even these protagonists conform to the prevailing representations of their peers. Almost every woman seen in volume 1 is either a prostitute, a fetish object, or a victim of sexual assault, and Mina plays all these parts in turn. In fact, Moore's interpretation of *Dracula*—a sound one, to be sure—casts Mina in this final role before *League* even begins. "Ravished by a foreigner and all that," her supervising officer tells her. "Quite against your will, of course, but then people do talk so, don't they?" (1: 1.3). Sexual assault becomes Mina's foundational trauma, her origin story, and it will hound her through the rest of the narrative, from her near rape in Cairo in volume 1 (which serves primarily to jolt Quatermain out of his torpor by prompting him to rescue her) to Griffin's brutal attack in volume 2 (2: 3.16–17). Griffin doesn't rape her, but his assault is nevertheless "degrading and sexualised," an attempt at asserting his power over Mina (Hilton 202–203); Hyde recognizes this when he takes revenge on her behalf by raping and murdering Griffin. In *Black Dossier* James Bond attempts to rape Mina, though for once she subdues him without any male assistance (6–7). In *Century* she is molested by Tom Riddle (better known as Voldemort) before being committed to a hypersexualized asylum run by the descendants of Rosa Coote. For all that Di Liddo and Hilton describe Mina as an independent New Woman, for all that Moore himself regards her as "probably the strongest member of the group" (Nevins, *Heroes* 230), Mina cannot escape the endemic misogyny, exploitation, and rape.

Similarly, the Asian and Middle Eastern characters in volume 1 (with the exception of tea shop owner Quong Lee) are depicted as rapists who assault a white woman, a murderous Arab mob, and an army of Chinese criminals who serve Dr. Fu Manchu, the ultimate Yellow Peril villain. Nemo is certainly more individuated than the teeming hordes, but as an exotic foreign criminal in his own right he is no less terrifying to the English people. Moore and O'Neill follow Jules Verne's characterization of Nemo in *The Mysterious Island* as an Indian prince who rebels against British rule and hates imperialism in all its forms (Nevins, *Heroes* 35–38). Mina describes him as the nightmare of the British empire (1: 1.15); when he finally has an opportunity to attack English soldiers, he mows them down with such ferocity that Mina declares him more monstrous than Hyde (1: 6.14–15).

Neither protagonist disproves the stereotypes they ostensibly challenge, yet they remain the only female or Asian characters of any prominence until they are joined by Janni Nemo in *Century: 1910*. Initially renouncing her father's piratical ways, Janni travels to London, where she works at a seedy hotel under the name Jenny Diver. After the men of the hotel gang-rape her, she assumes command of the *Nautilus* and exacts her bloody vengeance while sacking the docklands and killing a great many innocent people in the process. Janni Nemo is both the victimized woman and the Asian menace; Moore provides almost no other alternatives for his characters.

These tensions persist into volume 2. Written after the September 11th attacks and the subsequent war in Afghanistan (Nevins, *Blazing World* 250–251), released as the United States and the United Kingdom mobilized for the invasion of Iraq, volume 2 presents the Martian invasion of *The War of the Worlds* as an imperialism in reverse, an imperialism come home to roost in the heart of empire. The metaphor of alien invasion proves just as adaptable to the war on terror and the invasion of Iraq as it did to the imperial ventures of Wells's time. After Mycroft Holmes makes a rather contrived reference to the Mahdi uprising in the Sudan, Quatermain helpfully explains, "the Mahdi revolt's a perfect example of England's complacency. We warred on a culture we didn't understand . . . and we were massacred" (2: 3.10). The obvious parallel to recent events delivers the anti-imperial critique that Moorcock and Di Liddo describe, but the comic also tells another story about imperialism. The first issue of volume 2 is set almost entirely on Mars, detailing the efforts of the native Martians to drive off Wells's invaders (who are foreign imperialists even on the red planet). Those efforts are led by a pair of Earthmen, Edwin L. Arnold's Gullivar Jones and Edgar Rice Burroughs's John Carter. Both men are American, but Jones's flowing robes and headdress resemble Arab clothing and Carter is first seen sitting in a tent, smoking a hookah (figure 3.2). Nevins notes that O'Neill draws Jones's allies, the Hithers, to resemble Ottomans (*Blazing World* 31), while O'Neill remarks that he darkened the Hithers to give them "a touch of Arabian fantasy" (*Blazing World* 35). O'Neill and Nevins both comment on the unmistakable comparison of Jones and Carter to T. E. Lawrence—all of them white men who travel to foreign lands and become recognized as military leaders (*Blazing World* 25). While volume 2 decries British and American imperialism, it opens with an Orientalist fantasy of white Anglo-Saxon leadership and strategic superiority. As with so much else in the series, Moore and O'Neill are deeply invested in the very attitudes they criticize in the Victorians.

FIG. 3.2. *Alan Moore and Kevin O'Neill,* The League of Extraordinary Gentlemen, *vol. 2, issue 1 (America's Best Comics, 2002), p. 6.*

The back cover to the first issue of volume 1 expresses that ambivalence in a fictitious quote that could serve as the motto for the first two volumes: "The British Empire has always encountered difficulty in distinguishing between its heroes and its monsters." The first incarnation of the League is a gathering of monsters and undesirables: an invisible rapist, a murderous brute, a foreign terrorist, a fallen woman. Even Allan Quatermain, the great colonial explorer and hero of the empire, is written by Moore as an opium addict. The team initially works for M, the director of British intelligence, who turns out to be Professor James Moriarty, archenemy of Sherlock Holmes and the Napoleon of crime. As Moriarty explains, Holmes "thought me an enemy of the state . . . never reasoning that it might suit the state to create its own enemy" (1: 5.7). Working through an intermediary, Moriarty dispatches the League to steal an antigravity device from Fu Manchu so the devil doctor can't use it to power an airship and subject England to aerial bombardment, a common fear in Victorian science fiction (Nevins, *Heroes* 60–61). Once he retrieves the device, however, Moriarty uses it to power his own airship and subject the East End district of Limehouse (home to many Chinese immigrants and Fu Manchu's power base) to his own aerial bombardment. Just as the head of the secret service and the kingpin of the criminal underworld are the same man, so is his plan identical to that of the fiendish Oriental menace. Moore suggests British society is maintained at the highest levels by criminals and sociopaths who are indistinguishable from the enemies they guard against. To echo a later volume, the empire is kept alive by monstrous deeds.

Successive volumes show a growing loss of faith in the formulas of heroic adventure fiction and in the possibility of heroism itself. Volume 1 may question the Victorians' taste in heroes, but the League achieves a conventionally heroic victory against two of the greatest criminal masterminds in fiction and saves London in the process. From this height they descend to a decisive but unwitting and morally objectionable role in the war against the Martians, to abandoning the field and decamping for the Blazing World in *Black Dossier*, and finally to outright failure in *Century*. The farther the narrative travels from the Victorian era, the less competent the League becomes—and yet, the more likely Moore is to exalt the Victorian heroes he once criticized. Volumes 1 and 2 continually stress Quatermain's addiction, infirmity, and general incompetence; Moriarty calls him "a third-rate adventurer playing out of his league" (1: 6.17). By the time of *Black Dossier*, however, a rejuvenated Allan Quatermain expresses his contempt for the modern version of the British adventure hero, James Bond, and other characters such as Tom Swift and Harry Potter fare no better in *Century* and *Heart of Ice*. The more modern and popular the heroes are, and the more they have become intellectual property franchises, the less Moore seems to like them—another manifestation of his belief in the decline of Western culture (Hoberek 90).

Moore's long-standing criticism of James Bond, well noted in discussions of *Black Dossier* (Nevins, *Impossible Territories* 36), is worth revisiting in its original context:

> As our political and social consciousness continues to evolve, Alan Quartermain [*sic*] stands revealed as just another white imperialist out to exploit the natives and we begin to see that the overriding factor in James Bond's psychological makeup is his utter hatred and contempt for women. [. . .] The fact remains that we have changed, along with our society, and that were such characters created today they would be subject to the most extreme suspicion and criticism. ("Mark of Batman" n.p.)

While Moore implements this reading of Bond in *Black Dossier,* he largely ignores his earlier appraisal of Quatermain (not to mention his spelling), presenting instead a hero who criticizes British imperialism. Jess Nevins supports this interpretation, arguing that Quatermain and his creator, H. Rider Haggard, were "progressive relative to their contemporaries," both expressing ambivalence toward imperialism; he concludes that Quatermain was "emphatically not the Great White Hunter stereotype" (*Encyclopedia* 720–721). Nevertheless, Nevins must concede that Haggard and Quatermain are racist and paternalistic by twenty-first-century standards (720), and other scholars more familiar with the breadth of Haggard's output don't even grant him that qualifier. Wendy R. Katz has thoroughly documented Haggard's investment in racist beliefs and stereotypes, including xenophobic and anti-Semitic views that Nevins ignores. To acknowledge that Haggard "probably knew more about and had more sympathy for African society than most of his contemporaries," to grant that he "was very much a man of his time and his class" (Katz 148), is not to confuse him for a cultural relativist or a critic of empire. Despite Nevins's claims to the contrary, scholars such as E. Mandiringana and T. J. Stapleton have noted Haggard's contributions to the development of the Great White Hunter image, which romanticizes imperialism and promotes white supremacy (218).

Moore largely ignores these ideological dimensions of Quatermain's character in *League,* criticizing him instead for personal failings that are Moore's own invention. In *Century: 2009,* however, Allan sheds his despondency long enough to die in heroic (if mostly ineffectual) combat against the Antichrist; with his last words, he insists that he really is the hero Mina read about in books as a child, not the homeless drug addict he has become. Moore and O'Neill conclude *Century* with a full-page image of Quatermain's burial site in Africa, surrounded by the graves of other white explorers and jungle lords from Sir Henry Curtis to Tarna the Jungle Boy (plate 6). The image serves as a belated elegy for a dead genre, laying all the imperial adventure heroes to rest; curiously, it's crowned by a cloud in the shape of a lion. While this could be an ironic reference to a similar scene from Disney's *The Lion King,* a last-second dig at another mass-cultural juggernaut, the apparition of the heraldic symbol of Britain over the skies of Africa also reads as a sincere and even affectionate tribute to the imperial heroes of old. This puzzling image demonstrates the comic's uncomfortable relation to imperialism: *The League of Extraordinary Gentlemen* condemns Britain's imperial adventures while breathing new life into its antiquated views of foreigners, and lays its heroes to rest without questioning their ideological foundations.

LOVE AND THEFT

This tension is most apparent in Moore and O'Neill's use of the Golliwogg. Created by Florence Kate Upton in her 1895 children's book *The Adventures of Two Dutch Dolls and a Golliwogg*, the Golliwogg was an animate rag doll whose coal-black skin, bright red lips, bulging white eyes, and unruly hair mark him as part of the blackface and minstrel traditions in American culture (N. Davis 9). Immensely popular in Britain, the Golliwogg was quickly copied by other writers, artists, and merchandisers, including the doll manufacturers who changed the name to "golliwog" in an effort to avoid copyright—unnecessarily, as Upton never copyrighted her character (N. Davis 100). The golliwogs' minstrel appearance and association with the racial slur "wog"—British slang for any person with dark skin, especially a foreigner—have long made them lightning rods for criticism, but the controversy didn't deter Moore and O'Neill from using the Golliwogg in *Black Dossier*, where he rescues Allan and Mina and transports them to the Blazing World. This inclusion prompted blogger Pam Noles to chart the history of the Golliwogg and the minstrel figure in British and American culture (Noles pts. 1–4); by using the Golliwogg without any critical frame or context, Noles argues, Moore and O'Neill root *Black Dossier* in a tradition of racist iconography.

Some interviewers have raised these objections with Moore and O'Neill, though they tend to do so in the most passive and noncommittal manner possible. Jess Nevins tells Moore, "As you might imagine, the appearance and use of the Golliwog has been somewhat controversial with American fans" before immediately jumping to his "pure fanboy question" about the Golliwogg's powers and piratical dialect (*Impossible Territories* 201). Pádraig Ó Méalóid addresses the issue more directly, asking Moore, "The golliwogg is generally seen these days as being a racist character. Why did you decide that you wanted to use a character with a problematic history like that in your work?" (Ó Méalóid, "Last Alan Moore"); Douglas Wolk simply asks O'Neill, "[W]hat was up with the Golliwog's appearance in there?" ("Douglas Wolk"). These aren't critical interrogations, but invitations for the creators to defend their choices. In so doing, however, Moore and O'Neill only compound the problem. Moore tells Nevins,

> Kevin had turned up some material concerning Florence M. Upton's original Golliwog. Now, it seemed to us on looking over this material that the Golliwog as a figure had been grossly misrepresented. It seemed to us that Florence M. Upton's use of the word "Golliwog" preceded the later British use of the term "wog," to mean somebody of foreign extraction. [. . .] However she derived the term, the character of the Golliwog in those early books was, at least as far as we could see, one of the first black role models that you could name as such to ever appear in Western fiction. At the time, there were—you'd have your Uncle Toms and your Nigger Jims and you might even have the odd Umslopogaas, but these were fairly menial and in retrospect, even if well-intentioned, were fairly demeaning roles for black characters. Whereas the Golliwog was traveling fearlessly all around the world in a balloon, he was his own master, he'd got this string of continually naked, for the most part, Dutch dolls accompanying him everywhere. [. . .]
>
> So what we thought we'd like to do is take this perhaps needlessly controversial figure, strip him of the minstrel clothes that he was later, and not in any of Florence M. Upton's narratives, but he was later dressed in, to take all of those elements away, to restore him to the original figure, to give him a bit more of an interesting hot air balloon. (Nevins, *Impossible Territories* 201–202)

Remarkably, Moore mangles almost every statement of fact in this account, from Florence Kate Upton's middle initial to Jim's name to the exaggerated claims of the Golliwogg's priority in Western fiction.[10] His attempt to pardon the Golliwogg on the grounds that the character preceded the racial slur misses the point that the Golliwogg and his imitators most likely *inspired* the racial slur. The most common etymologies of "wog" identify it as an abbreviation of "golliwog"; folk etymologies that claim the term is an acronym (for "Westernized Oriental gentleman," "working on government service," etc.) are not supported by any evidence. However, the *Oxford English Dictionary* (2nd ed., 1991) entries for "golliwog" and "wog" provide several examples of "golliwogg" and its variations being used to refer to foreigners, all of which postdate the Upton books and predate Frank C. Bowen's 1929 citation of "wog" as nautical slang in *Sea Slang: A Dictionary of the Old-Timers' Expressions and Epithets*.

Upton's character proves equally impossible to separate from the minstrel and blackface traditions that, as Eric Lott has shown in *Love and*

Theft: Blackface Minstrelsy and the American Working Class, were central to American culture in the nineteenth century and beyond. Moore may claim the Golliwogg's minstrel clothes didn't originate in Upton's work (Nevins, *Impossible Territories* 203), but Noles observes that minstrelsy was part of both the Golliwogg books and the larger cultural climate in which they were produced (pt. 2). Even Norma S. Davis, clearly an admirer of Upton's books, concedes that the Golliwogg's appearance "associates him undeniably with the minstrel shows so popular earlier in the nineteenth century" (9) and notes that the other black characters are usually racist stereotypes, from Sambo dolls to African cannibals (109). The minstrel elements are primarily rooted in Upton's blackface design of the Golliwogg, which Moore and O'Neill have left largely intact (plates 7, 8). Moore, O'Neill, and Davis are generally correct when they observe that the Golliwogg was not written as a stereotype—although Davis notes that his schemes often fail and that he depends on the other dolls for rescue and comfort (15), not quite the heroic adventurer Moore describes. But he was certainly drawn as a racial stereotype, and that image is the part Moore and O'Neill have altered the least. As a character in illustrated children's books (and now comics), the Golliwogg can no more be separated from his visual representations than can *The League of Extraordinary Gentlemen* itself.

This should not imply that the writing is free of racial stereotypes. Moore may insist that he and O'Neill "wanted to dispel any racist notions" (Nevins, *Impossible Territories* 203) attached to the character, yet they have added to them by writing the Golliwogg as a prodigiously endowed, oversexed lover. Moore continually refers to his sportive sexual relationship with his bevy of wooden dolls; in passages written in Dutch in *Black Dossier* but translated into English in Nevins's annotations, the dolls call their companion "proud champion of love" (162n164) and "admiral of pleasure" (168n180). When asked why they sail with him, one of them boasts, "His penis is enormous" (166n175). O'Neill claims this lascivious behavior is merely an extrapolation from a veiled sexual subtext in the Upton books, but his only evidence is the observation that Upton's rudimentary, sexless wooden dolls spent most of their time naked (Wolk, "Douglas Wolk"). Their interaction with the Golliwogg in *Black Dossier* has much more in common with Moore's predilection for writing highly sexualized interpretations of literary characters—including other children's book characters, as seen in *Lost Girls*—to say nothing of Western culture's fascination with black sexuality and its long history of hypersexualized representations of black men (Noles pt. 5). By adding this stereotype to Upton's minstrel design, Moore and O'Neill have managed the neat trick of making the Golliwogg even more racist.

When questioned on this subject, however, they have ignored or dismissed the racial implications of their portrayal of the Golliwogg, attempting to shift the discussion to issues of creative ownership and free expression. In a 2014 interview, Ó Méalóid asks Moore, "How do you respond to the contention that it is not the place of two white men to try to 'reclaim' a character like the golliwogg?" (Ó Méalóid, "Last Alan Moore")—a generous prompt that misstates the criticisms of readers such as Noles, who in fact compliments several white writers and artists for their critically informed use of blackface and minstrel imagery (pt. 3). In response, Moore first expresses uncertainty that he and O'Neill were attempting to reclaim the Golliwogg, in direct contradiction to his earlier statements to Nevins. He then suggests that any objections to this reclamation

> would appear to be predicated upon an assumption that no author or artist should presume to use characters who are of a different race to themselves. Since I can think of no obvious reason why this principle should only relate to the issue of race—and specifically to black people and white people—then I assume it must be extended to characters of different ethnicities, genders, sexualities, religions, political persuasions and, possibly most uncomfortably of all for many people considering these issues, social classes. (Ó Méalóid, "Last Alan Moore")

Moore expands Ó Méalóid's misleading summary of the criticisms into even more outlandish assumptions of his own invention. He attempts to shift the grounds of debate from the particulars of his use of the Golliwogg to abstract principles of artistic representation—in this case, so abstract as to be irrelevant to the actual criticisms of *Black Dossier*. He also continues to insist that Upton's Golliwogg didn't contain any racial stereotypes or imagery, describing him as a "strong, likeable and positive figure" who was "black-identified if only by virtue of his skin colour." Moore maintains that the Golliwogg was "a heroic, romantic and fantastical being" who was never meant to represent black men, yet nevertheless continues to compare him favorably to Uncle Tom and "Nigger Jim." Moore claims that the Golliwogg is both a positive black character and not at all black; any racism is attributed solely to "the later Minstrel-attired racist-slur toy" (Ó Méalóid, "Last Alan Moore").

O'Neill also tries to separate Upton's Golliwogg from those of her imitators, associating racist imagery exclusively with the latter. He describes these imitations as an opportunistic exploitation of Upton's creative labor, telling Wolk, "I was talking to Alan and I said, 'This is very interesting: She never trademarked the Golliwogg, so as soon as the character became popular, people just changed the spelling a bit and ripped her off.' So all the Golliwogs that my sisters had when I was a kid, the whole industry of Golliwogs comes from her just not protecting her rights" (Wolk, "Douglas Wolk"). O'Neill casts Upton as a kindred spirit, another artist exploited by a culture industry that appropriated and profited from her character under the flimsiest legal pretexts. But he and Moore have also appropriated the Golliwogg, changed the spelling a bit (Moore calls him the "Galley-wag"), and added racial stereotypes and markers that are not original to Upton's work.[11] Even if it were possible to separate Upton's racial imagery from that of the later golliwogs, Moore and O'Neill's interpretation still has much in common with the other, overtly racist copies that earn their disdain. As Eric Berlatsky observes with regard to the sex scenes in *Black Dossier*, postmodern pastiche often faces the problem of reproducing the very ideologies it claims to parody. He detects the same problem in Moore and O'Neill's treatment of race, noting that in the absence of any critical commentary on Upton's character, the presence of the Golliwogg does more to maintain those racist caricatures than it does to oppose them ("Lone Woolf").

The reactionary politics and imagery in *The League of Extraordinary Gentlemen* are hardly limited to the Golliwogg: they also include the conflicted and occasionally nostalgic portrayal of imperialist heroes like Allan Quatermain, the figuration of recent history as a tragic fall from the vigorous culture and common purpose of the Victorians, and the meticulously refurbished fantasies involving victimized women and rapacious foreigners. The comic's reliance on characters who predate copyright has led to its replication of ideologies that predate civil rights, not to mention feminism, anticolonialism, and other equality movements of the twentieth and twenty-first centuries. While Moore and O'Neill sometimes present these characters and ideologies as subjects for critique, they are just as likely to indulge in them—or to abandon the criticism entirely, as they do in their depiction of the Golliwogg, and deny there are any grounds for controversy. In either case, Moore is quick to attribute any objectionable material to his faithful restoration of older literary sources, displacing all artistic responsibility onto them. While insisting fiction should be free from legal oversight and control, he attempts to remove his own work from critical scrutiny.

These attempts have been supported by some of his most prominent critics. Writing an afterword for Todd A. Comer and Joseph Michael Sommers's *Sexual Ideology in the Works of Alan Moore,* Annalisa Di Liddo responds not to the anthology's copious praise of Moore's handling of that subject but to the scant criticism that infiltrates its pages. After nodding toward the arguments of Orion Ussner Kidder and the few other contributors who offer oppositional readings of Moore's handling of gender, sexuality, and race, Di Liddo counters, "These controversial representations, though, are made all the more complex by the fact that they can be interpreted as criticism of the very social, historical, and cultural canons they appear to be based on" ("Afterword" 202). In other words, Di Liddo reassures us, whenever Moore appears to indulge in racist, heteronormative, or misogynistic representations, we can interpret those representations as critiques of racism or heteronormativity or misogyny—though she offers no reasons why we should do so or why we should discount her fellow contributors' judicious criticisms. In her only counterexample, Di Liddo suggests that the extended, brutal rape scenes in Moore's *Neonomicon* (2010) serve "to challenge common patterns of representation," as if rape scenes were not already a common pattern of representation in Moore's work, and she claims their interminable duration functions as a critique of the reader's voyeurism (203). Apparently there is no critique left for their author. Di Liddo insists that nothing is arbitrary in Moore's work, but she mistakes his cultivation of controversial subject matter for a moral condemnation that, in this case, remains purely notional.

Moore scholars have been equally willing to pardon these elements in *The League of Extraordinary Gentlemen,* when they have acknowledged their presence at all. Di Liddo doesn't mention the comic's frequent depiction of sexual violence except in a vague and indirect reference to Griffin's crimes (*Alan Moore* 107). Lloyd Isaac Vayo chooses to focus on Fanny Hill's more consensual escapades in *Black Dossier,* though he nevertheless manages to overlook the many intimations of bestiality, pedophilia, and other scenarios in which consent is impossible. Laura Hilton cites Mina's constant sexual jeopardy (including her near rape in Cairo) only as evidence of her "active and apparently fearless approach" and her willingness to go into the field (202), presenting the sexual assaults as proof of her competence and independence. Jackson Ayres subsumes these assaults wholly within Moore's themes of corporate ownership and creative autonomy, drawing a facile analogy between the purported "statutory violence" of copyright law (152) and the sexual violence that recurs throughout *League* (157). And while Jason B. Jones recognizes the scope of that violence, he justifies its omnipresence by approaching it, like Di Liddo, as part of Moore's critique of Victorian culture (115), not as an element ripe for critique in Moore's own comics.

Jones at least registers some of the contradictions and complications of the series, arguing (like Sean Carney) that they display Moore's heterogeneous model of history. For Jones, *League* illustrates "the complex relationship between fantasy, material conditions, and historical change" (101), retreating into idealistic celebrations of the power of the imagination but also providing more material critiques of history's capacity to reveal or occlude structures of violence (120–122). Where Jones sees a supple and sophisticated historiography, however, Hoberek detects an inability to distinguish between the aesthetic and the material—an inability that allows Moore to negotiate the contradictions between his criticisms of the corporate exploitation of intellectual properties and his advocacy for an intellectual commons in which autonomous creators are free to adapt and reinterpret their predecessors (Hoberek 103–104). While Moore draws a sharp distinction between artists who wish to work within this commons and corporations that seek to profit from it, his penchant for associating creative exploitation solely with corporate ownership or other impersonal institutions relieves those autonomous creators of their own artistic and ethical accountability.

From its unreflective racial caricatures to its rampant sexual violence, *The League of Extraordinary Gentlemen* serves as a reminder that cutting characters loose from their material ownership doesn't guarantee they won't be exploited—or that such exploitations won't extend to the cultures they depict and the audiences they hail. Voyages to the Blazing World notwithstanding, the characters in *The League of Extraordinary Gentlemen* don't inhabit a purely aesthetic realm of unconstrained imagination, but emerge from and exert influence on a world of material power relations in ways that Moore only recognizes intermittently. To truly understand the series, scholars must examine those extratextual relations as avidly as we pursue the network of intertextual references that serve as its building blocks. Otherwise, we are liable to repeat the oversights of a series that relies as much on Moore and O'Neill's studied neglect of the contexts and consequences of their fictional adaptations as it does on the adaptations themselves.

CHAPTER 4

THE LIMITS OF REALISM

ALTERNATIVE COMICS AND THE WORKSHOP AESTHETIC

The thirteenth issue of *McSweeney's Quarterly Concern*, published in the summer of 2004, captures the precise moment that comics took over the world. The dust jacket, an elaborately structured comic written and drawn by guest editor Chris Ware, chronicles the tribulations of a lonely cartoonist who, under pressure to meet a looming deadline, decides his comic strip "doesn't need a punchline at all! I mean . . . life doesn't have a punchline, right? Maybe I should just stop, let it end where it is . . ." ("God"). Thanks to a timely divine intervention, the cartoonist follows through on his idea and soon readers are praising the strip for its lifelike rhythms and realistic lack of resolution. "Who woulda thought," the cartoonist muses, "that in less than one week comic strips would supplant painting, sculpture, and movies as the world's dominant artform?" In short order, the cartoonist is living in palatial surroundings, followed by an adoring public, and hounded by mobs of female admirers, all because he has introduced realism into his strip, now inventively titled *Life of the Seated Cartoonist* (figure 4.1).

While Ware presents these developments with considerable irony (the seated cartoonist, dissatisfied with his overnight success, ponders painting still-life watercolors until he remembers that nonsequential art no longer holds any value in this parallel aesthetic universe), they are closely matched to the project of the anthology they envelop. By dedicating an issue of the innovative literary quarterly to comics, Ware and *McSweeney's* founder Dave Eggers advance the idea that comics are "increasingly recognized as the cutting edge of visual and literary culture"—perhaps not quite the world's dominant art form, but closing in fast (Worden 892). While the comics assembled within *McSweeney's* issue 13 display a variety of styles,

FIG. 4.1. *Chris Ware, "God,"* McSweeney's Quarterly Concern *issue 13 (2004), dust jacket.*

from sardonic humor to grotesque horror, the majority of the contributing artists strive for some form of realism, ranging from documentary journalism to psychological character study to confessional self-revelation. A later volume edited by Ware, *The Best American Comics 2007*, is even more heavily weighted toward autobiography and realistic fiction; a similar aesthetic governs many of Ware's own comics, such as *Building Stories* (2012), which self-consciously patterns itself after the observational and confessional culture of the contemporary writing workshop. Ware may jokingly exaggerate the cultural impact of realistic comics on his dust jacket, but his comics and anthologies—especially the introductory essays that outline his selection criteria and his vision for comics—promote realism to the exclusion of other modes of comics writing.

In so doing, they also sustain some of the hierarchies of literary and artistic value that have long marginalized comics. Thierry Groensteen tabulates the assumptions that have delegitimized comics, including fears of the seductive power of the image and a mistrust of comics' hybrid nature, which violates Western culture's long-standing separation of words and pictures (35–37). But artists such as Ware are more likely to celebrate comics for these formal attributes; to the extent that they share the culture's traditional suspicion of comics, it's because that culture has historically associated them with fantasy, escapism, and childhood reading (Groensteen 38–41). These sentiments, which equate realism with quality and artistic maturity, are echoed by many comics scholars, as when Hillary Chute asserts that nonfiction comics are "the strongest genre in the field" while simultaneously writing the commercial comics publishers and genres out of her brief history of American comics ("Comics" 452, 455). Such arguments demonstrate the overlap between populist and elitist critical approaches, both of which make excessive and exceptionalist claims for the genres they study, but they also illustrate their divergences—for only the latter seek to separate their chosen genres from the historical medium of comics. In this respect, they merely follow the precedents established by some of the comics artists whom they exalt. While Ware embraces the formal possibilities of comics, his fastidious avoidance of popular genres and his privileging of conventionally literary modes of writing perpetuate traditional and arbitrary divisions between high and low culture even as he seeks to position comics between the two. Ware is a key participant in the construction of comics' increasing cultural legitimacy, yet his comics and anthologies consistently reinforce many of the same assumptions and values—favoring the literary, the textual, the realistic—that denied comics such legitimacy in the first place.

REALISM AND ILLUSION

Ware's realist aesthetic can be traced to his roots in the alternative comics movement of the 1980s and 1990s. This movement, as described by Charles Hatfield in *Alternative Comics: An Emerging Literature*, was itself inspired by the underground comix of the 1960s and 1970s and was nourished by the direct market of comic book specialty stores that emerged in the late 1970s (6–31); unlike either the undergrounds or the superhero comics favored by the direct market, however, alternative comics renounced familiar genres in favor of formal experimentation, graphic and generic diversity, and the belief that comics could pursue the highest literary and artistic ambitions (ix–x). Noting that autobiography has been central to those ambitions, Hatfield traces its influence in comics to the work of Harvey Pekar, a pioneer in the development of "the quotidian autobiographical series, focused on the events and textures of everyday existence" (109). In *Comic Books as History*, Joseph Witek observes that this emphasis on the quotidian distinguishes Pekar's comics from their predecessors in the undergrounds and suggests that Pekar's style "is closer to the realists of prose literature than to anything that has appeared in comic books before" (128, 132).

Witek's claim that Mark Twain, Stephen Crane, Frank Norris, and other "masters of American realism" constitute "the wellsprings of [Pekar's] homegrown aesthetic" should indicate the extent to which comics artists and critics alike have framed the realism of the alternative comics movement in literary rather than visual terms (132). Indeed, Witek acknowledges that the artwork in Pekar's comics is often crude, unsophisticated, not "conventionally 'realistic'"—with the stylistic descriptor placed in quotes, as if to signal that the comic's realism lies in areas other than visual convention (126). This description highlights a tension within realism itself, between its ability to re-create the semblance of reality and its interest in exposing other truths that lie beyond mere appearance. In *Picture Theory: Essays on Verbal and Visual Representation*, W. J. T. Mitchell identifies this tension as a contrast between illusionism, the "simulation of the presence of objects, spaces, and actions," and realism, the "capacity of pictures to show the truth about things" and to offer "a transparent window onto reality, an embodiment of a socially authorized and credible 'eyewitness' perspective" (325). Mitchell's use of "realism" muddies the distinction, however, as both "illusionism" and "realism" are important elements of the realist style in literature and the visual arts. Art historian Linda Nochlin defines this style through its ambitions "to give a truthful, objective and impartial representation of the real world, based on meticulous observation of contemporary life" (13). Nochlin distinguishes between realism's traditions of faithful simulation and honest observation, characterizing them as, respectively, verisimilitude and objectivity, sincerity, or authenticity (19–21, 31–40). For many creators and critics of alternative comics, however, authenticity of observation takes precedence over verisimilitude in graphic representation—and, perhaps because comics are a visual medium, they tend to associate illusionism exclusively with visual representation, preferring to evaluate and praise their works' realism in predominantly narrative and literary terms.

Ware, one of the foremost figures to emerge from the alternative comics movement, recapitulates this aesthetic in his anthologies, most notably in the introduction to *Best American Comics 2007*. Although he exalts comics for their capacity for mimetic representation, which he contrasts against the rise of conceptualism in twentieth-century visual art, Ware generally favors narrative authenticity over visual verisimilitude. He says the qualities he looks for in art and literature ultimately boil down to "telling the truth"; he defends the "preponderance of autobiographical work" in contemporary comics as "a necessity [. . .] both for the artists and the medium" if they are to learn "how to express real human emotion"; he argues that autobiographical self-expression "is a necessary step towards understanding what communicates and works in a medium"; and he claims the contributors to his volume have all developed individual styles "with the aim of getting at something new or, more precisely, real" (xvii–xviii, xxi). To accommodate the experimental, decidedly nonillusionistic work of Gary Panter, C. F. (Christopher Forgues), and the Paper Rad collective, Ware suggests that these artists allow for "very strange yet oddly real associations and feelings" (xxi).

With a sufficiently flexible definition, the realist label can be made to fit any artist, and Ware inevitably bestows it as a term of high praise. However, these shifting applications mask a series of uncritical and misleading elisions: *Best American Comics 2007* conflates mimetic representation with quotidian realism, quotidian realism with autobiography, and both modes of writing with "telling the truth." Yet for all its claims to objectivity, realism does not and cannot offer a transparent window onto reality (Nochlin 14–15). Autobiography poses a particular challenge in this regard; while it may appear to provide the most honest and authentic representations, in practice it can also prove the most deceptive. As Hatfield cautions, autobiographies depend on the fictive as well as the factual, a paradox that comics can only exacerbate through the graphic presence of the cartoonist's self-image: "what passes for frankness in comics must be a matter of both subjective vision and graphic artifice, a shotgun wedding of the untrustworthy and the unreal" (*Alternative Comics* 118). Hatfield cites comics by Daniel Clowes, Robert Crumb, Gilbert Hernandez, and Harvey Pekar that subvert, exploit, or ridicule this inevitable slippage between truth and artifice, and Ware's own "Corrigenda" to his semiautobiographical *Jimmy Corrigan: The Smartest Kid on Earth* (2000) acknowledges, in his typically self-deprecating fashion, "the chasm which gapes between the ridiculous, artless, dumbfoundedly meaningless coincidence of 'real' life and my weak fiction—not to mention my inability at knitting them together" (n.p.). Yet his anthologies equate autobiography, honesty, and realism without question.

Ware instead reserves his skepticism for visual verisimilitude and illusionism. In his introduction to *McSweeney's* issue 13, he claims that "the more detailed and refined a cartoon, the less it seems to 'work,' and the more resistant to reading it becomes" (11). He elaborates on this judgment in comments to Daniel Raeburn: "Fundamentally you're better off using ideograms rather than realistic drawings, [. . .] There's a vulgarity to showing something as you really see it and experience it. It sets up an odd wall that blocks the reader's empathy" (Raeburn 18). Ware is hardly the only comics artist to make such claims; Scott McCloud argues that simplified, iconic images increase reader empathy and identification in chapter 2 of *Understanding Comics*, and Art Spiegelman describes *Maus* in similar terms to Joshua Brown (104).[1] While these comments reveal much about the artists' creative processes, Ware extrapolates his preference for simplified ideograms into a general renunciation of illusionistic art. Raeburn makes this renunciation explicit with his own gloss on Ware's comments, adding, "Realism is fine for telling tales about jut-jawed good guys in tights who sock dastards, but it is too explicit for anything emotional. It bullies the readers and their emotions, turning sentiment into sentimentality. Just as the old saw holds that in writing fiction you should show, not tell, in comics to show too much is to 'tell' too much" (19).

Although Raeburn eschews "realism" as a whole, he only targets realism in comics art, contrasting it with the literary variety; writers of fiction are supposed to favor dramatization and detail over exposition and didacticism, but comics artists must avoid overburdening their images lest the images themselves become didactic. Acting as Ware's interlocutor, Raeburn claims that realistic drawing and writing are antithetical, associating realistic pictures exclusively with the superhero adventures he and Ware decry. Ironically, some superhero boosters make the same association, though with approval rather than scorn; in *The Silver Age of Comic Book Art*, Arlen Schumer reserves his highest praise for the naturalistic figure drawing of Neal Adams and his imitators.[2] Whether laudatory or dismissive, such arguments tend to overlook the idealized and exaggerated anatomies, outré settings, and heroic subjects that would more than disqualify such comics from realism in the visual arts (Hatfield, review 352). The realism Raeburn derides is the illusionistic tradition of Neal Adams and Alex Ross, not the social observation of Alison Bechdel or Joe Sacco. While these traditions may be separated by their emphasis on different components of realism, the determining factor for Raeburn seems to be their occupation of different genres—superheroes versus autobiography, realistic fiction, and reportage—that aspire to different levels of authenticity and command radically different kinds of cultural capital.

Ware, too, misses no opportunity to distance the selections in his anthologies from superheroes and other genres traditionally associated with comics. This is a standard rhetorical strategy of the alternative comics scene, which has long defined itself against the fantasy, action, humor, and superhero genres that dominated the North American comics market at the time of that scene's emergence in the early 1980s. While subsequent generations of artists such as Michel Fiffe and Josh Bayer have demonstrated more interest in and affection for commercial comics, the early alternative scene derived "its raison d'être, its core readership, and its problematic, marginal, and self-marginalizing identity" from its rejection of the corporate mainstream (Hatfield, *Alternative Comics* 111). Witek incorporates this oppositional stance into his arguments in *Comic Books as History*, with many of his claims for the value of nonfiction comics predicated on their evident departure from "brightly colored breakneck fight scenes between cosmos-spanning power figures with the fate of the universe at stake"; his hyperbolic description re-creates many alternative comics artists' derision for the fantasies they reject (127). Although Ware once incorporated superhero characters into his own comics, including "Thrilling Adventure Stories" and *The ACME Novelty Library*, he inevitably did so with ambivalence, irony, or anxiety (see Brogan; Singsen), and it's no surprise that his anthologies can't disavow them often enough. *McSweeney's* issue 13 holds the commercial genres at arm's length both in Ware's comics contributions (one of the strips on his dust jacket is called "Adolescent Power Fantasy Man"; others poke fun at formulaic newspaper gag strips) and in his introduction, where he swears off any responsibility for those fellow contributors who refuse to follow suit: "none of the 'words-only' authors invited to contribute were asked to write about superheroes and their childhoods, though nearly all of them did" (12).

Ware faces no such embarrassments in *Best American Comics 2007*, which excludes superhero comics not simply for their generic features but also for their most common mode of production. Ware claims, "The traditional, commercially established mode of 'scripting' a story and then simply illustrating it does not admit to the endemic potential in comics to literally imagine and see on the page, to say nothing of plumbing areas of imagination and memory that, I think, would otherwise be left inaccessible to words or single pictures alone" (xix). Understandably, he privileges comics created by a single writer-artist, another key element of the alternative ethos that values comics as avenues for self-expression by a lone creator (Hatfield, *Alternative Comics* 16, 18). Ware goes far beyond this prioritization, however, when he implies that language, single images, and even comics created through the collaborative division of labor are all somehow less able to access their creators' imagination and memory. If Ware applied this principle across all genres of comics, then presumably he would have to conclude that the work of superhero writer-artists such as Todd McFarlane and Rob Liefeld possesses more of comics' "endemic potential" than that of Harvey Pekar, who never illustrated his own scripts and always collaborated with an artist—but these vexing exceptions don't intrude upon Ware's aesthetic. He extends the commercial division of labor to extreme lengths, separating these comics into their component words and pictures as a means of denying them the same capacity for expression, meaning, and depth, if not excluding them from full consideration as comics.

THE FINE ART OF RESENTMENT

Having dismissed the commercial genres, Ware also separates his chosen milieu from the world of fine arts. This time, however, the separation is not entirely voluntary. His *McSweeney's* introduction describes the humiliating judgments of his instructors at the School of the Art Institute of Chicago, who couldn't understand or accept his decision to create comics; in the comic-strip history of comics that runs parallel to his prose introduction, and acts at times as a visual commentary on it, the same page shows a Benday-dotting Roy Lichtenstein type who boasts that he uses comics "as a symbol for the spiritual poverty of American culture" (11). By the time of his *Best American Comics 2007* introduction, however, Ware seems almost grateful for this rejection, treating it as a fortunate fall that exempted comics from the abstractionist and conceptualist bent of twentieth-century art. In Ware's telling, modernism and its successors "all but stomped out the idea of storytelling in pictures," with comics the lone holdout; he even goes so far as to imply that the anti-comics crusade of the 1950s was some kind of retribution for daring to tell lurid stories in an age of abstraction (xix–xx). He regards comics as a locus, if not a haven, for mimetic and narrative art "during a period that art historical naysayers and doomsdayers sometimes label as suffering a 'crisis of representation'" (xxii). If the academy has rejected comics, it's the academy's loss.

Katherine Roeder has noted Ware's profound ambivalence about an art world that alienated him long before it welcomed his work. She chooses to frame that ambivalence in terms of his "advocacy for a greater awareness of comics" (65), though that advocacy takes a curiously double-edged form in anthologies such as the *McSweeney's* issue. The same history of comics that characterizes pop artists as condescending parasites also depicts the comics themselves as puerile mass entertainment (or, in the case of "Trippy," Ware's parody underground comic, puerile niche entertainment) good for little more than marketing or plagiarism; the Lichtenstein figure's appropriation of their iconography is only the latest instance in a history of theft (plate 9). In works such as the *McSweeney's* introduction or "Our History of Art"—a comic that originated as *The Whitney Prevaricator*, a poster Ware produced to commemorate and mock his participation in the Whitney Museum of American Art's 2002 Biennial—his advocacy is built around a performative denigration of the very form he promotes. The performance has become routine enough that Roeder, in discussing "Our History of Art," must concede that he reinforces the culturally prescribed (i.e., delegitimated) roles of comics even as he criticizes the art world for prescribing them (70).

Bart Beaty diagnoses Ware's dual antipathies to the worlds of art and comics as a textbook case of *ressentiment*, the tendency to blame external forces or authority figures for one's perceived inferiority. In *Comics versus Art*, Beaty describes this reaction as a typical one among cartoonists who feel marginalized by the art world; tellingly, most of his examples (Peter Bagge, Daniel Clowes, and Ware himself) became leading figures in the alternative comics scene of the late 1980s and early 1990s, about a decade before the art and literary establishments began to recognize and legitimate comics (51–55). As Beaty notes, however, Ware would seem to be the comics artist with the least cause to feel inferiority or resentment, and he tallies the many book awards, museum exhibitions, and prestigious fellowships Ware has won (214). Ware's comics, sketchbooks, and introductions nevertheless position him as an alienated and marginalized figure, performing his exile from an art world that has repeatedly validated him (215–216). This is not a paradox of Ware's success, Beaty argues, but rather its mechanism: Ware has ascended so rapidly not despite his performance of weakness and abjection, but because of it. By reasserting its worst assumptions about comics with undeniable narrative and artistic command, he notes, Ware "reaffirms the supremacy of the art world relative to comics by maintaining and reinforcing existing prejudices" in a display of *ressentiment* and self-loathing that only "makes him all the more acceptable by the art world that he claims to disdain" (222).

Ware's portrayal of comics is not always shaped by resentment, and the earlier *McSweeney's* introduction in particular draws some subtle distinctions between painting and comics art. After he argues that excessive visual detail hampers our ability to read comics, Ware suggests that the true art of comics resides in "the tactility of an experience told in pictures outside the boundaries of words, and the *rhythm* of how these drawings 'feel' when read"; he further claims that the comics artist's style is "expressed in how their characters move, how time is sculpted" (11, his emphasis). Although he relies on figurative, analogic descriptions borrowed from music and the plastic arts, his emphasis on rhythm, motion, and time suggests that, much like Scott McCloud, Ware believes the art of comics inheres in its ability to represent time through the juxtaposition and arrangement of images. This complicates his *Best American Comics* dichotomy of referentiality and conceptualism, indicating that comics are different not simply for representing the world mimetically but for representing it through multiple images that combine to form a unified narrative. In positioning alternative comics between popular culture and the fine arts, Ware has also raised, however indirectly, the intriguing possibility that comics could occupy a middle space between representation and abstraction—or a space that lies outside this binary entirely, neither beholden to referentiality nor bound to reject it.

Unfortunately, *Best American Comics 2007* devotes more energy to situating alternative comics between the popular and the elite and condemning both, a maneuver strikingly reminiscent of that made by the postwar middlebrow critics of mass culture, as described by Leslie Fiedler in "The Middle Against Both Ends." In that essay—prompted, as it happens, by the anti-comics crusaders of the 1950s—Fiedler notes that these critics were as suspicious of modernist literature as they were of the comics, leading him to conclude,

> The middlebrow reacts with equal fury to an art that baffles his understanding and to one which refuses to aspire to his level. The first reminds him that he has not yet, after all, *arrived* (and, indeed, may

> never make it); the second suggests to him a condition to which he might easily relapse, [. . .] even suggests what his state may appear like to those a notch above. (428, his emphasis)

The middlebrow critics aren't a perfect match for Ware: modernist and postmodernist art can hardly be said to baffle his understanding, and he doesn't reject "the intolerable notion of a hierarchy of taste, a hierarchy of values," as Fiedler maintains the anti-comics crusaders did (428). Quite the opposite, his anthologies reinforce the same hierarchies and stereotypes that denied comics any cultural capital in the past and caused Ware so much grief at art school.

In *McSweeney's*, Ware laments that "the associations of childhood and puerility are still hard to shake" for many cartoonists—but he blames the art form itself for creating these associations, since "the accumulated world-dump of comics is piled high with nonsense" (11). Both his dust-jacket strips and his introductory history of comics portray comics as a crass, despised, ephemeral, hopelessly commercialized medium; even God himself proclaims that cartoonists "sure got shafted" ("God" n.p.). Daniel Worden observes how this sense of shame at comics' vulgar history permeates the anthology, providing a common aesthetic for the contributors and defining the book's audience (893–894). It is also so common to Ware's own work that, in his preface, Ware's friend Ira Glass quips that "comic book artists often seem to think of themselves as marginal figures. I'm sure somewhere in this issue of *McSweeney's* Chris Ware is bemoaning how no one pays attention to comics, how they're not taken seriously, how they're seen as children's art" (7). One page later, Ware is doing just that. His issue of *McSweeney's* presents comics as an abject, shameful art form even as he castigates the art world for viewing it the same way.

Best American Comics 2007 is even more equivocal in its simultaneous defense and defensive belittlement of comics. Ware justifies the preponderance of autobiography in alternative comics (and in his anthology) by announcing that comics have entered their late adolescence as an art form and declaring autobiography "the most facile and immediate way" for novice artists to learn to write emotions (xviii). Some context might help illuminate these curiously backhanded arguments: Ware is defending autobiographical comics against a perceived slight in a *New York Times* review by John Hodgman, who writes, "For all the admirable effort to allow comics to tell different types of stories, there is also a creeping sameness to many of these comics: black-and-white, semi- or wholly autobiographical sketches of drifting daily life and its quiet epiphanies," and adds that "sometimes the epiphanies are so quiet as to be inaudible" (18).[3] Hodgman's criticisms, although delivered with considerable sympathy, suggest that some alternative comics have settled into a monotony that contravenes their own ethos; a movement that prides itself on generic diversity has reached the point where, according to Hatfield, "the appearance of bracing 'honesty' runs the risk of hardening into a self-serving, repetitive shtick" (*Alternative Comics* 114).

Perhaps the worst sting, however, is landed when Hodgman, after summarizing one particularly inert story by Jonathan Bennett (reprinted in *Best American Comics 2007*), yawns, "This is when I tend to reach for the pile of superhero comics" (18). Hodgman, tongue firmly in cheek, refuses to respect the hierarchies of taste maintained in Ware's introductions and in the world of North American alternative comics in general; the fact that these comics don't feature superheroes is no longer sufficient reason for Hodgman to ignore his feeling that many (though by no means all) of these alternative comics are "kind of boring" (18). Ware's response is not to refute the charge but to reassert the hierarchy. He reanimates the dismissals of his art school years with his claims that comics have entered their late adolescence—perhaps a marginal improvement over childhood, which Ware associates with superhero and humor comics—and that they have focused on autobiography out of convenience and a lack of any better ability to express emotion. If these defenses seem patronizing, even counterproductive, at least the hierarchy of taste they maintain places Ware's alternative comics in the middle: Hodgman's superhero comics are sent back to the bottom of the pile.

TABLES OF DISCONTENT

Ware's anthologies reinforce this hierarchy of genres through their selection and categorization of comics artists. Both volumes skew heavily toward various forms of literary realism or life writing: quotidian fiction, autobiography, diary comics, dream journals. These genres account for roughly half of the comics in *McSweeney's* issue 13, contributing to the anthology's "remarkably homogenous" thematic range (Worden 892). The trend is even more pronounced in *Best American Comics 2007*; with the absence of historical comics artists like Rodolphe Töpffer, George Herriman, or Charles Schulz (all featured in *McSweeney's*), nearly two-thirds of the artists work within some form of realism, and autobiographies alone account for more than a third of the collection. Ware draws even more attention to this narrow range by grouping his selections together by genre and style, exacerbating the impression that his collections are governed by only a few modes of writing.

Nowhere is Ware's tendency to promote autobiographical comics—and to pigeonhole alternative comics artists in a handful of genres—more apparent than in his handling of women artists. Of the thirty-two comics artists included in *Best American Comics 2007*, nine are women. (One, underground comix artist Aline Kominsky-Crumb, only appears in collaboration with her husband, Robert Crumb; their piece is followed by a page from their daughter, Sophie Crumb.) *McSweeney's* issue 13 is even less inclusive, with women accounting for only three out of thirty-seven artists. In 2005, when the *Masters of American Comics* exhibition sought to establish a canon of fifteen male comics artists (including Ware), Carly Berwick, paraphrasing Linda Nochlin, asked, "[W]hy have there been no great women comic-book artists?" To forestall such complaints about his *Best American Comics* volume, Ware wraps up the introduction with a preemptive and rather prickly defense of his selection process, stating, "I am not of the cut of the cloth to check an artist's genitalia at the door" and dismissing "those who still feel compelled to tally points for one or another chromosome" (xxiii)—typical reversals that seek to shift the blame onto anyone who wants to address issues of gender exclusion, based on the old fallacy that acknowledging difference is itself a form of discrimination. He adds, "Nor in the case of this book did I go out in search of a couple of hermaphrodites to even out the score," further trivializing any objections (xxiii). Ware confronts charges of exclusion more directly when he says he chose to include "work that I found to be the most interesting, honest, and revealing to be published in the past year, and that collection, as it turned out, included comics from the pens of both sexes" (xxiii). The detached posture and passive language ("as it turned out") imply that Ware was truly gender-blind in his selections, and pleasantly surprised with the equitable result.[4]

A look at the contents of *Best American Comics 2007* tells another story. Of the nine women Ware includes, eight are grouped together consecutively in the autobiography section, even though Lynda Barry's strip *Ernie Pook's Comeek* is not autobiographical. The ninth woman, Miriam Katin, also works in autobiography but is wedged between two other Jewish comics artists, Sammy Harkham and Ben Katchor, in a different but equally claustrophobic category. Ware's selections barely acknowledge that women create comics in other genres. Series editor Anne Elizabeth Moore appends a supplementary list of one hundred notable comics published during the eligibility period that includes history, biography, fantasy, fiction, and experimental comics by women such as Andrice Arp, Megan Kelso, Linda Medley, Danica Novgorodoff, and Becca Taylor, among several others, yet none of them made the cut in a collection that nevertheless has room for four David Heatley comics, three Ivan Brunetti pages, and the entire Crumb family. While the small number of women may reflect the relative paucity of female creators in North American comics at the time, this stark segregation by gender and genre is Ware's handiwork—most likely a consequence of his disproportionate emphasis on autobiography, which was then the genre of comics with the most prominent and prevalent work by women. Ware's ostensibly gender-blind selection process only perpetuates this ghettoization. The partitioning need not be malicious or deliberate, merely the most extreme example of a foreshortened vision of comics that focuses on "honest and revealing" work above all else—and naïvely equates those characteristics with their most obvious forms of expression in autobiography and quotidian realism.

Ware offers a different explanation of his aesthetic preferences in *Best American Comics 2007*. Contrasting the recent boom in comics with the rising popularity of prose fiction in the nineteenth century, he contends that in the past, "as geography, communication, and society became more tight-knit, individual perceptions and expression began to standardize" (xxi). Ware summarizes a complex but widely accepted argument, offered by Stephen Kern and David Harvey, among others, that the technological and social innovations of the second Industrial Revolution instituted universalized, ever-shrinking scales of time and space, providing the world, for the first time, with a common frame of reference.[5] He then makes his boldest claim when he asserts that this process of universalization "is more or less exactly the inverse of what's been happening in comics for the last few years [. . .] even a casual flip-through of the pages of this book will demonstrate a highly individual approach by each and every artist" (xxi), positioning alternative comics as running counter to modernity itself. Ware's thesis is admirable for its ambition, its scope, and its neat encapsulation of the changes wrought by modernity, but it also prompts a few immediate objections. First, modernity isn't solely the homogenizing force that Ware describes; Kern and Harvey observe that the same period in the late nineteenth and early twentieth centuries that saw the attempted regularization of time and space also produced modernism's highly personalized, idiosyncratic, fragmented modes of perception and artistic representation. Second, and more important to understanding Ware's aesthetic criteria, his claim that "each and every artist" in his anthology has a "highly individual approach" is belied by the comparatively narrow range of genres and art styles he has selected for inclusion. Although plenty of exceptions exist, too many of the *Best American Comics 2007* contributors present diaries, autobiographies, or quotidian realistic fiction, or draw in the same loose, deliberately unpolished DIY aesthetic, for Ware's claim of universal individuality to be more than hyperbole.[6] The majority of his contributors work within a set of generic and stylistic conventions that are as well defined as the commercial narrative techniques he rejects.

Ware may nevertheless be onto something when he locates his contributors within an aesthetic of the individual. Some of the selections, such as Sammy Harkham's imagination of life in a nineteenth-century shtetl or Dan Zettwoch's record of the 1937 Louisville flood, sketch entire communities, while others, like the free-associative experiments of C. F. and Paper Rad, abandon realistic narrative entirely. Most of the stories in *Best American Comics 2007*, however, are stories of individual dilemmas, individual epiphanies (or the lack thereof), individual artists or their surrogates lost in their own individual perceptions. Ware is not incorrect to place this emphasis on individual experience in opposition to the more social focus of nineteenth-century fiction, but he seems unaware that it's hardly limited to comics. In 1978, Christopher Lasch bemoaned the popularity of confessional literature in *The Culture of Narcissism*, excoriating it for what he viewed as its self-indulgence (16–21); Hatfield has observed how Lasch's arguments underwrite many common critiques of autobiographical comics (*Alternative Comics* 129–130). Contemporary realistic fiction has prompted similar critiques: as George Packer notes, "Recent American literature reflects this triumph of private life. The writing that has had the greatest influence in the past two decades [. . .] is a breakfast-table realism, focused inward on marital complaints, childhood troubles, alcohol, sex, general self-loathing and dissatisfaction" (390). By way of example Packer cites the *Best American Short Stories* series; had he written this passage seven years later, he could just as easily have cited *Best American Comics 2007*. The stories Ware has selected do cultivate an individual approach, not in their shared styles but through their common retreat into interior life, and Ware's introduction hints at the privatizing aesthetic at work in these comics even if he doesn't acknowledge that such an aesthetic exists. This undercuts many of his claims for comics' revolutionary break from prevailing aesthetic standards—for while they may challenge the postwar visual arts' focus on abstraction and conceptualism, his selections fall perfectly in line with postwar American literature's taste for the confessional and quotidian. Ware has simply exchanged one set of canonical standards for another.

WORKSHOP STORIES

This literary aesthetic also shapes Ware's comics, which promote the dominant values and practices of quotidian realism while positioning themselves as excluded from or marginalized by the institutions of the literary and art worlds. These comics maintain a delicate and sometimes paradoxical balance between their most ambitious formal experiments and their far more conventional subject matter. Martha Kuhlman notes that Ware's predilection for formal games suggests an affinity with European comics artists such as Oubapo, or L'Ouvroir de Bande Dessinée Potentielle (the Workshop of Potential Comics), a group dedicated to exposing and expanding the mechanisms of comics production (78). In terms of their content, however, Ware's comics share many commonalities with another type of creative workshop, one that carries far less positive associations with the factory or assembly line: the university writing workshop. This tension is especially prominent in *Building Stories*, which collects a decade's worth of comics that Ware created for the *New York Times Magazine*, the *New Yorker*, the *Chicago Reader*, *Nest*, and other magazines and newspapers (including his own issue of *McSweeney's*) along with several new pieces to form an overarching narrative—or rather, a set of interlocking narratives.

Building Stories consists of a box containing fourteen different comics (plus a few extra strips hidden around the inner side panels) that can be read in any order. Most of these pieces mimic the formats and publication outlets that historically fostered comics art: newspaper strips, broadsheets, comic books, and magazines (Kashtan 423–424). Others recall the artifacts of childhood: a fold-out game board, a cardboard-bound book that resembles the Little Golden Books. The pieces are printed just slightly out of scale, ten to twenty percent larger than their inspirations, perhaps to replicate the feeling of handling these texts as a child. Yet for all their physical variety, these childhood throwbacks largely adopt the narrative styles and subjects of literary realism. Ware's unnamed protagonist is a woman with a prosthetic leg who first harbors and then abandons her dreams of becoming an artist and a writer. Some stories trace her development from an isolated art school student to a dissatisfied mother and wife; others expand the point of view to focus on her elderly landlady or the other residents of her apartment building. Other than a few pieces that focus on the misadventures of an anthropomorphic bee (who may or may not exist only in the bedtime stories the protagonist tells her daughter), most of *Building Stories* operates within the narrow range of styles that enjoy the sanction of the literary world and its institutions, devoting particular attention to the standards and practices of the university creative writing workshop.

MFA writing programs have often been criticized for producing formulaic "paint-by-numbers fiction" and promoting an "assembly-belt aesthetic," to the point that the criticism itself has become a cliché (Julavits). Defenders insist that the MFA teaches more than just the quiet epiphanies and sanded-down prose of Raymond Carver, Richard Ford, and other "dirty realists." In *The Program Era: Postwar Fiction and the Rise of Creative Writing*, Mark McGurl charts the writing programs' influence on what he defines as the three major schools of postwar American fiction: "technomodernism," postmodernism that incorporates information technology as subject or style; "high cultural pluralism," which celebrates the authenticity of diverse racial and ethnic voices while joining them to the literary values of high modernism; and "lower-middle-class modernism," another name for dirty realism, which crafts minimalistic tales about socially, economically, or psychologically insecure characters (32). McGurl recognizes that these schools overlap more than his taxonomy might imply. The high cultural pluralists and the lower-middle-class modernists, for example, both work in the subjective and reflexive mode of high modernism and both locate writerly authenticity in the representation of difference or hardship. The fundamental compatibility between these schools may be observed by the ease with which Ware combines them, creating comics that depict the dreary routines of a lonely florist while also projecting himself into the point of view of a disabled woman. McGurl observes that in the program era, white male writers have been the most likely to adopt the voices of different subjectivities, while other writers have often found themselves pigeonholed into representing a single mode of experience (382). Ware's adaptation of these practices merely demonstrates that his work fits well within two writing program traditions that already have much in common.

He breaks newer ground in his efforts to integrate McGurl's third school of postwar American fiction, the postmodernist or technomodernist approach. Ware's comics have long pursued two goals once considered incompatible in the world of literary fiction, deconstructing and rebuilding their formal properties while simultaneously developing realistic narratives with psychologically complex characters. Ware, who has the advantage of working in a form that provides at least two different fields for narrative expression, is able to present conventionally realistic stories through his narration, dialogue, and characterization while tackling more experimental strategies in his visual design. However, *Building Stories* is not just postmodern but technomodern, as the narrative (especially in its later installments) explores the impact of information technology and social media on its characters. This focus extends to its form: although reviewers such as Rick Moody celebrated *Building Stories* as a defiant assertion of the material richness of the book and a rejection of the e-book, Aaron Kashtan observes that the work hybridizes print and digital reading technologies, replicating hypertextual structures through its scattered material forms (434–441) and adapting one story, "Touch Sensitive," that was originally created for the *McSweeney's* iPad app (441–445). By combining such bold formal innovation with the subdued epiphanies of quotidian realism and (somewhat willfully) the diversity of the pluralists, Ware unites McGurl's three reigning modes of the program era. *Building Stories* is almost perfectly pitched to the concerns and values of workshop fiction, and thus, through the workshops' influence, to contemporary American literary fiction as a whole. As Chad Harbach quips, "We are all MFAs now" (11), and *Building Stories* represents one of Ware's strongest bids for inclusion in the ever-expanding sphere of program fiction.

It's not at all surprising, then, that writing workshops, bookstores, and other sites of literary culture appear throughout *Building Stories*. More surprising, perhaps—for those unfamiliar with Ware's body of work—is the defensive and self-deprecating tone that marks their appearances. A common feature in Ware's comics, this tone also proves to be a key element in his bid for literary status: he demonstrates a writerly anxiety over his work's quality while also arguing for its radical break from the very tradition he seeks to join. However, the scenes that position his work in relation to the literary world display the sharp limits of his radicalism. At the conclusion of the shorter of the two large broadsheets (the one with the life-sized illustration of a baby in the centerfold—visually, Ware's innovation is unimpeachable), the protagonist, searching for a novel to take on vacation and daunted by the modernists and Russians on her bookshelf, laments, "Why does every 'great book' have to always be about criminals or perverts? Can't I just find one that's about regular people living everyday life?" The comment doubles as a description and implicit justification of *Building Stories*, but Ware oversells his work's novelty; for the past forty years, regular people living everyday life have been a staple of literary fiction, the sort of fiction taught in the workshops and the sort Ware aspires to produce.

Another, even less subtle articulation appears at the end of the magazine-format piece titled "Disconnect." The protagonist describes a dream in which, while browsing in a bookstore ("one of those big chain bookstores that don't exist anymore"), she discovers a copy of her own book:

> And it had everything in it . . . my diaries, the stories from my writing classes, even stuff I didn't know I'd written [. . .] All of the illustrations (and there were a lot of them—there seemed to be more and more the more I looked) were so precise and clean it was like an architect had drawn them . . . they were so colorful and intricate [. . .] And it wasn't—I dunno—it wasn't really a book either . . . it was in . . . pieces, like, books falling apart out of a carton, maybe . . .

This dream, which obviously describes *Building Stories* itself, is just one of many episodes that have prompted readers such as David Ball to speculate that the protagonist is also the author of *Building Stories* ("Beautifully Failing"). The fact that Ware himself conceived the structure of *Building Stories* in a dream only increases the similarities between character and creator (Gevinson). Yet the end of this scene, in which the middle-aged protagonist describes her dream to her now-grown daughter, strongly implies that she never finished any of these stories and that she looks back with regret on her decision to abandon her creative work. As Peter Sattler observes, she is "more like the *imagined* author of a book she did not or could not create. These fragments, *Building Stories* tells us, are something like the memories (or dreams) of what one woman *might* have made, the books and drawing[s] that she might have created" ("Building Memories," his emphasis). Her artistic life as actually depicted in *Building Stories* is instead a record of frustration, discarded ambition, and social ostracism, all the themes that constitute Ware's "rhetoric of failure" (Ball, "Failures" 45).

Surveying his earlier comics, Ball argues that Ware deploys the recurring theme of failure in a bid to join a literary canon that equates commercial rejection with artistic worth ("Failures" 46). In this self-affirming logic, acknowledging such failures—even in work that proves commercially successful, as Ware's comics have—offers comics artists a pathway to literary sophistication and institutional validation (53). Worden detects similar themes at work in Ware's issue of *McSweeney's,* but he additionally notes that Ware's model of the neglected (and implicitly male) comics artist practicing his shameful art reproduces modernist notions of artistic isolation and masculine melancholy, attempting to gain entry into the literary canon by replicating its prejudices (907). *Building Stories* transplants this affect of shame and regret onto an intergenerational succession of frustrated women artists (the protagonist, her landlady, and potentially her daughter) but otherwise leaves it intact, validating Ware's own art by presenting it as the story (and, implicitly, the product) of unrecognized genius. In fact, the protagonist's dream goes one step beyond the performances of failure in Ware's prior works, advertising not only their marginality but also their novelty: the comics we hold in our hands are so avant-garde that they could not possibly exist in the world he has depicted.

This double-voiced self-deprecation can also be found in the clothbound book that details the protagonist's struggles during her art school years and her early twenties. This volume, which was initially published at a smaller scale and with slightly different content as *ACME Novelty Library* issue 18, contains more ironic articulations of the components of *Building Stories,* explicitly figuring them as assignments intended for a writing workshop. In the page titled "This Morning," the protagonist contemplates turning her memories and experiences into fodder for her stories, but she pulls back for fear that they would mean nothing to anyone else. Those memories and experiences are the subject of this very page, much of the rest of the clothbound book, and *Building Stories* more broadly, but the protagonist's doubts discourage her from pursuing these subjects. A brief flashback to the workshop (conducted by an instructor who resembles Ware, one of the artist's many self-effacing cameos in his comics) finds the style and substance of *Building Stories* once again reflected in the students' critiques: a classmate's comment that the protagonist's story is too emotionally detached, in part because the protagonist doesn't have a name; the protagonist's unspoken retort that she doesn't care about the classmate's stories about raising her children or losing her virginity; and the protagonist's silent, scathing commentary on the instructor's own story, a tale of infidelity written from a male and a female point of view, not unlike Ware's story of the unhappy couple who live below the protagonist. The next scene in the *Building Stories* hardcover adds two pages not present in *ACME* issue 18, in which the protagonist attends her workshop and reads a story she has written about her landlady; the final line of the story, "Oh mama, what happened? What happened to me?," also concludes the third page of the comic book written from the landlady's point of view. Although she doesn't receive any formal critiques this time—the one comment is brief and complimentary—the protagonist supplies more than enough anxiety and self-doubt on her own as she laments the lack of authenticity in her adoption of an old woman's voice.

These convergences between workshop stories and *Building Stories* serve several purposes. By implying that the protagonist of *Building Stories* could also be its author, Ware insulates himself from his own work; any infelicities in his style may be written off as products of the aspiring but unpublished writer. But while some of the workshop critiques identify common problems in Ware's work, like his fondness for heavy-handed symbolism, most of the protagonist's doubts are notable for being so transparently inapplicable to the work that contains them. Her fears that her stories won't interest anyone, like her later regrets that she never completed them, are belied by the existence of *Building Stories* itself. Such comparisons are inescapably self-aggrandizing: the protagonist's timidity stands in implicit but stark contrast to her creator's decision to forge ahead with his identical project, and Ware shines by comparison against his own faulty proxy. These not-quite-self-criticisms serve to authenticate Ware's work, performing the rhetoric of failure and anxiety that Ball reads as the gateway to literary respectability while simultaneously demonstrating that his comics already belong to literary culture by virtue of their shared subjects and concerns: shame, alienation, trauma, memory, ordinary experience, and of course the writing workshop itself.

Most of the scholarship on *Building Stories* hasn't examined Ware's preoccupation with his own cultural status, focusing instead on more easily lauded topics such as his innovative use of material form or his representations of memory, disability, and architectural space.[7] Ariela Freedman takes up the issue of Ware's interactions with the art world, yet she accepts his defensive and misleading self-presentation from her first sentence, which positions comics as a "hybrid, upstart mode" in contrast to "canonical art and institutions" (337). This is precisely the sort of performative marginality that Hillary Chute and Patrick Jagoda warn against in their introduction to *Comics & Media* (3), but it doesn't quite match Ware's relationship to the art world: as Freedman notes, his pages have been exhibited by the Art Institute of Chicago, the same institution whose art school instructors once dismissed his comics (339n3). Those comics are even less marginal in the literary world, where *Building Stories* was published by Pantheon, reviewed with great acclaim in publications such as the *Los Angeles Review of Books* (by novelist Rick Moody), and promoted in venues like the New York Public Library (with novelist Zadie Smith). Although she suggests that comics artists and scholars have attempted to distinguish their critical language from "the measures and hierarchies of the art world," Freedman replicates the hierarchies of the literary world when she claims that comics scholarship has successfully argued "that comics be judged not as the lesser terrain where words and images meet, nor as loose collections of low-culture ephemera encompassed by sub-categories of genre, but as an art in its own right" (337). Comments such as these tacitly accept the very divisions they claim to challenge, implying that art and genre (or other types of low-culture ephemera) are mutually exclusive categories. Like Ware himself, Freedman builds her case for the aesthetic merit of a few select comics around the exclusion of other types.

She supports that case by arguing that Ware interacts with canonized artists working in consecrated forms. Her reading of *Building Stories* detects intertextual influences and allusions ranging from Joseph Cornell to Georgia O'Keeffe, an argument of artistic virtue by association. In her final example, however, Freedman maintains that the circular, captioned panels that bookend one of the fold-out strips function as dual allusions to the epiphanies of James Joyce and the single-panel cartoons of Bil Keane, the late artist and creator of *The Family Circus* (figure 4.2). There can be no doubt that Ware works in the epiphanic mode, crafting stories that build up to fleeting moments of transcendent insight into everyday experience, although this mode has been so predominant for so long in the world of literary fiction that the mere inclusion of an epiphany doesn't necessarily constitute a reference to Joyce; on the contrary, such moments are the buy-in for the entire genre, a token of entry. Similarly, the comics intertexts in this strip, while certainly nodding to Keane, also draw more broadly from the worlds of newspaper and magazine cartoons: one of the panels features a captioned exchange of dialogue, a rarity in *The Family Circus* but a common element in midcentury cartooning. Nevertheless, because Ware combines the narrative

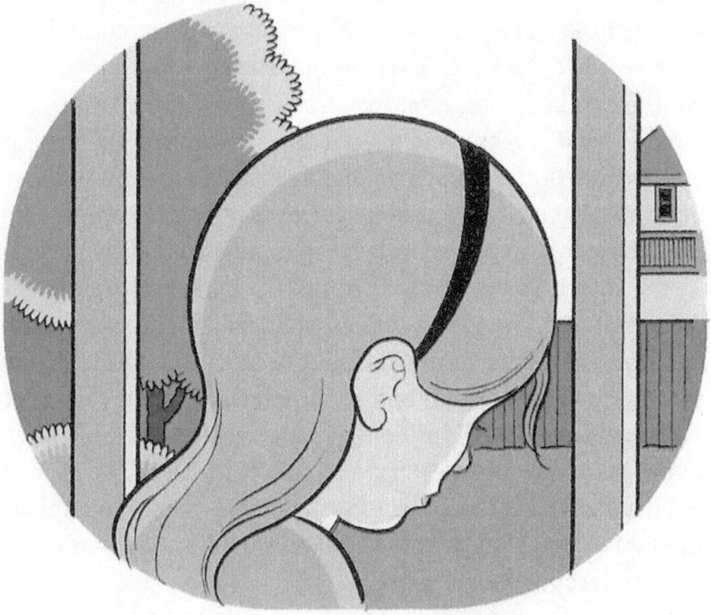

FIG. 4.2. *Chris Ware, untitled,* Building Stories *(Pantheon, 2012), fold-out strip.*

conventions of literary fiction with the visual iconography of "one of the most maligned and popular comics artists," Freedman argues that "The turn towards a devalued device—the Bil Keane capsule, or epiphanic circle, and a devalued experience—the domestic, rejects the internal hierarchies not only of the art world but also of the comics world, which is so often associated with masculine and public models of heroism" (355).

What Freedman describes here is less an internal hierarchy of the comics world than an external perception of it. It's true that Keane's *Family Circus* cartoons are not held in high regard by many comics artists or critics, but as numerous journal issues and Ware's own anthologies demonstrate, neither are the (presumably super-) heroic comics to which Freedman alludes. In the world of alternative and underground comics, the world Ware came from and the one that enjoys the most traction among art and literary institutions, Bil Keane is likely to receive far more respect, whether with irony or sincerity. Keane and *Zippy the Pinhead* artist Bill Griffith drew their characters for each other's comic strips, and Griffith wrote a tender appreciation for the *Comics Journal* after Keane's death (Griffith). Ware's portion of the comics world is ready and willing to valorize even the most banal daily comic strips—Griffith compares *The Family Circus* to Ernie Bushmiller's *Nancy* in terms of their "unconscious surrealism"—while still seeking to distance itself from the superhero tales that dominate public perceptions of comics in the United States. In other words, the Bil Keane capsule already holds greater status within the alt-comics world (and therefore enjoys easier access to the art world) just as the domestic does within the literary world, where stories of urban isolation and suburban desperation can hardly be described as devalued. Far from being upstart gestures, Ware's selection of his comics intertexts (the newspaper comic strip, the magazine cartoon and cover) dovetails with his conventionally literary subject matter as bids for continued respectability within the canons and institutions that have already proven receptive to his work.

Freedman suggests that by combining references to supposedly marginalized comics artists such as Bil Keane with allusions to venerated novelists like James Joyce, "Ware declares the war between comics and the canon, between low and high, over" (355). Yet widely syndicated artists such as Keane only look marginal when viewed from within a rhetoric of failure that suggests commercial success cannot coexist with cultural capital. In *Building Stories*, as in his anthologies, Ware doesn't challenge this rhetoric so much as argue that certain comics—and only certain comics—already meet its prevailing standards. Ware doesn't end the "war" between low and high; he simply makes his pitch to join the side with more institutional support.

"USUALLY EXCESSIVE"

Chris Ware isn't the only writer to project the literary world's preferences for realism and autobiography onto comics. Published almost simultaneously with *McSweeney's* issue 13 in that miraculous summer when comics took over the world, Charles McGrath's 11 July 2004 *New York Times Magazine* article on graphic novels, "Not Funnies," both recognizes and enables comics' newfound respectability. Yet McGrath also conflates a single mode of writing with an entire medium as he evaluates the graphic novel in the narrowest of literary terms, delegitimizing the art form he claims to praise

(Pizzino 33–35). After quickly dismissing the popular genres from consideration, McGrath asserts that the "better" graphic novels—"the comic book[s] with a brain"—inhabit "a place of longing, loss, sexual frustration, loneliness and alienation—a landscape very similar, in other words, to that of so much prose fiction" (30). He celebrates anomic alternative comics precisely because they conform to contemporary literary fiction's preferences for realism, interiority, self-reflection, and above all autobiography.

McGrath also reduces all autobiographical and semiautobiographical comics to a single "ur-narrative, which upon examination proves to be, with small variations, the real life story of almost everyone who goes into this line of work" (30). Or of the male artists he interviews, at least—for all the diversity of his examples, which range from the comics journalism of Joe Sacco to the superhero fantasies of Alan Moore, he cites just four female artists and quotes only two. The story McGrath tells is yet another iteration of Ware's masculine melancholy, a story of obsession, social ostracism, "usually excessive masturbation," "rage and depression and thwarted energy," a story so formulaic that by article's end McGrath has boiled it down to formula twice more and used it to sum up the lives of Daniel Clowes and Chris Ware: "broken home, comics obsession, friendless, dateless adolescence" (30, 33). While lauding these stories as the most literate and mature style of comics, McGrath confines them to a single plotline as predictable as anything produced by the superhero factories of DC or Marvel Comics. His article exceeds even Ware's *Best American Comics* introduction in its penchant for reinforcing the value judgments of the same cultural establishment he claims graphic novels are supplanting, beginning in the second paragraph, when he states that "if the highbrows are right, [comics are] a form perfectly suited to our dumbed-down culture and collective attention deficit" (24).

Ironically, those judgments no longer hold the same sway over much of the literary world. Authors of considerable skill and acclaim were challenging the privileged position of memoir, autobiography, and realistic fiction well before McGrath and Ware attempted to translate that privilege over to comics. Colson Whitehead dissected the formulaic repetitions, pandering metaphors, and always-muted epiphanies of the "Well-Crafted Short Story" in a 2002 *New York Times* book review (8); just a few weeks earlier Michael Chabon took to the pages of *McSweeney's* to describe his exhaustion with the epiphanic form in brutally Darwinian terms, lamenting the generic dominance of "the moment-of-truth story that, like homo sapiens, appeared relatively late on the scene but has worked very quickly to wipe out its rivals" (7). Chabon and Whitehead both observe that quotidian realism is a genre like any other, with as much potential for rigid formulas and tired conventions as any of the popular genres Ware and McGrath dismiss. If literary fiction is in fact on the wane, as McGrath speculates in his first paragraph, already on its way to becoming a niche genre for a shrinking audience, it seems counterintuitive that he and Ware should promote comics that adopt the standards and the genres that reign over its decline.

For all that Ware positions himself, in comics and in print, against art instructors, book reviewers, and other cultural gatekeepers, his comics and anthologies are less interested in exploding the gatekeepers' hierarchies of taste than they are in ascending within them, both by duplicating the conventions of more legitimized art forms and by distancing themselves from the kinds of comics that once earned the highbrows' scorn. While comics such as *Building Stories* thematize their own compatibility with the values of contemporary literary fiction, Ware's anthologies situate alternative comics in general as a new middlebrow, rejecting the demotic excesses of superheroes and funny animals while razzing the ossified conventions of the visual arts. Like Fiedler's middlebrow, Ware's anthologies rail against both high and low culture, but they do so in the interest of recycling rather than denying the culture's value judgments. They sustain the marginalization of most comics while prescribing limited ranges of aesthetic ambition and generic production for the few that are granted legitimacy. With their claustrophobic categories, their recirculated hierarchies, and their renunciation of both the fine arts and popular culture in favor of a homogenous and derivative middle ground, *Best American Comics 2007*, *McSweeney's* issue 13, and *Building Stories* do not reflect the full diversity and potential of comics; they only affirm that Ware's vision of alternative comics no longer offers much of an alternative.

CHAPTER 5

COMICS STUDIES IN MINIATURE

THE CANONIZATION OF *PERSEPOLIS*

Perhaps no single work better emblematizes the changing cultural view of comics than Marjane Satrapi's *Persepolis*. A memoir of Satrapi's life during and after the Iranian revolution of 1979, *Persepolis* began as a seven-page comic, "Le Foulard" (1999), published by the French small-press comics cooperative L'Association in its anthology *Lapin*. Satrapi developed the story into a longer narrative, which L'Association published in four volumes as *Persepolis* (2000–2003). The daily newspaper *Libération* serialized the third volume in the summer of 2002, giving Satrapi a national audience and fueling the memoir's sales; a two-volume English translation followed soon after (2003–2004), garnering instant critical acclaim in publications such as *Bookforum* and the *New York Times*. Arriving contemporaneously with Chris Ware's *McSweeney's Quarterly Concern* issue and Charles McGrath's *New York Times Magazine* profile, the favorable coverage not only canonized *Persepolis* in its own right but further advanced the critical acceptance of comics, as seen by the flood of scholarly articles that soon followed, with the first in English appearing in 2005—a remarkably short turnaround for such a new work.

However, much of that critical discourse has sought to authenticate Satrapi's work by locating it outside the traditions of comics. Journalists and scholars are more likely to discuss *Persepolis* in relation to Iranian memoirs or Persian miniatures, the historical avant-garde or expressionist cinema, than to mention her publishers and colleagues at L'Association. Some seek to downplay any influence from other comics artists, or else they attribute it solely to already-canonical works such as *Maus*. While Satrapi has drawn inspiration from a rich variety of sources, these interpreters read her work too selectively. Analogies to culturally specific forms such as Persian miniatures can invite reductive and unsustainable comparisons while tacitly limiting Satrapi to an isolated and unmediated national tradition. Other critical accounts may locate *Persepolis* in relation to other comics autobiographies, yet they rarely acknowledge Satrapi's departure from a staple of the genre: the comics autobiography typically seeks to authenticate itself through a self-deprecating and self-critical attention to the author's shortcomings, yet Satrapi devotes far more effort to exalting her autobiographical protagonist and endorsing all but the most naïve of her views. (I will follow the critical convention of referring to the author of *Persepolis* as Satrapi, and her autobiographical proxy as Marji.) By absenting it from comics influences, industry practices, and genre conventions, critics have extracted *Persepolis* from some of the contexts most necessary to its interpretation.

Though the widespread praise for *Persepolis* is well deserved, its saturation of the scholarly discourse has forestalled more incisive critical appraisals of Satrapi's work—not simply aesthetic evaluations of her style and technique, which some scholars have sought to foreclose as gendered criticisms of a female artist, but also ideological assessments of her promotion of heroic individualism. While autobiography always has the potential to glorify the individual subject that sits at the foundation of classical liberalism and market capitalism, *Persepolis* supports a more recent doctrine. Subordinating public tragedies to personal epiphanies, rejecting social solidarity in favor of an undefined universalism, and presenting the consumption of Western popular culture as a form of individualized revolt, *Persepolis* is fully consonant with the tenets of neoliberalism. Such a reading may seem incompatible with most scholarly discussions of the book, which tend to argue that it presents a collective focus on the lives of Iranians, especially Iranian women. However, these same readings typically neglect the material and generic contexts of *Persepolis*, leading them to overlook the self-aggrandizing focus that both distinguishes the book from other comics autobiographies and aligns it with the neoliberal elevation of private experience over public affiliation. A more informed critical reading of *Persepolis* must first seek to situate it as a comic—and to understand how and why it has been situated as everything else.

PERSEPOLIS WITHOUT COMICS

The separation of Satrapi from her origins and influences in comics has been a halting and uneven affair, one that is best seen in the critical handling of her publishers and peers at L'Association. Hillary Chute's discussion of *Persepolis* in *Graphic Women: Life Narrative and Contemporary Comics* provides an ideal case in point precisely because Chute, unlike many of the academics who write about Satrapi, is well-versed in those contexts and writes about them with authority. Unfortunately, she also reads them selectively, minimizing Satrapi's relationship to L'Association and obscuring her connections to the world of comics. Her account demonstrates the formation of an influential and ascendant critical narrative as certain contexts and antecedents are thrust into the spotlight while others are quietly shuffled offstage.

To underscore her argument that Satrapi makes collective and therefore political claims by asserting the normality of her experience, Chute foregrounds *Ms.* magazine's publication of an excerpt from the book in 2003 under the title "Tales from an Ordinary Iranian Girlhood"—though she labels this "the original title" (136), eliding the book's prior publication by L'Association. While she acknowledges the cooperative's role as publisher in the next paragraph, Chute describes their involvement as follows: "*Persepolis* was encouraged into existence, as [Satrapi] has explained, by French cartoonists in the L'Association comics publishing collective (particularly David B., of the autobiographical *Epileptic*), with whom she happened to share the Atelier des Vosges studio" (136). The L'Association artists are characterized as early supporters whose encouragement is essentially a matter of happenstance, not peers who motivated Satrapi to begin making comics and published her first comics work (Hill 15–17; Spurgeon, "Holiday Interview"). In another telling example, Chute repeats Satrapi's statement to Christian Hill that L'Association doesn't do any marketing or promotion for its books (Chute 136; Hill 29), but not the artist's description in that same interview of how L'Asso founder and president Jean-Christophe Menu critiqued some of her pages and prompted her to redraw them (17). Chute's account stresses what L'Association didn't do for Satrapi while ignoring Menu's editorial guidance.

These omissions are particularly egregious in the case of David B. One of the founding members of L'Association and a major figure in French independent comics, David B. (Pierre-François Beauchard) is routinely cited by comics critics as a profound influence on Satrapi's style.[1] Many of the elements found in *Persepolis*, particularly in its earliest chapters, can trace their antecedents to David B.'s comics: the flattened perspective, the use of undifferentiated crowds to represent mass action or violence, the depiction of historical combat and ancient warriors, and the creation of fantastic images to portray real events or emotional states, approaching realism by way of expressionistic distortion or invention. Nevertheless, much of the academic scholarship on Satrapi downplays or minimizes this influence when it doesn't ignore David B. outright. In *Graphic Women*, Chute largely relegates him to her endnotes, where she first refers to him as an "early champion of Satrapi's work" before claiming "too much" has been made of the similarities between his style and Satrapi's (242n4). Taking issue with Douglas Wolk's claim that Satrapi was David B.'s "former student" (Wolk, "L'Association"), Chute cites Satrapi's explanation that she enjoyed the support of other L'Association artists such as Émile Bravo and Christophe Blain as well as David B., who "helped me for the first two, three chapters of [. . .] *Persepolis*. He taught me a lot of things" (242n4; Hill 17). While these comments don't describe the kind of formal teacher-student relationship that Wolk implies, neither do they limit David B.'s role to the early booster who praised Satrapi's work in his introduction to the first French volume of *Persepolis*.

The minimization of Satrapi's comics influences extends to her comics reading in general. Citing an interview with Dave Weich, Chute notes that Satrapi avoided Tintin albums in favor of a comic book about dialectical materialism, supposedly the only comic she read as a child (*Graphic Women* 139; Weich). Other interviews tell a different story, however. In her conversation with Christian Hill, Satrapi reiterates that she never read any Tintin books, but she goes on to say that "as a young girl, I preferred Lucky Luke" (11), referring to the popular cowboy comic by Morris (Maurice De Bevere) and René Goscinny. She also mentions Goscinny and Albert Uderzo's Astérix, though she says she read only one volume and observes, "Once it's translated, a lot of the charm wears off" (11). Hill, a thorough scholar of other Satrapi interviews, mentions several comics Satrapi read when she was young: "*Astérix et Cléopâtre*, the *Marxist Dialectic*, and some Draculas in English." Satrapi's response: "Right" (11). While these seemingly scattered readings by no means establish Satrapi as a lifelong comics fan, they demonstrate a much broader familiarity than Chute describes. Chute calls Hill's piece "the most useful interview on the early publication history of *Persepolis*" (242n4), and so it is, but she quotes only those excerpts that cast *Persepolis* as an isolated creation with little or no connection to the comics culture in which it was produced.

Satrapi has been an accomplice in shaping this narrative. While she did tell Dave Weich that she had read only the comic on dialectical materialism (Weich), which appears in *Persepolis* and plays a role in Marji's developing political consciousness (1: 12–13), later interviews provide more expansive accounts of her youthful reading. The most radical expansion came in 2012, when Satrapi told Chiara Clemente, "I grew up with American comics—lots of *Dracula*, lots of *Batman*" (Clemente); in another interview later that year, Satrapi again volunteered that she had read "[l]ots of Batman comics" as a child (Saizarbitoria). These changing accounts demonstrate how carefully Satrapi has shaped her own image, downplaying her reading habits when comics for adults were still treated as novelties in most journalistic and academic discourse, then admitting to them after superheroes gained more cultural cachet—and long after Satrapi's own status as an author and artist was already assured. Her judicious and selective self-presentation when *Persepolis* first came to public attention allows Chute to characterize her, with equal selectivity, as a kind of savant who was almost wholly unfamiliar with the world of comics.

The same narrative has taken hold over accounts of Satrapi's adult reading. Chute implies that *Maus* was Satrapi's sole inspiration from the world of comics, noting that she started *Persepolis* "after a friend had given her *Maus* as a birthday present and after numerous children's book projects she developed met with rejection" (*Graphic Women* 136). No other comics are mentioned in Chute's account of the book's genesis, but Satrapi tells Hill that she also read comics by David B., Joann Sfar, and other L'Association artists (18). When she says "*Epileptic* was one among others. I read other books too" (19), a statement Chute cites to delimit and dilute David B.'s influence (243n4), Satrapi does so in the context of other comics and comics artists such as Sfar; in her next response, she mentions that she read *Epileptic* before she read *Maus*. She also specifically disclaims any artistic influence from *Maus*, describing it instead as "a revelation. I told myself, 'There! It's possible to do very serious work with this means of storytelling.' Same thing with *Epileptic*, with graphic novels by Joann Sfar, and with many other books" (19). In Chute's account, however, only *Maus* served this role. As Andrew Loman observes, *Maus* has long been recognized as one of the most lauded, respected, and anthologized American comics, securing its status in the literary canon (210–212); indeed, Chute herself would go on to play some small part in sustaining its canonization as the associate editor of *MetaMaus*, a companion volume collecting interviews, historical documents, sketches, and other archival material. To limit Satrapi's comics inspirations to *Maus* is to imply that *Persepolis* has an impeccable pedigree, one uncontaminated by other comics; it also further consecrates *Maus* as the sole comics influence on an author whom Chute otherwise places in the traditions of painting, cinema, and the fine arts.

In a flurry of references, Chute links *Persepolis* to Persian miniatures, murals, and friezes, the historical avant-garde, expressionist cinema, F. W. Murnau, Félix Vallotton, Paul Cézanne, German Expressionism, and even abstract expressionism (*Graphic Women* 144–146). Nor is she alone in making these comparisons: while Luc Sante acknowledges the formative influence of Henri Matisse, he suggests that Satrapi's "stylized layouts effortlessly evoke centuries of Persian art" (7). This claim has been made so often as to become a truism, the sort of statement that is repeated in both academic articles (Ostby; R. Davis) and journalistic reviews of *Persepolis* (McGrath; S. Ellis). Perhaps the first version of this claim appears in Fernanda Eberstadt's 11 May 2003 review for the *New York Times*:

> She paints a thick inky black-on-white, in a faux-naïf pastiche of East and West. "Persepolis" deploys all the paranoid Expressionism latent in the comic strip's juxtapositions of scale [. . .] but when Satrapi depicts a schoolyard brawl, it's straight from Persian miniature. (8)

Eberstadt doesn't elaborate on this comparison, but the terms of her description suggest that something is amiss: heavy inks and black-and-white printing are in no way characteristic of Persian miniatures, which are renowned for their vivid colors and fine detail (Welch 13; B. Gray 10). Following Eberstadt's review, however, the Persian miniature comparison quickly became conventional wisdom for Satrapi's most effusive proponents. David Hajdu doesn't even make this claim directly in his 2004 *Bookforum* profile of Satrapi, yet he titles the piece "Persian Miniatures"—suggesting the allusion has become such a commonplace that he no longer needs to explain it.

Not all the critics who invoke Persian miniatures are so blithe in their analogies. Marie Ostby connects the form to *Persepolis* on the grounds that some of Satrapi's panels "distort, break, or dispense with frames as narrative devices" (562); while Ostby attributes this ostensibly "transgressive pattern" (562) solely to Persian culture, Ann Miller observes that Satrapi's framing devices have a number of proponents and antecedents in the world of comics theory (41). Conversely, Chute notes that Satrapi's use of black and white distinguishes her work from Persian painting and suggests that it places her instead in the tradition of the (predominantly European) historical avant-garde, yet she also attempts to link *Persepolis* to Persian miniatures on the grounds that "both forms are physically 'miniature'" (*Graphic Women* 145). While the name encourages such specious comparisons, Persian miniatures can in fact be quite large compared to most comics. Stuart Cary Welch's *Wonders of the Age: Masterpieces of Early Safavid Painting, 1501–1576* collects many that are more than 300 mm (11.8 in) or even 400 mm (15.75 in) tall—in other words, larger than the dimensions of *Persepolis* itself. The term "miniature" simply describes any manuscript illustration that isn't incorporated into some other design element such as a border or initial; the term comes from the Latin word *miniare,* meaning to color with red paint, or *minium* (M. Brown 86). Nearly every review that attributes Persian influences to *Persepolis* overlooks the foundational role that color plays in true Persian miniatures.

Satrapi herself has made conflicting statements on the Persian influence in her art. In a September 2004 address in New York City, she said her simple drawing style and flat perspective were part of her "Iranian side" (qtd. in Chute, *Graphic Women* 145). One year earlier, in August 2003, she told Christian Hill that her cultural background inspired her techniques of "including little perspective, and that of characters becoming taller or smaller based on their importance. These devices very much evoke Persian miniatures" (20). The question that prompts this reflection, however, is worth examining:

> CH: During the 2003 BookExpo America [held 30 May–1 June], you joked about the fact that critics reading *Persepolis* traced back many influences over your work, from Persian miniatures to Matisse's style, and so on.
>
> MS: Right.
>
> CH: Is there nonetheless something in your style that is unique to your Persian cultural background? (20)

While Satrapi is comfortable with identifying certain aspects of her style as Persian or Iranian in origin, Hill's query suggests that she initially regarded the flood of artistic comparisons, including references to Persian miniatures, with some amusement.

Humorous or not, these comparisons are at best only partially accurate, and at worst culturally reductive. While Satrapi's art shares the flat, two-dimensional composition and the text-image interaction of Persian miniatures, it differs from them starkly in its lack of color, detail, and ornamentation. By making these miniatures their primary point of comparison, writers such as Eberstadt not only remove Satrapi from the comics cultures and institutions that inspired and supported her work, they also limit her wide range of influences to one simple, culturally determined source. As Theresa Tensuan observes,

> In the context of critical commentary on comics, processes and practices of domination and misrecognition are often played out in readings that cast the work of a particular artist as emblematic of a national ethos or aesthetic. In US and British reviews of *Persepolis*, one can see this dynamic at work not only in readings that imagine the work as a transparent rendition of an undiluted cultural tradition—that is the characterization of *Persepolis* as "a charming, poignant story, drawn in small black-and-white panels that evoke Persian miniatures" (McGrath 26) or a naïve version thereof, as in the suggestion that "[t]he art seems to be almost a cross between Persian friezes and children's doodles" (Cave 1). Such critical visions maintain an investment in a vision of Satrapi as an artist who maintains a direct relationship with an idealized Persian culture uncluttered and unaffected by Western cultural or commercial influences and forces. (956)

In fact, Satrapi is more likely to cite the influence of Western writers such as Gustave Flaubert or film directors such as François Truffaut, Ingmar Bergman, and F. W. Murnau (Hill 17–18, 22), but most of the writers who invoke Persian miniatures don't account for this complex accumulation of inspirations. In its most glib and fleeting invocations—which is to say, most of them—the comparison serves to exoticize Satrapi and her work, walling her off from the culture in which she made *Persepolis* and limiting its influences to the culture of her birth.

These comparisons also serve to further isolate Satrapi from the culture and institutions of French small-press comics. Tensuan notes that "only a handful of critics" discuss the influence of Satrapi's fellow artists at L'Association and therefore account for the transnational contexts of her work (956–957). A closer examination of these influences reveals that even some of the stylistic elements Satrapi attributes to Persian art also have antecedents in the work of other L'Association artists. David B., for example, doesn't simply inspire Satrapi's depictions of historical warriors, fantasy creatures, and the violence of crowds. He also varies the size of his characters to reflect their roles in the narrative, as seen in the first chapter of *Epileptic*, where children are drawn at massive scale when they romp through the streets of their neighborhood and adults swell to monstrous size when they terrify the young protagonist (figure 5.1). His use of flat perspective also anticipates Satrapi's, particularly when he visualizes stories of war and conquest in an iconography that evokes both medieval illuminated manuscripts and a child's drawings (figure 5.2). These scenes depict violent conflicts such as the Algerian War through the lens of a child's imagination, another technique Satrapi would later use in *Persepolis* to represent the violence of the Shah's police state and the fundamentalist regime that succeeded him (Chute, *Graphic Women* 151–152). Even the most distinctive and lauded elements of Satrapi's style can find precedents, if not direct inspirations, in the work of her colleague and studio-mate, complicating popular claims that her art is specifically or solely Persian in its origins.

The few reviewers who have made these connections, however, tend to be dismissed by scholars on the grounds that they are dismissing Satrapi. Chute suggests that "supporters of [David] B.'s work appear, in the face of Satrapi's enormous international success, invested in demonstrating the

FIG. 5.1. *David B.,* Epileptic, *translated by Kim Thompson (Pantheon, 2005), p. 18.*

FIG. 5.2. *David B.,* Epileptic, *translated by Kim Thompson (Pantheon, 2005), p. 14.*

indebtedness of her style to B., whereas his is actually denser and more decorative" (*Graphic Women* 243n4). These comments imply that any attributions of influence stem from sour grapes while citing the aesthetic differences between the artists as proof that no debt is owed. For other scholars, the mere observation of aesthetic difference (or valuation of the wrong party) is itself suspect. Tensuan cites Andrew Arnold as one of the handful of journalists to acknowledge the French influence, yet she responds to his suggestion that David B. has "the greater graphic skill" ("Iranian Girlhood") by implying that he is displaying "a gendered bias in critical estimations of women comic artists" (957). Tensuan observes, quite accurately, that male comics artists who work in spare, distorted, or unpolished styles are frequently regarded as challenging artistic conventions, "elevated to the realm of 'art brut' rather than marginalized as aesthetically immature or artistically incompetent" (957). Arnold has in fact praised such male artists—comics by Jeffrey Brown and Mark Beyer, both mentioned by Tensuan, made his list of the best comics of 2004 ("Top 10")—but his celebration of *Persepolis* one year earlier as "a gorgeous comicbook" and "one of the best graphic books of the year" ("Iranian Girlhood") neither marginalizes Satrapi nor brands her as incompetent. Tensuan raises the spectre of "patronizing evaluations" of female artists (957) to dismiss Arnold's appraisals of the drawing styles of Satrapi and David B., foreclosing on any comparisons that are less than wholly flattering to Satrapi even as she urges scholars to account for the influence of L'Association. Ironically, her sole graphic example from *Persepolis* is the procession of conquerors from the second chapter, "The Bicycle," one of the images most indebted to David B.'s style and one of the chapters that received his assistance (figure 5.3).

Tensuan and Chute both offer useful correctives to culturally reductive

FIG. 5.3. *Marjane Satrapi,* Persepolis, *vol. 1 (Pantheon, 2003), p. 11, translated by Mattias Ripa.*

readings by noting the diversity of influences on Satrapi's work, yet they also minimize the influences most proximate to the publication of *Persepolis*. The understandable desire not to denigrate the work of an acclaimed female artist has led to the dismissal of conflicting aesthetic preferences, if not the outright denial of David B.'s influence and his erasure from the critical narrative. Interestingly, scholars don't apply the same standard to Satrapi's influences from cinema and the fine arts (Vallotton, Matisse, Murnau), or even to more consecrated comics artists such as Spiegelman. But these artists confer respectability and legitimacy through comparison to Satrapi, whereas David B. was only translated into English one year before she was and can't offer the same cultural capital. Nor are any of the more consecrated artists, even Spiegelman, direct inspirations, guides, companions, or competitors in the manner of David B., and so their influence doesn't pose the same threat to Satrapi's autonomy or reputation. More so even than his colleagues at L'Association, David B. is the one artist it is most necessary to dismiss if Satrapi's relocation from the comics world to the fine arts is to be maintained.

AUTOBIOGRAPHICAL ASPIRATIONS

Efforts to classify *Persepolis* as literature have followed a similar pattern. Nima Naghibi and Andrew O'Malley observe that *Persepolis*, like *Maus* and other canonical comics, has achieved literary status precisely through its removal from and definition against the popular conception of comic books (227–228). Naghibi and O'Malley are more willing than most scholars to acknowledge Satrapi's comics influences, with none of the defensiveness that characterizes some discussions of David B. or L'Association, yet they still characterize comics as a marginalized art form—a characterization that, in their view, makes comics an ideal medium for representing the lives of marginalized people. Feminist critics Joan N. Radner and Susan S. Lanser call this strategy "trivialization," the masking of subversive messages in overlooked and undervalued media (19–20), and Naghibi and O'Malley readily apply it to Satrapi, pointing out that "by adopting a naïve, childlike drawing style, by using a child as the autobiographical subject, and by working in a medium associated primarily with either low-brow or juvenile readers and narratives, she effectively 'camouflages' the complex politics of identity and nation Marji's story raises in the guise of simplicity and universal accessibility" (234). In this interpretation, Satrapi's decision to work in the comics form is merely a demotic guise adopted to conceal her sophisticated content.

Once again, a look at the comic's production contexts tells a very different story about Satrapi's aspirations. *Persepolis* was published as part of L'Association's Collection Ciboulette, a line of black-and-white comics that had the dimensions and page count of trade paperback novels. In *Unpopular Culture: Transforming the European Comic Book in the 1990s*, Bart Beaty notes that this deliberate resemblance has helped L'Association position their comics as literature, and that *Persepolis* in particular "benefits from the perception that it is simply a novel with pictures" (38–39). Far from trivializing her subject matter or camouflaging its complexity, Satrapi worked with a publisher that advertised its literary ambitions. Nevertheless, scholars such as Jennifer Worth continue to assert the marginality of the comics form even when they note the high-end production values and literary aspirations of Satrapi's American publication:

> By choosing to present her story through the graphic novel, Satrapi is clearly placing herself outside the mainstream. The American editions of the books try to downplay this aspect by publishing *Persepolis* on thick, creamy paper in two hardback volumes as a way of marking its cultural cachet and seriousness as a piece of literature. (In France, where the graphic novel is slightly more accepted, four smaller, more economical paperbacks were released.) (153)

Note the tactically deployed presumptions of intentionality. Satrapi's decision to work in comics is an act of defiant nonconformity, not a consequence of her professional relationships with the L'Association artists in the Atelier des Vosges; the literary packaging, on the other hand, is an attempt to conceal this outsider status. The French volumes are simply smaller and cheaper paperbacks, not the novelistic line Beaty describes, and France itself is merely a place "where the graphic novel is slightly more accepted," since to concede *la bande dessinée* any more legitimacy would undercut the idea that Satrapi was attempting to shun the cultural mainstream. Worth thus attempts to turn the comic's sophisticated packaging by Pantheon, the publishers of Boris Pasternak and Simone de Beauvoir, into evidence of its marginalization. Interpretations such as these say far more about the scholarly view of comics (particularly in North America) than they do about Satrapi's ambitions in using the comics form.

Scholars have offered similar readings of the book's printing and coloring. Worth argues that the black-and-white printing reflects Satrapi's decision to simplify and universalize her images (154), as does Chute, who refers to "Satrapi's insistence on black and white" (*Graphic Women* 145) and suggests that the stark visuals soften the portrayal of traumatic violence (152). Satrapi herself has argued that vivid colors would dehumanize the victims of that violence, and claims the monochromatic printing and simplified backgrounds help to universalize their experiences (Hill 21). While she deftly exploits the advantages of working in black and white—including its association with alternative comics, art-house cinema, and other mature, serious works of art in mass media—neither Satrapi nor the scholars who discuss her refusal of color mention that the choice was largely out of her hands. L'Association printed nearly all its books in black and white (Beaty, *Unpopular Culture* 29–30, 37–39), both as a rejection of the standards of the mass-market comics industry and as an economic necessity for a small publisher with limited funding. Satrapi has no doubt benefited from the lack of color, but that printing is a standard feature of most small-press comics and doesn't fall solely under her creative control, no matter how it has been presented or received.

Packaging and production aren't the only elements that mark *Persepolis* as a respectable work of literature rather than a socially marginal comic book; Satrapi's chosen genre also plays an important role in her authentication. Beaty notes that autobiography "offers the most explicit promise of legitimizing cartoonists as authors" (*Unpopular Culture* 143) through its putative realism and its promotion of the comics artist as auteur. Satrapi's reception has certainly upheld this claim, and Beaty cites *Persepolis* as an example of the critical and financial clout of autobiographical comics (146–147). Emerging from the American underground comix tradition, the first comics autobiographies didn't stray far from the marginalized role that critics attach to Satrapi—see, for example, Justin Green's *Binky Brown Meets the Holy Virgin Mary* (1972), which was printed as a comic book, released through the comix publisher Last Gasp, and sold in head shops. Following an explosion of autobiographical work in the 1980s and 1990s, however, the genre became recognized as a legitimate mode of expression, as seen by the awarding of a Pulitzer Prize to *Maus* in 1992 (*Unpopular Culture* 144–145). Yet many scholars continue to discuss *Persepolis* as a breakthrough, not in its content or reception but in its very existence as an autobiography in comics form. Amy Malek suggests that the *Persepolis* books "blend the genres of memoir and graphic novel" (354) and claims that they subvert the genre of memoir itself (366), as if comics memoirs were not already an established and acclaimed genre. When she does acknowledge the many autobiographical comics that preceded *Persepolis*, she ignores most of the female artists who have worked in the genre in order to claim that comics autobiographies "have nearly all been written by men" (371). Oversights such as these are fairly common for scholars who come to *Persepolis* from other fields and are unfamiliar with the history of comics. Nevertheless, too many scholars maintain their claims for Satrapi's exceptionalism even after they demonstrate awareness of other comics autobiographies. Whether they position her against some imagined institutional disdain or erase the traditions she writes within, these critics have gone to great lengths to make her work appear more unique and transgressive than it actually is.

Reading Satrapi more fully within the traditions of autobiographical comics would help to distinguish those elements that are typical of the genre from those that are truly original to *Persepolis*. Much of the scholarship on the genre builds on the work of autobiography theorists, who argue that autobiographers assert their sincerity by questioning their own mediation as part of what Philippe Lejeune terms the "autobiographical pact," in which writers "establish authority according to subjective, rather than verifiable, truths" (Chaney, "Terrors" 22). In other words, autobiographers affirm their honesty and objectivity by openly taking up the issue of their honesty and objectivity. For the reviewers who introduced *Persepolis* to the American public, however, the book offered a transparent window onto an unfamiliar country, a thoroughly unmediated look at growing up in post-revolutionary Iran. Sante observes, "Satrapi's voice is as artfully artless as her graphic style, never giving any indication of effort or calculation but simply communicating, in a way that feels unmediated, like a letter from a friend, in this case a wonderful friend" (7). Sante knows that Satrapi's work only *feels* unmediated, that it only lacks the *indication* of effort, but aside from these hedging qualifiers he praises the book for an unpremeditated voice that he seems to know is a sham.

This sentiment is shared by some academics. Manuela Costantino admits that *Persepolis* is "easily accessible and seemingly transparent" (432), which would contravene most scholars' understanding of the autobiographical pact. Malek, who comes to the text from outside literary studies, dispenses with the qualifiers and assigns Satrapi a level of honest simplicity that no post-poststructuralist would ever admit to contemplating. Citing memoirist

Vivian Gornick, she maintains that "it is the *truth* of memoir that is the real key to its worth" (Malek 360, her emphasis) and quotes Gornick's claim that "a fictional 'I' can be, and often is, an unreliable narrator; the nonfictional 'I' can never be" (Gornick viii). Gornick issues this injunction as a statement of practical necessity, not ontological infallibility; the comment comes from her foreword to a popular guide to writing memoirs rather than from the copious scholarship on life writing, which acknowledges that autobiographers routinely commingle fictive elements with factual ones.[2] Indeed, some of these scholars suggest that fictive (by which they mean self-reflexive) elements offer a more honest accounting of the text's own artifice and provide an important bulwark against the kind of false transparency that Malek, Costantino, and Sante find in Satrapi. As Charles Hatfield summarizes, "The fictive, then, problematizes itself, while the merely fictitious strives for transparency" (*Alternative Comics* 124).

Most Satrapi scholars are therefore more circumspect about attributing such unvarnished truth to *Persepolis*. They have instead devoted considerable attention to Satrapi's graphic artifice, in keeping with autobiography theory's focus on the self-reflexive and self-revealing aspects of the fictive. Yet *Persepolis* also departs from a standard practice of autobiographical comics, one that goes largely unacknowledged in Satrapi scholarship. Comics scholars have long argued that autobiographical comics authenticate themselves through self-doubt and self-deprecation, establishing their honesty by baring their authors' flaws for all to see (Hatfield, *Alternative Comics* 111–114). This practice, which can range from the self-critical to the self-indulgent, includes Art Spiegelman's depiction of his violation of his father's trust in chapter 1 of *Maus*, Alison Bechdel's rigorous interrogation of her own epistemology in *Fun Home*, and Joe Sacco's self-positioning as a tourist and voyeur in *Palestine*, to say nothing of the more intimate, embarrassing, or downright shameful self-revelations of Julie Doucet, Chester Brown, and Joe Matt. Naghibi and O'Malley note that autobiographies in underground and alternative comics tend to emphasize "the inadequacy or ineffectualness of their subjects" (240), and they place Satrapi's child protagonist firmly within that tradition (241). But as Chute notes, Satrapi is never self-deprecating, which sets her apart from the comics artists who work in this mode. Chute suggests that Satrapi offers a "gentle self-critique of childhood notions," but this critique "never becomes a harsh motif, as it can in work by Spiegelman, Sacco, and Kominsky-Crumb" (*Graphic Women* 242n2).

Indeed, *Persepolis* routinely defies this common practice, favoring its protagonist with validation rather than criticism. Satrapi endorses Marji's beliefs and actions through the testimonies of friends, relatives, the autobiographical narrator, and even God himself. Nor are these validations limited to her childhood notions, as they extend into her young adulthood. Without concealing her mistakes, Satrapi encourages readers to accept rather than question her flattering self-representation; for all her graphic artifice, she actually evades questions of her own mediation. By the terms of autobiography theory, *Persepolis* leans toward the fictitious rather than the fictive. This is a judgment not on Satrapi's honesty but on her self-representational artifice: even if every event happened exactly as reported in the text, readers are invited only to accept Satrapi's interpretations, never to challenge them. Simply put, *Persepolis* doesn't engage in the self-questioning practice for which scholars routinely praise autobiography, yet this absence has gone virtually unacknowledged in Satrapi scholarship.

Satrapi authenticates herself through external testimony rather than unflinching self-examination. This becomes most apparent when she enlists her family to endorse her narrative mission, casting them as unimpeachable authorities who all but mandate the creation of the text in which they appear. These endorsements begin when her uncle Anoosh tasks her with preserving the family's memory, prompting young Marji to vow she will never forget (1: 60). This instruction is repeated as Marji prepares to leave Iran for Austria, when her father tells her, "Don't ever forget who you are" (1: 148), and, four pages later, "Don't forget who you are and where you come from" (1: 152). Satrapi echoes these sentiments in her own voice while broadening their focus beyond the purely personal in her introduction to the English translation, where she states, "I also don't want those Iranians who lost their lives in prisons defending freedom, who died in the war against Iraq, who suffered under various repressive regimes, or who were forced to leave their families and flee their homeland to be forgotten" (1: n.p.). Chute describes these injunctions not to forget as "the defining project of the text" (*Graphic Women* 143); other scholars such as Rocío Davis are equally likely to promote these "metaliterary imperatives" (275) as evidence of the comic's formal and thematic sophistication, praising Satrapi for her own self-authentication.

Satrapi expands these external validations to include friends, teachers, and no less an authority than God himself. The six-year-old Marji believes she is a prophet, but it's the adult artist who draws God cradling her and telling her, "You are my choice, my last and best choice" (1: 8). The rest of the family is once again mobilized to support this ambition: Marji's grandmother volunteers to become her first disciple (1: 7), and her parents defend her when her teacher suggests that Marji is disturbed (1: 8). Satrapi is careful to present this God-figure as a childish fantasy, not a literal deity; he vanishes on the night hundreds of citizens are killed in the Cinema Rex fire (1: 17) and Marji banishes him for good after Anoosh is executed (1: 70), reflecting her disillusionment with God in the face of suffering. Nevertheless, these measures haven't prevented critics from taking the fantasy seriously as part of Satrapi's self-validation: Chute cites the six-year-old's confidence in branding herself a prophet as part of the book's feminist content (*Graphic Women* 242n2). Unfortunately, recognizing that self-confidence has, in this case, forestalled any critical assessment of young Marji's self-aggrandizing fantasies.

The early chapters of *Persepolis* revolve around shocking Marji out of her childhood certainties—her belief in her future as a prophet, the Shah's divine ordination, and her own invulnerability. These pages are filtered through a child's imagination, depicting the Shah as a fairy-tale king with a giant crown (1: 23) and her own grandfather as a prince riding an elephant through a magical landscape (figure 5.4). Graphically as well as textually, these beliefs are set up for mockery and eventual abandonment, yet Satrapi presents them with a sincerity that is not to be dismissed lightly. As Chute observes, Satrapi's adoption of her childhood perspective allows her to "present the historical events of her childhood with a matter-of-factness that is neither 'innocent' nor 'cynical,' but a constant negotiation of these

FIG. 5.4. *Marjane Satrapi,* Persepolis, *vol. 1 (Pantheon, 2003), p. 22, translated by Mattias Ripa.*

[. . .] a conversation between versions of self" (*Graphic Women* 144). The comic balances ironic detachment with a deliberately naïve self-presentation in which Satrapi is fully invested; if the particulars of her fantasies are set aside, the conviction in her specialness is not. Far from challenging "the heroic figures of conventional comics, as well as [. . .] the triumphant celebration of the individual common to autobiographical narratives" (Naghibi and O'Malley 240–241), as traditionally self-deprecating comics autobiographies do, Satrapi positively relishes her self-portrayal as a heroic individual marked out for a special destiny.

The sincerity of Satrapi's investment in these childhood fantasies can be measured by one other factor, rarely mentioned in the criticism: they do not end with childhood. Reviewers and scholars almost always discuss *Persepolis* in terms of its "child's point of view" (Costantino 430) or its "childlike drawing style" (Sante 7), even when, like Sante, they review the second half of the story, in which Marji gets married and graduates from college; perhaps they overlook this transition because Satrapi's drawing style is harder to justify once it can no longer be attributed to Marji's youth and immaturity. Some of Marji's childhood notions also continue into adolescence and early adulthood: Satrapi credits prayers, miraculous premonitions, and other forms of divine intervention for her success on her exams in Austria (2: 69) and Iran (2: 129), her graduation from school (2: 72), and even her survival of her suicide attempt—with the last opinion voiced by a therapist who can think of no other explanation (2: 119). These divine intercessions appear graphically when God visits Marji during her studies and textually when Satrapi's narrator weighs in: "Each time that I asked my mother to pray for me, my wish was granted" (2: 69). No longer filtered through fallible characters or impressionable children, these sentiments receive the endorsement of the adult who narrates the tale retrospectively. Satrapi's irony can't fully obscure her validation of many of her childhood beliefs, particularly those that cast her as divinely ordained.

God always supports and encourages Marji, when he can be bothered to show himself, but the mortal authority figures in her family prove more demanding. When they reprimand her, however, it's generally for endangering herself, neglecting her studies, or otherwise failing to live up to her potential. They rarely challenge her ideas or her values, which receive steady affirmation—and when they discipline Marji, Satrapi manages to even the score by casting them as tyrannical figures in the vein of the dictators and militias who rule Iran before and after the revolution. Chute suggests that

FIG. 5.5. *Marjane Satrapi,* Persepolis, *vol. 1 (Pantheon, 2003), p. 39, translated by Mattias Ripa.*

these episodes blur the historical and the everyday, connecting Marji's personal experiences to political events (*Graphic Women* 153, 155), but in the course of conflating the traumas of revolutionary Iran with the growing pains of her own childhood and adolescence, Satrapi also downplays their grossly divergent consequences. In the chapter titled "The Letter," the Satrapis' maid, a sixteen-year-old girl named Mehri, takes young Marji to an antigovernment demonstration on "Black Friday," 8 September 1978, when the Shah's soldiers killed protestors in Tehran. When Marji and Mehri return home, Marji's mother slaps them both. Satrapi writes, "That day there were so many killed in one of the neighborhoods that a rumor spread that Israeli soldiers were responsible for the slaughter." The next panel corrects the record: "But in fact it was really our own who had attacked us" (1: 39). While the former panel shows the bodies of dead protestors, the latter shows Marji and Mehri sitting despondently, the sting of the maternal slap still lingering as a black handprint drawn on each face (figure 5.5).[3] The juxtaposition of the images, and the pairing of a narrative caption that nominally refers to the mass killing with an illustration of Marji and Mehri, blends public and private in the manner Chute describes, but it does so in ways that diminish the civic tragedy while hyperbolizing the family trauma. To compare her mother's punishment, corporal though it may be, to the massacre of protestors is to exaggerate the personal suffering and trivialize the public atrocity.

Satrapi asserts another false equivalence with even less cause when Marji's mother scolds her for cutting class in "The Cigarette." Her mother says, "You tell me the truth right now or else you'll be punished twice!" and Satrapi comments, "My mother used the same tactics as the torturers" (1: 113). This statement comes from the adult narrator, not the child protagonist; the conflation is especially galling given that Satrapi has already depicted the brutal, degrading, and even fatal abuses inflicted by the Shah's torturers (1: 51–52). Marji then berates her mother—"Dictator! You are the guardian of the revolution of this house!"—comparing her to the Army of the Guardians of the Islamic Revolution, the post-revolutionary government's Islamist militia (1: 113). Satrapi sustains this comparison a few pages later, when she juxtaposes the revolutionary regime's execution of dissidents with her own illicit smoking of her first cigarette: "Those who opposed the regime were systematically arrested . . . and executed together. As for me, I sealed my act of rebellion against my mother's dictatorship by smoking the cigarette I'd stolen from my uncle two weeks earlier" (1: 117). Significantly, the final panel shows Marji staring out of the page and addressing the reader directly: "With this first cigarette, I kissed childhood goodbye. Now I was a grown-up" (figure 5.6). The first line is spoken by twelve-year-old Marji, the second by the narrator, momentarily erasing any distinction between their voices. While Satrapi frames these pronunciations with a certain sarcasm—Marji's youthful appearance belies her claim to adulthood and clashes amusingly with her grim expression—they complicate any efforts to separate the adult narrator's views from the callow child's. For Chute, this blurring of voices complements the scene's blurring of personal and historical registers (*Graphic Women* 153), yet it also prevents us from reading the statement solely as authorial irony or self-criticism. The book's characteristic blend of irony and sincerity allows Satrapi to participate in her younger self's facile equation of mother and dictator—indeed, the equation is as much a product of the adult's graphic and narrative artifice

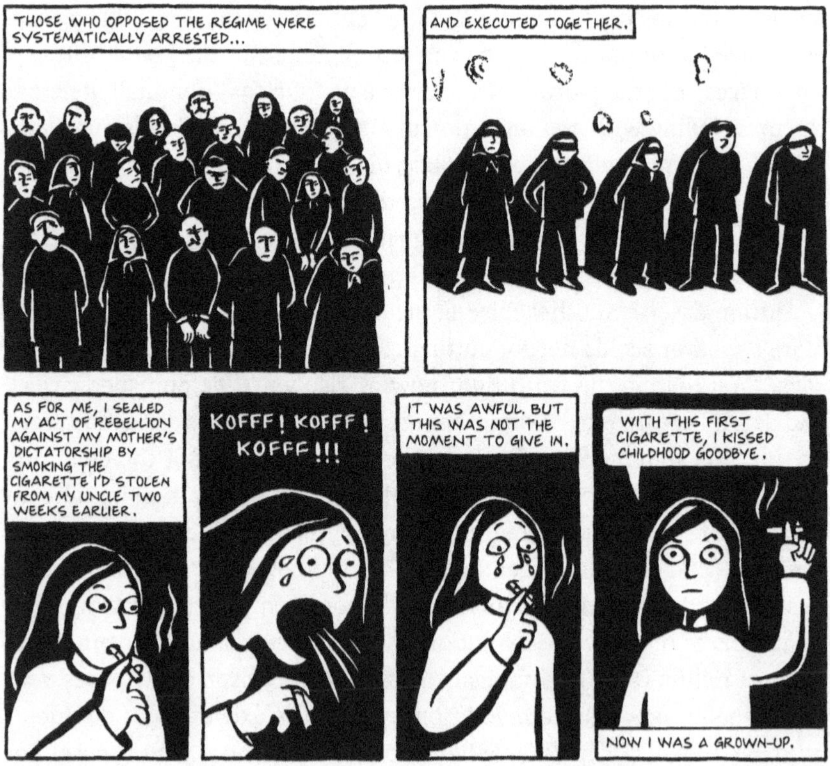

FIG. 5.6. *Marjane Satrapi,* Persepolis, *vol. 1 (Pantheon, 2003), p. 117, translated by Blake Ferris.*

as it is the preteen's self-absorption. Satrapi once again appropriates scenes of torture and mass death to adorn her more mundane rites of passage, valuing no one's trauma as highly as her own.

One scene late in *Persepolis* might appear to run counter to this trend, allowing another family member to challenge Marji without being compared to an executioner. It happens after Marji, caught in public wearing lipstick and waiting for her boyfriend, distracts some Revolutionary Guards by accusing a stranger of accosting her; the Guards arrest the stranger and Marji slips away, her lipstick unnoticed (2: 131–133). Impressed with her own cleverness, she relates the story to her grandmother, who upbraids her for being a "selfish bitch" (2: 137). This is one of the rare episodes in which Satrapi is self-critical in the tradition of Spiegelman or Sacco, but the reasons for that criticism ultimately reinforce rather than question her prevailing self-representation. The grandmother's censure focuses not on the false accusation of an innocent man, but on the lapse in Marji's familial memory and the abandonment of her mission to preserve it: "Have you forgotten who your grandfather was? He spent a third of his life in prison for having defended some innocents! And your uncle Anoosh? Have you forgotten him too???! [. . .] It's the blood of your grandpa and of your uncle that runs in your veins! Shame on you!" (2: 137). Rather than hold Marji accountable for the suffering she has inflicted on a stranger, the grandmother reinscribes Satrapi's narrative duty to her family. Kimberly Wedeven Segall, one of the few critics to discuss this scene, notes that Marji's subsequent introspection "focuses on [her] relocation of her identity along an intergenerational line of relatives who died for their beliefs" (46). Satrapi and her critics agree that her greatest mistake is her failure to honor her family, live up to her potential, and fulfill the mission that culminates in *Persepolis* itself; her lapse is most important not as an injury against another person, but as a failure of self-actualization.

THE NEOLIBERAL SELF

Critics have interpreted the personal focus of works such as *Persepolis* as a political choice that brings agency to the powerless and a voice to the unheard. Persis M. Karim suggests that memoir "may have particular resonance for Iranian and Iranian American women writers because it confers a kind of self-authorization that women in Iran have typically been denied" by Iran's patriarchal literary traditions (153). Beaty also observes that autobiography can serve as a liberating form in which oppressed people speak for themselves and assert their own subjectivity (*Unpopular Culture* 143–144); on the other hand, he notes that the form favors "personal expression above all else" (145), focusing on individual experiences rather than collective ones. Beaty characterizes autobiography's increasing dominance in alternative comics as "the turn towards the real and towards the self" (12), both of which are fair descriptions of *Persepolis*. Satrapi may challenge the silencing of Iranian women but she also prioritizes her own individual self-expression, converting public history into a backdrop for private experience. Contrary to readings that emphasize her role as a critic of Western society, these priorities are perfectly compatible not just with capitalism but with its most aggressive and ascendant doctrine, neoliberalism.

I use this term not as the all-purpose political slur it has become in certain quarters of the left, but as the most accurate description of a set of beliefs and priorities that shape Satrapi's text. David Harvey defines neoliberalism as "a theory of political economic practices that proposes human well-being can best be advanced by liberating individual entrepreneurial freedoms and skills within an institutional framework characterized by strong private property rights, free markets, and free trade" (*Brief History* 2)—usually accompanied by deregulation, privatization, austerity measures, and the erosion of social welfare programs. Beaty associates this ideology with commercially successful, mainstream comics creators such as Jean Van Hamme, author of the *Largo Winch* international finance thrillers and several other popular series in the Franco-Belgian comics market. Paraphrasing Bruno Canard, Beaty criticizes Van Hamme for "the neoliberal politics of his books—which are celebrations of masculine control and in which women are regarded as the tributaries of male power" and notes that these politics are "perfectly suited to the masculine subculture that is comic book reading" (*Unpopular Culture* 174). The description of Van Hamme's work is perfectly accurate, but such unreconstructed sexism is hardly the only face of neoliberalism. Wendy Brown suggests that neoliberalism is best understood not simply as a suite of economic policies but rather as a political rationality that implies an extreme and totalizing view of society. That rationality, "while foregrounding the market, is not only or even primarily focused on the economy; rather it involves *extending and disseminating market values to all institutions and social action*, even as the market itself remains a distinctive player" (par. 7, her emphasis).

Thus, while Satrapi doesn't subscribe to the neoliberal policy agenda, her individualism is perfectly amenable to its ideological foundations. Harvey contends that any political movement focused on individual freedoms in the manner of the New Left, the May 1968 protests, and other student-led movements of the 1960s is potentially more compatible with neoliberalism than with social justice, which "presupposes social solidarities and a willingness to submerge individual wants, needs, and desires in the cause of some more general struggle" (*Brief History* 41). Marji scoffs at these assumptions in *Persepolis*, accusing her fellow students in Austria of exaggerating the threat of the extreme right (2: 73) even as she castigates her boyfriend for not joining the protests against them (2: 75).[4] She distrusts any form of political expression or engagement that differs from her own, a sharp demonstration of how neoliberal rhetoric "has the power to split off libertarianism, identity politics, multiculturalism, and eventually narcissistic consumerism from the social forces ranged in pursuit of social justice through the conquest of state power" (*Brief History* 41). Neoliberalism, as Harvey and Brown outline it, is not solely the ideology of Jean Van Hamme, exalting male power and the free market; it is also the ideology of Marjane Satrapi, subordinating social justice to her individual experiences and freedoms. Satrapi may not share Van Hamme's values, but her vaguely feminist sentiments (which she refuses to identify by the name of feminism) and her staunchly individualist expression are far more acceptable to most scholars and critics.

That acceptance may be measured by the critics who cite the private focus of *Persepolis*, and autobiography more broadly, as proof of its political engagement and artistic daring. Rocío Davis concurs with Terri Sutton's earlier assessment that women's autobiographical comics are "the most adventurous of the genre" (Sutton 111) precisely because "their art is enacted most significantly in the private sphere" (Davis 268). Costantino claims that young Marji's decision to take a long bath in an attempt to understand her grandfather's experiences of water torture (1: 25) emphasizes "the importance of the personal over the political"—which she means as a term of approval, maintaining that Marji "personally experiences a part of national history," even though she notes that, technically, a long bath is not a form of torture but a luxury (444). For critics such as Costantino, the relentlessly personal focus of Satrapi's writing—in which stories of other people's traumas are frequently filtered through Marji's imagination—fosters understanding and identification. Yet her example demonstrates how easily this kind of identification slides into a self-centered appropriation, as Marji confuses her sheltered lifestyle with her grandfather's suffering and Satrapi claims moral authority through that confusion.

Naghibi and O'Malley, on the other hand, are well aware that autobiography tends to exalt the heroic individual and the bourgeois subject. Searching for alternative genre constructions, they briefly consider "life writing," noting that Marcie Frank "believes this term more accurately describes such underground comix as Julie Doucet's *Dirty Plotte*, which, she argues, demonstrate the unstable and performative nature of identity" (Naghibi and O'Malley 240); for Frank, such comics defy normalizing or totalizing models of identity because they "work through their refusal to speak on anyone's behalf" (260). But is this truly an alternative? While the destabilized, performative, poststructuralist mode of subjectivity hasn't quite attained the status of comforting platitude among the global elite, it does little to challenge the social and economic systems that sustain them. Indeed, the poststructuralist logic of unstable and indeterminate subjectivity complements the postmodern and neoliberal logics of disrupted and unregulated economies; both promote mobile identities for an increasingly volatile global society (D. Harvey, *Postmodernity* 350–352; see also Hardt and Negri 150). Much as neoliberal ideology anathematizes the collective values that undergird social justice movements, so can poststructuralist notions of the death of the subject work against the very kind of identity politics that Frank claims they empower. Noting this unfortunate confluence between poststructuralist thought and the liberation politics of the 1960s and 1970s, Nancy Hartsock asks, "Why is it that just at the moment when so many of us who have been silenced begin to demand the right to name ourselves, to act as subjects rather than objects of history, that just then the concept of subjecthood becomes problematic?" (163). Whatever name it goes by, any mode of autobiography or life writing is potentially consonant with the political quietism and social atomization of neoliberalism.

Frank's contention that certain modes of life writing refuse to speak "on anyone's behalf" is fully consistent with that atomization, though it complicates Chute's claims that Satrapi collectivizes her experiences. Chute locates this collectivization primarily in Satrapi's graphic form and style, perhaps because the narrative is focused so predominantly on the artist's own life: "the understated quality of Satrapi's line [. . .] rejects the visually laborious in order to departicularize the singular witnessing of the author as well as open out the text to readers" (*Graphic Women* 156). This is another version of Chris Ware's argument that ideogrammatic drawings promote reader identification (Raeburn 18), but even if representing traumas through simplified icons does render them more accessible to readers, it doesn't necessarily decouple them from Satrapi's subjective framing. Chute claims that Satrapi's witnessing in *Persepolis* "is, in part, an inclusive, collective ethos" (147), though she makes this claim immediately after quoting an interview in which Satrapi grounds that ethos in her personal experience, repeating "I was witness" four times in four consecutive sentences (Leith 12). In the next paragraph of the interview, Satrapi explains, "The reason the book stops in 1994 is that I don't live there any more," and she vows not to write a book based on "second-hand information" (12), further grounding her witnessing in the particularities of her own observations.

Chute stages this argument in the context of Satrapi's depiction of the infamous Cinema Rex fire, where she represents the deaths of hundreds of Iranians not through any collective testimony but through an expressionistic vision of flaming spectres and screaming skulls (figure 5.7). Chute describes this panel as "clearly a child's image of fiery death," a representation of Marji's imagination of the massacre, yet she also attributes its imagery to Iranian culture at large: "The author draws a scene of death not as a child perceives it empirically, but as she *imagines* it in a culture pervaded by fear of violence and retribution [. . .]. In this sense *Persepolis*—ostensibly a text about growing up and the private sphere—blurs the line between private and public speech" (*Graphic Women* 147, her emphasis). To blur these lines, and to maintain her implication that *Persepolis* is only ostensibly about the author's private life, Chute claims that Satrapi's representation of her own imagined terrors is somehow more public, more collective, than an empirical record of the event that inspired them. When even depictions of subjective, interior imagery are paraded as a kind of collective witnessing,

FIG. 5.7. *Marjane Satrapi,* Persepolis, *vol. 1 (Pantheon, 2003), p. 15, translated by Mattias Ripa.*

then the public sphere has been defined so broadly as to be meaningless. These claims of collective focus serve as a necessary fiction that aligns *Persepolis* with the political values shared by many scholars in the humanities. The text tells another story, filtering national history through Satrapi's individual subjectivity and sometimes conflating public tragedies with her more personal traumas (or imagined traumas, as in the case of the bath). *Persepolis* is an all-too-fitting example of what Gillian Whitlock terms, with no particular reproach, "the self-regarding art of graphic autobiography" ("Autographics" 976).

If Satrapi's focus on her own subjectivity is compatible with neoliberal ideals, then so too are her claims to universality, which she deploys to impede any form of collective political identification. Satrapi refuses to identify herself as a feminist, rejecting the label and branding herself a humanist instead (Solomon 28; Hill 24–25). However, her brand of humanism is not an ideological commitment to human autonomy (much less a preference for the rational over the divine) so much as a means of avoiding any interrogation of her own ideology. In an interview with Deborah Solomon, she demonstrates how this self-proclaimed humanism shades into a facile universalism that can't distinguish between different cultures or political systems:

> SOLOMON: Your books denounce Islamic fanaticism, particularly as it curtails the rights of women. Is that your main theme?
>
> SATRAPI: Oh, no, not at all. I don't consider myself as a feminist but more a humanist.
>
> SOLOMON: Still, in your work, you are constantly contrasting your love of food, smoking and sensual pleasures with the acts of self-denial demanded by the mullahs, like wearing a chador.
>
> SATRAPI: It's a problem for women no matter the religion or the society. If in Muslim countries they try to cover the woman, in America they try to make them look like a piece of meat.
>
> SOLOMON: Are you suggesting that veiling and unveiling women are equally reductive? I disagree.
>
> SATRAPI: We have to look at ourselves here also. Why do all the women get plastic surgery? Why? Why? (Solomon 28)

Paul Williams quotes this exchange with approval: "through Satrapi's humanist lens there can be no prioritizing of female humiliation" (141).

Apparently there can be no contextualizing either; while the structures of patriarchy and misogyny in the West have only become more visible in the years since the Solomon interview, most women in America don't get plastic surgery—and those who don't cannot be arrested for their transgressions, as Marji is arrested or disciplined for her appearance several times over the course of *Persepolis*. In Williams's sympathetic gloss on Satrapi's comments, "any strategic targeting of inequality is unethical because it starts from a position of cultural difference where there is only essential humanness" (141). This would seem to set an impossible standard in which inequality can only be challenged if it's targeted all at once, everywhere, with no attention to the legal and structural differences between societies. Satrapi's recourse to the humanist label obscures rather than interrogates systems of power and eschews any kind of collective or ideologically coherent project in favor of the more ad hoc protests of an individual writer who is focused chiefly on her own personal freedoms. Immediately after this exchange with Solomon, Satrapi moves from her superficially feminist comparison to the ultimate libertarian gripe, seizing the opportunity to rail against smoking bans along the same self-interested grounds (28).

Similar claims to universal humanism permeate *Persepolis*, posing a challenge to many of the book's interpreters. Although Satrapi is critical of Western capitalism and imperialism, she asserts several commonalities of experience that have proven highly appealing to Western readers. Any academics who are uneasy with Satrapi's universalism must therefore rationalize it within their own readings of a text that subverts exoticizing stereotypes and critiques Western culture. One common tactic is to compare *Persepolis* favorably to Azar Nafisi's prose memoir *Reading Lolita in Tehran*, which affirms the universality, portability, and moral utility of the English literary canon.[5] Measured against Nafisi's embrace of the Western canon, Satrapi doesn't look like much of a fan. Beyond her criticisms of European and American imperialism in Iran, she also addresses the West's propensities for prejudice and extremist politics, the difficulties of assimilation, and the overindulgence in vices great and small promoted by a culture of consumption—although these critiques must be weighed against her embrace of Western music and popular culture (R. Davis 273–274), her adoption of that culture as a form of individual resistance against fundamentalist oppression (Naghibi and O'Malley 234–238), and her many testimonies to the familiarity and normality of Iran's Westernized elites (Malek 371–372).

Another strategy has been to acknowledge Satrapi's appeals to universality while displacing them onto her readers. Chute notes that *Persepolis* has often been celebrated for its universalism, but she describes this reading as "a broad strain of discourse around her work," "an approach to the book," and a "generalizing, didactic notion of *Persepolis*," phrases that assign this interpretation to readers rather than to the text that prompts it (*Graphic Women* 138). Tensuan is equally critical of any reading that "celebrates the work as a universal coming-of-age story" (957) with no attention to the particularities of Satrapi's experience, which command much of the book's attention. However, Tensuan's discussion of the putative misreadings of Satrapi's mother, Taji Satrapi, reveals how far some critics are willing to go to exempt Satrapi from responsibility for any unwelcome interpretations:

> In casting her mother as an icon of heroic resistance, Marji could be aligned with readers of *Le Monde* or of the *Evening Standard* who would be cued to see Taji Satrapi as an emblematic representation of individual resistance, communal movements, and democratic progress. Following [Benedict] Anderson's model, French nationals could see Taji Satrapi's stance as part of a particular syntax of political activity based on memories of the student demonstrations and workers' strike of 1968, while English readers might invoke histories of the suffragist movement of the 1920s, assimilating her figure into familiar histories and placing her in a specific teleology of democratic progress. In these historical, political, and geographic contexts, Taji Satrapi is made into an icon of resistance to anti-democratic forces and cast as a representative figure in the ideological script in which an individual takes on a "regressive Muslim fundamentalist" regime. Satrapi complicates such a reading through a number of different gestures [. . .] (957–958)

Tensuan adroitly describes the process by which readers of *Persepolis* could indeed interpret Satrapi or her mother as liberal-democratic heroes who seize the power of free expression to protest repressive religious fundamentalism. Without any examples of such readings, however, Tensuan's readers are strictly hypothetical, astonishingly detailed fabrications (complete with memories of the May 1968 protests) who "could see" or "would be cued to see" or "might invoke" Western political history in order to place the Satrapis within its traditions. Since these interpretations are drawn only from Tensuan's reading of the text, her elaborate scenarios of what the hypothetical misreader *could see* are effectively discussions of what the book *actually says*, albeit on just one register that isn't highly prized by most literary scholars.

Other scholars have been more willing to attribute these universalist and liberal humanist readings to the book itself. Naghibi and O'Malley note that *Persepolis* invites readings that consolidate the Western subject by bringing Iranian culture into line with a normative Western experience (226). Malek, always inclined to take the text at face value as a transparent account of the author's life and beliefs, praises *Persepolis* for its universality (371) and describes how Satrapi grounds Marji's life in the commodities and signifiers of Western culture, fostering identification with her Western audience (372). Costantino observes how Satrapi caters to that audience by offering both "a sassy little girl" protagonist suitable for reader identification and a cast of antagonists whose portrayal as "uneducated, primitive, and narrow-minded brutes" enhances her connection with readers who may share that perception of Muslim extremists (432). In *Soft Weapons: Autobiography in Transit*, Whitlock observes that Western readers "take up autobiographical stories empathically, identifying in and through trauma and in terms of human rights campaigns for social justice that play to Western traditions of benevolence. [. . .] Discourses of human rights offer a universal and seemingly uncontested ethics of cross-cultural relations, an inevitable and natural moral grammar, which is part of the *doxa* of globalization" (12–13).[6] Costantino extends this observation to Satrapi's work, discussing how the marketing for the book and subsequent film promote the "general notion that Satrapi is telling a universal story of good and evil in which both the artist and her Western readers are on the 'right side'" (437).

These scholars typically nod to the text's universalism before moving on to consider the many ways Satrapi particularizes her experiences in Iran or criticizes Western images of the Middle East. Even Costantino, who unpacks Satrapi's highly successful positioning as a pro-Western artist suitable for audience identification, tends to attribute it to her marketing and audience reception rather than to the avowed humanist herself. Costantino goes on to describe how *Persepolis* debunks the exoticizing stereotype of the mysterious, veiled Oriental woman, and yet she observes that Satrapi does so by revealing commonalities of experience between Iranian and Western women (440–441); her challenges to Western ideology prove inseparable from her appeals to universalism. When scholars attempt to partition these arguments—to minimize Satrapi's universalism or to foist it off onto less enlightened readers—they ignore one of the major themes of *Persepolis* and an important part of its appeal. Satrapi scholars have promoted the ostensibly oppositional readings that hold the most capital in academia at the expense of the liberal humanist interpretations that made the book popular in the first place, exposing a stark divergence in the tastes and priorities of these audiences.

TOPICAL APPLICATIONS

A similar divide has formed between academic and journalistic treatments of the book's topicality. Nowhere is this clearer than in Beaty's account of the critical reception of *Persepolis* in *Unpopular Culture*, in which he defends Satrapi from criticisms leveled by French journalist Romain Brethes. Brethes contends that Satrapi was celebrated for her identity and her timely subject matter rather than her facility with the comics form:

> Doubly remarkable for her status as a woman and as an exiled Iranian in an artistic world that singularly lacks figureheads, Marjane Satrapi became an icon because the topic of *Persepolis*—schematically, her relationship to Iran and to the Islamist dictatorship—took steps towards the treatment of this subject. Comics as a cultural object are not directly valorized here because they disappear behind an individuality that is ideally wed to topicality, as is attested by the business relating to the Islamic hijab [. . .] (qtd. in and trans. by Beaty 246)

Beaty says Brethes is "thoroughly dismissive" of Satrapi's accomplishments (248), yet he follows this statement with a series of journalistic citations that partially prove Brethes's point about her public reception. American journalists such as Christopher Theokas and Fernanda Eberstadt did praise *Persepolis* for its topicality and timeliness, for the perspective it offered during a time of increased tensions with Iran and escalating military conflicts across the Middle East (Theokas, "*Persepolis*"; Eberstadt, "God"). Some of these same reviewers criticized Satrapi's art even as they extolled the book for its window onto post-revolutionary Iran, further validating Brethes's assessment (Beaty 248). These critics promoted *Persepolis* for its subject matter, not its graphic form.

While Beaty regards Brethes's comments as an attack on Satrapi's abilities, other scholars have been more willing to evaluate the book's topical appeal. Costantino notes that *Persepolis* became, to borrow Whitlock's phrase from *Soft Weapons*, a "highly valued commodity" for Western readers because it suited the geopolitical climate of the times (433); she refers to the American publication in 2003 and 2004, when France was debating whether to allow Muslim students to wear veils and headscarves in public schools and America was invading Iraq.[7] Not unlike Brethes, Costantino suggests that the issue of the veil drove the public reception of the book, including its adoption by various educational institutions, from French primary schools to North American universities. If the universities embraced Satrapi as "a liberal Middle Eastern viewpoint amidst radical unrest," Costantino implies, the French primary schools enlisted her "as a way of reinforcing the national political agenda," stressing the veil as a form of oppression and presenting Europe as a safe haven for Muslim women (433, 434). Although she argues that Satrapi complicates such readings (in part through her public opposition to the veil ban), Costantino at least addresses the many ways that timeliness, topicality, and compatibility with prevailing Western values have driven the book's public reception.

Even scholarly treatments have not proven immune to the lure of the topical hook. Whitlock opens her initial discussion of *Persepolis* with the claim (building on similar arguments by Marianne Hirsch in *PMLA*) that scholars must engage with visual narratives following the dissemination of images from the September 11th attacks, the invasion of Iraq, and the prisoner abuses at Abu Ghraib ("Autographics" 965–966)—none of which appear in *Persepolis*. Those scholars who don't rely on external calamities to validate their studies are drawn almost inexorably to Satrapi's treatment of the veil, and understandably so, as the veil is the subject of Satrapi's first chapter and several subsequent ones. These scholars tend to take antiessentialist, anti-Orientalizing approaches, but they devote as much attention to the veil as the marketers and publicists who serve as the heavies in Costantino's piece; they simply advertise a more rarefied topicality to a more discerning audience. Indeed, readings of the first page of *Persepolis*—specifically, Satrapi's images of herself in the veil, then of her self edged out of the panel that reproduces her class photograph—have become almost obligatory elements in Satrapi scholarship, appearing in the work of Chaney, Chute, Costantino, Ostby, Tensuan, Uchmanowicz, Whitlock, and Worth, among many others.

A handful of other images receive similarly recurrent and generally redundant analysis—the panel that shows Marji split between religious and secular identities (1: 6), the page that details her adolescent physical transformations (2: 35), and the juxtaposition of rich children partying while poor ones die in the Iran-Iraq war (1: 102) being foremost among them. These are hardly the only passages worthy of discussion, nor are they all newsworthy the way the veil was in 2003 and 2004, but they demonstrate the relatively narrow range of issues that Satrapi scholars have used to authorize the study of *Persepolis*: representations of oppression, narratives of personal development and maturation, and contrasts between East and West (especially those that are seen as subversive or antiessentialist), along with reflections of contemporary cultural debates. Even the most attentive formal close readings tend to stick to these subjects, suggesting the reasons for Satrapi's enthusiastic reception lie not simply in her work's topicality but in its easy rationalization and recuperation within the cosmopolitan values of cultural gatekeepers and tastemakers. In *Soft Weapons*, Whitlock discusses how the characteristics of the literary exile "lend themselves to commodification as signs of discrimination and taste: the respect for immigration, supreme individualism, and the cachet of the aesthetic" (183). *Persepolis* adds to this list the respect for cultural diversity and the validation of personal testimony as the ultimate expression of individualism, qualities that have made the book a prime candidate for canonization both inside and outside the academy.

Where Satrapi departs from these values, as in her suspicion of feminism or her rejection of graphic virtuosity, scholars have labored to rescue *Persepolis* from itself, reconciling it to prevailing academic standards while attempting to close off lines of criticism that would furnish genuinely oppositional readings. Generally speaking, however, *Persepolis* has been welcomed because it flatters academic ideals as well as liberal-democratic ones. These values, largely congruent to begin with, have equal claim on *Persepolis*, and those reviewers who embraced the book for its universalist sentiments are no more in error than the scholars who champion its subversion of distinctions between East and West. Indeed, these are two versions of the same claim, one delivered in the language of universal humanism, the other in the argot of antiessential poststructuralism. Both are consonant with the book's calls for tolerance and gender equality, and neither one complicates its promotion of heroic individualism. Scholars must begin to confront the possibility that *Persepolis* has become canonized precisely because it doesn't seriously challenge its audience, narratively or politically, while it presents a subject matter and point of view that academics, journalists, and other readers rich in cultural capital are likely to celebrate. Far from unsettling our beliefs or questioning our certainties, *Persepolis* reconfirms them at almost every turn—a project its interpreters have been all too ready to join.

CHAPTER 6

SHADOWS OF THE PAST

FICTIONS OF HISTORY IN *NAT TURNER*

Perhaps no tendency has been more characteristic of literature scholars' approach to comics studies than their penchant for canonizing comics written about traumatic experiences. Those traumas may be intimately personal or grandly historical, written onto individual bodies or into the chronicles of nations; the most lauded comics suggest these wounds are one and the same. The priorities that guided the reception of *Persepolis* have also driven critical attention to Kyle Baker's *Nat Turner*, even if the two books could hardly diverge more in their visual style or subject matter. Baker is a veteran comics artist who mixes work for Marvel and DC with independent projects such as his retelling of the life and death of Nat Turner, the leader of the 1831 slave rebellion in Southampton County, Virginia (Fischer 255–258). One of the most prominent African American artists in the comics industry, Baker has said that telling Turner's story all but dictated his decision to self-publish his comic, which he released in four issues in 2005 and 2006: "When creating a book denouncing slavery, it's kind of important that the guy who writes, draws, letters, colours and designs the book get most of the money. Any other situation would kind of render the book's argument moot" (Mathews). In his preface to the collected edition published by Harry N. Abrams in 2008, he notes, "I liked that one of my first books as an independent publisher would be about a self-freed slave" (6). While the creative and financial benefits of this decision are hard to dispute, Baker's comment also contains an intriguing historical judgment: in the most literal and pragmatic sense, Nat Turner was not a free man when he was executed for leading the Southampton rebellion. Before his narrative has even started, Baker has already cast Turner not just as a heroic figure but as a victorious one.

Prior to his execution, while he awaited trial in the Southampton County jail, Turner spoke to a local lawyer named Thomas Ruffin Gray, who recorded his testimony in *The Confessions of Nat Turner* (1831). Gray's pamphlet became the primary historical source on the rebellion, though by no means the only one; in addition to contemporary accounts in newspapers, journals, letters, and trial records, Turner's story was retold and reinterpreted by writers as diverse as the abolitionists Henry Highland Garnet and Thomas Wentworth Higginson, the proslavery historian William Sidney Drewry, and the novelists Harriet Beecher Stowe and William Wells Brown.[1] The late twentieth century saw a renewed interest in Turner, prompted by the civil rights and Black Power movements and by William Styron's controversial novel, also titled *The Confessions of Nat Turner* (1967), which Scot French suggests "remains the single most influential work on the subject" (4). That influence stems in large part from the heated criticism the novel provoked, most notably from the authors assembled in John Henrik Clarke's *William Styron's Nat Turner: Ten Black Writers Respond* (1968). The "Ten Black Writers" challenged Styron's historical inventions and inaccuracies as well as his appropriation of Turner's voice and his attribution of motives (including Turner's imagined lust for white women) that the authors found both baseless and repugnant. Following this controversy, the terms of debate included not just the morality of Turner's actions—which resulted in the deaths of at least 55 whites (roughly half of them children) and anywhere from 120 to 200 or more African Americans—but also the morality of representing Turner's actions, with the Styron discussion in particular revolving around competing claims over who was entitled to speak for Turner, to represent his consciousness and his history.

One of the remarkable features of the more recent scholarly discourse on Baker's *Nat Turner* is that it scarcely addresses these claims at all. Andrew Kunka connects Baker's work to the debate around Styron's *Confessions*, suggesting that the prior controversy serves as a powerful yet unnamed intertext for Baker's graphic novel, and scholars such as Jonathan W. Gray have attempted to frame the critical discussion around notions of the unspeakability of historical atrocity. For the most part, however, comics scholars have rarely engaged with the issues that preoccupied the Styron debate, with a particular reluctance to take up the question of Baker's historical accuracy—or rather, a reluctance to view it as a matter subject to questioning. Baker routinely imagines scenes that went unrecorded in the fragmentary and compromised archive of slavery, and occasionally depicts events that are known not to have happened in the somewhat more complete archive of the Southampton rebellion. Even when his dramatizations correspond to those archives, however, Baker represents Turner, his mother, and his companions through romanticized conventions that owe more to the popular fantasies of action movies, westerns, and superhero comics. Nevertheless, most of the scholars who discuss *Nat Turner* maintain that the book provides a historically accurate depiction of the Turner rebellion; some argue that Baker offers a knowing critique of the historical representation of slavery; and a few have even suggested that his graphic novel is more accurate than the testimonies of writers who were themselves enslaved. If the Styron controversy revolved around questions of historical fidelity and authorial license, the discussion around *Nat Turner* has attempted to rule out any objections along those grounds.

Yet such objections prove both vital and necessary, as *Nat Turner* goes beyond representing the experiences of the unrepresented in favor of fabricating a history that is more thoroughly documented than either Baker or his critics acknowledge. Baker fills his pages with visual and textual anachronisms, dramatizes actions that did not happen, downplays or ignores events that would complicate his heroic view of Turner, and generally demonstrates his indifference to the historical record. Unfortunately, comics scholars have been reluctant to discuss these fabrications—possibly because they don't regard them as fabrications, because they don't wish to violate the protocols of unrepresentability that govern our discussions of historical atrocities, or (perhaps most likely and most depressing of all) because they simply haven't done the historical research or formal close reading that would expose such shortcomings. *Nat Turner* caters to critical sensibilities that value the celebration of resistance above history's evidentiary obligations to verify its narratives, or its claim that those narratives represent a world external to the text. Ironically, while comics scholars have used *Nat Turner* to question the reliability of historical discourse, many of these same scholars have also endorsed Baker's claims to present a transparent and objective account of Turner's life. We do accept history's claims to referentiality, it turns out, but only when the history represented aligns with the narratives we prefer to tell ourselves about the past.

THE LAST ACTION HERO

Baker's investment in his heroic and inspirational narrative is not hard to discern. In the preface to the Abrams edition, he says he was drawn to Turner's story because it furnished the "opportunities for compelling graphics" that comics need, including "lots of action and suspense, also a hero with superhuman abilities" (6). Characterizing Turner as a kind of superhero, he then extends the superhuman descriptors to other slaves, whom he labels "bigger, stronger [. . .] a physically superior majority" created, he maintains, by selective breeding (7). After Baker pivots from celebrating this eugenic vision of physical refinement to praising Turner's intellect, he suggests Turner's "sole strength was his superior brain" (7). As Michael A. Chaney observes, the preface revalues black masculinity by approaching it through the generic vocabulary of superhero comics ("Slave Memory" 281–282). However, Kunka cautions that Baker's descriptions of his work are sometimes parodic, citing a facetious comment in *Nat Turner: Encore Edition* (a collection of the first two issues, published in 2005) where Baker claims his story is "presented in a historically accurate & educational presentation which is quite stimulating to the adrenal system through inventive depictions of such things as beheadings & eviscerations" (qtd. in Kunka 176). But this prior irony inheres in the mock-Victorian bombast of Baker's antiquated language; if his tongue is lodged firmly in cheek, it's for the assertion that the violence is both stimulating and educational, inventive and historically accurate, not the observation that the book is preoccupied with action and grisly violence.

In fact, Baker had already promoted the violent fantasies of *Nat Turner* elsewhere. Comparing the then-unfinished project to his recent work on his graphic novel *King David*, Baker told Ed Mathews,

> Both biographies have all the elements that make a good story. Guys from extremely humble beginnings who go on to become great and powerful men despite impossible odds. Lots of action, chasing and fighting, which all of the best comics need. Romance. Great, all-powerful, unbeatable Villains. Interesting visual elements, lots of outdoor scenes. [. . .] Nat Turner's got guys chopping each other's heads off and people being eaten by sharks. That's good comics! (Mathews)

If this is ironic, it's an irony that Baker has maintained with remarkable consistency over the years—less a matter of presenting and subverting ideas he doesn't hold than of maintaining an insulating distance from those he does. Scholars such as Chaney and Conseula Francis have read Baker's preface as a sincere and straightforward expression of his heroic view of Turner, and with good reason. From its opening depiction of action-packed slave raids to its sensationalized portrayal of the Southampton rebellion, *Nat Turner* is exactly the book Baker describes.

That book calls upon the conventions of action movies, superhero comics, and other adventure genres to romanticize its subjects. These genre transplants are especially visible in chapter 1, "Home," which departs from the fragmentary record of Turner's life to depict events that took place in Africa and during the Middle Passage, years before he was born in Virginia. This doesn't mean the events shown in the first chapter are wholly fictitious; most of them are drawn from the broader history of slavery, allowing Baker to expand the scope of his narrative beyond Turner to encompass that history, from Africa to the Americas (J. Gray 187, 192). In addition to the extrapolations and condensations that are necessary for such expansion, however, "Home" also presents a heroic narrative that owes less to the historical record than it does to recent popular fictions. This narrative begins with the sequence in which the woman who will one day become Turner's mother first fights and then flees from the raiders who attack her village in search of captives to sell. This sequence draws heavily from the visual language of action movies and their predecessors in the western: one panel shows a raider bearing down on a child, brandishing a pistol in one hand and a lasso in the other while the shadow cast by his headwear resembles nothing so much as a cowboy hat (figure 6.1). In the chase that follows, Turner's mother ambushes two raiders by lunging down on them from the forest canopy and using one man as a human shield while she seizes his shotgun and shoots the other. (One-handed and with no apparent priming, unremarkable in a John Woo movie but quite a feat in a time of flintlock weapons.) Surrounded by more raiders, she comes upon a cliff and decides to leap off it, choosing death before capture—at least until another lasso descends from above and snares her ankle (21–28). Jonathan Gray and Howard Rambsy II both suggest that the image of Turner's mother diving off the cliff evokes myths of flying Africans (Rambsy 288), although as Gray notes, Baker alters and reverses even his legendary sources, relocating the flight from the Sea Islands off the Atlantic coast to Africa itself (187). Building on the folk traditions reported by Stephen B. Oates in *The Fires of Jubilee: Nat Turner's Fierce Rebellion*, Baker represents Turner as coming from a lineage of African resistance (Oates 11), but his visual and narrative vocabulary comes from the fantasies of popular cinema.

FIG. 6.1. *Kyle Baker,* Nat Turner *(Abrams, 2008), p. 18.*

FIG. 6.2. *Kyle Baker,* Nat Turner *(Abrams, 2008), p. 55.*

The cinematic spectacle continues into Baker's representation of the Middle Passage, which both builds on and reacts against the precedents established in Steven Spielberg's film *Amistad*. Baker tells Rich Watson in an interview that he used *Amistad* as a visual reference, but he credits himself for including a detail Spielberg omitted—the trails of sharks that followed the slave ships in search of human carrion. He goes on to criticize Spielberg for sidelining the slave revolt on the *Amistad* in favor of a conventional legal drama featuring heroic white attorneys, but his other comments, including his fears that "I hope nobody's done the sharks. [. . .] I'm really worried that I gotta top Steven Spielberg and sharks" and his statement that Spielberg "knows how to wring the most drama out of a situation" (Watson)—to say nothing of his consultation of *Amistad* for reference material—suggest that his argument is primarily dramatic rather than historical in nature; he describes his competition with Spielberg in terms of novelty and spectacle, not historical fidelity. Those concerns appear to be foremost during the climactic scene of the Middle Passage sequence, in which a mother throws her child to the sharks rather than consign the infant to a life of slavery (figure 6.2). Shark heads lunge out of the water on three pages (52, 53, 55), as if Baker were re-creating Spielberg's dramatic reveal of the shark in *Jaws* not once but three times. Fundamentally, the artist's quarrel with *Amistad* is not that Spielberg sanitized his history but that he didn't make it melodramatic enough.

The lurid quality of these images serves to amplify them from isolated incidents to dramatic condensations of the history of slavery and the Middle Passage: the violence is so extreme and stylized because it represents not one death but many. In that sense, images like the child's final plunge into the shark's perpetually upturned maw can be compared to the cut-paper silhouettes of Kara Walker, which represent slavery through exaggerated or impossible figures engaged in garish, unsettling violence. Baker's reliance on silhouette, particularly in some of his most gruesome scenes, further invites the comparison. But Walker's art marshals this imagery to form surreal allegories of the past, not historical narratives that aspire to realism. Even paintings and installations based on historical personalities such as John Brown or literary texts such as *Uncle Tom's Cabin* abandon realistic illusionism in favor of a gothic reimagining or "rememory" of the past (Shaw 42–43); Walker represents the legacy of slavery through metaphor and allegory, not historical documentation. Baker, too, calls upon metaphors, myths, and stereotypes, but he claims the authority of history for his images through his citation of historical texts even as he draws his imagery from contemporary popular media.

Baker provides another metaphoric condensation of the history of slavery in chapter 2, "Education," when he depicts an elderly slave being beaten, tortured, and maimed for playing a drum. The image of the slave's severed hands lying next to his broken drum not only illustrates the violence of slavery, it provides a succinct and gory visual trope for the slaves' forcible separation from African cultures and traditions (68). However, Rambsy's inclination to link this scene to the amputation of Kunta Kinte's foot in Alex Haley's *Roots* serves as a reminder that Baker invokes and recycles modern representations of slavery as much as he dramatizes historical experiences (290). A scene depicting Turner's first, abortive attempt at fleeing slavery deploys yet another cinematic antecedent, but with no metaphorical purpose: the image of Turner submerged up to his eyes in water, dangerously exposed to the patrollers and hounds who pass within feet of him, doesn't match the sparse accounts of Turner's flight and return (95). Turner instead resembles action heroes like Sylvester Stallone's John Rambo or Arnold Schwarzenegger's Dutch Schaefer in those moments when they crouch in jungle waters and prepare themselves for battle. If images like the severed hands or the sacrificed bodies of the Middle Passage serve as condensations of slavery, this one functions only as cliché—a cliché that primes readers to interpret Turner as another action hero, awaiting his moment.

The promised violence arrives in chapter 3, "Freedom," which depicts the events of the Southampton rebellion with a visual grammar that blurs the lines between history and fantasy. This chapter includes the most graphic and hyperbolic depictions of violence in *Nat Turner*, including the full-page image of Turner's follower Will beheading a smiling child (135), yet it also consigns some of the grisliest acts to small inset panels, silhouettes, and tiny cameo-like illustrations that serve to confine and contain the violence (148–153). Once the narrative returns to a more conventional scene-by-scene dramatization of the final battle, however, the action movie clichés return in full force; Baker depicts the leader of the white militia firing his musket one-handed in a posture and framing almost identical to those used earlier for Turner's mother (167). A few pages later, Will is given an extended death scene in which he charges his foes with a firearm in one hand and an axe in the other, killing several militiamen and injuring countless others in an eight-page frenzy of blood and gore before he is finally gunned down (171–178). This scene trades the cinematic influence for one closer to Baker's own career: Craig Fischer observes that the battle owes much to the hyper-violent abstractions of Frank Miller, whose aesthetic has served as "a source of homage, parody, and/or inspiration" for several comics by Baker (266). Nor is Miller the only comics intertext operating here, as Chaney describes Will as "a kind of Black Incredible Hulk" ("Slave Memory" 281) and compares Baker's composition and character placement with a typical Marvel Comics cover (282). Baker's Will is easily the most incredible and exaggerated character, or caricature, in a book prone to romantic exaggeration.

Like the combat and chase scenes in chapter 1, these pages mark Baker's abandonment of history in favor of mythology. His rendition of the final battle combines events from three different confrontations on two consecutive days, at the houses of James W. Parker, Simon Blunt, and Newit Harris; it also credits the rebels with fatalities that never happened. Although Will's lethal last stand is commemorated in the folklore of the Southampton rebellion and presented as fact in William Wells Brown's 1867 account (24), Henry Irving Tragle reports that no whites were killed in the final battle and suggests that "the validity of [Brown's] work must be seriously questioned" (412n14). Once again, however, Baker's narrative template is drawn not from the historical records of the Southampton rebellion but from the action-adventure fantasies of film and comics. This romantic logic is so pervasive that Kunka argues it extends even to the unnamed white militia leader, a figure he identifies as Benjamin Phipps. According to Kunka, Baker represents Phipps not just as a conventionally "strong, handsome, romantic" white hero but as a Christlike savior to the whites of Southampton County. Kunka suggests this portrayal represents "Baker's most troubling and intense irony in this work," one that calls the artist's heroic view of Turner into question (186). However, reading Baker's initially heroic and Christlike presentation of this figure against other scenes featuring the same character suggests that Baker's portrayal is neither as romantic nor as ironic as it seems—or rather, that the irony cuts in a somewhat different direction. First, however, it's important to note that this character probably isn't Benjamin Phipps at all.

Benjamin Phipps was a local farmer who captured Turner some two months after the rebellion (Oates 117); he isn't recorded as playing any role in the militias that quelled the rebellion and he certainly wasn't their leader. If Baker's character has a historical antecedent, it's likely either Captain Alexander Peete or Captain James Bryant, who led the militia at the James W. Parker house (Oates 89), where Baker locates his final battle (160);

Thomas Gray names Peete as the commander in *Confessions* (15). But Kunka's confusion is both understandable and telling: most of Baker's characters go unnamed, and Phipps's sole appearance in *Nat Turner* is drawn at a distance, with a particularly murky line that makes identification difficult (184). Kunka's confusion also reveals much about the narrative logic that is presumed to operate in *Nat Turner*, a logic in which the militia leader must be Benjamin Phipps not only because Phipps is the only name Baker gives to any of Turner's antagonists, but because the militia leader is Turner's chief antagonist and the chief antagonist must be the man who captures him. This is the economy of character that rules the contemporary Hollywood action movie, a form that dictates a brutal narrative efficiency amidst the spectacular visual bloat, and Kunka assumes this is the economy that governs *Nat Turner*. Given all the other Hollywood formulas on display, I don't think he is wrong in that assumption—only this particular application.

Kunka also argues that the heroic portrayal of the militia leader complicates Baker's otherwise sympathetic portrayal of Turner, contributing to the text's ambivalence and irony (185–186). Captain Peete (or Bryant) first appears exactly as Kunka describes him, a muscular, square-jawed hero who is seen petting his dog while his child looks on. Summoned by a church bell, he grabs his gun and rushes off to defend his family and his community from the menacing rebels, the very picture of the classic western hero (Baker 144). Baker's later depiction of Captain Bryant (or Peete) in the same pose once struck by Turner's mother might imply that he, too, is fighting to protect his family from raiders—although this assumes that Baker has reused the pose with the intention of drawing a parallel, and not simply because he thinks it looks badass. Between these scenes, however, another appearance by the captain thoroughly undermines this seemingly heroic portrayal. In this scene, the captain and two other militiamen approach a house after Turner's rebels have passed through and killed the occupants.[2] Shocked by the carnage within, the captain stumbles outside to retch—and runs straight into the sights of a lone rebel, armed with a musket. The captain's heroic tale almost ends there, when he is horrified and powerless, but the rebel takes a swig of something from a flask and drinks so deeply that he knocks himself clean off his horse. The rebel vomits in the grass while the captain seizes his musket, victorious through absolutely no virtue of his own (154–159). This scene, it must be noted, is a fabrication. Oates depicts the fight at the Parker house as something of a comedy of errors in which both Captains Peete and Bryant were unable to control their horses (89), and he reports an earlier scene of militiamen retching at the Waller farm (85), but he describes no incidents in which the rebels were able to surprise any member of the militias.[3]

Baker's invention serves a twofold purpose: it undercuts the image of the militia captain as a courageous western hero—an image Baker establishes in large part to be undercut—and it conforms to a general pattern in which Turner's rebels are defeated through either their own drunken incompetence or the actions of other slaves, or both. Baker twice shows the rebels drinking when they should be marching or fighting, first in the flush of early victory (142–143) and again when the militia catches them unawares at the Parker house (164–165). In the general melee that follows, slaves fight for both sides; one top-hatted slave is shown shooting another, more humbly dressed rebel in the back (168), a clear visual trope for Baker's view of those slaves who protected their owners or fought in their defense.[4] He depicts these slaves not only as servile minstrel caricatures but as key players in Turner's defeat, further reducing the militia captain's role in quashing the rebellion; indeed, Tim Bruno suggests that the captain is decapitated during Will's last stand, though no other scholars have made this identification (947n75). Whatever his fate, the captain disappears midway through the battle, his role supplanted first by the turncoat slaves and then by the anonymous, silhouetted militiamen who bring down Will in a fight that never happened.

Kunka argues that Baker's depiction of internecine conflicts among slaves contradicts the "mythical, inspirational vision" of the Ten Black Writers, who criticized Styron for making similar claims of internal dissension and betrayal (Kunka 185). Although Baker breaks from the Ten Black Writers in this regard, he does so in the service of portraying a Turner who is otherwise very much in keeping with their views—a man of action who doesn't hesitate in his rebellion and who can't be defeated by white men, only by the vices and treacheries of his fellow slaves. This mythical and inspirational vision is sustained into Baker's fourth and final chapter, "Triumph," which presents a Turner who endures his execution with supernatural stoicism and (in a staging of an exchange in *Confessions*) answers a question from Gray by comparing himself to Christ. Nothing in the chapter contradicts Turner's self-representation as a martyr for his cause. But while Baker's presentation of the interrogation and hanging draws from Gray's *Confessions* and other historical accounts, he is just as willing to abandon those sources in favor of fantasy, mythology, and pop-cultural cliché. Whether he follows the historical record or discards it, the only constant is the romanticized image of Turner.

AN ART OF TENSIONS

This friction between Baker's narrative and his source material has not gone unnoticed. Many scholars have argued that Baker places his images in conflict with the historical texts they cite in order to call their authority and objectivity into question, creating what Qiana Whitted terms an "ideological tension between word and image" (87). That tension is certainly upheld by the book's first narrative interaction between image and text, in which Baker quotes Theodore Canot's memoir *Twenty Years of an African Slaver* on a page that shows Turner's mother being restrained in preparation for her forcible shaving. As Jonathan Gray notes, the violence of the image—the slaver's tensed muscles and clenched teeth, the mother's fearful expression, the intense light that glints off the brandished razor—contradicts Canot's genteel language, in which the men and women are "neatly shaved," hot branding irons are merely "impressed" onto their bodies, and even the stripping of the slaves simply ensures that "women as well as men go out of Africa as they came into it—naked" (Baker 36), a process almost as natural as childbirth. Baker's imagery exposes the dehumanizing violence concealed by Canot's decorous descriptions, unmasking the "archival language of slavery" (J. Gray 188).

The academic discussion of *Nat Turner* has chosen to highlight such examples, extending their critical function to nearly all of the comic's text-image interactions. Kunka suggests this function is built into the very structure of the book, in which the dominance of images over text "sets the reader up to be skeptical of [Thomas] Gray's narrative when Baker's images contradict or otherwise differ from it" (177). He cites the passage where the young Nat Turner, caught reading a Bible, pantomimes ignorance and illiteracy in order to escape punishment (Baker 88–90), a scene that doesn't correspond with any part of Gray's *Confessions*, though it quotes passages from *Confessions* that include information that isn't depicted in the scene. These disjunctions serve two generally divergent portrayals of Turner, as Baker depicts "a conventional trickster figure in contrast with the pious and somber figure that emerges from Turner's testimony" (Kunka 178). However, this doesn't mean that Baker has primed readers to be skeptical of Gray's account. Despite the variance in their details, the excerpts from Gray bear a loose thematic relationship to the scenes they accompany: Baker places the quote about Turner's reading and self-education immediately after a multi-page sequence that shows him reading the Bible at great personal risk (85–89), while the successful conclusion of Turner's deception is paired with the passage in which Turner confesses that he regularly took part in the "roguery" of his neighbors, helping them plan their schemes (90). Baker cites Gray to establish the drive for education and the capability for trickery featured in the Bible scene; if they don't fit the action perfectly, that may not imply skepticism so much as an inability to find a better quote in Baker's limited source material.

The most significant contradictions, revisions, and departures from Gray occur on those pages where Gray isn't cited at all—for example, in Baker's depiction of Turner's marriage and his forcible separation from his wife and children at the auction block (97–99). Turner's family is well documented (Oates 29–30), but he doesn't appear to have mentioned them to Gray and so they appear nowhere in *Confessions*. By including them in his narrative, Baker highlights Thomas Gray's omissions in the manner Jonathan Gray describes, although the selective and sporadic nature of his excerpts from *Confessions* means that he never explicitly identifies these absences as absences; it's difficult to tell whether Gray has left them out or Baker simply hasn't included those passages. When he does cite *Confessions*, however, he generally selects passages that complement his narrative, even if he has to strain to make them fit. This includes one of his most vivid and disturbing additions to Turner's story, the shocking scene of the infant thrown to the shark during the Middle Passage. The tale appears nowhere in any history of Turner, yet Baker folds it within Gray's account by asserting that this is the prophetic story Turner mentions in which, as a child, he once related events that happened before he was born—events that remain unspecified in Turner's testimony (Baker 57). This is the first use of Gray's text in *Nat Turner*; Baker doesn't cite the passage to undercut Gray, but rather uses Gray to rationalize his own contributions to the story. In so doing, he establishes a pattern that repeats itself throughout *Nat Turner* whenever he invents scenes or transplants material from other accounts of slavery.

The next page to cite Gray juxtaposes a quote from *Confessions* with a seemingly unrelated image of the young Turner looking on while other children are fed corn mush from a trough (figure 6.3). No such scene appears in Gray; Baker's scant endnotes identify its source in a passage from *Narrative of the Life of Frederick Douglass, an American Slave* (Baker 204 note to p. 70).

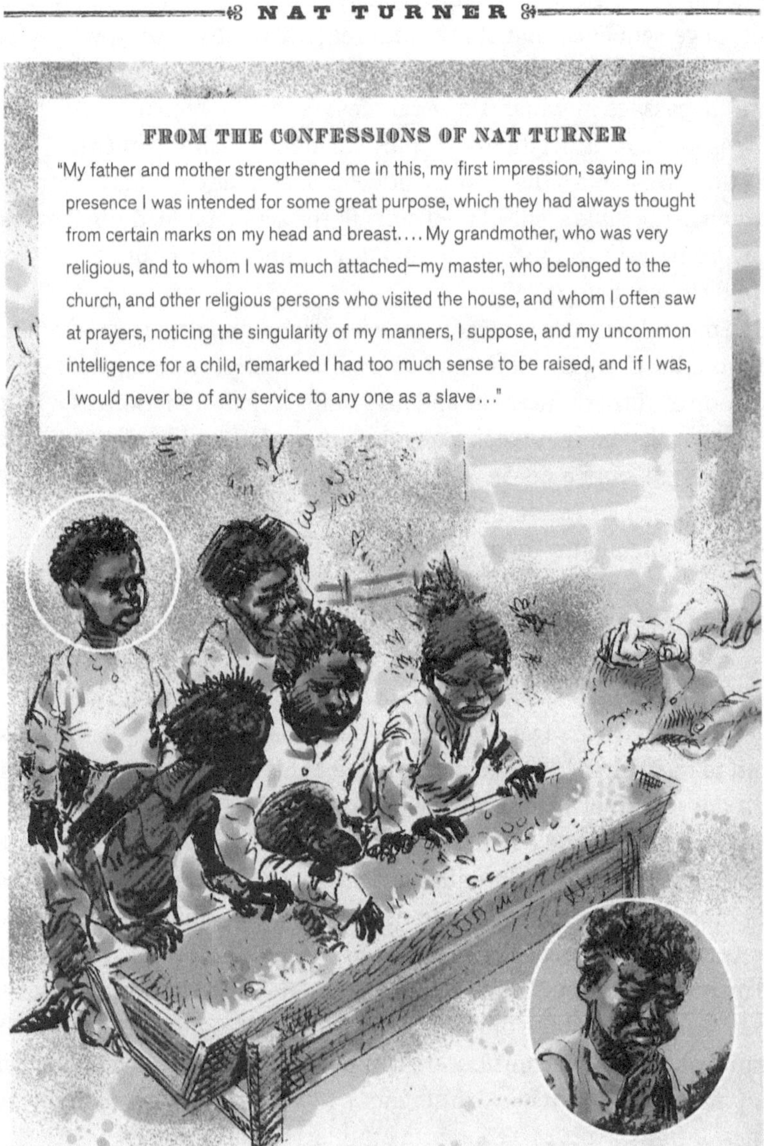

FIG. 6.3. *Kyle Baker,* Nat Turner *(Abrams, 2008), p. 70.*

Nevertheless, the image illustrates certain themes in the quoted testimony. Turner describes his parents' conviction that he was marked for a great purpose, and the sentiments of many other adults who noticed "the singularity of my manners [. . .] and my uncommon intelligence for a child," qualities that gave Turner "too much sense" to be raised as a docile slave (Baker 70). The quote foreshadows his future rebellion, but it also contributes to Baker's mystical, prophetic interpretation of Turner's character (Kunka 177–178)—a portrayal that originates in Turner's own confessions to Gray (Whitted 86). Two elements in Baker's visual design support this portrayal. The first is a white circle or panel border that encloses Turner's head, graphically setting him apart from his peers and calling attention to his singularity: while the other children line up at the trough in anticipation of their meal, he stands apart and refuses to abase himself. The other is an inset panel that shows Turner at prayer, emphasizing his religious and prophetic qualities. While the imagery comes from Douglass's narrative, Baker composes it to reinforce those qualities he highlights in Gray's account.

For a mostly wordless comic, *Nat Turner* displays a remarkable dependence on the written word. Jonathan Gray, in the course of arguing that Baker's visuals serve as a criticism or corrective to the historical record of slavery, observes that "Baker supplements the archival text with images designed to call attention to perspectives the archive cannot represent" (189). While those images may expand on or occasionally overrule the words, in keeping with Kunka's claim that the book privileges the visual over the verbal (177), the scenes in *Nat Turner* that feature quotations tend to present the images as supplements to the anterior written text. Sometimes these images are additive, filling in the details unmentioned in *Confessions*, as when Baker illustrates Turner's youthful reading with dramatic scenes of captivity and escape from the book of Exodus (86–87). Sometimes they amplify Gray's narrative for dramatic effect, like the thunderstorm that drenches Turner in his moment of spiritual revelation (102–103). Sometimes they are orthogonal to the text, like the scenes of Turner attending a religious meeting that accompany a quote in which he describes his solitude (91)—or, in a curious converse, the scene two pages later in which images of Turner tilling a field in solitude accompany a quote that describes his efforts to influence his fellow slaves (93). But no matter how disjointed they are, these images rarely contradict Gray's account. Baker's purest additions or inventions tend to appear on their own, wordless pages, while the quotes from Gray usually offer some form of corroborating detail for the adjacent visuals. One page after he depicts the religious meeting, Baker cites a passage in which Turner mentions his attendance at such gatherings; in the same passage Turner describes a revelation that came to him while he prayed at his plow, setting up the images on the next page (Baker 91–93). Similarly, Turner mentions a thunderstorm as part of his revelation, though it appears only in his visions of spirits warring in the heavens; Baker may render the figurative literal, but he doesn't challenge Gray here either. The quotes instead provide license (however slender) for his interpretations and embellishments. The pictures do supplement the words in *Nat Turner*, but the words also supplement the pictures; as Janet Neary observes, the visual and verbal cannot easily be separated in this book, where even the passages that clash with Baker's images nevertheless serve to authenticate their historical claims (169).

Frequently, this interdependence is much less complicated than I and other critics have made it out to be: many of Baker's images function as straightforward illustrations of Gray's text. These include virtually all of the text-image juxtapositions in chapter 3's rendition of the Southampton rebellion. Several pages in this chapter invert the book's normal preference for image over text, presenting lengthy quotes from *Confessions* punctuated by small inset panels (Baker 127, 129, 133, 148, 160). These drawings neither challenge nor expand Gray's narrative; they dramatize it. Baker's rendering of Turner's first escape from slavery (94–96) is less dependent on Gray's account, but it doesn't question his veracity, even when Turner cites Luke 12:47 ("For he who knoweth his Master's will, and doeth it not, shall be beaten with many stripes") to explain his voluntary return to enslavement. The inclusion of this verse reinforces Baker's portrayal of Turner as a religious mystic without contradicting Gray's depiction of Turner as a religious fanatic who never seriously questions the moral rightness of slavery; Baker doesn't balk at Gray's citation (in Turner's voice) of a line of scripture that was routinely used to justify slavery in antebellum America.[5]

This is because Baker generally presents *The Confessions of Nat Turner* as a record of Turner's life told in his own words, not as a narrative shaped by Thomas Ruffin Gray. He rarely considers that Gray might be editing or distorting Turner's testimony, even though historians have long cast doubt on Gray's accuracy and his motives in publishing Turner's confessions. Tragle casts him as a canny self-promoter in search of a best-selling story and notes that his presentation of Turner's trial doesn't match the court records (402–406). In *The Confessions of Nat Turner and Related Documents*, Kenneth S.

Greenberg concurs about Gray's financial motives but also argues that the lawyer and slaveholder attempts to impose his preferred ideological narrative on the Southampton rebellion, presenting it as the work of a religious fanatic and not as a response to the conditions of slavery (8–10). Greenberg suggests that *Confessions* should be regarded as "a joint production" between Gray and Turner (8), one in which both parties shaped the narrative—for Turner, too, withheld information, most notably the existence of his wife and children, and Greenberg warns that he likely "engaged in a kind of self-censorship" (11) in his statements to Gray. Even Oates, who regards Gray's *Confessions* as a reliable source that largely matches contemporary trial records and newspaper accounts, concedes that Gray attributes his own language to Turner and frames the rebellion in a manner that doesn't trouble his own investment in the system of slavery (122–123). Tragle therefore has good reason to ask, "[W]ho can say, with reference to *The Original Confessions*, where Gray stops and Nat begins?" (409). But Baker never raises this question, treating *Confessions* as an unvarnished (if incomplete) account of Turner's life.

The one time that Baker directly contradicts *Confessions* is also the only time he quotes Gray in his own words, as opposed to his channeling of Turner's voice. Baker opens chapter 4 with Gray's description of his visit to the imprisoned Turner:

> The calm, deliberate composure with which he spoke of his late deeds and intentions, the expression of his fiend-like face when excited by enthusiasm, still bearing the stains of the blood of helpless innocence about him; clothed with rags and covered with chains; yet daring to raise his manacled hands to heaven, with a spirit soaring above the attributes of man; I looked on him and my blood curdled in my veins. (T. Gray 19; Baker 188).

The face that dominates the next page in close-up doesn't appear especially enthusiastic, much less fiend-like; the disjunction calls attention to Gray's sensationalistic language, which he uses to demonize his subject. On the other hand, the image also complements Gray's simultaneous account of Turner's "calm, deliberate composure," as do the pages that follow, which show Turner meeting his execution with beatific tranquility. We don't see Turner literally raising his manacled hands to heaven, but he displays all the sanctity (or sanctimony) that Gray describes. When even the most direct challenge to Gray also calls upon other portions of the same passage for confirmation and authentication, then it's safe to say that *Nat Turner* simply isn't as skeptical as most scholars have claimed.

HISTORY AS FICTION

Nevertheless, comics scholars have maintained that *Nat Turner* performs a critical intervention on its primary source. Kunka compares the interplay between Baker's images and Gray's text to the use of intertextuality in historiographic metafiction (169), which Linda Hutcheon defines as narratives that metatextually interrogate both fiction and history as human constructs (5). Jonathan Gray and other scholars who discuss Baker's disruption of the archival language of slavery offer similar readings, whether explicitly or implicitly. But while individual scenes may perform this disruptive work, the text as a whole doesn't interrogate its subject, its sources, or its own formation of historical narrative in the manner Hutcheon describes. Even if *Nat Turner* conformed perfectly to these models, however, the text would still be open to critical interrogation as Hutcheon's articulations of historiographic metafiction, like her articulations of postmodernism more generally, are dehistoricized in ways that call her critique of historical discourse into question.

Hutcheon develops her analysis of historiographic metafiction in response to Fredric Jameson, Terry Eagleton, and other critics of postmodernism who regard the movement solely as a series of blank parodies or empty gestures that erase historical memory and naturalize the ideological assumptions of late capitalism. Her account provides a useful corrective to these oversimplifications; unfortunately, in reacting against their determinism Hutcheon also offers some oversimplifications of her own. She dismisses any efforts to define postmodernism through temporal or economic signposts (3), such as those that attribute it to the rise of post-Fordist capitalism, although she concedes that these signposts are generally correct (6). Showing no apparent interest in postmodernism's historical origins, she defends a postmodernism without a history. That effort is aided by some eccentric and highly selective definitions: her inventory of postmodern genres includes such characteristically modernist experiments as the linked short story sequence and the fictional biography (9–10), while her examples of postmodernist artists include Bertolt Brecht and René Magritte (7, 142) but exclude the surfictionists of the 1970s and 1980s (40) on the grounds that the former practice the type of referential metafiction Hutcheon champions and the latter do not. Postmodernism, then, is exactly what Hutcheon wishes it to be, and historiographic metafiction is what defines her brand of postmodernism.

This indifference to historical causation and chronology is no mere oversight or lapse on Hutcheon's part; it rests at the foundations of her analysis. According to Hutcheon, historiographic metafiction "refuses the view that only history has a truth claim, both by questioning the ground of that claim in historiography and by asserting that both history and fiction are discourses, human constructs, signifying systems, and both derive their major claim to truth from that identity" (93). Like any truth that threatens to become a truism, this observation is accurate on its own terms yet also dangerously incomplete. History and fiction are both discourses, but they are discourses with very different standards of evidence and verification—standards that Hutcheon reduces to "positivist and empiricist assumptions" (95) with no greater claims on the truth. Like most literary scholars who discuss history as a narrative and ideological discourse, Hutcheon cites the work of Hayden White, who expresses a similar skepticism about history's claims to represent the real without mediation and an equal conviction that literature may also help us make sense of the world (H. White 98–99). As Eric Berlatsky has suggested, however, even White's earliest and most strident pronouncements about the narrative character of history only call for new and nonnarrative forms of historical writing; he neither denies the possibility of accessing the past nor implies that history and fiction are interchangeable (*Real* 21–23). The lengthy (though still truncated) quote from "The Burden of History" that Hutcheon includes in her deconstruction of historical discourse, in which White urges historians to "expose the historically conditioned character of the historical discipline" (H. White 29; qtd. in Hutcheon 95), affirms the importance of historical causation and contextualization—the first things Hutcheon rejects in her own definition of postmodernism. White may focus on the narrative methodologies that link the discourses of literature and history, but he also recognizes the different claims they make to access and represent the real. Hutcheon's attempt to level these discourses, to render them not just equally valid but, in the form of historiographic metafiction, functionally indistinguishable, has less in common with White's critique of history than it does with the more general academic backlash against empiricism and expertise that accompanied the rise of cultural studies.

As Catherine Liu notes, that backlash had difficulty distinguishing between legitimate critiques of cultural or institutional bias and wholesale rejections of specialized knowledge, critical methodology, or even empirical confirmation itself. In its most extreme forms, the skepticism of academic elites shaded into a suspicion of scientific facts. Cultural studies scholars found their criticisms mirrored by creationists and climate change deniers (Liu 188–190), while in the case of the infamous "Sokal affair," the journal *Social Text* published a hoax article that made nonsense claims about the social and linguistic construction of physical reality, couched in the language of poststructuralist theory (Liu 193–200). To be sure, Hutcheon doesn't make such claims herself: she stresses that postmodernist historiographers and philosophers of history aren't radical relativists or subjectivists and they don't lack concern for history (90). She insists that history and fiction are not equivalent modes of discourse—at least not within what she terms historiographic metafiction, though she acknowledges that other "combinations of history and fiction [. . .] do attempt such equivalence" (112). These fleeting disclaimers aside, Hutcheon opens the door to such equivalencies, particularly through her characterization of empiricism as just another discursive assumption used by historians to maintain their autonomy and authority among the humanities. Her willingness to conflate the discourses of fiction and history, and her indifference to the evidentiary practices that distinguish them, has made her work a source of theoretical support for the historical inventions seen in *Nat Turner*.

Yet Baker's graphic novel doesn't fit her model of historiographic metafiction. Hutcheon observes that postmodern novelists and historiographers both abandon the pretense of objectivity, foregrounding their own ideological perspectives, their discursive situations, and the roles they play in fashioning their narratives (91–92). However, she is careful to stress that historiographic metafiction (unlike the more semiotic metafictions of the surfictionists) never loses sight of its reference to the real world and real events. In fact, it highlights that referentiality: "Historiographic metafiction, like both historical fiction and narrative history, cannot avoid dealing with the problem of the status of their 'facts' and of the nature of their evidence, their documents" (122). For Hutcheon, the primary subject of historiographic metafiction is the process by which events become fashioned into historical narratives; the genre argues that such processes are never neutral and seeks to problematize any belief in the objectivity or transparency of history, most of all its own. One characteristic technique is its appropriation of "the paratextual conventions of historiography (especially footnotes) to both inscribe and undermine the authority and objectivity of historical sources and explanations" (123). Turning history's own techniques against itself, refusing any and all claims to empirical validation, historiographic metafiction asks readers to consider how we make history and how we come to think we know the past.

Nat Turner doesn't do this. True, there are isolated moments—all of them thoroughly tabulated and discussed in the criticism—in which Baker challenges the archival language of slavery or, in Chaney's reading, the power of language itself to narrate and memorialize slavery ("Slave Memory" 291–292). But these moments are few and far between in a book that otherwise remains credulous of its sources and convinced of its history, and invites readers to adopt the same stance. As already noted, Baker doesn't question Gray so much as write around him, augmenting his narrative with other stories and relying on Gray to authenticate his own story in turn. Baker does, in fact, avoid dealing with the status of his facts and evidence, not in the least by adopting a narrative form (the nearly wordless comic) that resists documentation. By reading his partial rejection of language as a critique of historical discourse while neglecting his profound and unquestioning reliance on his primary source, comics scholars have let Baker off the hook for the critical and self-critical interrogations that are also part of historiographic metafiction.

Those interrogations include a refusal of generalized characters and broad historical types, which Hutcheon maintains have little place in historiographic metafiction, "except as something to be undercut" (114). Kunka extends this renunciation to Baker's handling of historic stereotypes, noting that the aforementioned Bible scene, in which young Turner feigns illiteracy to escape punishment, turns the "Sambo" stereotype on its head and converts it into a mode of resistance (Kunka 178). This reading is absolutely correct as far as this particular scene goes, but other scenes deploy equally stereotypical imagery without any such critical function. The slaves who alert white slaveholders to the rebellion are drawn as minstrel caricatures, complete with bulging eyes and shabby clothes that serve as parodies of genteel white dress (Baker 130, 136). They adopt broad grins and theatrical hand gestures (132) and they run in a loping, bowlegged gait, arms splayed wide like cartoon characters (figure 6.4). Turner's adoption of the Sambo pose may be a subversive stratagem, but these characters fully inhabit the minstrel role in deference to white authority. Other stereotypes appear in

FIG. 6.4. *Kyle Baker,* Nat Turner *(Abrams, 2008), p. 136.*

Nat Turner as well: Craig Fischer notes that Will is "a hulking golem, a visual crystallization of the Big, Black Buck figure used to justify slavery" (265)—and, I would add, of the "physically superior majority" Baker envisions in his own preface (7). Everyone in *Nat Turner,* with the exception of Turner himself (and perhaps his mother), functions as a type: the cruel overseer, the sycophantic turncoat, and so forth. Far from renouncing historical types, Baker relies on type and stereotype alike to outline characters, dispense moral judgments, and articulate his eugenic theory of slavery.

Finally, Baker adopts the paratextual conventions of historiography, but he does so in a manner that is both fitful and misleading, one that inscribes the conventions of historical authority without undermining them. The Abrams edition of *Nat Turner* includes a bibliography and endnotes, marking it as work of historical method and substance—yet each of these supplements is barely a page long, hardly substantive documentation for a two hundred-page book. Kunka notes that Baker's bibliography is extremely limited, containing just three sources specifically about Turner (one of which, Terry Bisson's *Nat Turner,* is a children's book) and some notable omissions (Kunka 188n8). The endnotes are similarly sparse, annotating just ten pages and providing only a single source (the aforementioned passage from Douglass). These notes assert historical claims without sourcing them, even when those claims are remarkably specific: in his note to page 196, which depicts the crowd at Turner's execution, Baker writes, "Onlookers were reportedly unsettled by the fact that Turner did not die kicking and suffering as hanged men usually do. He simply rose into the air, breathing his last, peacefully without twitching a muscle" (204). Baker provides no indication of where these reports came from, how he found them, or how reliable they are.[6] He has simply gone through the motions, adopting the conventions of historical discourse without doing or sharing the evidentiary work. This is not the critical self-examination of historiographic metafiction; this is the specious confidence of fiction that claims to be history.

FICTION AS HISTORY

Contrary to the historiographic arguments of some comics scholars, Baker presents a traditionalist view of history—or rather, his own historical narrative—as an objective record of the past. Explaining his research process to Rich Watson, Baker says, "I didn't want anyone to call me a liar. I made sure I wasn't gonna have anything in these books that didn't actually happen for real" (Watson). He made similar comments in a symposium at Howard University in the spring of 2010, when he stated that he simply drew what happened without taking an editorial stance or offering any commentary (Singer, "Week 8"). I organized that symposium, and my presence for those comments may go a long way toward explaining why I read Baker's text so differently from so many of my colleagues. His confident declarations of accuracy and objectivity gloss over the many inventions, omissions, and condensations in his narrative, which he presents as a fact-based contribution to the historical discourse. Baker has also made the absurd claim that "You read books about slavery, very few of them are published by black people" (Watson), erasing not only the testimonies of former slaves but the production of countless writers and scholars. Far from presenting his work as historiographic metafiction, he casts *Nat Turner* as an impartial, transparent, and isolated record of the history of slavery.

Many scholars have been willing to accept these claims at face value. Frances Gateward and John Jennings refer to *Nat Turner* in passing as "historically accurate" (13), while Jan Baetens and Hugo Frey attest repeatedly to its authenticity (234, 237, 239). Howard Rambsy II goes one step further. Describing his experiences reading *Nat Turner* with a group of black college students, he says they regarded Baker's work as *more* instructive than actual historical sources written by former slaves:

> Members of our reading group were hardly aware that black people could have been so rebellious and courageous at every stage of enslavement and along the Middle Passage, nor had we adequately imagined just how far some slaves would go in order to resist enslavement. We had read Frederick Douglass's narrative and we knew of his fight with Covey, as well as Douglass's eventual escape. We had also heard, like many black folks, about the heroics of Harriet Tubman. Baker, however, gave us rare and dramatic visual accounts of anonymous black people engaged in multiple forms of resistance, and his depictions of Africans resisting enslavement long before they arrived in the Americas reminded us that well known figures like Douglass, Tubman, and Turner were the descendants of a host of unacknowledged freedom fighters. (Rambsy 289–290)

Citing one of the most overtly romanticized portions of the narrative, Rambsy suggests Baker improved his group's understanding of slavery.

At no point does metafictional self-reflection on the nature of historical discourse enter the picture.

On the contrary, Rambsy implies that Baker offers an unfiltered and more easily accessible representation of the past: "We had of course all heard of Nat Turner before reading Baker's book. However, how many of us actually considered the look of determined rage on Turner's face as he raised his axe to strike his master?" (292). He assumes that he and his group have seen the look of determined rage on Turner's face, and not Baker's rendition of Turner's emotional state—or, for that matter, Baker's rendition of his face.[7] Those assumptions reveal a strange double standard in which Rambsy acknowledges that Thomas Gray "inevitably presented Turner's testimony to fulfill his own interests" and states that "the reliability of Turner's 'confession' has always been the subject of debate" (294), yet he argues that Baker—who calls on Gray for confirmation and corroboration throughout his narrative—merely "utilizes creative license" to create "more dramatic scenes from Turner's life than what his actual confessions suggest" (294-295). The primary historical source is unreliable, but the ancillary narrative that relies on it manages to improve on its record. Rambsy attempts to paper over this contradiction, writing, "Of course, Baker had likely read or viewed various works on slave rebellions" (295). That "likely" is doing a lot of work here, as is the "various"; anybody who has viewed Baker's bibliography (which Rambsy cites later in this same sentence) knows exactly how many sources he has read.

Conseula Francis describes Baker's research more accurately when she notes that "Baker consulted several primary and secondary documents in addition to the 1831 *Confessions*" (127). Francis nevertheless surpasses Rambsy when she argues that *Nat Turner* is not just dramatically superior to the slave narratives but more historically accurate as well. She maintains that Baker "gives voice to the silences in the traditional slave narrative," a form that, because it was calibrated to appeal to white audiences through the performance of respectability, "cannot adequately express the physical and psychological violence of slavery" (114). For these reasons, Francis contends that "Baker's *Nat Turner*, ultimately, is able to tell the story that the enslaved man himself could not" (114)—a claim she initially makes with respect to Turner's jailhouse confessions but quickly expands to encompass all slave narratives. Indeed, she vacillates between suggesting that Turner's unapologetic reports of brutal violence separate his confessions from the rhetorical performances of nineteenth-century slave narratives (116) and claiming his confessions as one of them: "The form Turner speaks in, the slave narrative (not to mention the jailhouse confession), cannot tell the full story of slavery or of Turner's life" (127). Francis may be ambivalent on whether Turner's confessions constitute a slave narrative, but she is consistent in maintaining that the genre could not offer an honest accounting of the routine, structural violence of slavery, let alone the aberrant violence of Turner's rebellion.[8]

Francis suggests that the authors of the slave narratives, fearful of alienating their white readers, had to learn "how to write about violence using code and metaphor" (118), yet she chooses as her examples Harriet Jacobs and Frederick Douglass, both of whom write in decidedly literal terms about the violence they witnessed and experienced firsthand. Francis claims that because Jacobs was not raped herself, her story of sexual degradation "functions primarily as *metaphor* for all the different sorts of degradations and humiliations suffered by female slaves" (118, her emphasis), a symbolic substitution for and condensation of a larger system of violence. This is exactly the mode of representation Baker uses in chapter 1 of *Nat Turner*, in which the (imagined) experiences of Turner's mother stand in for the larger historical experiences of African slavery and the Middle Passage, but Francis regards those metaphors as an expansion and critique of Gray's *Confessions*, not a limit on Baker's representation (127). Douglass's fight with Edward Covey similarly "stands in for the routine physical violence of slavery" (Francis 119), a description that implies the fight is not also part of that routine violence; the many other violent acts described in vivid detail by Douglass, from his near maiming at Gardner's shipyard to the brutal punishments inflicted on Aunt Hester and other female slaves, go unmentioned. Scholars of the slave narratives generally don't regard Douglass as derelict in his depictions of violence; on the contrary, critics such as Deborah E. McDowell have claimed that his recitations of violence against women are so graphic and voyeuristic as to symbolically participate in that violence (203). Saidiya Hartman declines to reproduce the scene of Aunt Hester's beating for similar reasons, arguing that such reproductions become implicated in their dehumanizing violence (*Scenes* 3–4)—an argument that would, if applied to Kyle Baker, carry troubling implications for his own sensationalistic visuals. In one respect, however, Baker is far more reticent than either Douglass or Jacobs: they delineate structures of violence that never intrude upon his graphic novel, most notably the systematic degradation and rape of enslaved women. Yet Francis views these descriptions only as semantic codes, not as depictions of actual violence recorded by actual eyewitnesses; she chides them for representing that violence through metaphor when Baker doesn't represent it at all.[9]

Nevertheless, Francis insists that it is Turner and Baker, not Douglass or Jacobs, who offer the most uncoded, unfiltered representations of the violence of slavery. Never mind that Turner's confessions, as presented by Gray, detail only the violence done *by* the rebels, glossing over the violence done *to* them, along with all the other abuses of slavery; to claim that Turner offers readers a more complete picture, Gray's editorial role must necessarily be muted. While Francis acknowledges that Gray was a slaveholder and that he may have shaped Turner's narrative to suit his own ends (114), most of these admissions are curiously equivocal. She concedes that "Gray's rhetorical goals are markedly different than Douglass's and Jacobs's" (118) and comments that Gray doesn't "seem particularly motivated by abolitionist zeal, or perhaps, even by the desire to record Turner's words accurately" (134), yet she rarely ventures to suggest exactly what did motivate him or why it might call his narrative authority into question. Gray occupies a strangely indeterminate role in Francis's article, as in other critical treatments of *Nat Turner*: he is both there and not there, like a quantum superposition or the Cheshire cat. His editorial hand is light enough that it never calls Turner's confessions into question, but just heavy enough to ensure there are silences and gaps in his story—gaps that only Kyle Baker can fill through his lurid depictions of graphic violence. Thus, Francis concludes, "Baker's slave narrative completes the picture merely sketched in draft in the 1831 *Confessions*" (136).

Francis's contention that *Nat Turner* is more honest and historically complete than the slave narratives rests on a series of selective and heavily freighted comparisons in which Baker's text, and only Baker's text, is held to be free of mediation and rhetorical performance. On the other hand, Rambsy's point about the greater dramatic value of Baker's narrative is indisputable. The graphic expression, the formal daring, the emotional intensity, to say nothing of the superheroic slugfests and gravity-defying chase sequences—these make for a far more stirring story than Turner's impassive retelling in Gray's account. Fiction allows more opportunities for excitement, catharsis, and empathic identification than most historical primary sources do, and readers generally allow writers of fiction to create such opportunities even at the expense of historical accuracy. But this distinction merely reaffirms one of the key differences between the discourses of fiction and history and the varying truth claims they make. However much some scholars present *Nat Turner* as a transparent window onto the history of slave resistance, Rambsy's acknowledgment of Baker's creative license concedes all the ways he has reshaped, distorted, or departed from the historical record. In the end, *Nat Turner* is neither the historiographic metafiction described by Kunka nor the history that Baker and his most ardent defenders proclaim: it is historical fiction of a particularly dishonest kind, one that freely invents and reshapes history while declaring its accuracy and objectivity.

TEXTURES OF AUTHENTICITY

Those declarations have generally been accepted by critics, in part because some critics have assumed that as a visual narrative, *Nat Turner* offers a more complete and accurate representation of the past. That assumption has led to some outlandish claims on Baker's behalf, such as James Braxton Peterson's flatly false assertion that "his art is the only visual depiction of Nat Turner in history" (217), an assertion that ignores both the one surviving sketch of Turner from his lifetime (Tragle iii) and the many images produced after his capture and execution. Peterson nevertheless remains resolute in his belief that "Baker's reconstructed historical narrative lends the text a palpably authentic aura" (218). That aura is as much a product of Baker's art as it is of his frequent citations of Gray's *Confessions*—and yet the moments when Baker strives to simulate historical authenticity are responsible for some of the most revealing slippages between the historical record and Baker's fictionalized representation. These slippages are not always errors of historical fact, but rather telling lapses that show Baker has little interest in historical representation as such.

One of the most apparent of these slippages can be found in chapter 3, when the militia captain grabs his gun and sets out to quell the rebellion (figure 6.5). The top panel shows a close-up of a cartoonish hand reaching for a weapon that Baker has rendered through photographic reproduction; the image reinforces the book's claims to historical authenticity by depicting what appears to be a period gun. But appearances can be deceiving. A closer examination of the weapon reveals the manufacturer's name, the "Union Fire Arms Co."—a company that operated in Toledo, Ohio, from 1903 to 1913, more than seventy years after the Southampton rebellion ("Union Fire Arms 1907 Catalog"). The image provides further evidence of its anachronism: the

FIG. 6.5. *Kyle Baker,* Nat Turner *(Abrams, 2008), p. 145.*

gun barrel is marked with the words "choke bored," referring to the tapering of a shotgun's bore for greater accuracy, an innovation that wasn't patented until 1866 (Greener 256). Finally, Baker compounds the error with another image that isn't anachronistic but is just as poorly conceived and executed: while the top panel shows a hand, presumably the militia captain's, grabbing a double-barreled shotgun, the bottom one shows the captain running off with a single-barreled musket or rifle, complete with a ramrod that would be of absolutely no use to a breech-loading weapon like the one shown above it.

My point is not to nitpick a single mistake, nor to chastise Baker for his lack of knowledge of nineteenth-century firearms (though such knowledge might have been useful for a comic about a nineteenth-century rebellion). This image is merely one example, albeit a richly layered one, of the many lapses, shortcuts, creative distortions, and outright errors that punctuate Baker's narrative. Those lapses are most easily identified when Baker includes "period" details that appear to originate from the Southampton rebellion or its era but on closer examination almost always turn out to be anachronistic. An image of a bloodied axe clearly shows the maker's mark and label of W. M. Marples & Sons of Sheffield, England (Baker 152); William Marples was making tools as early as the 1820s, but his sons didn't join his company until 1860 ("William Marples and Sons"). Similarly, the small inset photos of houses dotted throughout chapter 3, presumably to indicate the homes visited by Turner's rebels, don't match the photographs provided by Tragle or Bisson, nor those preserved in Sarah N. Roth's digital archive, *The Nat Turner Project*. They appear instead to be stock photos of generic nineteenth-century homes, and considerably grander ones than those documented by Tragle, Bisson, and Roth. Baetens and Frey suggest that these images contribute to the realism of *Nat Turner* (237–239), but such fake period details provide only a shoddy simulacrum of the past.

Baker further contributes to that simulacrum with an antiquated design sensibility that recalls nineteenth- and early twentieth-century visual media. He prints *Nat Turner* in black ink and a sepia wash that evokes late Victorian photography. He frequently represents characters in silhouette and depicts much of the rebellion in small oval panels that derive their form, if not their macabre subject matter, from cameo portraiture. He sometimes frames characters (61, 84, 101) or their thoughts (120) in round panels that mimic cinematic iris shots, a distinctive element in the style of D. W. Griffith and other silent-film directors. Finally, in a visual parallel to his incorporation of text from Gray and Canot, he integrates F. O. C. Darley's engraving "Nat Turner & His Confederates in Conference" into his own images (Baker 111). As the inclusion of anachronistic media and artworks should indicate, however, Baker is less interested in ensuring historical fidelity to Turner's life or his times than in creating a general aura of antiquation. The silhouette was a contemporary art form in 1831, but the Southampton rebellion preceded all but the earliest photographic experiments: daguerreotypes weren't introduced to the public until the end of the decade. The first motion pictures were exhibited in the 1890s, and cinematic conventions like the iris shot weren't developed until the early twentieth century. Similarly, Darley's engraving was first published in 1863, a full generation after the rebellion (French 126). While reprints of the image were frequently painted in full color, Baker makes a different adjustment, rendering it in the same sepia as the rest of his book while altering Turner's features. Even the sepia tones function as a retrospective convention, a chromatic shorthand for the pastness of the past. Chaney comments on the "intrinsic temporal duality of the text, which imagines itself to be not just about but also to originate from the nineteenth century" ("Slave Memory" 280), but that duality produces only a foreshortened modern view of the past.

The same principles govern Baker's graphic representations of historical text. He opens chapter 1 with a reproduction of the title page from the 1832 Richmond printing of Gray's *Confessions*—a relevant and historically proximate image, but one Baker has edited to make it appear even more proximate. As Whitted notes, he has cropped the year, printer, and place of publication (87), unmooring this page from its publication history so efficiently that some critics have misattributed it to the original and distinctive 1831 Baltimore edition (Francis 120). Whitted argues that these alterations, along with the page's relocation to the interior of the text, serve to minimize Gray's role, but they can just as easily support another interpretation: Francis suggests that the placement of the facsimile casts the following pages as part of Gray's *Confessions*, as if Baker were simply illustrating Gray's text rather than composing his own narrative (Francis 120–121). More significantly, Baker has faded the image even though perfectly legible facsimile reproductions are available.[10] These alterations both obscure the page's provenance and exaggerate its age and decrepitude, overselling the historicity of his sources and his subject. Other quotations of Gray's text, such as the mock title page of the abbreviated three-page excerpt that runs in the back of the Abrams edition (Baker 205), take even greater liberties with the layout, typography, capitalization, and other design elements. The list of the white victims of the insurrection printed in chapter 3 draws its text from Gray's *Confessions*, but its format is Baker's invention: where Gray lists the dead in paragraph format, Baker arranges them in a column, and while Gray's typesetters used standard mixed-case letters, Baker prints the heading and the final tally of the dead in screaming capitals and smudged, faux-distressed type (Baker 179). His list of the names of the dead is more prominent, more sensationalized, and more falsely antiquated than Gray's; the most relevant comparison is not the text of *Confessions* but the wanted posters immortalized in western legends and boardwalk photography stands everywhere.

Whether real, fake, or wildly anachronistic, these images of past objects, texts, and art forms serve a common purpose. Unlike the brazen anachronisms of an actual work of historiographic metafiction (such as Ishmael Reed's *Flight to Canada*, in which escaped slave Raven Quickskill flees north on a jumbo jet), Baker conceals his creative license: he doesn't force us to question our construction of historical narrative so much as ask us to accept his narrative as history. That so many of his images are historically inaccurate or chronologically impossible is irrelevant for these purposes, as the critical reaction demonstrates. What Baker offers his readers is not the past but a sense of pastness, not authenticity but the texture of authenticity, the "palpably authentic aura" that Peterson lauds. The most relevant comparison for *Nat Turner* is therefore not history or historiographic metafiction, but—as his description of *Amistad* as both source and competitor should indicate—the period movie.

In his essay "*Django Unchained*, or, *The Help*: How 'Cultural Politics' Is Worse Than No Politics at All, and Why," Adolph Reed Jr. observes that the modern period movie typically strips the past of historical particularity, reducing it to a backdrop for ostensibly timeless themes of love, compassion, or revenge. Echoing the film critic Manohla Dargis, Reed suggests that Hollywood only values historical accuracy in its costume and production design—although in the case of *Nat Turner*, even the prop master has abandoned that responsibility. These creative liberties assume a particularly moralistic character in the case of what Reed terms "black-interest films," which stake claims to education, uplift, and social significance even as they neglect material and institutional forms of oppression in favor of purely interpersonal evils. For Reed, such films "read the sensibilities of the present into the past by divesting the latter of its specific historicity. They reinforce the sense of the past as generic old-timey times distinguishable from the present by superficial inadequacies—outmoded fashion, technology, commodities and ideas—since overcome." Had Reed turned his attentions from film to comics, he would have found these characterizations equally applicable to *Nat Turner*. Baker's prefatory description of his story as a testament to a forgotten historical hero projects exactly the sort of hollow profundity Reed detects in the period film, casting the violent revenge tale that follows as a work of inspiration and empowerment. Similarly, the mélange of anachronistic images and design sensibilities, almost none of which can be traced back to Southampton County, Virginia, in 1831, still serve to signify pastness to readers not inclined to look any further. These are old-timey times; you can tell by the font.

What Baker has created in *Nat Turner*, then, is not history or historiographic metafiction or even historical fiction. It is historicism, but only in the most critical, Jamesonian sense of "the random cannibalization of all the styles of the past" (*Postmodernism* 18). Baker has built a simulacrum of historicity but has put little effort into representing the historical past beyond recycling the clichés of the comics and film genres that were closest at hand. His claims to careful research and historical inspiration, like his "period" imagery, amount to little more than stylistic gestures. Yet the form of history hasn't been vacated of its content so much as inundated, flooded with fictions: Baker freely mingles fact, extrapolation, and invention without distinguishing between them or even acknowledging their copresence in his text. *Nat Turner* is neither beholden to historical accuracy nor openly defiant of it in the manner of Hutcheon's metafictions; it is indifferent to historical accuracy, in a sense very much akin to the indifference to factuality, to truth itself, that philosopher Harry G. Frankfurt calls bullshit.

In his invaluable book *On Bullshit*, Frankfurt suggests that bullshit is something quite distinct from lies. Lies accept the importance of objective constraints of truth, which is why they seek to conceal their violation; bullshit, on the other hand, isn't concerned with the truth at all (33–34). Whereas lies are specific and tactical, presenting certain falsehoods as truths, bullshit is more expansive, improvisational, even artistic, fabricating a context for its more particular fabrications—first and foremost by misrepresenting the bullshit artist's own enterprise as something else entirely (52–54). For all that he publicizes his research in interviews and adopts the markers of historical discourse in his paratextual materials, Baker blends fact, fiction, and cliché with no regard for their truth or falsehood, claiming the mantle of history for them all. The parts of *Nat Turner* that are grounded in historical fact don't alter this pattern of misrepresentation. As Frankfurt observes, "[T]he essence of bullshit is not that it is *false* but that it is *phony* [. . .] although it is produced without concern for the truth, it need not be false. The bullshitter is faking things. But this does not mean he necessarily gets them wrong" (47–48). This passage may be less relevant to Baker's comic, which gets a great many things wrong and fakes many more, than it is to his preface, which has produced such divergent interpretations among scholars. Baker has thrown off his critics by adopting a self-consciously sarcastic tone while describing his book and his beliefs with perfect sincerity; in other words, he even bullshits us about bullshitting.

The challenge of determining Baker's sincerity or insincerity is exacerbated by his indifference to the premises of evidence and verification that rest at the foundation of scholarly inquiry. Because it ignores not just the truth but the authority of the truth, bullshit, Frankfurt argues, "is a greater enemy of the truth than lies are" (61). Of course, some scholars in the humanities have already rejected such appeals to the authority of truth. Frankfurt suggests that a loss of belief in the knowability of truth leads inevitably to either intellectual paralysis or bullshit (61–62); he makes this critique even more explicit when he traces the "contemporary proliferation of bullshit" to "various forms of skepticism which deny that we can have any reliable access to an objective reality and which therefore reject the possibility of knowing how things truly are" (64). He refers specifically to the antirealist doctrines of analytic philosophy, but five decades of cultural studies and poststructuralist theory have expanded this skepticism to the sciences, as demonstrated by the "science wars" of the 1990s; to history, as seen in Hutcheon's skepticism of "positivist and empiricist assumptions" (95); and to comics, as seen in that skepticism's ready adaptation to the critical discussion of *Nat Turner*. An intellectual climate that disdains truth claims has allowed comics scholars not only to accept Baker's poor history but to defend and compound it.

Those scholars might well object that asserting the authority of the truth is one thing, but claiming to represent it is quite another; we can accept the possibility of reference to an external reality and still maintain that history, like any other kind of narrative, is a subjective and ideological construct, always open to reinterpretation and debate. Yet Baker's lapses extend even into the rather less subjective field of astronomy. At various points in *Nat Turner*, Baker uses a multipanel graphic of the phases of the

FIG. 6.6. *Kyle Baker,* Nat Turner *(Abrams, 2008), p. 183.*

moon to signify the passage of time (29, 33, 183). These graphics show the moon waxing and waning from left to right in a "C-O-D" pattern (figure 6.6); assuming the viewer is in the northern hemisphere, as Turner certainly is when he is depicted in one of these scenes, the moon actually illuminates from right to left in a "D-O-C" pattern.[11] To complicate the matter further, in the midst of these lunar errors Baker once gets the phase pattern right (95). His narrative's internal consistency is no more immune to his indifference than are the laws of nature. These are hardly the most significant errors in *Nat Turner*, but they are the most empirically measurable ones, evidence of Baker's careless disregard for truth, accuracy, and referentiality; they are bullshit written on a cosmic scale.

FAILURES OF INSPIRATION

Most scholars have ignored Baker's problem with the truth, largely because they have made no effort to read *Nat Turner* against the historical record (let alone the astronomical one). Some critics argue that record is so incomplete or unreliable as to license almost any artistic invention, a claim Baker himself invites: in his preface, he asserts that he never found more than "a few sentences" about Turner in any book (6), a statement that says more about his research than about the volume of historical scholarship on Turner. As Greenberg cautions in "Name, Face, Body," the obliteration of Turner's identity has deprived historians of some of the most basic information about him, including his appearance and the disposition of his remains. However, the Southampton rebellion has yielded a wealth of historical documentation and research that belies Baker's anemic bibliography; Greenberg and Tragle have collected copious primary and secondary sources into convenient editions. Nevertheless, those sources haven't prevented Francis from citing Baker's comment about those "few sentences" as justification for his project, not once but three times (113, 114, 120). Peterson (216) and Jonathan Gray (184) similarly overstate the incompleteness of the historical record, particularly in comparison to what little Baker shows of it. If scholars choose to accept his narrative as history, it's not because he writes into a void, but because he writes what they are ready to hear.

Rambsy and his college reading group praise *Nat Turner* for highlighting "the notion of black resistance as central to the circumstances of slavery" (289) and for allowing them to visualize such resistance. As Adolph Reed points out, filmmakers and critics have used similar inspirational claims to justify the period films' erasure of ideology, of material power, of politics as anything other than the story of individual struggle and achievement; he particularly singles out films that use black heroes or narratives of black resistance for those purposes, concealing their ideological evasions behind the guise of cultural uplift. Reed argues that these films typically participate in "a discourse that displaces a politics challenging social structures that reproduce inequality with concern for the feelings and characteristics of individuals." For Reed, critics who prioritize and valorize such cultural politics—often at the expense of structural and institutional politics—share the culture industry's "fetishization of heroes and penchant for inspirational stories" in which exceptional individuals triumph against overwhelming opposition. In Deborah McDowell's words, such stories also promote "the myth of the male slave as militant, masculine, dominant, and triumphant in both private and public spheres," a narrative that served to challenge the Stanley Elkins thesis of slave passivity and docility at the cost of enshrining patriarchy as a revolutionary practice (196). These assumptions are legible not only in Rambsy's approving descriptions of black resistance in *Nat Turner*, but also in those critical accounts that cast Baker's Turner as a moral exemplar: Peterson, for example, claims that *Nat Turner* "chronicles the history of one of Black Nationalism's greatest heroes" (216).

To make Turner conform to this preference for tales of inspiration, uplift, and triumph, however, critics must affirm the success of his rebellion while obscuring or ignoring its disastrous consequences. Peterson tempers his praise with a rough tally of the hundreds of African Americans who were murdered in the brutal backlash, yet just two pages later he refers to Turner as "a successful revolutionary" and "a paragon of Black Nationalist ideology" (216, 218). Turner's admirers emphasize his symbolic value out of necessity, as his rebellion failed utterly in its strategic objective of seizing the town of Jerusalem and inspiring a larger revolt among slaves in Southampton County (Oates 68). Instead, news of the rebellion sparked a violent panic across the region; Oates reports that at least 120 slaves and free black people who had no involvement in the rebellion were killed in the immediate backlash (100), though Greenberg suggests this figure is "probably a minimum" and notes that "the revolt was far more a tale of the death of slaves than of masters" (*Confessions* 19). The panic continued well after the rebellion was quashed, with rumors of a nonexistent slave army fueling lynchings and executions in North Carolina (Oates 107). Including those who were killed in the fighting or executed after the fact, Oates estimates that "Nat Turner's rebellion cost the lives of approximately sixty whites and more than two hundred Negroes" (126).

Nor were the rebellion's consequences limited to its body count. White Virginians, including Governor John Floyd, blamed the violence on northern agitators, abolitionists, black preachers, black religious meetings, and black literacy itself. Free black people were subject to particular persecution, leading to a mass exodus from Southampton County; Greenberg reports that as much as one-fifth of that population emigrated to Liberia following the revolt (*Confessions* 22). While the Virginia legislature considered a proposal to end slavery in the state through graduated emancipation and removal, they instead passed legislation that further restricted black religious meetings and slave schools (Oates 140; French 60). These repressive measures soon spread to other Southern states, which expanded their militias and tightened their slave codes (Oates 142). Harriet Jacobs offers a firsthand account of the immediate reaction in Edenton, North Carolina, more than fifty miles away from Jerusalem, where white militias whipped and tortured black residents while looting their homes (chap. 12). In the weeks that followed, white citizens placed further restrictions on the movements of slaves and destroyed the black church in Edenton. Contrary to Francis's claim that the slave narratives represent violence only in metaphor, Jacobs details the South's increasing radicalization and mobilization in defense of slavery in the wake of the Southampton rebellion. As Oates would write more than a century later, "Thanks to white intransigence and to those oppressive new codes, Virginia's blacks were more shackled to the rack of slavery than they had ever been" (141).

The critical discussion of *Nat Turner* has failed to account for these consequences, largely because Baker himself neglects them. While he shows some of Turner's followers dying in the fighting (most notably Will), he doesn't depict any of the executions other than Turner's, let alone the violent panic or the increased legal restrictions that followed. Although his preface and his frontispiece image of a slave reading a pilfered copy of Gray's *Confessions* frame his story as a testament to the power of reading, he doesn't address the closing of the slave schools and religious meetings. And, as previously mentioned, he graphically amplifies Gray's list of the white victims of the rebellion but lavishes no such attention on the many black victims of the backlash. Comics scholars, generally content to accept Baker's myopic account as history, have followed his lead in avoiding these subjects. Francis mentions the rebellion's white victims multiple times

(114, 127, 133) but never addresses the black ones, presumably because they don't appear in Baker's narrative. By ignoring their deaths and otherwise overlooking the backlash, Baker and his critics both promote the inspirational narrative of Turner's rebellion at the expense of a full accounting of its costs.

Turner's victories, such as they were, also pose a dilemma for scholars. His rebellion is commemorated as the most successful slave uprising in American history, but in practice it accomplished little more than the murders of dozens of civilians, predominantly children. Some critics manage these contradictions by arguing that the violence in *Nat Turner* achieves a kind of retributive balance. Francis repeatedly stresses the horrific nature of the violence seen in chapter 3 (133–135), but she adds that "Baker first spends 100 pages focusing that same unflinching gaze on the institution of slavery and the violence and destruction it inflicts. Turner's violence is not an aberration, then. It is a consequence of slavery" (134). What Francis proposes is not simply a historical context in which slavery created the conditions that impelled Turner to act, but a moral causality in which that institution bears sole responsibility for those actions, even at a generation's remove: "Consequently, the death of the Travis baby in Book 3 was written all the way back in Book 1 when Turner's mother's suicide attempt to escape slavery is thwarted by that slaver's rope around her ankle" (135). Chaney offers a similar reading of the book's causality, noting how Baker traces a chain of events from one infanticide on the Middle Passage to another in the Travis house, "making Turner an intelligible cipher of retributive justice" ("Slave Memory" 293). Francis and Chaney read Baker's moral logic accurately, though not critically—not in the sense that Jonathan Gray observes how Will's splash-page murder of the child at the Francis house "can be understood in Žižekian terms as the inevitable response to systemic violence," but adds, "it is difficult to locate the heroism in these actions" (196). If we choose to apply Baker's moral logic, it is just as impossible to attribute any heroism to Turner and his followers as it is to level the more censorious readings that Francis attempts to discount in her essay. To depict Turner's actions as inevitable and retributive consequences of historical causality is to remove him from moral agency or culpability, turning him into a mere instrument—or, as Chaney says, a cipher.

This exculpatory logic is only one of the ways *Nat Turner* shrinks away from a truly unflinching account of its protagonist's actions. Francis's argument that Baker offers a conflicted, morally ambiguous representation of

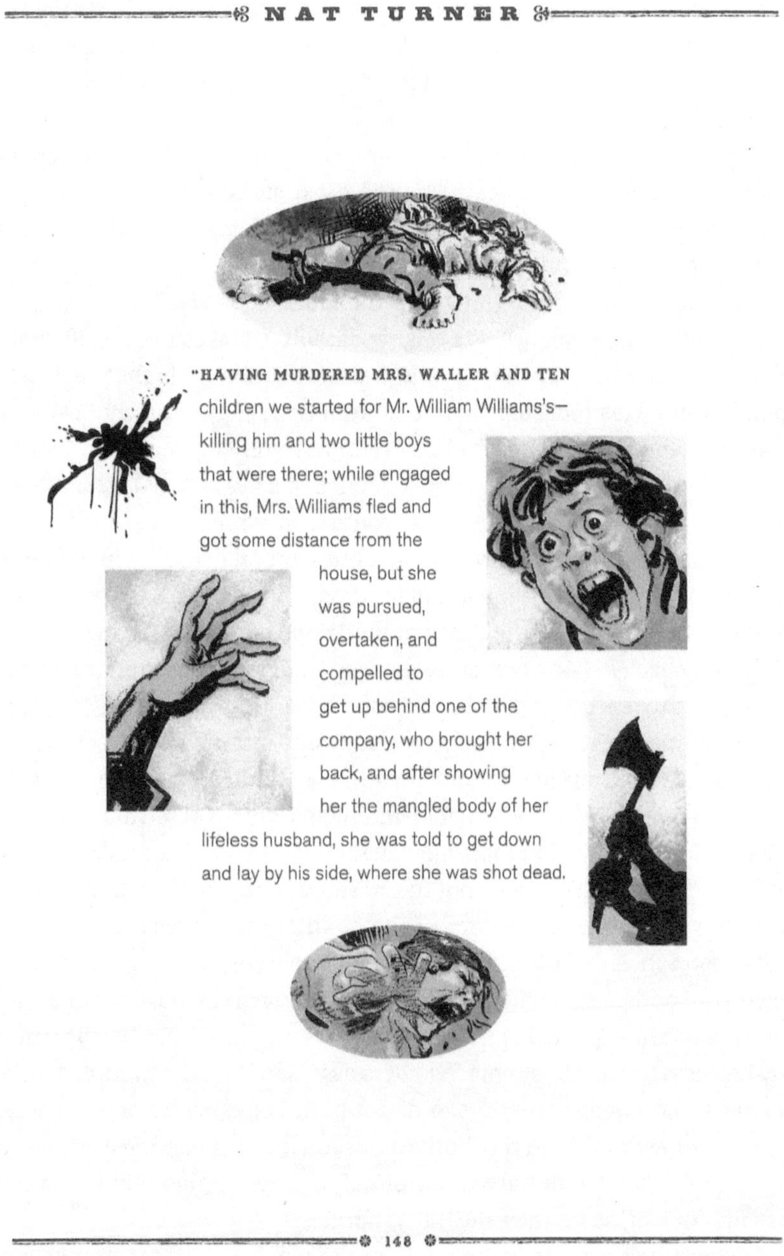

FIG. 6.7. *Kyle Baker,* Nat Turner *(Abrams, 2008), p. 148.*

the rebellion, and her contrast of that representation with the nineteenth-century slave narratives, rests on her claim that Baker "does nothing to sugarcoat the violence of Turner's 1831 raid on the people of Southampton County" (114). This is true of some individual scenes like the grotesque image of Will beheading the child (135), an image that, like so many other grotesques in *Nat Turner*, serves as a metaphoric condensation of a larger pattern of violence. However, the overall representation of the rebellion is so spotty, inconsistent, and reliant on Gray's text that it does occlude or minimize much of the brutality, keeping other instances of violence against children discreetly off-panel. Baker shows Will raising an axe over the sleeping Travis infant, but the completion of the swing is left to the reader's imagination and to the terse narration from Gray's *Confessions* (Baker 121). The murder and decapitation of ten schoolchildren at the Levi Waller farm happens across a page break; on one page Turner is sending his men ahead of him on horseback and on the next the children are already dead (147–148), replicating a similar elision in *Confessions*. The inset panels, which accompany Turner's narration of a subsequent killing, form a collage of fragmentary images: an upraised axe, a splatter of blood, an outstretched hand, the terrified face of a still living child, the fallen bodies of the dead (figure 6.7). Baker's intense cropping displays parts but not wholes, causes and consequences but not actions, obscuring the violence most likely to disturb readers. These omissions become silent partners to the book's retributive causality, enabling readers, if not to justify the displaced violence, then certainly to remove it from moral judgment.

UNSPEAKABLE THINGS SPOKEN

Some critics have extended this absolution to Baker's graphic adaptation, arguing that his willingness to represent the unspeakable violence of slavery outweighs any challenges to his historical accuracy. Used by scholars such as Francis to denote both the systemic violence of slavery and the anomalous violence of the Turner rebellion, invocations of the unspeakable are not simply descriptions of scale or intensity but ideologically loaded claims. For Naomi Mandel, the unspeakable "is not merely an entity toward which we can gesture, with compelling injunctions to speak, witness, testify, or remember; it is, moreover, a discursive production that is re-created and reinforced whenever the limits of language, of comprehension, and of thought are evoked" (4). The unspeakable doesn't simply describe acts of atrocity; it makes claims on how such atrocities should be represented while declaring the limits of representability itself. Jonathan Gray, expanding on Mandel's formulation, observes that unspeakable historical events command deference from artists and scholars, who must acknowledge that "the magnitude of these atrocities can never truly be apprehended or appreciated—even as they plumb these sites of trauma for narrative inspiration" (193). He contends that slavery has only recently attained this status, following the controversy over Styron's novel and the battle for control over Nat Turner's memory and legacy (193).

Given Americans' long-standing refusal to acknowledge the horrors of slavery or to account for their centrality to our history, it doesn't seem quite right to suggest that slavery has only newly become unspeakable. Rather, it has acquired a new stature of unspeakability, one that complements but has not wholly replaced the old one. Toni Morrison addresses this older sense in her essay "Unspeakable Things Unspoken: The Afro-American Presence in American Literature" (briefly referenced by both Gray and Francis), in which she discusses not only slavery but race itself—by which she means blackness—as a "prescribed absence" in early American literature (14), a great unspoken that informed that literature in ways that subsequent generations of scholars have only recently begun to acknowledge. Morrison's definition of the unspeakable is more expansive than Gray's, historically speaking, and yet these accounts are not mutually exclusive. Gray describes a more recent phenomenon, a capacity to deny comprehension and to compel silence not in the name of avoiding the unspoken but, ostensibly, of respecting it—even if the end result is much the same. In order for slavery to be unspeakable in this latter, Mandelian sense, Gray argues, it must be "capable of demanding deference from the very people who seek to address it sympathetically" (193). This capability seems both fairly recent and eminently applicable to the critical discussion of *Nat Turner*.

The precepts of unspeakability are not, however, the only rhetoric available to comics. In "Comics as Literature? Reading Graphic Narrative," Hillary Chute argues that comics are particularly adept at depicting historical trauma because artists refuse to follow the protocols of unspeakability, rendering trauma visible while recognizing the challenges it poses to representation (459). She expands on this argument in *Graphic Women*, tracing the rhetoric of unspeakability to its roots in poststructuralist theory and suggesting that comics can offer a counternarrative:

> the force and value of graphic narrative's intervention, on the whole, attaches to how it pushes on conceptions of the unrepresentable that have become commonplace in the wake of deconstruction, especially in contemporary discourse about trauma. Against a valorization of absence and aporia, graphic narrative asserts the value of presence, however complex and contingent (2).

For Chute, that complex and contingent presence can lead to "new possibilities for writing history," suggesting that in comics, "historical accuracy is not the opposite of creative invention; the problematics of what we consider fact and fiction are made apparent by the role of drawing" ("Comics" 459). She describes something akin to Saidiya Hartman's "critical fabulation," a creative imagining that exposes the limits of the historical archive, although without Hartman's emphasis on the impossibility of such a project or its antipathy to historical discourse ("Venus" 11). These practices would seem to be relevant to *Nat Turner*, although Baker's drawings rarely address the problematics of historical representation in the manner Chute describes. With the exception of Andrew Kunka, most comics scholars haven't applied Chute's observations about fictionality and history to the discussion of *Nat Turner*, perhaps because Chute (unlike Hartman) also removes the primary argument they have applied in defense of Baker's fabrications: the sanctity of the unspeakable.

Mandel notes that assertions of the unspeakability of Turner's narrative take on political overtones, allowing contemporary readers and critics "to participate in what they perceive as the rebellion's historical and ethical stakes" (143). This too seems applicable to the critical discussion of *Nat Turner*, not in the least for Mandel's subtle distinction between what readers perceive those stakes to be (the dismantling of slavery and white supremacy) and the material consequences of the rebellion and its backlash. But here, too, there are significant differences between Mandel's reading of unspeakability and the forms of unspeakability invoked by comics scholars. Mandel suggests that modern readers of Gray's *Confessions* use the unspeakable "to distinguish between the literary and the historical, representation and experience" (143)—in other words, to separate Gray's literary voice from Turner's historical testimony and experience, preserving a space for Turner's narrative agency while maintaining contemporary literary theory's suspicion of representation. Comics scholars have done just the opposite, collapsing distinctions between the literary and the historical or assuming the accessibility of Turner's experience through Gray's narrative representation. Even those scholars who presume the impossibility of objective historical representation end up reaffirming Baker's affirmation of the historical truth of his narrative. This contradiction may be explained, though not resolved, by the observation that Baker leaves them little choice. He claims the authority of the historian so baldly, and in the face of such obvious fabrications, that his critics must either follow him in collapsing the distinction between history and fiction or else hold him accountable for it—and comics scholars have worked hard to ensure that passing that sort of critical judgment on any comic, particularly one with such politically and historically charged subject matter, is simply not an option.

Thus Francis, noting that "readers might question whether the events of Book 1 are true," offers this in reply: "I would answer that the factuality of Turner's mother's life, as depicted by Baker, is beside the point" (126). Her response to any questions or criticisms of Baker's historical inventions is to remove them from consideration on the grounds of the narrative's unspeakability: "The point is that Baker uses the comics form, the interdependence of verbal and visual elements, to highlight the ways *Confessions* fails to tell us what we want to know, and perhaps fail[s] to tell us Turner's actual story" (126–127). The unspeakable is evoked here not as a barrier to any and all representation—for Francis exempts *Nat Turner* from the silencing she detects in the nineteenth-century slave narratives—but as a defense against any criticisms of Baker's fabrications and any evaluations that don't align with dominant critical readings of the text. Citing my comments on teaching *Nat Turner* (Singer, "Week 8"), Francis claims that my "wish that *Nat Turner* 'had the courage to judge or condemn its hero as easily as it praises him' suggests a longing for the same kind of moral certainty, one in which lashing out violently against a pervasive system of dehumanizing and degrading oppression is always wrong" (118).[12] A less contentious paraphrase might have said that lashing out violently, even against a pervasive system of dehumanizing and degrading oppression, is always subject to critical interpretation and judgment, but that statement might well have received the same response. Francis attempts to link my objections to Baker's equivocations to the "respectability test" and the "morality test" that nineteenth-century audiences applied to slave narratives (116)—tests that supposedly silenced their authors and limited their ability to represent the violence inherent in slavery. If those slave narratives aren't as evasive as she implies, neither is *Nat Turner* as direct as she claims. For Francis, the unspeakable is not an absolute historical condition of Turner's experience, but a mutable rhetorical standard that she uses to present Baker's loose imagining of Gray's heavily edited record of Turner's incomplete testimony as the most unmediated version of his story.

This is the unspeakable, not in Morrison's sense of a prescribed absence, but in Mandel's sense of willed deference. Whatever its aims, its effect is not to expose the systemic horrors of slavery and their centrality to American history and culture, but to enforce a set of social norms as to how those horrors may be represented and how those representations may be discussed. Baker's romantic inventions and blithe indifference to the historical record don't trouble scholars who view Turner as a successful revolutionary or a nationalist icon; they share Baker's romantic view of his subject and so praise his comic for its authenticity. Only when Baker's story is measured against the historical archive is that archive suddenly rendered incomplete and unreliable. Only then does Turner's narrative become unspeakable and inaccessible, except through Baker's creative and heroic interventions, which stand as far beyond judgment as Turner's own actions.

Mandel observes that both critics and defenders of Styron's *Confessions* invoked notions of an objective history in order to condemn or praise Styron's work (144–148). Both factions stressed the historical Turner's inaccessibility, his muteness, his unspeakability and unspokenness, as a means of either castigating Styron for his appropriation of Turner's voice or releasing him from any obligations to emulate Thomas Gray's suspect narrative. By contrast, many of the scholars who write on *Nat Turner* dismiss the notion of history entirely—not just the outmoded belief that an objective record exists independent of any cultural or ideological influence, but the idea that the discourse of history, by virtue of its regimes of evidence and verification, both allows for and demands qualitatively different sorts of truth claims than are permitted in the discourse of fiction. Ironically, even as they echo the Ten Black Writers' investment in a heroic Nat Turner, some of these scholars adopt the same position as Styron's most passionate defenders: if the historical record were truly as incomplete as they claim, then Baker and Styron would both have the freedom to invent any Turner they please. In fact, the archival work of Tragle, Oates, Greenberg, and other historians demonstrates that the events of the Southampton rebellion and its aftermath are quite well documented, even if Turner's thoughts and motivations remain accessible only through Gray's editorially mediated account and an equally subjective and unreliable folk tradition. Baker simply chooses to ignore these archives—to the extent that he bothered to explore them in the first place—in favor of presenting a heroic fiction more in keeping with his background and his audience in the comics market.

History is never a static discourse, much less an infallible one. For years, scholars believed that the Thomas Gray who wrote *The Confessions of Nat Turner* was a planter in his sixties who owned dozens of slaves. Those beliefs were upended in 1978, when Southampton County historian Thomas C. Parramore discovered that Turner's confessor was actually thirty-one-year-old lawyer Thomas Ruffin Gray; the elder Gray was his father, who died shortly after the rebellion (Parramore 105–107). Such revisions are both a normal part of historical discourse and a chastening reminder that even the most carefully researched accounts may still contain false assumptions or faulty information. Unfortunately, Baker's research is anything but careful. Following the lead of Terry Bisson, who described Gray as "an elderly white man" (101) a full ten years after Parramore's revelations, Baker draws Gray as an older man (188–190), adhering to assumptions that were nearly thirty years out of date. We don't need to hold any illusions about history's objectivity to find Baker's version of history equally illusory and misleading.

Similarly, I don't emphasize the importance of the historical record in order to dictate the limits of representation in the manner of the Ten Black Writers and their respondents (Mandel 154–155). Whether their purpose is to rule out particular interpretations or to maintain a general suspicion of representation itself, such appeals to a narrowly conceived historical fidelity seek to make the past unspeakable. I hope that bringing the rich and frequently contentious historical discourse about Nat Turner into dialogue with the sparse and historically ill-informed comics discourse around *Nat Turner* will help render at least part of that past speakable again. I also hope it will expand the range of arguments and interpretations in the discussion of *Nat Turner*—a discussion that must begin to recognize how and where Baker departs from the historical record, what he invents in its place, why he makes these changes, and why so many comics scholars have either ignored or defended them. The absence of such recognition has fostered a contradictory and self-negating consensus in which Gray's *Confessions* is at once an incomplete and unreliable record and a perfectly accurate primary source, in which Turner is unknowable but his testimony to Gray is more credible than any narrative written by a former slave, in which Kyle Baker transcends the failings of his sources to provide the most historically accurate narrative by disregarding the historical evidence. All that matters is the veneer of historicism, the palpably authentic aura, and most importantly the inspirational tale of black resistance that obviates even these empty gestures toward historicity.

In *The Return of Nat Turner: History, Literature, and Cultural Politics in Sixties America*, Albert E. Stone charts how generations of novelists, critics, historians, and readers interpreted and reinterpreted Nat Turner from the 1960s to the 1980s, with each faction finding the Turner who most spoke to their own values. As Greenberg says in "Name, Face, Body," "Our search for Nat Turner repeatedly directs us down a hallway lined with endless mirrors in which we are forever destined to see little more than the reflections of our own faces" (23). Baker's graphic novel and the critical discussion it has generated have continued that pattern into the twenty-first century. Unfortunately, because they generally eschew historical methods and sources even as they make historical claims, Baker and his critics offer a portrayal of Nat Turner and the Southampton rebellion that ranges from the incomplete to the mythical. Even the most fictionalized historical fictions can still tell us truths, but the insights they yield reveal far more about our culture than Turner's. They tell us about our values, our priorities, our suspicion of history, our disdain for reference, and our fear of judgment: the truths we ignore, and the lies we cherish.

AFTERWORD

NEVER APOLOGIZE, NEVER DEFEND

The indifference to facts, evidence, and regimes of verification is hardly limited to the critical discussion of *Nat Turner* or even to comics studies in general. In recent years, a number of scholars in the humanities and social sciences have voiced their frustration with the suspicion of reference and the hostility to empirical description that they see as endemic to critical theory in its present form. This includes some erstwhile promoters of that suspicion, such as sociologist Bruno Latour, who once regarded scientific rationality, objectivity, and even facts themselves as contingent social constructs (Liu 188–189). Taking note of the rhetorical confluence between his critiques and the willful but unscientific skepticism mustered by climate change deniers, Latour came to regret the iconoclastic impulses of critical theory (Latour 226–227). His recantation, along with literary critic Eve Kosofsky Sedgwick's call for a turn from paranoid to reparative modes of reading, has sparked a trend toward "postcritical reading" in the humanities. But while this trend offers an important corrective to extreme formulations of social constructionism, antirealism, and the refusal of empiricism, it also threatens to devalue the social and intellectual purposes of critical reading. We should question the reflexive suspicion of referentiality—or reflexive suspicion of anything else, including suspicion itself—but if any single claim animates this book, it is that comics scholarship needs more criticism, not less.

Literary scholars have nevertheless taken up the project of postcritical reading in works such as *The Limits of Critique*, in which Rita Felski laments the dominance of what Paul Ricoeur termed the hermeneutics of suspicion: the demystifying, debunking sensibility that approaches every text as a set of problematic assumptions waiting to be revealed. Despite the radical and oppositional stances adopted by most critical readers in the humanities, nothing guarantees those hermeneutics will always be applied to radical purposes, particularly when they are marshaled against the authority of facts, evidence, or empirical methods; Felski also uses the example of the climate change denier who attributes inconvenient data to hidden bias (3, 45). She identifies this mode of critique as "antinormative normativity: skepticism as dogma" (9), but as the denialists demonstrate, skepticism that is selectively applied to one's enemies and untethered to any kind of evidentiary standard is not skeptical at all: it is dogma masquerading as skepticism. Comparisons to climate change denial may seem extreme, as comics scholarship (like most cultural studies scholarship) would appear to be neither as empirical nor as consequential as environmental science. But this view slights our subjects and our own scholarly work. As the critical discussion of *Nat Turner* demonstrates, questions of empirical and historical fact are not alien to the humanities; while the forms of confirmation are less positivistic, the Southampton rebellion was no less real. Unfortunately, this belief in the evidentiary power of referentiality has been devalued in contemporary critical theory, which often presumes—and sometimes insists—that not only texts but whole interpretive frameworks are governed solely by social and linguistic determinations, with no possibility of external verification.

This doesn't mean, however, that readings that avoid taking oppositional stances are wholly free of the hermeneutics of suspicion. The tools of critique may be enlisted to praise as easily as they condemn, provided we can make the objects of our study participate in the critique themselves. As Felski points out, literature is now routinely commended "for its power to defamiliarize and demystify, to lay bare the banality of the commonplace, to highlight the sheer contingency and constructedness of meaning. We did not need to be suspicious of the text, in short, because it was already doing the work of suspicion for us" (16). This is the mechanism by which a liberal-humanist memoir is transformed into a critique of liberal humanism, a series that embraces Victorian stereotypes is recast as an attack on Victorian values, or a work of romantic mythologization is hailed for its historical accuracy. Features that are readily apparent in the text are overlooked in the interest of uncovering a deeper, less obvious critique of the expected targets of critique: universalist principles, for example, or cultural values now considered repugnant, or a belief in the referentiality of historical discourse. If such beliefs are voiced by the texts themselves, or if evidence of their critical function is thin on the ground, that need not alter the end result.

In short, we have fallen into the habit of locating critiques in comics that cannot bear their weight. A jaded observer might attribute this to simple self-interest on the part of scholars: we would be out of work if we couldn't demonstrate that texts are filled with hidden meanings in need of revelation. Beyond its narrow and reductive sense of the work of scholarship, however, this interpretation is itself an example of the reflexive suspicion that Latour and Felski deplore, the cynical iconoclasm that seeks to expose and denounce everyone else's motives without subjecting our own to the same scrutiny. A more charitable (and, I think, accurate) explanation would suggest that scholars have attempted to transpose the professional habits of critique onto the comics we study as a means of securing their status as objects fit for academic inquiry. In this view, critique serves as the passport to intellectual credibility, and comics that can be shown to reward the patterns and practices of critical analysis have rapidly found a place within the academy. As that place becomes more established, however, the cause of academic legitimation becomes less urgent. As comics embed themselves more deeply in universities, libraries, museums, galleries, and other cultural institutions, comics studies can accept—and those institutions may eventually demand—more oppositional critical stances. An institutionally mature comics studies could not only highlight the ways comics already flatter academic sensibilities but address all the ways they do not. Better yet, it could call those sensibilities into question, starting with the assumption that discovering a critique in a text constitutes a form of critique in and of itself—particularly when the text refuses to cooperate.

Felski further observes that critique is not just a function of adopting any particular theoretical doctrine or ideological position, but also a matter of following recognizable conventions of affect and tone. Critique is a familiar set of narrative structures, rhetorical postures, scholarly voices, and shared critical moods that threatens to occlude alternative ways of approaching texts. Readings may adopt these discursive formulas while applying their associated conceptual tools in only the most desultory fashion, if at all, placing the style of critique before its substance. One of the solutions Felski considers is changing the affect of criticism, swapping negativity and suspicion for positivity and affirmation. Such an approach can be especially relevant for fields that seek to open the canon to new works or new interpretive strategies; as Felski observes, feminist criticism, queer theory, and cultural studies have celebrated the affective aspects of reading as part of their mission to promote the study of previously neglected texts, to the benefit of the entire field of literary criticism (29–30).

Unfortunately, this particular remedy wouldn't cure what ails comics studies. We have enthusiasm and positive affect in abundance, and they have merely redirected our suspicions away from the comics we study and onto the critical paradigms we might have used to apprehend them. Henry Jenkins's call for a return to the treehouse is inseparable from his distrust of academic disciplinarity; W. J. T. Mitchell's patronizing nostalgia is mirrored by his blithe dismissal of basic genre theory; and Angela Ndalianis's skeptical (if not especially accurate) reading of Eco is not leavened by her fondness for *Smallville*. Felski is well aware of the anti-intellectualism that runs through the populist strain of cultural studies, pronouncing it a "weirdly self-hating and self-canceling form of argument" (139) that has led academics to advocate their own irrelevance. Nor does this oppositional stance constitute, in the end, much of an opposition; as Felski points out, cultural studies shares this iconoclastic posture with the academic discourse that it otherwise claims to reject (141). The major schools of comics scholarship tend to bear out this formulation: though the literary and media studies approaches typically prioritize different types of comics, both schools seek to legitimate their subjects by demonstrating that they challenge cultural hierarchies, historical narratives, or other forms of received wisdom. The palpable affection these scholars have for their chosen subjects has not reduced their dependence on the hermeneutics of suspicion.

Other scholars, dissatisfied with the limitations of suspicious reading, have sought to change their tools rather than their tone. Stephen Best and Sharon Marcus suggest broadening the scope of criticism from symptomatic readings that root out hidden meanings to surface readings that account for the manifold ways texts present themselves to and interact with readers. Comics studies could benefit from an infusion of such reading practices, and to some extent it already has. Amy Malek stands out among Satrapi scholars for her willingness to take *Persepolis* on its own terms, recognizing its appeals to universalism and liberal humanism without attempting to contort the book into a critique of its own values. Significantly, Malek is a sociocultural anthropologist writing for the journal *Iranian Studies*, not a literature or cultural studies scholar indebted to the hermeneutics of suspicion. While her background in the social sciences results in certain blind spots (such as her belief in the transparency of memoir), it also exempts her from the habits of symptomatic reading—and as a result, she is better positioned to read *Persepolis* than some experienced book reviewers and literature scholars. This is not to say that English professors can't also follow the practices of surface reading. Conseula Francis and Michael Chaney both take Kyle Baker's preface to *Nat Turner* at face value, reading it as a sincere statement of his beliefs rather than a performance of distancing irony; they approach the preface as a key to Baker's romanticized vision of history, not a barrier. Surface reading, in these applications, is not a movement from the depths of interpretation to the shallows of mere description, but a means of refocusing our attention from what we can make the text say to what it already says without our intervention.

For all its obvious advantages, however, an attention to manifest meanings can also shade into unreflective or overly credulous appraisals. This would include Malek and Francis, who both assume they are reading transparent accounts of real events rather than mediated narratives or romantic fabrications. Ironically, this credulity can also sustain the same critical practices that Best and Marcus, Felski, and other critics of critique seek to challenge; Francis's dismissal of historical sources and rejection of historicized criticisms (necessary moves to maintain Baker's claims to historicity) serve as reminders that even surface readings can be suspicious ones. These problems persist into some of the theoretical rationales for postcritical reading, which denounce the hermeneutics of suspicion in favor of an analytics of description. The most extreme advocates may nevertheless retain the cynical assumptions, the inflexible theoretical models, and above all the distrust of referentiality that have characterized suspicious modes of reading. Indeed, they may apply them not just to the practices of literary interpretation but to the values of humanism and humanistic inquiry more broadly.

Heather Love, for example, takes as one of her models the sociologist Erving Goffman, whose method of "thin description" leaves no room for symptomatic interpretation. Yet while Love describes herself, Bruno Latour, and other practitioners of the "new sociologies of literature" as evidence of a renewed empiricism in literary studies, her citation of Goffman suggests that the spectre of suspicion has not quite been exorcised:

> A good example of Goffman's abstract, thin form of description can be found in his essay "The Insanity of Place," in which he argues that

> mental illness does not inhere in persons but in places, situations, and institutions. His larger point is that the "deepest nature of an individual is only skin-deep, the deepness of his others' skin." (379)

Reducing human identity to social habits and interactions, this passage is hardly exempt from the debunking impulse and "destruction of sacred meanings" that characterize the hermeneutics of suspicion (Love 382). Nor is Love free of their indifference to referentiality and empirical fact: she omits Goffman's important concessions that mental illness can also have physiological or psychological origins and the equally important context that his work largely preceded the development of psychotropic medications that treat mental illness by altering the patient's brain functions (Shalin 126–127). In her telling, Goffman characterizes mental illness as a strictly social and relational phenomenon—a dangerously incomplete description that Love enlists to ratify her own animosity toward any theory of interpretation that presumes an essential human self (or, indeed, a biologically constituted one). But while Goffman's hypothetical examples of the different types of attention given to a "black wino" and a "blond model" certainly highlight the social composition of race and gender roles, his model of mental illness disavows the physiological factors that also attend alcoholism and other disorders (375n26). Although Love is careful to pardon Goffman for his use of stereotyped figures, she merely amplifies his totalizing social-constructionist position. The same reflexive skepticism that once questioned the truth claims of literature and history has expanded to include the fields of biology and medicine.

That position sits ill at ease with Love's declared interest in bringing a renewed focus on empiricism back to the humanities.[1] Quite the contrary, she has further partitioned empiricism off from the traditional tools of humanistic inquiry. Associating empirical knowledge exclusively with sociological methods such as thin description and quantitative methods such as statistical analysis and data mining, Love fails to consider that humanistic methods such as close reading or archival research also rely on observation and evidence to test claims, support theories, and yield valid insights about objects and conditions that extend beyond the domain of the signifier. If Love's selective amplification of Goffman's constructivist views demonstrates a questionable commitment to empiricism, then her broader invocation of the discourses of sociology is openly hostile to humanism: she exalts Latour's and Goffman's methods for being "corrosive of humanist values" (381). What emerges from her account is a mode of reading that devalues both empirical observation and humanistic interpretation. (In this light, it's worth remembering that before he turned his attention to rethinking the tools of humanistic inquiry, Latour was busy discrediting the authority of scientific inquiry.) In Love's brand of descriptive reading, empiricism seems to function primarily as a cudgel to wield against the humanities, not a commitment to referentialism in its own right.

This partitioning of descriptive and interpretive methods has carried over into comics studies, even among scholars who aren't looking to corrode the values of the humanities. In *The Greatest Comic Book of All Time*, Bart Beaty and Benjamin Woo challenge the insularity of a comics canon that has been dictated primarily by the interests of literary critics. Making the case for expanding that canon beyond the narrow range of authors, genres, and production methods that currently dominate it, they necessarily prioritize the study of social and material culture above the thematic and formalist close readings that have elevated auteurist creators. In the course of decentering these literary methodologies, however, Beaty and Woo also gloss over their insights; though well attuned to the ideological assumptions that shape the comics canon, they tend to downplay the ideologies of the actual comics they discuss. While their focus on the construction of cultural value unquestionably participates in the new sociologies of literature, Beaty and Woo also demonstrate the continued relevance of literary close reading and the importance of critical skepticism, as seen in their discussion of two comics artists who command radically different forms of cultural and economic capital: Dylan Horrocks and Rob Liefeld.

Although Liefeld was one of the most popular comics artists of the 1990s, his stellar sales never translated into critical acclaim. Fans today remember him as an exemplar of the worst excesses of the nineties, from paper-thin characterization to wildly exaggerated anatomies, while scholars, according to Beaty and Woo, have chosen not to remember him at all: their survey of peer-reviewed scholarship uncovered "a complete absence of the artist from the literature on comics," as they expected (73). This finding says as much about the interpretive limits of their quantitative methodology (a simple keyword search of two databases) as it does about Liefeld's lack of critical stature. Scholarly work on Liefeld's comics is admittedly scarce, but hardly nonexistent; most of it appears in journals of intellectual property law (Vashko) or library science (Lavin), fields that tend not to be indexed in humanities databases. These articles focus on the commerce of comics publishing, exactly the topic Beaty and Woo prescribe for a comics scholarship that values Liefeld's work, although their descriptions of Liefeld's exploitative business practices are anything but validating. The creations of Liefeld and his contemporaries at Image Comics also play significant if supporting roles in two of the earlier critical studies of superhero comics, Scott Bukatman's "X-Bodies: The Torment of the Mutant Superhero" and Jeffrey A. Brown's *Black Superheroes, Milestone Comics, and Their Fans.* Though they only mention Liefeld himself in passing, and thus don't show up under the blunt instrument of database searches, both studies examine the caricatured and highly polarized gender representations that Beaty and Woo barely acknowledge while making their case for Liefeld's importance as a commercially successful comics artist.

Beaty and Woo aren't interested in disputing these criticisms of Liefeld so much as they are in asking a different set of questions entirely: why did so many fans love Liefeld's comics, and what might a comics criticism that shares those values look like? In other words, they are conducting another type of surface reading—one focused more on reception and cultural value, but still a mode of reading that examines the text's manifest content and appeal to its core audience. In the process, however, they opt to discuss Liefeld's artwork on his own preferred terms (those of artistic realism and excess rather than, say, technical competence or narrative legibility) while devoting little attention to critical perspectives that might evaluate his content as well as his style. These two approaches are hardly incompatible: Brown conducts a brief ethnography of some young Image fans to discover why they like the company's comics (125–127) while also holding the comics accountable for their reliance on hyperbolically stereotyped depictions of masculinity and femininity (176–180). Many of his examples are drawn from comics or characters created by Liefeld, and Brown doesn't spare them from critical analysis even as he attempts to identify the source of their appeal; in fact, he locates it in precisely the features Beaty and Woo gloss over, their violent and cartoonish hypermasculinity. Brown's work suggests that comics scholarship is already more methodologically varied than Beaty and Woo acknowledge, but also that such variety doesn't have to preclude or displace the traditional methods of humanities critique.

Those methods may yield just as much insight when applied to comics that already enjoy greater critical prestige. *The Greatest Comic Book of All Time* closes with an extended reading of Dylan Horrocks's *Hicksville*, the story of a mythical New Zealand town where almost everybody loves comics, which

Beaty and Woo ably interpret as a map of the total field of comics production and a dramatization of the conflicting polarities of economic and cultural value that shape it. Notably, of the four characters they map onto different sectors of comics production, the two who most closely match Horrocks's own values are defined by their symbolic association of cultural legitimacy with forms of racial or gender difference. Beaty and Woo describe Kupe, the Māori lighthouse keeper who tends to a secret library of unpublished comics masterpieces, as a mysterious guardian who "has no journey in the story" and functions as "an ideal, more than a character" (136). Grace, the woman whose romantic advances and rejections motivate several of the male characters, plays a similarly abstracted role as the personification (and, they note, the sexualization) of artistic value (137). Less developed as characters than as compass points on Horrocks's map, Grace and Kupe suggest the obvious limitations of a narrative that reduces characters solely to indices of cultural value—and the implications of Horrocks's decision to locate the highest value in racialized, sexualized, exoticized figures.[2] Kupe in particular has little internal life or narrative agency of his own, but, like Grace, he serves as a facilitator for the characters who actually grow and change: if she is their motivator, then he is the waypoint by which they measure their progress or failure. In other words, he is just another wise, magical native, just as the most prominent female character is both artistic muse and femme fatale. Both serve as examples of the pandering, ostensibly "positive" stereotyping that writes women, indigenous people, and other socially marginalized groups as moral consciences responsible for guiding the white male protagonists at the center of the story. If Horrocks's social cartography is unusually well suited to illustrating Beaty and Woo's survey of the comics world, his social imagination is sadly typical in its use of romanticized alterity as a shortcut to moral authority.

The interpretation I have briefly sketched out here may strike some readers as an obvious, even pedestrian application of some of the most basic practices of ideological criticism—which unfortunately doesn't make it any less accurate. Indeed, it is the obviousness of this reading that makes its scarcity in the scant critical literature on *Hicksville* all the more troubling. My point, however, is not to argue that Horrocks's reliance on exoticizing stereotypes should dominate the scholarly conversation, but rather that it highlights the ongoing need for critical, skeptical, and even suspicious modes of reading in comics studies and the humanities more broadly. (Without them, these characters might be read as neutral indicators of cultural value and not as culturally loaded figures in their own right.) This mode of interpretation also underscores the tension that connects surface and symptomatic readings, which are more interdependent than some critics have acknowledged. Pointing out the stereotypical dimensions of Horrocks's characters might be more oppositional than retracing his map of comics, but it is no less descriptive, and a reading that settled for simply tabulating the ideologically problematic aspects of his work would be no more critical, in the broadest professional sense, than one that settled for explaining his sociology of value. Placing the two in conjunction, however, grants context and critical purpose to both observations, as it illuminates how Horrocks stakes his case for artistic value—most of all the value of autonomous cultural production—on hollow and demeaning cultural formulas. Description and interpretation are mutually constitutive, not exclusive; criticism can and should delineate the artist's work with care while subjecting it to the most discerning scrutiny. Doing so, however, means recognizing the value of interpretive methods and a humanistic mission that contemporary critical theory has all but abandoned.

The humanities have become a popular target of late, not only from academics seeking to debunk their values but also from legislators eager to defund higher education, granting agencies that emphasize economic impact over social good, administrators looking to reduce faculty positions, pundits ready to promote STEM fields as the wave of the future, and venture capitalists hoping to replace the university entirely. Humanities scholars have not been slow to recognize these trends, from Felski's acknowledgment of the loss of public support (179) to Martha Nussbaum's more sweeping indictment of a global crisis in education (*Not for Profit*). The resulting flurry of defenses of the humanities has grown so voluminous, and so potentially counterproductive, that some humanists are beginning to tune them out or pleading with their colleagues to stop.[3] Whatever their position on the public crisis, scholars must acknowledge that some of the earliest and most sustained attacks on the humanities have come from within the academy. We have moved from challenging the unquestioned assumptions and false universalisms that once pervaded the field to disparaging and delegitimizing the tools, methods, and even the purposes of the humanities themselves. Perhaps politicians and the academic-managerial class wouldn't have found us such ripe targets if we hadn't spent the past three or four decades arguing against our own existence. To justify our place in the academy and the culture at large, we must be able to articulate a mission and a sense of purpose for the humanities—or else we can't be surprised when the public directs our perpetual suspicion back upon us.

We have to be clear, however, on exactly which part of our work needs defending. Some of the more exasperated responses to the crisis in the humanities recall Joseph Witek's dictum, repeated at countless conferences and panel sessions over the years: "Never apologize, never defend." As he elaborates in "Seven Ways I Don't Teach Comics," Witek sees little purpose to preemptive defenses or justifications for studying comics: students who have signed up for his courses don't need such rationalizations, he argues, while hostile colleagues are unlikely to be swayed (218–219). He draws on his experience teaching comics at a time when they found little purchase in the academy, but his comments are just as applicable to the current era of hard-won legitimacy: as he notes, "Little is accomplished by rhetorically positioning comics as either culturally victimized or heroically ascendant" (219). Our own professional decisions to study and teach comics assume (and help establish) their importance and worth; little is gained by belaboring the point. Witek's answer, at least in the classroom, is to let the work speak for itself and argue for its own artistic value or cultural significance.

I share his resolution never to apologize for studying comics, nor to concede any doubts about the importance of our scholarly work—doubts, I would add, that underwrite many of the populist attacks on academic discourse. But while comics don't, at this particular moment in cultural history, require any special defense on our part, our own institutional place as comics scholars is as precarious as any in the university. The current political, economic, and administrative climate has forced scholars from every discipline to become advocates for our profession. These challenges are especially urgent for those of us who study popular culture, both because our place within the university is still tenuous and because our work is particularly liable to charges of indolence or indulgence. Traditionalists cite comics scholarship as proof of the decline of the university, the canon, civilization itself (Yardley 81–84); vanguardists regard it as the ultimate in false consciousness (T. Frank 283–284). Both share the presumption that it substitutes the pleasures of affective reading for the hard work of scholarship, a charge that has long haunted all literary scholars. As Best and Marcus note, symptomatic reading and the hermeneutics of suspicion served the purpose of elevating literary criticism from a form of leisure to a form of labor, a heroic endeavor that wrestles the highest meaning from the most duplicitous texts (5–6). While scholars today have ample reason to be skeptical of this heroic criticism and the reflexive skepticism it engenders, a retreat into criticism-as-leisure is not an option either. If comics no longer require us to justify their existence, neither do they particularly need us to sing their praises. That position will not survive the instrumentalist imperative that drives the modern university: why do students need to study comics? But it also evades the larger philosophical question that all comics scholars should ask themselves sooner or later: why do *we* need to study comics?

Academic disciplines, though much derided by scholars of a populist bent, can supply a number of possible answers to this question, from the sociological (we explore comics as art world or subculture) to the economic (we examine comics as drivers of the culture industry) to the strictly practical (we study comics to make better comics). But if we wish to understand what this or any other art form can teach us about the world or ourselves, if we want to know what art means or why it matters, then we must be able to address these questions in the language of the humanities. This means reconciling ourselves to the methods of humanistic inquiry, including close reading, historical contextualization, depth hermeneutics, and other forms of critical thinking. These practices generate more than just the intellectual pleasures or credentialing effects cited by their detractors. Critical readings can challenge existing cultural hierarchies and question faulty assumptions; in Felski's terms, critique can "say no to the world" and "carve out a space of negative freedom," preserving its independence while clearing the ground for new ideas (143). But its values are not purely oppositional: critical methods can also serve explanatory purposes, opening new ways of reading and introducing new texts for us to read. They can serve civic purposes, teaching us to view the world and its people from perspectives other than our own, or curatorial ones, preserving the artifacts of the past and passing them along to present and future audiences. Perhaps most important of all—and certainly the most overlooked—they can serve purposes of verification as scholars propose and test competing truth claims, seeking to describe the world accurately and ensuring that other texts do the same. Latour, for all his protests, seeks to reclaim a realist attitude in criticism, and Felski's survey can't help but circle back to the fundamental role of referentiality in sorting valid readings from irresponsible ones: "We cannot afford to be quite so cavalier about the differences between finding things out and making them up" (115). Reference, evidence, and regimes of verification stand at the foundation of good criticism and good scholarship, though a glance at current research in the humanities—especially in comics studies—would not always indicate that this is the case.

The challenge for contemporary scholars is to shed the knee-jerk reactions and axiomatic assumptions that characterize both the paranoid and the credulous modes of reading while embracing the evidentiary standards that underwrite an authentically critical stance. Best and Marcus, Felski, and Latour each call for a more expansive and empirical mode of criticism that gathers facts, builds associations, and creates interpretive frameworks rather than tearing them down: a criticism in which, as Latour writes, “The critic is not the one who debunks, but the one who assembles” (246). Such assemblies may rely on close reading and surface reading, affective response or critical theory, along with philosophy, psychology, history, sociology, economics, linguistics, and any other relevant field of study. A genuinely multidisciplinary field can draw on the methods and insights of all its constituent disciplines without rejecting disciplinarity itself as an implement of academic elitism; a truly empirical one should recognize the importance of evidence and verification regardless of their disciplinary applications. These are the aspirations that drive the readings I have offered here, whether they focus on describing comics and their critics with greater precision, locating comics within their literary or historical contexts, interpreting them in relation to their ownership practices, unpacking their claims to cultural authority, or, on the most fundamental level, evaluating their historical and representational claims to measure their truthfulness and accuracy. Any scholarship that doesn’t recognize the possibility of such evaluation, or the role of evidence in sustaining it, isn’t scholarship at all.

Disciplinarity, with its attendant professional ethics and practices, can offer comics scholars another frame for understanding our role in the academy. We don’t have to view our scholarship as either a heroic struggle or a leisurely pastime, just as a responsibility to maintain the highest standards and social purposes of our respective fields. This will mean rededicating ourselves to our disciplinary methods, embracing them as strategies that work to produce or reveal meaning instead of running from them as signs of elitism. Indeed, as recent crises from the sciences to the humanities all demonstrate, we must welcome the role of expertise in the pursuit of knowledge and assert rather than demean our authority as scholars. We must also earn that authority through a renewed commitment to empirical observation, evidence, and argument. And we must bring together the many practices and concerns that define comics studies—not individually in the work of any single scholar, but collectively as a truly multidisciplinary field—to form a better understanding of comics: their texts and contexts, their producers and audiences, their historical development and capacities to make meaning in the twenty-first century and beyond.

Comics scholars, assemble.

NOTES

INTRODUCTION

1. See Art Spiegelman, "Ballbuster" and "Forms Stretched to Their Limits."
2. This work is just as necessary for lifelong fans, who are sometimes steeped in intensely personal attachments or erratic conventional wisdom, as it is for novices—as seen, for example, in the ongoing critical evaluations of the notorious anti-comics crusader Fredric Wertham, which diverge widely from popular caricatures. See Amy Kiste Nyberg, *Seal of Approval: The History of the Comics Code*; Bart Beaty, *Fredric Wertham and the Critique of Mass Culture*; and Carol Tilley, "Seducing the Innocent: Fredric Wertham and the Falsifications that Helped Condemn Comics."
3. These covers are not all equivalent. The covers from the earlier period (issues 152 to 176, published in 1965 to 1968) are more likely to present Wonder Woman in conflict with various female monsters, evil doppelgangers, and older or younger versions of herself. These battles are far less sexualized than the covers of the late 1960s and early 1970s that pit her against other women—but this is the sort of interpretive distinction that gets lost when Robinson refuses to engage with the content beyond the most cursory summaries.
4. To distinguish their use of "graphic narrative" from other potential applications, Chute and DeKoven state that they "use graphic narrative here specifically to denote a comics text" (779n1)—raising the question of why they don't simply use the term "comics text."
5. See Loman, "'That Mouse's Shadow': The Canonization of Spiegelman's *Maus*"; Gordon, "Making Comics Respectable: How *Maus* Helped Redefine a Medium"; Beaty, *Comics versus Art*; and Beaty and Woo, *The Greatest Comic Book of All Time: Symbolic Capital and the Field of American Comic Books*.

CHAPTER 1: THE MYTH OF ECO

1. Alan Moore pokes gentle fun at this convention in his introduction to the Superman story "Whatever Happened to the Man of Tomorrow?": "This is an IMAGINARY STORY . . . Aren't they all?" (Moore, Swan, and Pérez 423.1). For an explanation of the system I use for citing volume, issue, and page numbers in comics, see chap. 2, n. 2.
2. Spider-Man first appeared in *Amazing Fantasy* issue 15, cover-dated August 1962 and released in May 1962. His second appearance, in *The Amazing Spider-Man* issue 1, was cover-dated March 1963 and released in December 1962. "Il mito di 'Superman'" was published in 1962 as part of the proceedings of a conference held in Rome that January.

   Marvel's Daredevil first appeared in *Daredevil* issue 1, cover-dated April 1964. Another superhero named Daredevil was published by Lev Gleason in the 1940s, but because Eco calls his "Devil" a "more recent" character, groups him with the Fantastic Four and Spider-Man, and associates him with Marvel's distinctive irony, it seems likely that Jeet Heer and Kent Worcester are correct in assuming Eco refers to the Marvel character.
3. Michael Goodrum similarly notes how parodic superheroes such as Squirrel Girl, whose mildly metafictional adventures are only partly rationalized within Marvel's shared continuity, serve to reinscribe the limits of that continuity even as they expose its construction (100–101).
4. Spider-Man's unmasking was undone in the "One More Day" storyline (2007); Captain America's death was reversed in *Captain America: Reborn* (2009–2010).
5. Technically, this isn't even a departure from the comics; writers had been depicting Lois Lane's adolescent meetings with Clark Kent as early as *Adventure Comics* issue 128, cover-dated May 1948, although these stories have been purged from recent continuities.
6. Resnais and Robbe-Grillet were affiliated with the Left Bank group of filmmakers, generally regarded as contemporaries of the New Wave (Farmer 2009).
7. Thomas Schatz has observed that genres almost always produce self-conscious parodies as soon as the audience becomes familiar with their conventions (39). The first superhero parody, the Red Tornado, appeared in Sheldon Mayer's humor feature *Scribbly* in *All-American Comics* issue 20 (cover-dated November 1940), just two years after Superman's debut (Coogan 27–28).
8. Other claims in Eco's essay, unacknowledged by Collins, show even more potential for agreement between the two critics. When Eco suggests that films like *E.T. the Extra-Terrestrial* demand an audience expertise that "is not only intercinematic, it is intermedia, in the sense that the addressee must know not only other movies but all the mass media gossip about movies"

("*Casablanca*" 210), he anticipates Collins's questionable claim that postmodern hyperconsciousness differs from prior reflexivities by moving across different media and different forms of discourse.

9. This omission is all the more puzzling because Collins is clearly familiar with "The Multiplication of the Media," having already cited it favorably in his book *Uncommon Cultures: Popular Culture and Post-Modernism* (16–17, 146). Eco's concluding remarks serve as Collins's epigraph (v).
10. Wally West was replaced by his cousin Bart Allen in *The Flash: The Fastest Man Alive* (2006); Barry Allen returned in *Final Crisis* (2008–2009), a development that was explained in *The Flash: Rebirth* (2009); Supergirl reappeared in "The Supergirl from Krypton" in *Superman/Batman* (2004); Jason Todd died in the *Batman* storyline "A Death in the Family" (1988) and was brought back in that same title's "Under the Hood" (2005); Bucky Barnes was declared dead in *The Avengers* issue 4 (1964) and returned as the Winter Soldier in the "Out of Time" storyline in *Captain America* (2004–2005).

CHAPTER 2: THE ABUSES OF HISTORY

1. Busiek and Coogan both draw on the problematic but popular use of the term "deconstruction" to describe the project of the revisionist superhero comics. Few of these comics were deconstructionist in the theoretical sense of identifying and exploding the genre's internal contradictions; however, the term had gained popular currency in the early 1990s after conservative journalists and activists began to condemn the rise of deconstructionist theory in the academy. (Michael Bérubé's *Public Access: Literary Theory and American Cultural Politics* offers a spirited and thorough rejoinder to these attacks, particularly in the essay "Winning Hearts and Minds.") Because its application to revisionist superhero comics presumes the misapprehension that deconstruction is inherently hostile to texts, and because it doesn't describe those comics accurately, I can't endorse the "deconstructionist" label. I use its cognate "reconstructive" in this chapter purely for the sake of clarity in responding to Coogan's formulation.
2. I have cited serialized comics by issue number and page number, with volume number set off with a colon when necessary. For example, (*Planetary* 7.6) refers to *Planetary* issue 7, page 6, while (*League* 2: 5.8) refers to *The League of Extraordinary Gentlemen* volume 2, issue 5, page 8. In this case, the anecdote in question appears in issue 8, page 20 of *Watchmen*.
3. It would be harder to find such rebuilt conventions in the wave of imitations that followed the groundbreaking revisionist works; the copies tended to emphasize the sex and violence, not the critical examination of the genre. However, even Image Comics series such as Rob Liefeld's *Youngblood*

(1992–1994) featured recognizable (read: derivative) character types, prefabricated continuities, and superheroes as celebrities.

4. The comedian Patton Oswalt refers to this new stage of permanence, plenitude, and pop-cultural surplus as Etewaf: "Everything That Ever Was—Available Forever" (Oswalt). The only comics that remain doggedly unavailable in this climate are those built around expired licenses, such as Marvel's *Micronauts* (1979–1984) and *Rom: Spaceknight* (1979–1985), which were based on toys produced by Mego and Parker Brothers. As Marvel no longer holds the comic book rights to these properties, it can't reprint those series. Even comics that are trapped in legal limbo, however, are still available via illegal downloads and file-sharing sites.
5. See Torin Monahan's "Just-in-Time Security: Permanent Exceptions and Neoliberal Orders," along with several other essays collected in Steven Peacock's *Reading 24: TV against the Clock*, particularly those by Anne Caldwell and Samuel A. Chambers, and Christopher Gair. On the political contexts and uses of 24, see Jane Mayer, "Whatever It Takes."
6. The protagonist's name poses a particular challenge for critical discussions of *Marvelman/Miracleman*. The character (originally a British copy of the American Captain Marvel) was first published as Marvelman in 1954; Moore and artist Garry Leach revived him under that same name for the British anthology series *Warrior* in 1982. When Eclipse Comics reprinted the stories in the United States, however, legal objections from Marvel Comics forced them to change the names of both character and series to *Miracleman*. Carney and most other comics scholars who write about the character use the name Marvelman—perhaps out of a sense of solidarity with Moore, or possibly under the assumption that the original name is more historically accurate. Yet the original material from *Warrior* ran out midway through the sixth issue of the Eclipse series. Everything that happened after that point, including the birth of Miracleman's daughter, the creation of his utopia, all of Neil Gaiman's issues, and nearly everything else Carney discusses, was published under the title *Miracleman*. The misleading nomenclature is a minor but telling example of how comics scholars have allowed fannish affiliations to override scholarly fidelity to the comic's tangled publication history.
7. This dialogue is made even more disturbing by the comic's lettering, which emphasizes Selene's supposed consent and Pan's lack of control over his own actions: "it's almost like she *wanted* that. Like he *had* to." I assume Moore added these lines to imply that the rape was consensual and therefore not really rape at all—but this, of course, is the same justification used in the real world to exempt many rapes from legal prosecution or moral condemnation.

Moore's apparent discomfort at his own cosmogony also raises another question: why not simply change his creation story to omit the rape? Prior to his work on *Promethea*, Moore publicly dedicated himself to the worship of Glycon, a Roman snake-god known to be a hoax perpetrated on worshippers, as a means of illustrating and committing to his belief that all gods exist as stories invented by humanity (Campbell 4–5). Given the self-consciously fictive nature of Moore's beliefs, he might just as easily have chosen or invented a creation story that did not naturalize, universalize, and arguably legitimize rape.

CHAPTER 3: PROPERTIES OF THE IMAGINATION

1. The pagination of *The League of Extraordinary Gentlemen* is complicated, obscure, and ever-changing. Volume 1 is paginated by issue; I have followed the same numbering system for volume 2, which is otherwise published in an identical format. *Black Dossier* is paginated sporadically but consistently, as seen in "Shadows in the Steam," "What Ho, Gods of the Abyss," and the reference key to the fake Underground map at the front of the volume. I have chosen to follow this numbering system rather than the one used by Jess Nevins in *Impossible Territories*, which starts from the frontispiece rather than the first story page. The *Century* and *Nemo* trilogies are unpaginated.
2. The rewritten lyrics also contain a number of references or near references to Moore's other comics. His version of "Mack the Knife" is filled with allusions to the same Ripper murders he explored in more detail in *From Hell*. When he turns to "Pirate Jenny," Moore refers to the oncoming ship as "the black raider" (n.p.); Marc Blitzstein's English translation calls it "the black freighter," a name Moore had already used in "Tales of the Black Freighter," the pirate comic threaded through the pages of *Watchmen*. The pointed refusal, in the first volume of *League* published by Top Shelf and Knockabout, to allude to a work still owned by DC Comics is even more conspicuous than a direct reference. These nested allusions span a career that has long been influenced by Brecht and Weill—Moore's early comic strips for *Sounds* magazine were written and drawn under the name "Curt Vile" (Khoury 37).
3. Eric Berlatsky discusses Moore's replication of poststructuralist discourses of gender in "Lone Woolf and Cubs: Alan Moore, Postmodern Fiction, and Third-Wave Feminist Utopianism." He also provides a thoughtful response to the poststructuralist suspicion of referentiality and "withdrawal of the real" in his book *The Real, the True, and the Told: Postmodern Historical Narrative and the Ethics of Representation* (3–9).
4. Moore had already castigated the Tom Swift stories for their racism,

xenophobia, violence, anti-intellectualism, and muscular pro-capitalist message in "Frankenstein's Cadillac," an essay that ran in his short-lived magazine *Dodgem Logic*. I am indebted to Joe McCulloch, who first linked this essay to *Heart of Ice* in his podcast with Chris Mautner and Matt Seneca, aptly named *Comic Books Are Burning in Hell* ("Wizard"). McCulloch also observes the retrograde gender politics of *Heart of Ice*, which begins with Janni's attempt to outdo her father and ends with her abject failure, her total dependence on her male crew, and her acceptance of her father's patriarchal values.

5. The passage also hints at Moore's earlier criticisms of another genre entirely. *Heart of Ice* exposes the bigotry and sadism of Reade, Swift, and their ilk, much as *Watchmen* and its peers once dismantled the ideology of the superheroes in Moore's somewhat premature imagining of their own twilight. Indeed, since "science-hero" was Moore's preferred euphemism for "superhero" in the America's Best Comics titles, Janni's reference to "the science-champions" could serve as an oblique linkage between the two genres, a reminder that the Edisonade heroes embodied many of the same values and that their industry ran on the same exploitative practices.
6. The prurient and misogynistic elements of this presentation cannot be understated. In *The Roses of Berlin*, Moore and O'Neill lavish considerable attention on the disrobing and dismemberment of female bodies, both mechanical and biological. That violence is largely reserved for the robots in *River of Ghosts*, which nevertheless continues their simultaneous sexualization and mutilation.
7. George V was actually coronated in 1911, the year after he succeeded to the throne. *Black Dossier* compounds this error by referring to the events of 1910 as taking place during the coronation of George VI (105), which didn't occur until 1937. These discrepancies serve as useful reminders that *The League of Extraordinary Gentlemen* offers only a semblance of historicism, a simulation of the periods and literatures it depicts as filtered through the modern imagination and a sometimes erratic historical memory.
8. After some readers criticized Mina's comments, Moore issued a tentative retreat from his position, telling Pádraig Ó Méalóid,

> The things that I did hear in a couple of the reviews that I got sent of the *League 2009*, were a couple of people who were talking about, specifically about the line where I've got Mina saying, "*how did culture fall apart in a hundred years?*" and they were saying, "*This is easily the most reactionary line Alan Moore has ever written.*" This is the equivalent of saying, "*It were all fields around here when I were a lad.*" They may have understood me too quickly. ("Interview: Alan Moore," his emphasis)

After insisting his words shouldn't be taken too literally, however, Moore says this in the very next paragraph:

> I would say, that if you're talking about a line of progress, if it can be called progress, that runs from Berthold [*sic*] Brecht's *Threepenny Opera*, to Donald Cammell's *Performance*, to *Harry Potter*, I don't think you can really see that as anything but a decline. [. . .] This is not actually cultural progress. Anyway, that was my feelings [*sic*]. Yes, I'd stand by the sentiments expressed in *League 2009*. I think that it was something that possibly needed saying.

Measuring a culture's history by drawing a line from epic theater to children's books could be seen as rigging the outcome. It would be just as easy, and just as misleading, to trace a path from *Winnie-the-Pooh* to *Get Carter* to *The Wire* (all of which are also referenced in *Century*) and conclude that Western culture can only be progressing to more complex, sophisticated, and socially conscious art forms—but Moore is not inclined to make that argument.

9. In a similar vein, the most prominent and visible depiction of the poor in *Century: 2009* doesn't actually depict the poor, but a group of actors who are known for portraying or impersonating the poor on British television shows; one of them even holds a sign reading "will Mockney for food" (n.p.), referring to his appropriation of the Cockney working class accent. Nevins's online annotations for *2009* hold an extensive discussion of this image and its antecedents (note to p. 34).

10. The name "Nigger Jim" was never used by Mark Twain, only by later interpreters and commentators such as Ernest Hemingway. Moore's dismissal of Jim and Uncle Tom is equally careless. Harriet Beecher Stowe's Uncle Tom, though impossibly saintly and excessively self-sacrificing, also defies Simon Legree and inspires his fellow slaves through nonviolent resistance; the modern sense of an "Uncle Tom" as a subservient collaborator in his own oppression derives from the illustrations, stage adaptations, and films of the late nineteenth and early twentieth centuries, many of them performed by white actors in blackface (Morgan). Similarly, while Twain's Jim is prone to minstrel comedy and buffoonish stereotypes, including his frequent subordination to a fourteen-year-old boy, he is also a canny operator who pursues his own freedom and fools Huck at least as often as he is fooled (F. Robinson; Chadwick-Joshua). Moore overlooks these nuances, to say nothing of the many black protagonists created by black authors such as William Wells Brown (in *Clotel*, 1853), Charles Chesnutt (in "The Goophered Grapevine," 1887), or Frances E. W. Harper (in *Iola Leroy*, 1892), all of whom preceded the Golliwogg. Norma S. Davis argues that the Golliwogg was the first black protagonist and role model in children's fiction (106–110); by expanding this claim to Western fiction as a whole, Moore ignores the complexity and diversity of nineteenth-century literature.

11. Moore calls him the Galley-wag because, as he reveals in the text feature that runs in the back pages of *Century*, his version of the Golliwogg is a fugitive galley slave, an escapee from a trans-galactic slave ship. The more Moore tries to alter the Golliwogg from Upton's original, the more he stamps him with racialized markers.

CHAPTER 4: THE LIMITS OF REALISM

1. While many comics scholars accept these judgments, some have challenged the association between simplicity and empathy, arguing that iconographic style does not determine reader involvement; see Jonathan Frome, "Identification in Comics."
2. Schumer also makes the questionable argument that Adams's expressive anatomical realism was a necessary precursor for superhero comics to tackle more complex and realistic subjects (20-21), quite the opposite of Ware's and Raeburn's separation of the two.
3. Ware doesn't cite Hodgman by name, but he refers to "a June 2006 roundup of various recent comics" and quotes Hodgman's review. He also neglects to mention that Hodgman praises several comics in the epiphanic style, including two, by Carol Tyler and Kevin Huizenga, that are excerpted in *Best American Comics 2007*.
4. David Foster Wallace explains the selection process for the *Best American* series in his introduction to *The Best American Essays 2007*. The series editor—in the case of *Best American Comics 2007*, Anne Elizabeth Moore—culls the submissions down to roughly one hundred finalists, and the guest editor—in this case, Ware—chooses which pieces will be published in the anthology.
5. See Kern, *The Culture of Time and Space, 1880–1918*, chap. 1, and Harvey, *The Condition of Postmodernity*, chap. 16.
6. Dave Eggers identifies many of the hallmarks of this style, then ascendant in alternative comics, in his catalogue for a 2008 gallery show of such works. He cites their lighthearted tone, scrawled writing, uncorrected spelling, "casual, even sloppy" drawings, "loose draftsmanship," and "intimate and disarming" ethos. Unfortunately, he declines to give a name to this affected unaffectedness, choosing (in a fitting example of the style) to title his exhibition and catalogue *Lots of Things Like This*.
7. In addition to the authors cited here, see Torsa Ghosal, "Books with Bodies: Narrative Progression in Chris Ware's *Building Stories*," and the chapters by

Daniel Worden, Matt Godbey, Margaret Fink Berman, and Peter Sattler in Ball and Kuhlman, *The Comics of Chris Ware: Drawing Is a Way of Thinking*.

CHAPTER 5: COMICS STUDIES IN MINIATURE

1. See Douglas Wolk, *Reading Comics*, 144–145, and Andrew Arnold, "An Iranian Girlhood." In an academic context, Ann Miller also documents the influence of David B. and L'Association on Satrapi's work (50).
2. See Timothy Dow Adams, *Telling Lies in Modern American Autobiography*, as well as Charles Hatfield, *Alternative Comics* 112–113. Contrary to her pleas for truth and authenticity, Gornick admitted in 2003 that she created composite characters and invented scenes both for her memoir and in some of her articles for the *Village Voice* (Sterling).
3. Curiously, Mehri's slap mark migrates from one cheek to the other in the span of three panels—a sign of the generally weak composition skills that have been excluded from most critical discussions of Satrapi.
4. These protests are motivated by the election of Austrian president and former Wehrmacht officer Kurt Waldheim. Marji claims that her fellow students overstate "the return of Nazism," though Satrapi confesses that at that point in her life she couldn't distinguish between Nazism and socialism (2: 73).
5. See Gillian Whitlock, "Autographics" 972–973, as well as Naghibi and O'Malley; Chute, *Graphic Women*; and Malek.
6. David Harvey also connects the discourse of human rights to the ideologies of globalization and neoliberalism. Drawing on the work of David Chandler, Harvey argues that appeals to universal human rights have been enlisted in support of political, economic, and military interventions in developing countries (*Brief History* 178–179). While he refuses to concede the field of human rights to neoliberalism, Harvey notes how its rhetoric may be co-opted in ways that actually set back the causes of social justice and self-determination.
7. *Persepolis* first gained widespread exposure somewhat earlier in France, when *Libération* serialized the third volume in 2002. This serialization preceded the public debate over the veil, though not the increased attention to the Middle East in the wake of the September 11th attacks and subsequent war in Afghanistan. Beaty has also observed that volume 3, which details Satrapi's time as an émigré in Austria, "was the perfect chapter in terms of content to reach that mass audience" in Europe (Spurgeon, "Holiday Interview").

CHAPTER 6: SHADOWS OF THE PAST

1. Scot French provides an overview of these and many other interpretations of Turner in *The Rebellious Slave: Nat Turner in American Memory.*
2. Baker opens the scene with a graphic that implies that this is either the Jacob Williams house or the Rebecca Vaughan house; the same image previously appeared in a montage depicting the violence at both homes (150–151). However, Baker's image doesn't match photographs of either home, which appear in Bisson (80–81) and Tragle (164).
3. Thomas C. Parramore offers a somewhat different account of the battle, in which it was local attorney and militiaman James Strange French who lost control of his horse (92–93), although this story wasn't recorded until 1877 (248n47). I have chosen to cite Oates's version of events here and elsewhere in this chapter because *The Fires of Jubilee* is the most carefully researched account of the Southampton rebellion listed in Baker's slender bibliography. The many discrepancies between *The Fires of Jubilee* and *Nat Turner* highlight Baker's tendency to depart from his own sources, not to mention the larger historical record.
4. No such combat between slaves occurred at the Parker or Harris houses, where the rebels fought white militias. Turner's men fought other slaves at the Blunt house (Oates 94–95), a battle that doesn't appear in *Nat Turner.*
5. See, for example, Frederick Douglass's description of Thomas Auld quoting this same verse while whipping a disabled woman in chapter 9 of *Narrative of the Life.*
6. Presumably Baker draws these accounts from Oates or from Bisson, who likely drew them from Oates (see Oates 125; Bisson 13). Oates and Bisson quote the same eyewitness, who reported, "Not a limb nor a muscle was observed to move"; Bisson cites no sources himself, but Oates attributes this quote to an article in the *Petersburg Intelligencer* that was quoted in the *Richmond Enquirer* on 22 November 1831 (Oates 176n41). One week earlier, the *Norfolk Herald* had reported that "but a few people" came to see Turner hanged (Tragle 140), but Oates follows the *Intelligencer*'s report of an "immense crowd" at the execution (French 50) and Baker follows Oates in turn. He also relies on Bisson's claim that the crowd was "spooked" by Turner's stoic death, a claim that Bisson, like Baker, offers with no documentation or support.
7. The lone surviving drawing of Turner from his lifetime, a newspaper illustration from 1831, doesn't much resemble Baker's protagonist (see Tragle iii; Greenberg, *Confessions* cover). In chapter 3, Baker reprints another illustration of Turner, F. O. C. Darley's 1863 engraving "Nat Turner & His Confederates in Conference" (Baker 111). However, he has altered the illustration, lengthening Turner's jaw and sharpening his widow's peak, to bring Darley's

image into line with his own portrayal. That portrayal is not a composite of historical sources, but rather a fabrication that Baker has altered his references to match.

8. There are many reasons, beyond its jailhouse composition and its contested authorship, not to classify Gray's *Confessions* as a slave narrative. Francis, who cites James Olney's authoritative study of slave narratives as autobiographical performances (116), doesn't mention that of the twelve narrative conventions and five paratextual conventions Olney attributes to slave narratives, *The Confessions of Nat Turner* exhibits fewer than half. Some of these conventions, such as the narrator's recounting their successful escape and adoption of a new last name, are obviously impossible in Turner's case; others, such as testimonials from white abolitionists or editors attesting to the narrative's authenticity, are obviated or subverted by Gray's legalistic framing. But Olney also notes that slave narratives typically contain detailed descriptions of the routinized oppressions of slavery, including the work required of slaves, the inadequate resources provided to them, the enforcement of illiteracy, the destruction of slave families, and the physical violence, including the "description of a cruel master, mistress, or overseer, details of first observed whipping and numerous subsequent whippings, with women very frequently the victims" (153). None of these appear in Gray's *Confessions*, not in the least because Gray seeks to explain and delimit the aberrant violence of the Southampton rebellion, not the structural violence of slavery. When Francis suggests that *Confessions* is limited by the "form Turner speaks in, the slave narrative" (127), she miscategorizes Turner's (and Gray's) narrative in an attempt to criticize another genre for its shortcomings.

9. Before he completed the project, Baker told Ed Mathews that "somewhere in there will be heads on pikes and slaves being raped by their masters." No such scenes appear in *Nat Turner*.

10. In fact, Baker used one such reproduction (with his own name and publishing house replacing the original) as the title page to the first issue of the original serial publication of *Nat Turner*. The placement of that facsimile suggests Baker wasn't burying or minimizing Gray's role, but rather presenting his own work as a faithful adaptation of Gray's narrative; the altered page states that the text is "adapted and illustrated by Kyle Baker," whereas the Abrams edition simply presents him as the author.

11. The location of the African scenes is more ambiguous. As reported by Oates, some sources claim Turner's mother came from "the North's Nile River country" (11), which would place those scenes in the northern hemisphere as well.

12. Craig Fischer offers a different objection to my comments, noting that "the interpretive field goes beyond the praise/judge valence, and the result is a text that provokes dissent and response, an eminently teachable book" (272). Setting aside the fact that my post already called for a wider interpretive field (judgment encompasses both praise and condemnation but is hardly limited to them), Fischer is rather sanguine about the possibilities for dissent in the current criticism and pedagogy on *Nat Turner*. A critical discourse that refuses to recognize the legitimacy of historical or ethical critique is unlikely to encourage dissenting views in the classroom.

AFTERWORD

1. In much the same manner, Sedgwick's declared interest in dethroning paranoid modes of reading sits ill at ease with her shrugging indifference to what she calls "the rather fixated question" of whether any given piece of knowledge is true—the particular "knowledge," in this case, being the conspiracy theory that the United States military created AIDS (124). If empirical standards are applied speciously and inconsistently in Love's critique of paranoid reading, they are almost wholly absent in Sedgwick's.
2. Grace may also have Māori ancestry; her last name, Pekapeka, is a Māori term for a bat native to New Zealand.
3. For just a few examples of this burgeoning genre, the anti-defense of the humanities, see David McCabe, "How Not to Defend the Humanities"; Wendy Earle, "Let's Stop Being Defensive about the Value of Arts Degrees"; and Simon During, "Stop Defending the Humanities." The harshest nondefense comes from During, who minimizes the challenges faced by the humanities while chastising them for their role in maintaining class and ethnic hierarchies. Such opportunistic attacks are hardly surprising, as During is an outspoken advocate for the populist and exceptionalist schools of cultural studies (T. Frank 287).

BIBLIOGRAPHY

Adams, Timothy Dow. *Telling Lies in Modern American Autobiography*. U of North Carolina P, 1990.

"Alan Moore Talks *Dodgem Logic*." *Mustard*, Oct. 2009. Archived at web.archive.org/web/20091026171315/http://www.mustardweb.org/dodgemlogic.

Alaniz, José. "Into Her Dead Body: Moore & Campbell's *From Hell*." *Alan Moore: Portrait of an Extraordinary Gentleman*, edited by smoky man and Gary Spencer Millidge, Abiogenesis, 2003, pp. 145–149.

Amacker, Kurt. "Opening the Black Dossier: The Alan Moore Interview," pt. 1. *Mania*, 7 Nov. 2007. Archived at archive.li/xCwqx.

———. "Opening the Black Dossier: The Alan Moore Interview," pt. 2. *Mania*, 14 Nov. 2007. Archived at archive.li/jLcda.

Arnold, Andrew. "An Iranian Girlhood." *TIME.com*, 16 May 2003, content.time.com/time/arts/article/0,8599,452401,00.html.

———. "Top 10 Everything 2004: Comix." *TIME.com*, 17 Dec. 2004, content.time.com/time/specials/packages/0,28757,1999700,00.html.

Asma, Stephen T. "Looking Up from the Gutter: Philosophy and Popular Culture." *Chronicle of Higher Education*, vol. 54, no. 7, 12 Oct. 2007, p. B14.

Ayers, William, and Ryan Alexander-Tanner. *To Teach: The Journey, in Comics*. Teachers College Press, 2010.

Ayres, Jackson. "The Integrity of the Work: Alan Moore, Modernism, and the Corporate Author." *Journal of Modern Literature*, vol. 39, no. 2, Winter 2016, pp. 144–166.

Baetens, Jan, and Hugo Frey. *The Graphic Novel: An Introduction*. Cambridge UP, 2015.

Baker, Kyle. *Nat Turner*. 2005–2006. Abrams, 2008.

Ball, David. "Beautifully Failing, Anew." *Comics Journal*, 15 Oct. 2012, tcj.com/beautifully-failing-anew.

———. "Chris Ware's Failures." *The Comics of Chris Ware: Drawing Is a Way of*

Thinking, edited by David M. Ball and Martha Kuhlman, UP of Mississippi, 2010, pp. 45–61.

Ball, David M., and Martha Kuhlman, eds. *The Comics of Chris Ware: Drawing Is a Way of Thinking*. UP of Mississippi, 2010.

Banerjee, Subhajit. "Alan Moore: An Extraordinary Gentleman—Q&A." *Guardian*, 25 July 2011, theguardian.com/books/2011/jul/25/alan-moore-league-extraordinary-gentlemen.

Barthes, Roland. *Mythologies*. 1957. Translated by Annette Lavers, Hill and Wang, 1972.

Beaty, Bart. *Comics versus Art*. U of Toronto P, 2012.

———. *Fredric Wertham and the Critique of Mass Culture*. UP of Mississippi, 2005.

———. *Twelve-Cent Archie*. Rutgers UP, 2015.

———. *Unpopular Culture: Transforming the European Comic Book in the 1990s*. U of Toronto P, 2007.

Beaty, Bart, and Benjamin Woo. *The Greatest Comic Book of All Time: Symbolic Capital and the Field of American Comic Books*. Palgrave Macmillan, 2016.

Bechdel, Alison. *Fun Home*. Houghton Mifflin, 2006.

Berlatsky, Eric. "Lone Woolf and Cubs: Alan Moore, Postmodern Fiction, and Third-Wave Feminist Utopianism." *The Gay Utopia*, Dec. 2007, gayutopia.blogspot.com/2007/12/eric-berlatskylone-woolf-and-cubsalan.html.

———. *The Real, the True, and the Told: Postmodern Historical Narrative and the Ethics of Representation*. Ohio State UP, 2011.

Bérubé, Michael. *Public Access: Literary Theory and American Cultural Politics*. Verso, 1994.

Berwick, Carly. "Why Have There Been No Great Women Comic-Book Artists?" *Art News*, 1 Nov. 2005, artnews.com/2005/11/01/why-have-there-been-no-great-women-comic-book-artists.

Best, Stephen, and Sharon Marcus. "Surface Reading: An Introduction." *Representations*, vol. 108, no. 1, Fall 2009, pp. 1–21.

Bisson, Terry. *Nat Turner*. Chelsea House, 1988.

Bloom, Harold. *The Anxiety of Influence*. Oxford UP, 1973.

Bowen, Frank C. *Sea Slang: A Dictionary of the Old-Timers' Expressions and Epithets*. Sampson Low, Marston, 1929.

Bridwell, E. Nelson. Introduction. *Superman from the Thirties to the Seventies*. Bonanza, 1971, pp. 7–15.

Brogan, Jacob. "Masked Fathers: Jimmy Corrigan and the Superheroic Legacy." *The Comics of Chris Ware: Drawing Is a Way of Thinking*, edited by David M. Ball and Martha Kuhlman, UP of Mississippi, 2010, pp. 14–27.

Brown, Jeffrey A. *Black Superheroes, Milestone Comics, and Their Fans*. UP of Mississippi, 2001.

Brown, Joshua. "Of Mice and Memory." *Oral History Review*, vol. 16, no. 1, 1988, pp. 91–109.

Brown, Michelle P. *Understanding Illuminated Manuscripts: A Guide to Technical Terms*. The J. Paul Getty Museum, 1994.

Brown, Wendy. "Neo-liberalism and the End of Liberal Democracy." *Theory & Event*, vol. 7, no. 1, 2003, muse.jhu.edu/journals/theory_and_event/toc/tae7.1.html.

Brown, William Wells. *The Negro in the American Rebellion: His Heroism and His Fidelity*. Lee & Shepard, 1867.

Brunetti, Ivan. "Cartooning Will Destroy You." *Schizo* issue 4, 2006, Fantagraphics, n.p.

Bruno, Tim. "Nat Turner after 9/11: Kyle Baker's *Nat Turner*." *Journal of American Studies*, vol. 50, no. 4, Nov. 2016, pp. 923–951.

Bukatman, Scott. "X-Bodies: The Torment of the Mutant Superhero." 1994. Rpt. in *Matters of Gravity: Special Effects and Supermen in the 20th Century*, by Scott Bukatman, Duke UP, 2003, pp. 48–78.

Busiek, Kurt, and Alex Ross. *Marvels*. Marvel Comics, 1994.

Campbell, Eddie. "Alan Moore." *Eddie Campbell's Egomania*, no. 2, Dec. 2002, pp. 1–32.

Carney, Sean. "The Function of the Superhero at the Present Time." *Iowa Journal of Cultural Studies*, vol. 6, no. 1, Spring 2005, pp. 100–117.

———. "The Tides of History: Alan Moore's Historiographic Vision." *ImageTexT*, vol. 2, no. 2, 2006, english.ufl.edu/imagetext/archives/v2_2/carney.

Carroll, Noël. *Theorizing the Moving Image*. Cambridge UP, 1996.

Chabon, Michael. "The Editor's Notebook." Introduction. *McSweeney's Quarterly Concern*, no. 10, 2002, pp. 5–8.

Chadwick-Joshua, Jocelyn. *The Jim Dilemma: Reading Race in Huckleberry Finn*. UP of Mississippi, 1998.

Chaney, Michael A. "Slave Memory without Words in Kyle Baker's *Nat Turner*." *Callaloo*, vol. 36, no. 2, Spring 2013, pp. 279–297.

———. "Terrors of the Mirror and the *Mise en Abyme* of Graphic Novel Autobiography." *College Literature*, vol. 38, no. 3, Summer 2011, pp. 21–44.

Chute, Hillary. "Comics as Literature? Reading Graphic Narrative." *PMLA*, vol. 123, no. 2, Mar. 2008, pp. 452–465.

———. *Graphic Women: Life Narrative and Contemporary Comics*. Columbia UP, 2010.

Chute, Hillary, and Alison Bechdel. "Bartheses: Barthesian Doubt Edition." Chute and Jagoda, p. 52.

Chute, Hillary, and Marianne DeKoven. "Introduction: Graphic Narrative." *Modern Fiction Studies*, vol. 52, no. 4, Winter 2006, pp. 767–782.

Chute, Hillary, and Patrick Jagoda, eds. *Comics & Media*, special issue of *Critical Inquiry*, vol. 40, no. 3, Spring 2014.

Cicci, Matthew A. "Marvel Team-Up: Hawkeye, Loki, and the Inescapable, Innate Resistance of the Female Superhero Comic Fan." *Journal of Comics & Culture*, vol. 1, Spring 2016, pp. 95–122.

Clarke, John Henrik, ed. *William Styron's Nat Turner: Ten Black Writers Respond*. Beacon, 1968.

Clemente, Chiara, dir. *Beginnings: Marjane Satrapi*. 2012. Sundance TV. *Nowness*, 8 Mar. 2012, www.nowness.com/day/2012/3/8/1978/beginnings-marjane-satrapi.

Collins, Jim. "Batman: The Movie, Narrative: The Hyperconscious." *The Many Lives of the Batman: Critical Approaches to a Superhero and His Media*, edited by Roberta E. Pearson and William Uricchio, Routledge, 1991, pp. 164–181.

———. *Uncommon Cultures: Popular Culture and Post-Modernism*. Routledge, 1989.

Comer, Todd A., and Joseph Michael Sommers, eds. *Sexual Ideology in the Works of Alan Moore*. McFarland, 2012.

Coogan, Peter. *Superhero: The Secret Origin of a Genre*. MonkeyBrain, 2006.

Cooke, Darwyn. *DC: The New Frontier* issues 1–6, 2004, DC Comics.

Costantino, Manuela. "Marji: Popular Commix Heroine Breathing Life into the Writing of History." *Canadian Review of American Studies/Revue canadienne d'études américaines*, vol. 38, no. 3, 2008, pp. 429–447.

Dargis, Manohla. "War Is Heaven." *Los Angeles Times*, 28 Dec. 2003, articles. latimes.com/2003/dec/28/entertainment/ca-dargis28.

David B. *Epileptic*. 1996–2004. Translated by Kim Thompson, Pantheon, 2005.

Davis, Norma S. *A Lark Ascends: Florence Kate Upton, Artist and Illustrator*. Scarecrow, 1992.

Davis, Rocío. "A Graphic Self: Comics as Autobiography in Marjane Satrapi's *Persepolis*." *Prose Studies: History, Theory, Criticism*, vol. 27, no. 3, 2005, pp. 264–279.

De Haven, Tom. *Our Hero: Superman on Earth*. Yale UP, 2010.

Devitt, Amy J. *Writing Genres*. Southern Illinois UP, 2004.

Dierick, Charles, and Pascal Lefèvre, eds. *Forging a New Medium: The Comic Strip in the Nineteenth Century*. Vrije Universiteit Brussel UP, 1998.

Di Liddo, Annalisa. "Afterword: Disgust with the Revolution." *Sexual Ideology in the Works of Alan Moore*, edited by Todd A. Comer and Joseph Michael Sommers, McFarland, 2012, pp. 201–206.

———. *Alan Moore: Comics as Performance, Fiction as Scalpel*. Jackson: UP of Mississippi, 2009.

Douglass, Frederick. *Narrative of the Life of Frederick Douglass, an American Slave, Written by Himself*. 1845. Edited by Houston A. Baker Jr., Penguin, 1982.

During, Simon. "Stop Defending the Humanities." *Public Books*, 1 Mar. 2014, publicbooks.org/nonfiction/stop-defending-the-humanities.

Earle, Wendy. "Let's Stop Being Defensive about the Value of Arts Degrees." *The Guardian Higher Education Network*, 23 May 2014, theguardian.com /higher-education-network/blog/2014/may/29/study-arts-humanites -enrichment.

Eberstadt, Fernanda. "God Looked Like Marx." *New York Times Book Review*, 11 May 2003, p. 8, nytimes.com/2003/05/11/books/god-looked-like-marx.html.

Eco, Umberto. "*Casablanca*: Cult Movies and Intertextual Collage." 1984. *Travels in Hyperreality*, translated by William Weaver, Harcourt Brace, 1986, pp. 197–211.

———. "Il mito di 'Superman' e la dissoluzione del tempo." *Demitizzazione e immagine*, edited by Enrico Castelli, CEDAM, 1962, pp. 131–148.

———. "The Multiplication of the Media." 1983. *Travels in Hyperreality*, translated by William Weaver, Harcourt Brace, 1986, pp. 145–150.

———. "The Myth of Superman." Translated by Natalie Chilton. *Diacritics*, vol. 2, no. 1, 1972, pp. 14–22.

Eggers, Dave. *Lots of Things Like This. McSweeney's Quarterly Concern*, no. 27, 2008, n.p.

Ellis, Samantha. "Less of Your Lipgloss." *Observer*, 6 Nov. 2004, theguardian.com /books/2004/nov/07/biography.comics.

Ellis, Warren, and John Cassaday. *Planetary* issues 1–27, 1999–2009, WildStorm Productions.

Ellis, Warren, and Jerry Ordway. *Planetary/JLA: Terra Occulta*. WildStorm Productions, 2002.

Falconer, Duncan. "A Hall of Mirrors II: The Prismatic Age." *Mindless Ones*, 3 Aug. 2008, mindlessones.com/2008/08/03/a-hall-of-mirrors-ii-prismatic-age/.

Farmer, Robert. "Marker, Resnais, Varda: Remembering the Left Bank Group." *Senses of Cinema*, no. 52, 2009, sensesofcinema.com/2009/52/marker-resnais -varda-remembering-the-left-bank-group.

Felski, Rita. *The Limits of Critique*. U of Chicago P, 2015.

Fiedler, Leslie. "The Middle Against Both Ends." *Encounter*, Aug. 1955. Rpt. in *The Collected Essays of Leslie Fiedler*, vol. 2, Stein and Day, 1971, pp. 415–428.

Fischer, Craig. "Provocation through Polyphony: Kyle Baker's *Nat Turner*." *The Blacker the Ink: Constructions of Black Identity in Comics and Sequential Art*, edited by Frances Gateward and John Jennings, Rutgers, 2015, pp. 255–273.

Fiske, John. *Reading the Popular*. 1989. Routledge, 1991.

Ford, Sam, and Henry Jenkins. "Managing Multiplicity in Superhero Comics: An Interview with Henry Jenkins." *Third Person: Authoring and Exploring Vast Narratives*, edited by Pat Harrigan and Noah Wardrip-Fruin, MIT P, 2009, 303–311.

Foucault, Michel. *The Archaeology of Knowledge*. 1969. Translated by A. M. Sheridan Smith, Pantheon, 1972.

Francis, Conseula. "Drawing the Unspeakable: Kyle Baker's Slave Narrative."

Comics and the U.S. South, edited by Brannon Costello and Qiana J. Whitted, U of Mississippi P, 2012, pp. 113–137.

Frank, Marcie. "'How Did I Get So Anal?'": Queer Self-Authorization at the Margins." *Queer Diasporas*, edited by Cindy Patton and Benigno Sánchez-Eppler, Duke UP, 2000, pp. 245–262.

Frank, Thomas. *One Market Under God: Extreme Capitalism, Market Populism, and the End of Economic Democracy*. Doubleday, 2000.

Frankfurt, Harry G. *On Bullshit*. Princeton UP, 2005.

Freedman, Ariela. "Chris Ware's Epiphanic Comics." *Partial Answers: Journal of Literature and the History of Ideas*, vol. 13, no. 2, June 2015, pp. 337–358.

French, Scot. *The Rebellious Slave: Nat Turner in American Memory*. Houghton Mifflin, 2004.

Frome, Jonathan. "Identification in Comics." *Comics Journal*, no. 211, 1999, pp. 82–86.

Gabilliet, Jean-Paul. *Of Comics and Men: A Cultural History of American Comic Books*. 2005. Translated by Bart Beaty and Nick Nguyen, UP of Mississippi, 2010.

Gateward, Frances, and John Jennings, eds. *The Blacker the Ink: Constructions of Black Identity in Comics and Sequential Art*. Rutgers, 2015.

Gevinson, Tavi. "Work Hard and Be Kind: An Interview with Chris Ware." *Rookie*, 29 Nov. 2012, rookiemag.com/2012/11/chris-ware-intervie/2/.

Ghosal, Torsa. "Books with Bodies: Narrative Progression in Chris Ware's *Building Stories*." *StoryWorlds: A Journal of Narrative Studies*, vol. 7, no. 1, Summer 2015, pp. 75–99.

Gibson, Timothy A. "Beyond Cultural Populism: Notes Toward the Critical Ethnography of Media Audiences." *Journal of Communication Inquiry*, vol. 24, no. 3, 2000, pp. 253–273.

Glass, Ira. Preface. *McSweeney's Quarterly Concern*, no. 13, 2004, p. 7.

Gloeckner, Phoebe, Justin Green, Aline Kominsky-Crumb, and Carol Tyler. "Panel: Comics and Autobiography." Moderated by Deborah Nelson. Chute and Jagoda, pp. 86–103.

Goffman, Erving. "The Insanity of Place." *Relations in Public: Microstudies of the Public Order*, by Erving Goffman, Harper Colophon, 1971, pp. 335–390.

Goldman, Jonathan E. "The Superhero Genre and Celebrity Culture in *The League of Extraordinary Gentlemen*." *The Rise and Reason of Comics and Graphic Literature: Critical Essays on the Form*, edited by Joyce Goggin and Dan Hassler-Forest, McFarland, 2010, pp. 142–153.

Goodrum, Michael. "'Oh C'mon, Those Stories Can't Count in Continuity!' Squirrel Girl and the Problem of Female Power." *Studies in Comics*, vol. 5, no. 1, 2014, pp. 97–115.

Gordon, Ian. *Comic Strips and Consumer Culture, 1890–1945*. Smithsonian Institution Press, 1998.

———. "Making Comics Respectable: How *Maus* Helped Redefine a Medium." *The Rise of the American Comics Artist: Creators and Contexts*, edited by Paul Williams and James Lyons, UP of Mississippi, 2010, pp. 179–193.

———. *Superman: The Persistence of an American Icon*. Rutgers UP, 2017.

Gornick, Vivian. Foreword. *Living to Tell the Tale: A Guide to Writing Memoir*, edited by Jane Taylor McDonnell, Penguin, 1998, vii–x.

Gray, Basil. *Persian Painting from Miniatures of the XIII.-XVI. Centuries*. B. T. Batsford, 1947.

Gray, Jonathan W. "'Commence the Great Work': The Historical Archive and Unspeakable Violence in Kyle Baker's *Nat Turner*." *Afterimages of Slavery*, edited by Marlene D. Allen and Seretha D. Williams, McFarland, 2012, pp. 183–200.

Gray, Thomas R. *The Confessions of Nat Turner*. 1831. Facsimile of the 1832 Richmond, VA, edition, UMI Books on Demand, 1993.

Green, Justin. *Binky Brown Meets the Holy Virgin Mary*. Last Gasp, 1972.

Greenberg, Kenneth S., ed. *The Confessions of Nat Turner and Related Documents*. Bedford/St. Martin's, 1996.

———. "Name, Face, Body." *Nat Turner: A Slave Rebellion in History and Memory*, edited by Kenneth S. Greenberg, Oxford UP, 2003, pp. 3–23.

Greener, W. W. *The Gun and Its Development*. 1910. Skyhorse, 2013.

"Greetings from Astro City." *Kurt Busiek's Astro City*, vol. 1, no. 5, 1995, Image Comics, n.p.

Griffith, Bill. "Bil Keane: An Appreciation." *Comics Journal*, 14 Nov. 2011, tcj.com/bil-keane-an-appreciation.

Groensteen, Thierry. "Why Are Comics Still in Search of Cultural Legitimization?" Translated by Shirley Smolderen. *Comics & Culture*, edited by Anne Magnussen and Hans-Christian Christiansen, Museum Tusculanum Press, 2000, pp. 29–41.

Gunning, Tom. "The Art of Succession: Reading, Writing, and Watching Comics." Chute and Jagoda, pp. 36–51.

Hajdu, David. "Persian Miniatures." *Bookforum*, Oct./Nov. 2004. Rpt. at mutualart.com/OpenArticle/Persian-Miniatures/66A209E1F044F4EA.

Halsall, Alison. "'A Parade of Curiosities': Alan Moore's *The League of Extraordinary Gentlemen* and *Lost Girls* as Neo-Victorian Pastiches." *Journal of Popular Culture*, vol. 48, no. 2, 2015, pp. 252–268.

Harbach, Chad. "MFA vs NYC." 2010. *MFA vs NYC: The Two Cultures of American Fiction*, edited by Chad Harbach, n+1/Faber and Faber, 2014, pp. 9–28.

Hardt, Michael, and Antonio Negri. *Empire*. Harvard UP, 2000.

Hartman, Saidiya. *Scenes of Subjection: Terror, Slavery, and Self-Making in Nineteenth-Century America.* Oxford UP, 1997.

——. "Venus in Two Acts." *Small Axe*, no. 26, June 2008, pp. 1–14.

Hartsock, Nancy. "Foucault on Power: A New Theory for Women?" *Feminism/Postmodernism*, edited by Linda J. Nicholson, Routledge, 1990, pp. 157–175.

Harvey, David. *A Brief History of Neoliberalism.* Oxford UP, 2005.

——. *The Condition of Postmodernity.* Blackwell, 1990.

Harvey, Robert C. *The Art of the Comic Book.* UP of Mississippi, 1996.

Hatfield, Charles. *Alternative Comics: An Emerging Literature.* UP of Mississippi, 2005.

——. *Hand of Fire: The Comics Art of Jack Kirby.* UP of Mississippi, 2012.

——. Review of *The Silver Age of Comic Book Art*, by Arlen Schumer. *International Journal of Comic Art*, vol. 6, no. 1, Spring 2004, pp. 350–355.

——. "Studies in Graphic Selfhood: A Review Essay." *Studies in Comics*, vol. 5, no. 2, Fall 2014, pp. 405–424.

Heer, Jeet, and Kent Worcester, eds. *Arguing Comics: Literary Masters on a Popular Medium.* UP of Mississippi, 2004.

——. *A Comics Studies Reader.* UP of Mississippi, 2009.

Hill, Christian. "Marjane Satrapi Interviewed, August 24, 2003." *International Journal of Comic Art*, vol. 8, no. 2, Fall 2006, pp. 6–33.

Hilton, Laura. "Reincarnating Mina Murray: Subverting the Gothic Heroine?" *Alan Moore and the Gothic Tradition*, edited by Matthew J. A. Green, Manchester UP, 2013, pp. 195–212.

Hirsch, Marianne. "Editor's Column: Collateral Damage." *PMLA*, vol. 119, no. 5, Oct. 2004, pp. 1209–1215.

Hoberek, Andrew. *Considering Watchmen: Poetics, Property, Politics.* Rutgers UP, 2014.

Hodgman, John. "Comics Chronicle." *New York Times Book Review*, 4 June 2006, pp. 18–19.

Horrocks, Dylan. "Inventing Comics: Scott McCloud's Definition of Comics." *Hicksville: The Website of Dylan Horrocks*, June 2001, www.hicksville.co.nz/Inventing%20Comics.htm.

Hutcheon, Linda. *A Poetics of Postmodernism.* Routledge, 1988.

Irwin, William. "Philosophy and/as/of Popular Culture." *Philosophy and the Interpretation of Pop Culture*, edited by William Irwin and Jorge J. E. Gracia, Rowman & Littlefield, 2007, pp. 41–63.

Jacobs, Harriet. *Incidents in the Life of a Slave Girl.* 1861. Edited by Jean Fagan Yellin, Harvard UP, 1987.

Jameson, Fredric. *Postmodernism: Or, the Cultural Logic of Late Capitalism.* Duke UP, 1991.

Jenkins, Henry. "Introduction: Should We Discipline the Reading of Comics?"

Critical Approaches to Comics: Theories and Methods, edited by Matthew J. Smith and Randy Duncan, Routledge, 2012, pp. 1–14.

——. "'Just Men in Tights': Rewriting Silver Age Comics in an Era of Multiplicity." *The Contemporary Comic Book Superhero*, edited by Angela Ndalianis, Routledge, 2009, pp. 16–43.

Jones, Jason B. "Betrayed by Time: Steampunk & the Neo-Victorian in Alan Moore's *Lost Girls* and *The League of Extraordinary Gentlemen*." *Neo-Victorian Studies*, vol. 3, no. 1, 2010, pp. 99–126.

Julavits, Heidi. "Rejoice! Believe! Be Strong and Read Hard!" *Believer*, vol. 1, no. 1, March 2003, pp. 3–15. Rpt. at believermag.com/issues/200303/?read=article_julavits.

Karim, Persis M. "Talking with a Pioneer of Iranian American Literature: An Interview with Nahid Rachlin." *MELUS*, vol. 33, no. 2, 2008, pp. 153–157.

Kashtan, Aaron. "'And It Had *Everything* in It': *Building Stories*, Comics, and the Book of the Future." *Studies in the Novel*, vol. 47, no. 3, Fall 2015, pp. 420–447.

Katz, Wendy R. *Rider Haggard and the Fiction of Empire*. Cambridge UP, 1987.

Kern, Stephen. *The Culture of Time and Space, 1880–1918*. Harvard UP, 1983.

Khoury, George. *The Extraordinary Works of Alan Moore: Indispensable Edition*. TwoMorrows, 2008.

Kidder, Orion Ussner. "Historicizing the Superhero: Alan Moore's *Supreme* and Warren Ellis/John Cassaday's *Planetary*." *Journal of the Fantastic in the Arts*, vol. 21, no. 1, 2010, pp. 77–96.

Klock, Geoff. *How to Read Superhero Comics and Why*. Continuum, 2002.

Kuhlman, Martha. "In the Comics Workshop: Chris Ware and the Oubapo." *The Comics of Chris Ware: Drawing Is a Way of Thinking*, edited by David M. Ball and Martha Kuhlman, UP of Mississippi, 2010, pp. 78–89.

Kukkonen, Karin. "Navigating Infinite Earths: Readers, Mental Models, and the Multiverse of Superhero Comics." *Storyworlds: A Journal of Narrative Studies*, vol. 2, 2010, pp. 39–58.

——. "Warren Ellis's *Planetary*: The Archaeology of Superheroes." *The Rise and Reason of Comics and Graphic Literature: Critical Essays on the Form*, edited by Joyce Goggin and Dan Hassler-Forest, McFarland, 2010, pp. 154–163.

Kunka, Andrew. "Intertextuality and the Historical Graphic Narrative: Kyle Baker's *Nat Turner* and the Styron Controversy." *College Literature*, vol. 38, no. 3, Summer 2011, pp. 168–193.

Kunzle, David. *The History of the Comic Strip*. 2 vols. U of California P, 1973, 1990.

Kuskin, William. "Introduction: Continuity in Literary Form and History." *English Language Notes*, vol. 46, no. 2, Fall/Winter 2008, pp. 5–13.

Laity, K. A. "'Avast, Land-Lubbers!' Reading *Lost Girls* as a Post-Sadeian Text." *Sexual Ideology in the Works of Alan Moore*, edited by Todd A. Comer and Joseph Michael Sommers, McFarland, 2012, pp. 138–149.

Lasch, Christopher. *The Culture of Narcissism*. Norton, 1978.

Latour, Bruno. "Why Has Critique Run Out of Steam? From Matters of Fact to Matters of Concern." *Critical Inquiry*, vol. 30, no. 2, Winter 2004, pp. 225–248.

Lavin, Michael R. "Comics Publishers in Decline: A Tale of Two Companies." *Serials Review*, vol. 24, no. 3–4, 1998, pp. 94–106.

——. "A Librarian's Guide to Image Comics." *Serials Review*, vol. 24, no. 2, 1998, pp. 79–92.

Leith, Sam. "A Writer's Life: Marjane Satrapi." *Daily Telegraph*, 27 Nov. 2004, p. 12.

Lepore, Jill. "Looking at Female Superheroes with Ten-Year-Old Boys." *New Yorker*, 7 May 2015, newyorker.com/culture/cultural-comment/marvel-a-force-female-superheroes.

Lewis, A. David. "One for the Ages: Barbara Gordon and the (Il-)Logic of Comic Book Age-Dating." *International Journal of Comic Art*, vol. 5, no. 2, 2003, pp. 296–311.

Liu, Catherine. *American Idyll: Academic Antielitism as Cultural Critique*. U of Iowa P, 2011.

Loman, Andrew. "'That Mouse's Shadow': The Canonization of Spiegelman's *Maus*." *The Rise of the American Comics Artist: Creators and Contexts*, edited by Paul Williams and James Lyons, UP of Mississippi, 2010, pp. 210–234.

Lopes, Paul. *Demanding Respect: The Evolution of the American Comic Book*. Temple UP, 2009.

Lott, Eric. *Love and Theft: Blackface Minstrelsy and the American Working Class*. Oxford UP, 1993.

Love, Heather. "Close but Not Deep: Literary Ethics and the Descriptive Turn." *New Literary History*, vol. 41, no. 2, Spring 2010, pp. 371–391.

Lukács, Georg. *History and Class Consciousness*. 1967. Translated by Rodney Livingstone, MIT P, 1971.

Malek, Amy. "Memoir as Iranian Exile Cultural Production: A Case Study of Marjane Satrapi's *Persepolis* Series." *Iranian Studies*, vol. 39, no. 3, 2006, pp. 353–380.

Mandel, Naomi. *Against the Unspeakable: Complicity, the Holocaust, and Slavery in America*. U of Virginia P, 2006.

Mandiringana, E., and T. J. Stapleton. "The Literary Legacy of Frederick Courteney Selous." *History in Africa*, vol. 25, 1998, pp. 199–218.

Mathews, Ed. "Interview: Kyle Baker." *PopImage*, 2005, popimage.com/content/kylebaker2005.html.

Mayer, Jane. "Whatever It Takes." *New Yorker*, 19–26 Feb. 2007, pp. 66–82.

McCabe, David. "How Not to Defend the Humanities." *Huffington Post*, 23 May 2014, huffingtonpost.com/david-mccabe/how-not-to-defend-the-hum_b_5366150.html.

McCloud, Scott. *Understanding Comics: The Invisible Art*. Kitchen Sink, 1993.

McCulloch, Joe, Chris Mautner, and Matt Seneca. "Wizard versus Bagpiper? FIGHT." *Comic Books Are Burning in Hell* (podcast), 14 Mar. 2013, factualopinion.com/the_factual_opinion/2013/03/wizard-versus-bagpiper-fight.html.

McDowell, Deborah E. "In the First Place: Making Frederick Douglass and the Afro-American Narrative Tradition." *Critical Essays on Frederick Douglass*, edited by William Andrews, G. K. Hall, 1991, pp. 192–214.

McGrath, Charles. "Not Funnies." *New York Times Magazine*, 11 July 2004, pp. 24–33, 46, 55–56.

McGuigan, Jim. *Cultural Populism*. Routledge, 1992.

McGurl, Mark. *The Program Era: Postwar Fiction and the Rise of Creative Writing*. Harvard UP, 2009.

Miller, Ann. "Marjane Satrapi's *Persepolis*: Eluding the Frames." *L'Esprit Créateur*, vol. 51, no. 1, Spring 2011, pp. 38–52.

Miller, Frank, Klaus Janson, and Lynn Varley. *Batman: The Dark Knight Returns* issues 1–4, 1986, DC Comics.

Miller, John Jackson. "*Superman* Sales Figures." *Comics Chronicles*, 25 Oct. 2009, comichron.com/titlespotlights/superman.html.

Mitchell, W. J. T. "Comics as Media: Afterword." Chute and Jagoda, pp. 255–265.

———. *Picture Theory: Essays on Verbal and Visual Representation*. U of Chicago P, 1994.

Mitchell, W. J. T., and Art Spiegelman. "Public Conversation: What the %$&# Happened to Comics?" Chute and Jagoda, pp. 20–35.

Molotiu, Andrei. *Abstract Comics: The Anthology*. Fantagraphics, 2009.

Monahan, Torin. "Just-in-Time Security: Permanent Exceptions and Neoliberal Orders." *Reading 24: TV against the Clock*, edited by Steven Peacock, I. B. Tauris, 2007, pp. 109–118.

Moody, Rick. "Fugue for Centrifuges: On Chris Ware's *Building Stories*." *Los Angeles Review of Books*, 25 Oct. 2012, lareviewofbooks.org/article/fugue-for-centrifuges-on-chris-wares-building-stories/#!.

Moorcock, Michael. "Homage to Cornucopia." *Alan Moore: Portrait of an Extraordinary Gentleman*, edited by smoky man and Gary Spencer Millidge, Abiogenesis, 2003, pp. 51–54.

Moore, Alan. "Frankenstein's Cadillac." *Dodgem Logic*, no. 4, June/July 2010, pp. 2–11.

———. "The Mark of Batman: An Introduction." *Batman: The Dark Knight Returns*, by Frank Miller, Klaus Janson, and Lynn Varley. DC Comics, 1986, n.p.

———. "Twilight of the Superheroes." Archived at archive.org/stream/TwilightOfTheSuperheroes/TwilightOfTheSuperheroes_djvu.txt.

Moore, Alan, Stephen Bissette, and John Totleben. *The Saga of the Swamp Thing* issue 24, May 1984, DC Comics.

Moore, Alan, and Jacen Burrows. *Neonomicon* issues 1–4, 2010, Avatar.

Moore, Alan, and Eddie Campbell. *From Hell*. 1989–1998. Eddie Campbell Comics, 1999.

Moore, Alan, and Melinda Gebbie. *Lost Girls*. 1991–2006. Top Shelf Productions, 2009.

Moore, Alan, and Dave Gibbons. *Watchmen* issues 1–12, 1986–1987, DC Comics.

Moore, Alan, Garry Leach, et al. *Marvelman*. *Warrior* issues 1–18, 20–21, 1982–1984, Quality Communications. Rpt. and cont. as *Miracleman* issues 1–16, 1985–1989, Eclipse Comics.

Moore, Alan, Rob Liefeld, et al. *Judgment Day* issues 1–3, 1997, Awesome Entertainment.

Moore, Alan, and David Lloyd. *V for Vendetta*. 1982–1989. DC Comics, 1990.

Moore, Alan, and Kevin O'Neill. *The League of Extraordinary Gentlemen*, 2 vols., 1999–2003, America's Best Comics.

———. *The League of Extraordinary Gentlemen: Black Dossier*. America's Best Comics, 2007.

———. *The League of Extraordinary Gentlemen Century* issues 1–3, 2009–2012, Top Shelf Productions/Knockabout Comics.

———. *Nemo: Heart of Ice*. Top Shelf Productions/Knockabout Comics, 2013.

———. *Nemo: River of Ghosts*. Top Shelf Productions/Knockabout Comics, 2015.

———. *Nemo: The Roses of Berlin*. Top Shelf Productions/Knockabout Comics, 2014.

Moore, Alan, and Dave Sim. "Correspondence: *From Hell*, Part Two." *Alan Moore: Portrait of an Extraordinary Gentleman*, edited by smoky man and Gary Spencer Millidge, Abiogenesis, 2003, pp. 319–329.

Moore, Alan, and Don Simpson. "In Pictopia!" *Anything Goes*, no. 2, Fantagraphics, 1986.

Moore, Alan, Curt Swan, and George Pérez. "Whatever Happened to the Man of Tomorrow?" pt. 1. *Superman* issue 423, Sept. 1986, DC Comics.

Moore, Alan, Rick Veitch, et al. *Supreme* issues 41–56, 1996–1998, Image Comics, Maximum Press, and Awesome Entertainment. Cont. as *Supreme: The Return* issues 1–6, 1998–2000, Awesome Entertainment.

Moore, Alan, J. H. Williams III, and Mick Gray. *Promethea* issues 1–32, 1999–2005, America's Best Comics.

Moore, Anne Elizabeth. "100 Distinguished Comics from August 31, 2005 to September 1, 2006." *The Best American Comics 2007*, edited by Chris Ware and Anne Elizabeth Moore, Houghton Mifflin, 2007, pp. 328–330.

Morgan, Jo-Ann. "Picturing Uncle Tom with Little Eva—Reproduction as Legacy." *Journal of American Culture*, vol. 27, no. 1, March 2004, pp. 1–24.

Morrison, Toni. "Unspeakable Things Unspoken: The Afro-American Presence in American Literature." *Michigan Quarterly Review*, vol. 28, no. 1, Winter 1989, pp. 1–34.

Mouly, Françoise. "Talk on *Blown Covers*." Panel with Daniel Clowes, R. Crumb, and Chris Ware. Chute and Jagoda, pp. 187–197.

Murray, Christopher. "Superman vs Imago: Superheroes, Lacan, and Mediated Identity." *International Journal of Comic Art*, vol. 4, no. 2, Fall 2002, pp. 186–208.

Naghibi, Nima, and Andrew O'Malley. "Estranging the Familiar: 'East' and 'West' in Satrapi's *Persepolis*." *English Studies in Canada*, vol. 31, nos. 2–3, 2005, pp. 223–248.

Ndalianis, Angela. "Enter the Aleph: Superhero Worlds and Hypertime Realities." *The Contemporary Comic Book Superhero*, edited by Angela Ndalianis, Routledge, 2009, pp. 270–290.

Neary, Janet. *Fugitive Testimony: On the Visual Logic of Slave Narratives*. Fordham UP, 2017.

Nevins, Jess. "Annotations to *League of Extraordinary Gentlemen* Volume III Chapter Three, a.k.a. *Century: 2009*." *JessNevins.com*, jessnevins.com/annotations/2009annotations.html.

———. *A Blazing World: The Unofficial Companion to The League of Extraordinary Gentlemen, Volume Two*. MonkeyBrain, 2004.

———. *The Encyclopedia of Fantastic Victoriana*. MonkeyBrain, 2005.

———. *Heroes and Monsters: The Unofficial Companion to The League of Extraordinary Gentlemen*. MonkeyBrain, 2003.

———. *Impossible Territories: The Unofficial Companion to The League of Extraordinary Gentlemen, The Black Dossier*. MonkeyBrain, 2008.

———. "*Kingdom Come* Annotations." Archived at "Annotations for DC Comic Books." *Enjolrasworld*, enjolrasworld.com/Annotations%20for%20DC%20Comics.htm.

Nochlin, Linda. *Realism*. Penguin, 1971.

Noles, Pam. "The Golliwogg in the *Black Dossier*." *And We Shall March*, Nov. 2007–Aug. 2011, andweshallmarch.typepad.com/and_we_shall_march/the_black_dossier/index.html.

Nussbaum, Martha. *Not for Profit: Why Democracy Needs the Humanities*. Princeton UP, 2010.

Nyberg, Amy Kiste. *Seal of Approval: The History of the Comics Code*. UP of Mississippi, 1998.

Oates, Stephen B. *The Fires of Jubilee: Nat Turner's Fierce Rebellion*. 1975. HarperPerennial, 1990.

Olney, James. "'I Was Born': Slave Narratives, Their Status as Autobiography and as Literature." *The Slave's Narrative*, edited by Charles T. Davis and Henry Louis Gates Jr., Oxford UP, 1985, pp. 148–175.

Ó Méalóid, Pádraig. "Interview: Alan Moore on *Providence*, *Jerusalem*, *League* and

More—Part 1." *The Beat*, 16 Apr. 2013, comicsbeat.com/interview-with-alan-moore-part-1.

——. "Last Alan Moore Interview?" *Pádraig Ó Méalóid AKA Slovobooks*, 9 Jan. 2014, slovobooks.wordpress.com/2014/01/09/last-alan-moore-interview.

Orbán, Katalin. "A Language of Scratches and Stitches: The Graphic Novel between Hyperreading and Print." Chute and Jagoda, pp. 169–181.

Ostby, Marie. "Graphics and Global Dissent: Marjane Satrapi's *Persepolis*, Persian Miniatures, and the Multifaceted Power of Comic Protest." *PMLA*, vol. 132, no. 3, 2017, pp. 558–579.

Oswalt, Patton. "Wake Up, Geek Culture. Time to Die." *Wired*, 27 Dec. 2010, wired.com/magazine/2010/12/ff_angrynerd_geekculture/all/1.

Packer, George. *Blood of the Liberals*. Farrar, Straus and Giroux, 2000.

Park, Hye Su. "Art Spiegelman's *Maus: A Survivor's Tale*: A Bibliographic Essay." *Shofar*, vol. 29, no. 2, 2011, pp. 146–164.

Parramore, Thomas C. *Southampton County, Virginia*. UP of Virginia, 1978.

Peterson, James Braxton. "Graphic Black Nationalism: Visualizing Political Narratives in the Graphic Novel." *The Rise and Reason of Comics and Graphic Literature: Critical Essays on the Form*, edited by Joyce Goggin and Dan Hassler-Forest, McFarland, 2010, pp. 202–221.

Phipps, Keith. "Chris Ware." *The Onion A.V. Club*, 2 May 2001, avclub.com/article/chris-ware-13711.

Pizzino, Christopher. *Arresting Development: Comics at the Boundaries of Literature*. U of Texas P, 2016.

Radner, Joan N., and Susan S. Lanser. "Strategies of Coding in Women's Cultures." *Feminist Messages: Coding in Women's Folk Culture*, edited by Joan Newlon Radner, U of Illinois P, 1993, pp. 1–29.

Raeburn, Daniel. *Chris Ware*. Yale UP, 2004.

Rambsy, Howard, II. "Reading Kyle Baker's *Nat Turner* with a Group of Collegiate Black Men." *Contemporary African American Literature: The Living Canon*, edited by Lovalerie King and Shirley Moody-Turner, Indiana UP, 2013, pp. 285–301.

Reed, Adolph, Jr. "*Django Unchained*, or, *The Help*: How 'Cultural Politics' Is Worse Than No Politics at All, and Why." *Nonsite.org*, no. 9, 25 Feb. 2013, nonsite.org/feature/django-unchained-or-the-help-how-cultural-politics-is-worse-than-no-politics-at-all-and-why.

Reed, Ishmael. *Flight to Canada*. 1976. Atheneum, 1989.

Reynolds, Richard. *Super Heroes: A Modern Mythology*. UP of Mississippi, 1992.

Reynolds, Simon. *Retromania: Pop Culture's Addiction to Its Own Past*. Faber and Faber, 2011.

Robinson, Forrest G. "The Characterization of Jim in *Huckleberry Finn*." *Nineteenth-Century Literature*, vol. 43, no. 3, 1988, pp. 361–391.

Robinson, Lillian S. *Wonder Women*. Routledge, 2004.

Roeder, Katherine. "Chris Ware and the Burden of Art History." *The Comics of Chris Ware: Drawing Is a Way of Thinking*, edited by David M. Ball and Martha Kuhlman, UP of Mississippi, 2010, pp. 65–77.

Rosenberg, Robin S. "Superman's Personality: From Krypton, Kansas, or Both?" *The Psychology of Superheroes*, edited by Robin S. Rosenberg with Jennifer Canzoneri, BenBella, 2008, pp. 29–49.

———. "What's Wrong with Bruce Wayne?" *Batman Unauthorized*, edited by Dennis O'Neil, BenBella, 2008, pp. 145–156.

Roth, Sarah N. "The Path of the Rebels." *The Nat Turner Project*, Sarah N. Roth, Widener University, 2015, natturnerproject.org/path-of-rebels.

Sabin, Roger. *Adult Comics: An Introduction*. Routledge, 1993.

———. *Comics, Comix & Graphic Novels*. Phaidon, 1996.

Sacco, Joe. *Palestine*. 1993–1995. Fantagraphics, 2001.

Sacco, Joe, and W. J. T. Mitchell. "Public Conversation." Chute and Jagoda, pp. 53–70.

Saizarbitoria, Jauretsi. "*Chicken with Plums* Director Marjane Satrapi Thinks Depression Is Great." *The Standard*, "Culture," 21 Aug. 2012, www.standardhotels.com/culture/chicken-with-plums-director-marjane-satrapi-thinks-depression-is-great.

Sante, Luc. "She Can't Go Home Again." *New York Times Book Review*, 22 Aug. 2004, p. 7, nytimes.com/2004/08/22/books/she-can-t-go-home-again.html.

Satrapi, Marjane. "Le Foulard." *Lapin*, no. 25, Oct. 1999, pp. 83–89.

———. *Persepolis*. 2000–2003. Translated by Mattias Ripa, Blake Ferris, and Anjali Singh, 2 vols., Pantheon, 2003, 2004.

———. "Tales from an Ordinary Iranian Girlhood." *Ms.*, Spring 2003, pp. 87–91.

Sattler, Peter. "Building Memories: Mine, Hers, and Ours." *Comics Journal*, 2 Nov. 2012, tcj.com/building-memories-mine-hers-and-ours.

Saunders, Ben. *Do the Gods Wear Capes? Spirituality, Fantasy, and Superheroes*. Continuum, 2011.

Schatz, Thomas. *Hollywood Genres: Formulas, Filmmaking, and the Studio System*. McGraw-Hill, 1981.

Schumer, Arlen. *The Silver Age of Comic Book Art*. Collector's Press, 2003.

Schwartz, Ben, ed. *The Best American Comics Criticism*. Fantagraphics, 2010.

Sedgwick, Eve Kosofsky. "Paranoid Reading and Reparative Reading, or, You're So Paranoid, You Probably Think This Essay Is About You." *Touching Feeling: Affect, Pedagogy, Performativity*, by Eve Kosofsky Sedgwick, Duke UP, 2003, pp. 123–151.

Segall, Kimberly Wedeven. "Melancholy Ties: Intergenerational Loss and Exile in *Persepolis*." *Comparative Studies of South Asia, Africa and the Middle East*, vol. 28, no. 1, 2008, pp. 38–49.

Shalin, Dmitri N. "Goffman on Mental Illness: *Asylums* and 'The Insanity of Place' Revisited." *Symbolic Interaction*, vol. 37, no. 1, 2014, pp. 122–144.

Shaw, Gwendolyn DuBois. *Seeing the Unspeakable: The Art of Kara Walker*. Duke UP, 2004.

Siegel, Jerry, Ed Dobrotka, and John Sikela. "Case of the Funny Paper Crimes." *Superman* issue 19, 1942. Rpt. in *Superman Archives*, vol. 5, DC Comics, 2000.

Siegel, Jerry, Joe Shuster, Ed Dobrotka, and John Sikela. "Superman, Matinee Idol." *Superman* issue 19, 1942. Rpt. in *Superman Archives*, vol. 5, DC Comics, 2000.

Singer, Marc. *Grant Morrison: Combining the Worlds of Contemporary Comics*. UP of Mississippi, 2012.

———. "Week 8: Kyle Baker, *Nat Turner*." *I Am NOT the Beastmaster*, 18 Mar. 2010, notthebeastmaster.typepad.com/weblog/2010/03/week-8-kyle-baker-nat-turner.html.

Singsen, Doug. "An Alternative by Any Other Name: Genre-Splicing and Mainstream Genres in Alternative Comics." *Journal of Graphic Novels and Comics*, vol. 5, no. 2, 2014, pp. 170–191.

Solomon, Deborah. "Revolutionary Spirit." *New York Times Magazine*, 21 Oct. 2007, p. 28, nytimes.com/2007/10/21/magazine/21wwwln-Q4-t.html.

Spiegelman, Art. "Ballbuster." *New Yorker*, 22 July 2002, pp. 72–74.

———. "Commix: An Idiosyncratic Historical and Aesthetic Overview." *Print*, vol. 42, no. 6, Nov./Dec. 1988, pp. 61–73, 195–196.

———. "Forms Stretched to Their Limits." *New Yorker*, 19 Apr. 1999, pp. 76–85.

———. *Maus*. 1980–1991. 2 vols., Pantheon, 1986, 1991.

———. "Picturing a Glassy-Eyed Private I." Introduction. *City of Glass*, by Paul Auster, Paul Karasik, and David Mazzuchelli, Picador, 2004, n.p.

Spurgeon, Tom. "CR Holiday Interview #3—Bart Beaty on *Persepolis*." *Comics Reporter*, 22 Dec. 2009, comicsreporter.com/index.php/cr_holiday_interview_03.

Station, Elizabeth. "Comics City." Interview of Hillary Chute. *University of Chicago Magazine*, 22 May 2012, mag.uchicago.edu/arts-humanities/comics-city.

Sterling, Terry Greene. "Confessions of a Memoirist." *Salon*, 1 Aug. 2003, salon.com/2003/08/01/gornick.

Stone, Albert E. *The Return of Nat Turner: History, Literature, and Cultural Politics in Sixties America*. U of Georgia P, 1992.

Styron, William. *The Confessions of Nat Turner*. Vintage, 1967.

Sutton, Terri. "Adventures in Adult Comic Land." *Utne Reader*, no. 59, Sept.–Oct. 1993, pp. 111–114.

Tensuan, Theresa M. "Comic Visions and Revisions in the Work of Lynda Barry and Marjane Satrapi." *Modern Fiction Studies*, vol. 52, no. 4, Winter 2006, pp. 947–964.

Theokas, Christopher. "*Persepolis* Paints Iran from a Kid's Perspective." *USA Today*, 6 Aug. 2003, usatoday30.usatoday.com/life/books/reviews/2003-08-06-persepolis_x.htm.

Thoss, Jeff. "From Penny Dreadful to Graphic Novel: Alan Moore and Kevin O'Neill's Genealogy of Comics in *The League of Extraordinary Gentlemen*." *Belphégor*, vol. 13, no. 1, 2015, belphegor.revues.org/624.

Tilley, Carol. "Seducing the Innocent: Fredric Wertham and the Falsifications that Helped Condemn Comics." *Information & Culture: A Journal of History*, vol. 47, no. 4, 2012, pp. 383–413.

Torner, Evan. "The Poles of Wantonness: Male Asexuality in Alan Moore's Film Adaptations." *Sexual Ideology in the Works of Alan Moore*, edited by Todd A. Comer and Joseph Michael Sommers, McFarland, 2012, pp. 111–123.

Tragle, Henry Irving. *The Southampton Slave Revolt of 1831: A Compilation of Source Material*. U of Massachusetts P, 1971.

Turner, Julia. "When Harry Met Osama." *Slate*, 20 July 2005, slate.com/articles/arts/culturebox/2005/07/when_harry_met_osama.html.

Uchmanowicz, Pauline. "Graphic Novel Decoded: Towards a Poetics of Comics." *International Journal of Comic Art*, vol. 11, no. 1, Spring 2009, pp. 363–385.

"Union Fire Arms 1907 Catalog." *Cornell Publications*. cornellpubs.com/old-guns/item_desc.php?item_id=748.

Upton, Florence K., and Bertha Upton. *The Adventures of Two Dutch Dolls and a Golliwogg*. Longmans Green, 1895.

Vashko, Robert E. "Exploitation of the Comic Book Superhero." *Loyola Intellectual Property & High Technology Law Quarterly*, vol. 3, no. 1–2, 1998, pp. 37–51.

Vayo, Lloyd Isaac. "I Remain Your Own: Epistolamory in 'The New Adventures of Fanny Hill.'" *Sexual Ideology in the Works of Alan Moore*, edited by Todd A. Comer and Joseph Michael Sommers, McFarland, 2012, pp. 189–200.

Waid, Mark, and Barry Kitson. *JLA: Year One* issues 1–12, 1997–1998, DC Comics.

Waid, Mark, and Alex Ross. *Kingdom Come* issues 1–4, 1996, DC Comics.

Wallace, David Foster. Introduction. *The Best American Essays 2007*, edited by David Foster Wallace and Robert Atwan, Houghton Mifflin, 2007.

Ware, Chris. *Building Stories*. Pantheon, 2012.

———. "God." *McSweeney's Quarterly Concern*, no. 13, 2004, dust jacket.

———. *Jimmy Corrigan: The Smartest Kid on Earth*. 1995–2000. Pantheon, 2000.

———, ed. *McSweeney's Quarterly Concern*, no. 13, 2004.

———. "Ruin: Your Life, Draw: Cartoons!" *The ACME Novelty Library Final Report to Shareholders and Saturday Afternoon Rainy Day Fun Book*, Pantheon, 2005, p. 25.

Ware, Chris, and Anne Elizabeth Moore, eds. *The Best American Comics 2007*. Houghton Mifflin, 2007.

Watson, Rich. "UVC Out-Takes: Kyle Baker (part 1)." *Pop Culture Shock*, 16 May

2007. Archived at web.archive.org/web/20070523050133/http://www.popcultureshock.com/uvc-out-takes-kyle-baker-part-1/41789.

Weich, Dave. "Marjane Satrapi Returns." 17 Sept. 2004. *PowellsBooks.Blog*, 10 Oct. 2006, powells.com/blog/interviews/marjane-satrapi-returns-by-dave.

Weida, Courtney Lee. "Wonder(ing) Women: Investigating Gender Politics and Art Education within Graphica." *Visual Culture & Gender*, vol. 6, 2011, pp. 99–108.

Welch, Stuart Cary. *Wonders of the Age: Masterpieces of Early Safavid Painting, 1501–1576*. Fogg Art Museum, Harvard University, 1979.

Whaley, Deborah E. *Black Women in Sequence: Re-inking Comics, Graphic Novels, and Anime*. U of Washington P, 2015.

White, Hayden. *Tropics of Discourse: Essays in Cultural Criticism*. Johns Hopkins UP, 1978.

White, Mark D., ed. *Watchmen and Philosophy: A Rorschach Test*. Wiley, 2009.

Whitehead, Colson. "The End of the Affair." Review of *A Multitude of Sins*, by Richard Ford. *New York Times Book Review*, 3 Mar. 2002, 8.

Whitlock, Gillian. "Autographics: The Seeing 'I' of the Comics." *Modern Fiction Studies*, vol. 52, no. 4, Winter 2006, pp. 965–979.

——. *Soft Weapons: Autobiography in Transit*. U of Chicago P, 2007.

Whitted, Qiana. "'And the Negro Thinks in Hieroglyphics': Comics, Visual Metonymy, and the Spectacle of Blackness." *Journal of Graphic Novels and Comics*, vol. 5, no. 1, 2014, pp. 79–100.

"William Marples and Sons." *Grace's Guide to British Industrial History*, 30 Sept. 2014, gracesguide.co.uk/William_Marples_and_Sons.

Williams, Paul. "Questions of 'Contemporary Women's Comics.'" *The Rise of the American Comics Artist: Creators and Contexts*, edited by Paul Williams and James Lyons, UP of Mississippi, 2010, pp. 135–149.

Wilson, G. Willow. "Dr. Lepore's Lament." *G. Willow Wilson*, 12 May 2015, gwillowwilson.com/post/118822887543/dr-lepores-lament.

Wilson, G. Willow, Marguerite Bennett, and Jorge Molina. *A-Force* issue 1, July 2015, Marvel Comics.

Witek, Joseph. "American Comics Criticism and the Problem of Dual Address." *International Journal of Comic Art*, vol. 10, no. 1, Spring 2008, pp. 218–225.

——. *Comic Books as History*. UP of Mississippi, 1989.

——. "Seven Ways I Don't Teach Comics." *Teaching the Graphic Novel*, edited by Stephen E. Tabachnick, Modern Language Association, 2009, pp. 217–222.

Wolk, Douglas. "Douglas Wolk Interviews Kevin O'Neill Part Four (of Five)." *Comics Journal*, 19 Feb. 2010, classic.tcj.com/superhero/douglas-wolk-interviews-kevin-oneill-part-four-of-five.

——. "L'Association Brings French Comics to the U.S." *PW Comics Week*,

6 Dec. 2005, publishersweekly.com/pw/by-topic/industry-news/comics/article/27883-l-association-brings-french-comics-to-the-u-s.html.

———. *Reading Comics: How Graphic Novels Work and What They Mean.* Da Capo, 2007.

"Wonder Woman." *Grand Comics Database,* comics.org/series/277/covers.

Woo, Benjamin. "An Age-Old Problem: Problematics of Comic Book Historiography." *International Journal of Comic Art,* vol. 10, no. 1, 2008, pp. 268–279.

Worden, Daniel. "The Shameful Art: *McSweeney's Quarterly Concern,* Comics, and the Politics of Affect." *Modern Fiction Studies,* vol. 52, no. 4, Winter 2006, pp. 891–917.

Worth, Jennifer. "Unveiling: *Persepolis* as Embodied Performance." *Theatre Research International,* vol. 32, no. 2, 2007, pp. 143–160.

Wright, Bradford. *Comic Book Nation: The Transformation of Youth Culture in America.* Johns Hopkins UP, 2001.

Yardley, Jonathan. *Monday Morning Quarterback.* Rowman & Littlefield, 1998.

Yockey, Matt. "Retopia: The Dialectics of the Superhero Comic Book." *Studies in Comics,* vol. 3, no. 2, 2012, pp. 349–370.

INDEX

www.ingramcontent.com/pod-product-compliance
Lightning Source LLC
LaVergne TN
LVHW100024310826
846742LV00012B/29
* 9 7 8 1 4 7 7 3 1 7 1 0 5 *